The International Politics of Eastern Europe

edited by
Charles Gati

Studies of the Institute on East
Central Europe and The Research
Institute on International Change,
Columbia University

The International Politics of Eastern Europe

PRAEGER SPECIAL STUDIES IN INTERNATIONAL POLITICS AND GOVERNMENT

Praeger Publishers   New York   Washington   London

Library of Congress Cataloging in Publication Data
Main entry under title:

The International politics of Eastern Europe.

(Praeger special studies in international politics
and government)
    Bibliography: p. 292
    Includes index.
    1. Europe, Eastern—Foreign relations—Addresses,
essays, lectures. I. Gati, Charles. II. Columbia
University. Institute on East Central Europe.
III. Columbia University. Research Institute on
International Change.
JX1542.I58   327.47   75-23963
ISBN 0-275-55960-2
ISBN 0-275-89500-9 student ed.

PRAEGER PUBLISHERS
111 Fourth Avenue, New York, N.Y. 10003, U.S.A.

Published in the United States of America in 1976
by Praeger Publishers, Inc.

Printed in the United States of America

This book is based on papers presented at the March 1975 Columbia University conference on the international politics of Eastern Europe. The conference was sponsored by the Joint Committee on Eastern Europe of the American Council of Learned Societies and Columbia University's Institute on East Central Europe. The editor of this book, who served as organizer of the conference, is pleased to acknowledge his gratitude to those who made the conference possible: the Joint Committee and Istvan Deak, director of the Institute on East Central Europe. The editor's own work on the subject began at Columbia University's Research Institute on International Change, and he is pleased to express his gratitude for the Institute's financial support and particularly for the intellectual stimulation provided by its members and by its director, Zbigniew Brzezinski.

As the title indicates, this book deals with the international relations of Eastern Europe. Both the editor and the contributors realize that no single book can explore all aspects of this vast topic. Therefore, we have decided to concentrate on the contemporary scene, focusing on the post-1968 era characterized by the East-West detente and the consequences of the 1968 invasion of Czechoslovakia by the Soviet Union and its supporters.

As far as substantive focus is concerned, we have sought to concentrate on the place of Eastern Europe within the communist subsystem (Part II), with particular emphasis on Soviet-East European relations. The main question we posed was whether Eastern Europe is still an asset or whether it has become a liability to the Soviet Union; but that question, as expected, has led to a series of additional questions about detente, the role of China and Yugoslavia, the meaning of the Conference on European Security and Cooperation (CSCE), and so on.

The chapters in Part III view Eastern Europe from the perspective of the West and of Western approaches to the region. The main question we posed here had to do with Western objectives: What could the West reasonably expect to achieve through "peaceful engagement," Ostpolitik, CSCE, mutual force reductions in Europe, or East-West trade?

Finally, in Part IV we raise a number of analytically discrete questions about the international politics of Eastern Europe: In comparison with NATO, what functions does the Warsaw Pact serve as an alliance system? Can the foreign policies of the Eastern European states be explained, in part at least, by their respective domestic political cultures? How can we go about evaluating or measuring non-Soviet external influences? Is it possible to construct a model for the study of the Eastern European decision-making process?

As the reader will certainly find, there are no easy answers to any of these questions. Since the publication of Zbigniew Brzezinski's *The Soviet Bloc*—a monumental study that dealt with pre-1968 international politics in Eastern Europe—the subject of our study has been rather neglected. What we can offer, therefore, is an introduction: our questions are exploratory and our answers are tentative. In fact, our answers are not only tentative, they tend to contradict each other, since the several authors often arrive at different conclusions.

Anticipating at least two reasonable criticisms, a word should be added about what is not in this book. First, we do not have a separate chapter devoted to the study of economic integration or the Council on Mutual Economic Assistance (CEMA). There are a number of reasons for this omission, none completely satisfactory; but the reader will find, especially in Chapters 4 and 10, detailed discussions on some aspects of CEMA and Eastern European economic integration. Not incidentally, this is a subject extensively dealt with in the scholarly literature. Second, we do not have a separate chapter devoted to the systematic and comparative study of the foreign policies of Eastern Europe. Again, the reader will find that practically every chapter in the book touches on similarities and differences among foreign policies in the region. So little has been done thus far on this important subject that it seemed premature to present the results of sketchy or incomplete data in book form. In addition, our primary, though not exclusive, focus here is "the view from the outside"—that is, how Eastern Europe is perceived—rather than "the view from the inside," meaning how Eastern Europe perceives the outside world. That may be the subject of another work.

With the exception of Chapter 11, a different version of which appeared before, all materials in this book are published here for the first time.

CONTENTS

LIST OF TABLES AND FIGURES

I

EASTERN EUROPE
IN THE
POSTWAR WORLD

CHAPTER

1

FROM COLD WAR ORIGINS TO DETENTE: INTRODUCTION TO THE INTERNATIONAL POLITICS OF EASTERN EUROPE
Charles Gati

EASTERN EUROPE AND WORLD POLITICS

The region that is usually identified as Eastern Europe or East Central Europe—extending from the Baltic to the Balkans and from Germany to the Soviet Union—has been the enfant terrible of the international politics of this century. It has probably caused, contributed to, or been victimized by more wars and international conflict than any other region in the world, even the always volatile Middle East. World War I started in what is now Yugoslavia; Poland was the *causus belli* of World War II; and it was largely over the fate and future of the whole region that the Cold War began.

Since the beginning of the Cold War in 1945-48, several of the dramatic crises and developments in Eastern Europe have involved, directly or indirectly, some or all of the great powers of the postwar world. The February 1948 communist coup in Czechoslovakia, for example, signified not only the end of all reasonable hope for the region's democratic evolution, but it also had such major international repercussions as the formation of NATO in 1949. Particularly because Czechoslovakia used to have a liberal democratic order, unlike much of the rest of Eastern Europe, its forceful Sovietization served to mobilize Western efforts against the possibility of further Soviet advances in Central and Western Europe.

Some of the ideas developed in this chapter were previously touched on by the author's "Soviet Tutelage in East Europe," *Current History*, October 1971, pp. 206-09; "East Central Europe: Touchstone for Detente," *Journal of International Affairs*, Fall 1974, pp. 158-74; "The Forgotten Region," *Foreign Policy*, Summer 1975, pp. 135-45; and in his "Introduction: But Was the Cold War Really Necessary?" in Charles Gati, ed., *Caging the Bear: Containment and the Cold War* (Indianapolis: Bobbs-Merrill, 1974), pp. xiii-xxvi.

Simiarly, the Soviet-Yugoslav break of 1948-49 did more than reveal fissures in what was then called the Soviet bloc; it also had an impact on such Western states as Italy, England, and the United States, which made a pragmatic political decision to help sustain a communist-led state (Yugoslavia) against the combined pressures of the Soviet Union and its Eastern European supporters. In the process, a still important feature of Western diplomacy surfaced in Eastern Europe: the willingness of the West to distinguish between those communist states that presented a threat, real or potential, to the European status quo and those that did not. Then as now, the West was concerned about aggressive foreign policy behavior rather than hostile or incompatible communist ideology. Tested in Yugoslavia, this Western attitude was to provide the essential background for subsequent Western appreciation of genuine differences within the once monolithic communist world; it helped guide Western policies toward polycentrism in the 1950s and the Sino-Soviet rift in the 1960s.

The Yugoslav deviation had major implications for the rest of the world as well. For the Soviet Union, it was a novel and traumatic experience, demonstrating the very real limits on Soviet power even in Eastern Europe. In addition, Yugoslavia also contributed to substantial innovation in Soviet ideology; by the mid-1950s, the Soviet Union at least verbally accepted the proposition that there could be different roads to socialism, hence conceding that the Soviet model did not have universal validity and applicability. Moreover, the Yugoslav defiance had several implications for the Third World, of which the most damaging to the Soviet Union was the Yugoslav emphasis on building a nominally socialist society without Soviet assistance and, indeed, in spite of Soviet pressures. Finally, it goes without saying that the Yugoslav experience provided a very compelling lesson to the other countries in Eastern Europe whose subsequent flirtation with independent or semi-independent socialism revealed the magnetism of the Yugoslav heresy.

Other regional events with considerable consequences for Soviet-American and, indeed, East-West relations included the Hungarian revolt of 1956 and the Czechoslovak "Prague Spring" of 1968.

The Hungarian revolt had been preceded by the first seemingly serious opportunity in the Cold War era to overcome or at least mitigate the prevailing atmosphere of international tension and hostility. The post-Stalin years of 1953-56 witnessed the beginnings of de-Stalinization in the Soviet Union, the partial reconciliation with Yugoslavia, the evolution of more moderate policies in Eastern Europe identified as the "New Course," the Austrian Peacy Treaty of 1955 (followed by the neutralization of and the removal of Soviet troops from Austria), the Geneva Summit of 1955 that gave rise to the hopeful "Spirit of Geneva," and finally the 20th Congress of the Communist Party of the Soviet Union in February 1956, with its momentous revelations about the Stalin era. In some ways, this was the first postwar attempt at detente between East and West. Its failure was due to a number of factors and circumstances, of which not the least important was continued Soviet domination over Eastern Europe. Specifically, the emerging spirit of East-West accommodation died on the streets of Budapest, as if the people of Eastern Europe wanted to indicate that the global relaxation of international tension must include the relaxation of Soviet dominance over Eastern Europe.

In 1968, another opportunity for Soviet-American rapprochement was in the offing. For the first time since the end of World War II an American president, Lyndon B. Johnson, was about to announce a forthcoming trip to the Soviet Union. That announcement was never made, nor did Johnson visit the Soviet Union, primarily because the Soviet Union and its Warsaw Pact supporters had just invaded Czechoslovakia. The brutal suppression of a more humanistic socialist experiment and the display of Soviet military might in the heart of Central Europe renewed skepticism about the prospect of even limited accommodation with the Soviet Union. As in 1956, Eastern Europe reminded the West of the fundamental differences still dividing East and West, and as a result important negotiations were postponed.

COLD WAR ORIGINS IN EASTERN EUROPE

The significance of Eastern Europe for the international system was already evident at Yalta, at Potsdam, and at other postwar conferences. Western, Soviet, and Eastern European scholars all tend to agree that while the Cold War had many origins, sources, or causes, it began and was fueled by events in Eastern Europe. Scholars do not agree, however, about who should be held responsible for the Cold War. The "traditionalist" Western interpretation viewed Soviet aggression and subsequent Soviet unwillingness to abide by the popular will in Eastern Europe as the primary cause. This view has since been countered not only by Soviet historians and propagandists, who have consistently blamed American imperialism for the Cold War, but also by Western "revisionist" historians who have argued that Soviet actions in Eastern Europe were essentially defensive rather than offensive—that the Soviet Union in fact only responded to American provocations.

This is not the place to analyze or reconcile these conflicting interpretations. The interested reader can consult the voluminous literature on his own.[1] It may be useful, however, to indicate some of the salient features of the Eastern European political scene through the following propositions:

1. Having liberated Bulgaria, Romania, Hungary, Poland, Czechoslovakia, and part of Germany from Nazi control, the Soviet Union played a vital role in the political life of Eastern Europe from the very beginning.

2. The Western powers never had any illusions about Soviet influence over Eastern Europe in the postwar world. In that oft-quoted meeting between Churchill and Stalin, held at Moscow in the fall of 1944, Stalin consented to

Churchill's proposal concerning the distribution of influence in Eastern Europe. In Greece, it was to be 90 percent Western influence, 10 percent Russian influence; in Yugoslavia and Hungary, 50-50; in Bulgaria, 25-75; in Romania, 10-90. The future of Poland, Czechoslovakia, and Germany was not reduced to such mathematical formulas, but it would be fair to assume that Western interest there at least matched Western interest in Yugoslavia and Hungary.

3. The American decision to drop two atomic bombs on Japan in 1945 was intended to end the war in the Pacific and to impress the Soviet Union with Western power and determination. Although this happened after the Soviet Union had begun to move toward exclusive control over Eastern Europe, especially in Bulgaria, Romania, and Poland, Stalin could have interpreted the American decision as an attempt to deprive him of influence in Eastern Europe. There is no evidence to sustain or reject this hypothesis; the fact remains, however, that the Soviet Union had begun to Sovietize Eastern Europe before Hiroshima and Nagasaki and continued to do so afterward.

4. Even if the West did not object to some or (in the case of Bulgaria and Romania) even extensive Soviet influence over Eastern Europe, it did object to Soviet domination. Simply put, the Western notion of "sphere of influence" was fundamentally different from what Stalin apparently had in mind. In any case, Western objections were based primarily on fear of Soviet expansion into Western Europe and, thus, the preponderance of Soviet power in Europe.

5. In point of fact, American diplomats were repeatedly instructed by the State Department to avoid confrontation with the Soviet Union in the Eastern European capitals. The U.S. ambassador to Bucharest, for example, was forbidden to meet with any Romanian politican or even advise the king "regarding his present difficult position" in the fall of 1944. Secretary of State James F. Byrnes cabled the ambassador: "We hope no action will be taken which might seem to give ground for Soviet suspicion that crisis was brought about by 'Anglo-American intervention.' "[2] By and large, the West followed a low-key approach to Eastern Europe throughout 1944-45, hoping to persuade the Soviet Union of peaceful and reasonable Western intentions and expectations.

6. It is possible to speculate, therefore, that what prompted the Soviet drive towards hegemony in the region was not Western persistence or provocation—but the lack of it. It may be that the Soviet Union accelerated its drive because it found no Western resistance and regarded the existing political vacuum as too tempting to overlook.

7. By late 1946, and especially after the Truman Doctrine of 1947, the West did begin to assert itself and to protest Soviet behavior in Eastern Europe. Western diplomats were in touch with the non-communist politicians of Hungary, Poland, and Czechoslovakia, and the official statements were increasingly critical, even anti-Soviet. But neither at that time nor since then did the West do much about Eastern Europe. It used Soviet hegemonical policies in Eastern Europe to mobilize the reluctant Western publics for the defense of

Western Europe (for instance, the formation of NATO was explained by the Soviet-inspired coup in Czechoslovakia).

THE SOVIET ROLE IN EASTERN EUROPE

By the February 1948 coup in Czechoslovakia, all the countries of Eastern Europe had been Sovietized. The subsequent era of Stalinist hegemony—lasting until the mid-1950s—was characterized by a certain simplicity, in the sense that the Soviet Union issued detailed instructions and directions to the leaders of Eastern Europe, who, in turn, implemented them. To leaders like Boleslaw Bierut of Poland, Klement Gottwald of Czechoslovakia, Matyas Rakosi of Hungary, or Walter Ulbricht of East Germany, the Soviet word was sacred; Soviet policies were always correct and applicable; and Stalin's wisdom was beyond the slightest doubt. They diligently took their cues from Moscow, so that differences between Soviet and Eastern European political patterns and priorities were of minor significance. The only exception was Yugoslavia's Marshal Tito, who, as a result of his more independent, national political course, was condemned as a deviationist and expelled from the communist movement in 1948-49.

The Stalinist phase in Soviet-Eastern European relations stemmed from certain Soviet imperatives and preoccupations. It was an era of ideological jubilance as the Soviet Union could, and did, demonstrate the utility and applicability of its own model of socialism and thus justify its ideological pretensions. It was an era of considerable political advancement, for after nearly three decades of building "socialism in one country," the Soviet Union could now claim to have contributed to the building of "socialism in one region." It was an era of military promise, not because the Eastern European armed forces could be regarded as reliable allies of the Soviet Union, but because the Soviet Union had fulfilled its historic ambition by erecting a buffer zone on its western frontiers. Finally, the Stalinist phase in Eastern Europe also offered economic benefits to the Soviet Union, partly in the form of extensive reparations, partly through imposed and eminently unfair trade agreements.

On the other hand, events in the 1950s clearly demonstrated that the Stalinist approach to Eastern Europe was too domineering to serve Soviet interests. The anti-Tito purges in Hungary, Czechoslovakia, and elsewhere instilled widespread fear, as was intended; but they also left a residue of considerable elite tension and barely internalized doubt. The imposition of collectivization resulted in an agricultural crisis throughout the region. The exploitation of the Eastern European economies proved to have been counter-productive, for ultimately the Soviet Union had to bail out its Eastern European clients in order to avoid political uprisings. Indeed, the East Berlin riots of 1953, the dramatic Polish events in 1956, and especially the Hungarian revolution of

1956 clearly suggested that the Stalinist conception of Soviet-Eastern European relations had to give way to a less imperious, more tutelary type of relationship.

The search for a new type of interstate relations—a change from the arbitrary, ad hoc arrangements of the Stalin era to a routinized relationship—led to the notion of a "socialist commonwealth" and to a series of new multilateral and bilateral treaties and agreements between the Soviet Union and the countries of Eastern Europe, on the one hand, and among the various Eastern European countries, on the other. In addition, existing relationships were formalized, institutionalized, or revived—CEMA, the Danubian Commission, the Organization for International Cooperation of Railway Administrations, and others. Concurrently, Eastern Europe obtained a larger degree of internal autonomy for experimentation; indeed, departure from Soviet patterns of governance, in economic and even political matters, became a common feature of Eastern European political life.

No advocate of the emerging diversity, the Soviet Union nonetheless seemed willing to tolerate it on two conditions. First, it insisted that its junior partners consistently support Soviet foreign policy, including that toward China. Second, the Soviet Union insisted that no Eastern European country promote its experiments or patterns as a "new model" of socialism to be followed by others beyond its frontiers. Such were the Soviet-imposed limits on the autonomy of Eastern Europe in the more mature, institutionalized phase of development after 1956.

During the mid-1960s, however, the countries of Eastern Europe on occasion rejected or at least violated the Soviet Union's two limits on their autonomy. As to the first, most Eastern European regimes violated the Soviet foreign policy line during the 1968 Czechoslovak crisis. Romania simply refused to participate in the invasion. Hungary contributed only a token force, and strongly hinted at its disagreement with the action taken. East Germany and Poland, on the other hand—led at the time by Ulbricht and Wladyslaw Gomulka, respectively—seemed more antagonistic, more volatile, and more zealous than the Soviet Union itself. Only Bulgaria seems to have followed faithfully the zigzag course of Soviet policy.

As to the second Soviet-imposed limitation, the sanctity of the Soviet model of socialism was also challenged, if one considers the scope of economic experimentation and innovation in the area during the 1960s and the pride with which some of the new models or policies were announced. (To be sure, Eastern European politicians and commentators always publicly underemphasize the novelty of their models and emphatically reject foreign commentary pointing to Eastern European divergence from the Soviet model—so emphatically, in fact, that these denials serve only to call attention to the new policy or the novel approach.)

From 1964 to 1968 in particular—during the transition from Nikita Khrushchev to Leonid Brezhnev—there was considerable Soviet tolerance toward

Eastern Europe. This was the time when Romania could express its anti-integrationist (and thus anti-Soviet) position by refusing to take economic direction from CEMA. Romania also failed to support the Soviet line against China (1964), opposed supranational planning in the Warsaw Pact (1966), criticized all military alliances (1966), and established diplomatic relations with West Germany (1967), hence facilitating the evolution of Ostpolitik before the Soviet Union was prepared to do so. This was also the time of economic reforms in Hungary and Czechoslovakia (both emulating the Yugoslav and not the Soviet model), featuring decentralization, the introduction of market mechanisms, indicative planning, membership or participation in the General Agreement on Tariffs and Trade (GATT), the World Bank, and the International Monetary Fund (IMF), as well as increased Western trade and tourism. Finally, this was the time of cautious political steps (primarily in Czechoslovakia and Hungary) toward reducing the all-pervasive involvement of the Communist party in all affairs, major or minor, enlarging the scope of parliamentary activities, and accepting the existence and merit of a three-tier interest structure (social, group, and individual interests) within the one-party political system.

Thus, despite continued expressions of unity and solidarity with the Soviet Union, there was more widespread experimentation, divergence, and optimism about increasing independence in the mid-1960s than any other time in the postwar era. Opposition to strict Soviet control, economic reform, relative moderation in the political and cultural realms, and emulation of the Yugoslav brand of socialism were broadly perceived to have been made possible by Soviet restraint within the "socialist commonwealth." That restraint, in turn, was viewed as partly self-imposed—a somewhat belated Soviet reaction to Stalinism in intrabloc relations—and partly the result of a combination of internal and external pressures on the Soviet leadership. Of the external pressures, the emerging American-Soviet detente, and particularly West Germany's Ostpolitik, were expected to be directly beneficial to, or indeed dedicated to, the cause of greater independence for Eastern Europe.

Yet the Soviet Union apparently felt compelled to intervene militarily in Czechoslovakia, and that action illustrates the Soviet dilemma in Eastern Europe. Although it could not then, and cannot now, return to the era during which Eastern Europe was the political appendage of the Soviet Union, the Soviet leadership must control regional aspirations for more autonomy and independence. If it is unduly strong and assertive, and especially if it resorts to the use of force, it has to accept the consequences: Western protests, including the possibility of a more critical Western posture toward detente, and vigorous condemnation by communist parties in Western Europe and even in China. If, on the other hand, the Soviet Union takes a more lenient position toward, and indeed tolerates, "different roads to socialism" in Eastern Europe, it has to accept different consequences: the erosion and possible disappearance of its authority and influence in this vital region. Faced as it has been with persistent and moderately successful Eastern European attempts to circumvent its hegemonical endeavors, the Soviet Union has therefore engaged in intricate maneuverings, delicate balancing, and considerations of alternative courses of action.

Paradoxically, however, the years of detente so far have not reduced Soviet insistence on uniformity and allegiance. Having expected far more dynamic and purposeful Western actions on behalf of Eastern Europe, the Soviet Union has treated the region as if Western policies were undermining the Soviet position there. In other words, the Soviet Union has used detente to react to the potentially erosive qualities of detente, reverting once again from tutelary to imperial behavior and attitudes. In comparison with the era before detente, opposition to Soviet control and values cannot surface as often and as openly. As a result of direct and indirect Soviet pressures, economic and political reforms have come under increasing criticism, and have been all but reversed. Since the West is not prepared to use detente in order to back Eastern Europe in opposition to the Soviet Union, the region—divided into nine relatively weak states—is unable to obtain more leeway from its powerful neighbor or even to maintain the tendencies of the mid-1960s.

On the whole, these tendencies have been arrested or reversed since Czechoslovakia, whose lesson (called the Brezhnev Doctrine in the West) was rather explicitly drawn by Sergei Kovalev in *Pravda* (September 25, 1968), a month or so after the intervention:

> There is no doubt that the peoples of the socialist countries and the Communist Parties have and must have freedom to determine their country's path of development. However, any decision of theirs must damage neither socialism in their own country nor the fundamental interests of the other socialist countries nor the worldwide workers' movement, which is waging a struggle for socialism. This means that every Communist Party is responsible not only to its own people but also to all the socialist countries and to the entire Communist movement. Whoever forgets this in placing sole emphasis on the autonomy and independence of Communist Parties lapses into one-sidedness, shirking his international obligations. . . . The sovereignty of individual socialist countries cannot be counterposed to the interests of world socialism and the world revolutionary movement.

The concept of limited sovereignty was hardly novel; it reflected long-standing Soviet policy toward Eastern Europe. What was important was the Soviet willingness to state it so clearly and unequivocally, and that willingness in turn reflected the new confidence of the Brezhnev regime. For all practical purposes, then, the "golden age" of experimentation in Eastern Europe—that lasted from 1964 to 1968—is now over, as the Soviet leadership reasserts the primacy of its political, security, and ideological interests in the region over other global interests and considerations.

EASTERN EUROPE AND THE WEST

Western reactions to the invasion of Czechoslovakia and to the subsequent assertion of the concept of limited sovereignty were quite illustrative of the postwar dilemma facing the West in Eastern Europe. From the Czechoslovak coup of 1948 to the invasion of Czechoslovakia in 1968—and, for that matter, since then—the West has been caught between its desire to alter or modify the Eastern European status quo and its inability to do so. The Western "desire" cannot be fulfilled without resorting to war; and no one, of course, has advocated the use of force to change Soviet policies in Eastern Europe. In 1968, as on other occasions, the dilemma was resolved by verbal expressions of indignation coupled with no consequential action aside from the cancellation of President Johnson's planned summit conference in Moscow.

Indeed, this discrepancy between word and deed and between hope and resignation has characterized the Western posture since 1948. In the 1950s, the emphasis was on hope, since there was much official talk about the "liberation" of Eastern Europe and the "rollback" of Soviet power. Often prompted by political emigres from Eastern Europe, the American political spectrum, for example—ranging from Secretary of State John Foster Dulles to the editorial writers of the New York *Times*—made Soviet behavior in Eastern Europe the criterion by which Soviet foreign policy would be judged. It was rather widely assumed that the relaxation of Soviet control in Eastern Europe, if not the pullback of Soviet forces from the region, was the precondition of genuine East-West talks and accommodation. Accordingly, there was a verbal commitment to changing the political status quo in Eastern Europe, a commitment often justified in idealistic or anti-communist terms. Dulles declared, for example: "To all those suffering under communist slavery, the intimidated and weak peoples of the world, let us say this, you can count upon us." Yet the Western interest in Eastern Europe was more than ideological. It was also based on the expectation that the post-Stalin leaders of the Soviet Union would prefer East-West detente to rigid imperial control over Eastern Europe, and that if they knew they had to make that choice, they might at least allow their "sphere of dominance" to become a "sphere of influence."

The expectation that Eastern Europe might thus be "Finlandized" was made more explicit in the 1960s, when the American policy of "bridge-building" and the West German policy of Ostpolitik developed, and when President Charles de Gaulle of France spoke of his vision of Europe extending from the Atlantic to the Urals. What was common in these Western approaches and concepts was the desire to convince the Soviet leaders that it was in their self-interest to relax their tight reign over Eastern Europe, whose seemingly permanent instability could spill over the Soviet Union itself. Thus the aim of Ostpolitik, in particular, was to influence the course of events in Eastern Europe by reaching the region through the back door, as it were—through Moscow. Under Chancellor Willy Brandt, West Germany first normalized its relationship with the Soviet Union, and only after that was more or less accomplished did the Federal Republic seek to establish—or, indeed, to reestablish—its presence in Eastern Europe.

Whether the West has or has not succeeded in Eastern Europe is a question of considerable complexity. Citing a degree of diversity in the region, most of the chapters in this book implicitly applaud Western efforts. It would indeed be hard not to recognize that the monolithic unity of the past is gone in Eastern Europe. With its emphasis on consumerism, for example, the Hungarian regime of Janos Kadar differs from its neighbors and from the Soviet Union; the intricate, almost Byzantine maneuverings of Romanian foreign policy are duplicated nowhere in Eastern Europe; and (to use a different sort of example) East German efficiency and productivity have made that country unique in the region. There is, moreover, Western presence everywhere—through trade, tourism, and radio broadcasts (particularly Radio Free Europe). Especially in the cultural realm, the West presents strong competition to Russian ideas and influences.

It is also true that traditional, pre-communist antagonisms have surfaced in the 1960s and 1970s. Romanian-Hungarian and Yugoslav-Bulgarian relations are at least cool, for example. Judging by the remarkable testimony of former Polish leader Wladyslaw Gomulka's personal interpreter, there is deep-rooted hostility among several of the leaders of Eastern Europe.[3] Prior to the Warsaw Pact decision to invade Czechoslovakia, for example, not only did the party leaders disagree about what to do, but Walter Ulbricht of East Germany lost his temper and shouted at Janos Kadar of Hungary for the latter's apparent concern about, and hence implicit opposition to, taking "drastic actions" against the reformist regime of Alexander Dubcek in Czechoslovakia.

While these are signs of diversity (and there are many others), trade and cultural exchange have probably not led to increased Western political influence. In this connection, it is useful to cite Adam B. Ulam's perceptive observation:

> Perhaps a moment will come when some of the prophecies about the corrosive effect of "convergence," certain common traits of all "post-industrial" societies, "consumerism," etc., on Communist authoritarianism will be fulfilled. There are, to be sure, forces of economic and social change constantly pushing against the walls of the authoritarian state. *Yet the controlling factor has always been the political one.* . . . It is at least premature, then, to expect that the

increased volume of economic and cultural contacts will produce a diminution of authoritarian controls in the East or crucially affect the pattern of relations between the Communist states in the area and the USSR. In fact, the local regimes—like the Soviet regime during the last few years—may well tighten their ideological and political controls to protect themselves from any undesirable fruits of more extensive contacts with the West, and they may also be *less willing to seek emancipation from their great friend and protector.*[4]

Indeed, the lesson of Czechoslovakia and detente for Eastern Europe is that in its search for more autonomy, it should not count on energetic Western assistance. During and after Vietnam and Watergate, the United States opted for detente with the Soviet Union without "liberalization" in Eastern Europe. In 1970 President Richard Nixon assured the Soviet Union that the United States would not "seek to exploit Eastern Europe to obtain strategic advantage against the Soviet Union" because the American "pursuit of negotiation and detente is meant to reduce existing tensions, not to stir up new ones." Thus the old point of departure was being reversed: instead of making Eastern Europe a test of Soviet intentions and a precondition of East-West detente, the United States entered into a detente relationship with the Soviet Union and assured Moscow of Western disinclination to "exploit" its difficulties in Eastern Europe. In a sense, this change in Western policy was officially and publicly promulgated in the summer of 1975 at the Helsinki Conference on European Security and Cooperation.

Even if Western political influence has remained minimal, the formation of foreign policy in, and thus the international politics of, Eastern Europe no longer resemble the Stalinist process. In at least one important area, perhaps the most important area, the Eastern European states can and do act as participants in a process of genuine give-and-take: economic decision-making within CEMA. This point was documented by William R. Kintner and Wolfgang Klaiber, who noted that economic integration was not making much progress in Eastern Europe despite Soviet encouragement, thus indicating "a significant development in Soviet bloc relations":

A decisionmaking process has evolved for blocwide programs and policies in which East European leaderships have risen to the de facto status of participants rather than the pawns they once were in the Soviet design. No doubt, the Soviet Union remains much more equal than any of the East European countries in the decisionmaking councils of the bloc, but the latter have gained the ability, individually and collectively, to advance or protect their own national interests against those of the Soviet Union and other bloc countries.[5]

Not the pawns they used to be, nor autonomous as most would like to be, the Eastern European states have obtained some leverage vis-a-vis the Soviet Union in the 1960s and 1970s. Accordingly, they seem to respond to similar pressures and restraints, and to live within the confines of some of the same ambiguities, that other small or medium-size countries must take into account in the formulation and implementation of their foreign policies. It is this tendency more than any other that makes the study of the international politics of Eastern Europe quite complicated—and exciting.

NOTES

1. For an excellent introduction, see Toby Trister, "Traditionalists, Revisionists, and the Cold War: A Bibliographical Sketch," in Charles Gati, ed., *Caging the Bear: Containment and the Cold War* (Indianapolis and New York: Bobbs-Merrill, 1974), pp. 211-22. Also see J. L. Richardson, "Cold-War Revisionism: A Critique," *World Politics* 25, no. 4 (July 1972): 579-612.

2. As cited by Richardson, op. cit., p. 584.

3. Erwin Weit, *At the Red Summit: Interpreter Behind the Iron Curtain* (New York: Macmillan, 1973), esp. pp. 193-217.

4. Adam B. Ulam, "The Destiny of Eastern Europe," *Problems of Communism* 23, no. 1 (January-February 1974): 12.

5. William R. Kintner and Wolfgang Klaiber, *Eastern Europe and European Security* (New York: Dunellen, 1971), p. 207.

EASTERN EUROPE
AND THE
COMMUNIST WORLD

2

HAS EASTERN EUROPE BECOME
A LIABILITY TO THE SOVIET UNION?
(I)—THE POLITICAL-IDEOLOGICAL ASPECTS
Vernon V. Aspaturian

CONCEPTUAL ISSUES

Periodically, one hears the almost plaintive rhetorical observation that Eastern Europe has finally become, or is about to become, a liability to the Soviet Union and hence might be jettisoned by the Soviet behemoth in its own self-interest, much as some giant conglomerate might abandon a once profitable, but now foundering, banana plantation or exhausted copper mine lest it become a source of financial vulnerability endangering the conglomerate as a whole.

The dictionary definition of "liability" is replete with financial connotations and denotes debt, debit, arrears obligation, burden, disadvantage, and drawback, as well as strongly suggesting the sense of vulnerability and exposure. It would be tempting to use the financial model of liability for a political analysis, since it would lend itself easily to metaphorical cuteness; but for purposes of this analysis, the financial model of liability will be employed only marginally, and the term "liability" will be employed in the more restrictive senses of burden, disadvantage, drawback, and vulnerability.

The principal antonym of "liability" is "asset," and indeed it is virtually impossible to conceive of liability without implying the corresponding concept of asset. The two, in many respects, must be viewed as the ends of a single continuum; and thus the central thrust of this analysis is to determine the degree to which Eastern Europe has become, or may become, a burden, disadvantage, drawback, or vulnerability for the Soviet Union. Correspondingly, of course, this involves an evaluation of Eastern Europe as an asset (something valuable, resources, means, possessions, advantage) to the Soviet Union. We must start with the assumption that Eastern Europe is viewed by the Soviet leaders as an asset, but an asset that under certain conditions can erode until it becomes a liability.

Hypothetically, of course, one can envision a concatenation of circumstances, contextual situations, or imaginative scenarios in which Eastern Europe might change from an asset into a liability and confront the Soviet leadership with the traumatic dilemma of abandoning a wasting asset or engaging in salvage operations. Great Britain, France, the Netherlands, Belgium, and Portugal have all suffered through the agonies of having valuable assets erode into liabilities, and, to a lesser degree, so has the United States, with respect to South Vietnam. Empires do not last forever, and certainly the Soviet empire is not immune to the ravages of inevitability; in the manner of other empires, it should at some point start breaking apart. The specific causal mechanisms that trigger the disintegration of empires may differ in individual instances, and the consequences vary in each case; but what they all have in common is the progressive erosion of assets (colonies, dependencies, clients, satellites) into liabilities because of war, political turmoil, diplomatic pressures, or economic costs.

Defining a liability within an international political context is an extremely complex and treacherous enterprise that lends itself with equal ease to oversimplification and overcomplication. Isolating the major variables and dimensions for separate analysis, although both possible and heuristically valuable for analytical purposes, necessarily distorts the concept of liability, since the latter is the sum total of all its dimensions—ideological, political, diplomatic, financial, economic, military, and strategic—which at different times and under varying conditions may reflect different values and weights in the overall calculation. (The military-strategic and economic aspects of liability are treated separately in Chapters 3 and 4.) Eastern Europe as an asset or liability to the Soviet Union, either as a whole or individually, may wax or wane as such in its various dimensions; and at different times the overall net value may reflect varying balances among the dimensions. Thus, it would not be unusual for Eastern Europe to become increasingly important as a strategic asset while its political and ideological liability increases, or vice versa. This can apply to individual countries in Eastern Europe as well, and again can reflect varying balances or mixes from one country to another. In each case, the Soviet leaders must weigh assets against liabilities as they devise policies and make decisions.

Thus, ideological and political liabilities cannot be treated as absolute and exclusive entities in the calculation of liability, but must be measured and balanced against economic, military, strategic, and other considerations. Furthermore, it is rare in politics for something to be a pure or absolute asset; every asset has a liability, although it may not be equally true that every liability retains a residue of asset; many liabilities do, however, particularly in international politics. Great wealth and power, among states as among individuals, always carry with them liabilities of some sort; and while they are substantially different from the liabilities that burden the poor and the weak, they are liabilities nevertheless. All assets are subject to degrees of diminishing value, in response to a multitude of changing situations and contexts; and at some point they can be transformed into liabilities. More appropriately, perhaps, it would be better to deal with diminishing or increasing liabilities and/or assets rather than with "liability" in isolation.

To add to the complexity of the conceptual problem, it must be noted that the terms "liability" and "asset" are perceptual in character; and thus their use may be highly subjective and judgmental. Not only liability in what context or dimension, but also liability for whom and for what purpose are highly critical questions. Different perceptions of liability can coexist simultaneously; and all of these perceptions may ultimately affect the objective situation, since states and leaders act essentially upon their perceptions of reality and interests rather than upon an abstract, objectively measurable reality. The Soviet leaders, those of Eastern Europe and of the Peoples' Republic of China (PRC), American policy-makers and those in Western Europe and the Third World, may have differing perceptions of Eastern Europe's value to the Soviet Union; and, depending upon how their perceptions affect their particular interests, they will shape policy accordingly. Within individual countries, including the Soviet Union and Eastern Europe, differing perceptions of liability may be held by factions, groups, observers, or analysts. As a consequence of these subjective factors, there is ample latitude for the operation of the self-fulfilling prophecy or expectation, whose dynamic in this case would tend more to erode assets into liabilities than to convert liabilities into assets, although the latter process is not entirely unknown. As any economist knows, solid assets can be transformed into liabilities by pessimistic expectations, just as any good con artist or swindler knows that the optimistic expectations of a victim can convert lead into gold for the swindler.

CHINESE AND U.S. INTERESTS IN EASTERN EUROPE

Among the uncertainties confronting the Soviet leaders today, as they pursue a detente arrangement with the United States and an increasingly hostile and adversative relationship with China, is the impact these developments will have on the countries of Eastern Europe and their relationship, collectively and individually, with the Soviet Union. (The PRC impact on and interest in Eastern Europe is covered in detail in Chapter 5.) Will these contrasting Soviet relationships with China and the United States work symbiotically, if inadvertently, to create contextual situations that may enable Eastern European leaders to skillfully orchestrate a triangular power minuet that will bring about a significant transformation of their relationship with Moscow? The degree to which they succeed in this venture will depend in large measure upon the ability of the Eastern European leaders to generate perceptions in Moscow that an unchanging relationship with Eastern Europe will be a serious liability to the Soviet leaders as they enter into changing relationships with Peking and Washington.

Since both China and the United States, for purposes that are not only different but perhaps even contradictory, seem interested in loosening the bond between Moscow and Eastern Europe, and this is well known in both Moscow and Eastern Europe, the Eastern European states are transformed from pawns and objects of Soviet foreign policy into actors and subjects of international politics. The Moscow-Peking-Washington triangle creates a latitude for maneuver and even limited autonomy for the Eastern European countries, and thus improves their bargaining leverage with Moscow—that is, creates new burdens or liabilities for the Soviet leaders.

The character of Eastern Europe as a liability or asset to the Soviet Union is closely interwoven with the precise nature of the contrasting interests and purposes of China and the United States in Eastern Europe. It is the fortuitous intersection of these uncoordinated Chinese and American purposes in the area that maximizes the flexibility of Eastern European leaders in tailoring their bargaining strategy vis-a-vis Moscow. Because China challenges the Soviet Union both within the subsystem of communist states and parties and in the general interstate system (principally in the Third World), the Eastern European leaders can also operate simultaneously in both systems and bring leverage to bear from one to another. In many respects, the Helsinki Agreement of 1975 and the preceding conference meetings legitimized the participation of the Eastern European states in their individual capacities rather than as members of a bloc. The agreement itself provides ample opportunity for the Eastern European states to increase their bargaining leverage with Moscow because many key provisions contradict the principles of socialist internationalism and particularly the Brezhnev Doctrine. As signatories of the Helsinki Agreement and as subscribers to the principles of socialist internationalism, the Eastern European leaders are provided with an international legal lever to use against the Brezhnev Doctrine, and hence the Helsinki Agreement emerges as a potential instrument for creating additional burdens for the Soviet Union in its relationship to Eastern Europe. This does not mean that Eastern Europe is diminished as an asset, or that it will necessarily use its legal lever, but it does imply that the costs of preserving Eastern Europe as an asset and precluding it from becoming a liability may increase. Or, to put it another way, in order to retain Eastern Europe as an asset for strategic purposes, the Soviet leaders may have to make concessions to Eastern Europe that will create political and ideological liabilities for Moscow.

Since the United States and the Western European states are also signatories to the Helsinki Agreement, the Eastern European states have a quasi-legal justification for involving them in their relations with Moscow, if the opportunity arises for invoking the Helsinki Agreement against the Soviet Union. Correspondingly, since China is part of the world communist movement and the socialist commonwealth, the states of Eastern Europe can use her as a lever against Moscow within the communist subsystem. The coexistence of the Helsinki Agreement with the principles of socialist internationalism creates a new dynamic of intersection and interaction; and the behavior of the United States as the principal partner in one arena and China in the other may coalesce to transform Eastern Europe into a liability, diminish it as an asset, or force the Soviet Union to pay an increasing cost to preserve it as a residual asset.

What, then, are the Chinese and American interests in the Soviet-Eastern European relationship and how can they affect the status of Eastern Europe as an asset or liability? Generally speaking, the Chinese interest has four objectives: (1) to weaken Soviet posture with respect to China by depriving the Soviet Union of an important reserve of human and natural resources; (2) to render the Soviet Union vulnerable to attack from the West, as the Soviet threat to China grows, and thus to slow or deter a possible Soviet attack on China; (3) to call into question Moscow's credentials as a communist revolutionary power by depriving the Soviet Union of its principal ideological extension in the world; and (4) to create a community of ideological interests between China and a group of small communist states in search of a new communist power that can provide protection without the risk of domination. Of course, this latter objective is a reflection of the fantasies that agitate the Chinese leaders at this particular moment. For some reason, they seem to believe that the regimes in Eastern Europe are bona fide communist regimes, however corrupted and contaminated by Soviet revisionism, that would like to break away from the Soviet Union and find a genuine communist revolutionary protector: China, which is sufficiently distant so that it cannot become a dominant power. To a certain degree, the relationship between China and Albania represents the kind of fantasy model that the Chinese leaders would like to see emerge: an Eastern European group of communist states looking to China for leadership rather than to the Soviet Union.

What are the American interests in loosening the bonds between Moscow and Eastern Europe, and how do they coincide with the Chinese purpose? (For a detailed analysis, see Chapter 7.) First and foremost the United States has, until recently, sought to disassociate the Soviet Union from Eastern Europe, not so much for ideological anti-communist purposes but, rather, to deprive the Soviet Union of a forward geopolitical springboard for possible invasion or intervention in Central and Western Europe. That is, its objective has been to remove once and for all the threat of direct Soviet intervention in Germany and in Western Europe, in response either to communist uprisings within these individual countries or to vulnerabilities and openings that might entice the Soviet Union to move its own forces directly into the area. What the United States seeks is the transformation of Eastern Europe from a potential Soviet springboard into a buffer zone between Soviet power and West Central Europe.

A second purpose has been to diminish Soviet power by depriving the

Soviet Union of the human and material resources of more than 100 million people who live in the region, although the current reliability and usefulness of these resources is questionable. No one knows exactly how the armies of Eastern Europe would react in the event of a war. The Soviet leaders themselves view the reliability of the Eastern European states with considerable skepticism.

A third purpose would be to deprive the Soviet Union of its credentials as the leader of a world revolutionary movement. If Eastern Europe were alienated from the Soviet Union, Soviet communism would be transformed from an international ideology into a parochial one. This is a very important point. Since the mid-1960s, given the fractured character of world communism and its near dissolution as a movement, the only residual credential of universality that the Soviet Union possesses in the worldwide movement is its ideological leadership in Eastern Europe. The Eastern European communist states are in many ways an extension of the Soviet system, and as such they perform an important function in validating the main ideological purpose of the Soviet Union.

Needless to say, the Soviet leaders are not about to accommodate either China or the United States by relinquishing their Eastern European empire. Indeed, as time passes, Eastern Europe will become more, not less, important to the Soviet Union. Nevertheless, if its detente relationship intensifies with the United States, there may be important changes in this relationship. No one knows at this point, either in Moscow or in Washington, exactly how the Eastern European states will be affected by detente. It remains to be seen how the Soviet Union will justify its military presence in the area without a credible threat from Western Europe, Germany, or the United States and to what degree this lack of threat will stimulate boldness and dissidence in the Soviet Union's Eastern European empire, thus increasing that empire's liability quotient.

Of course, to the degree that the detente relationship intensifies, the American interest in loosening the bonds between the Soviet Union and Eastern Europe may diminish as well, because the absence of a credible Soviet threat to Western Europe will have a similar corrosive impact upon NATO. Therefore, as detente develops—if it does develop—important changes probably will take place in both alliance systems, although their precise character cannot be predicted in detail.

As the Soviet Union's credibility as a revolutionary power erodes, and much of that erosion is due to the criticism and denunciation of the Chinese (who are now their principal challengers), the Soviet leaders are likely to be more obsessive about the importance of Eastern Europe as a validation of their system and their original pretensions. By keeping Eastern Europe within the Soviet orbit, Moscow retains the fig leaf of communist internationalism although it may stand exposed naked as an imperialist global power in all other respects.

SOVIET INTERESTS IN EASTERN EUROPE

At this point, perhaps it would be wise to state some fundamental and obvious propositions that might be otherwise obscured as we strive for a more sophisticated analysis. The Soviet position in Eastern Europe has always served, and continues to serve, two distinct but interdependent purposes that are in a relationship that changes continuously not only over time but also in response to circumstances and events.

The first is a purely strategic security purpose connected intimately with national defense and security. Eastern Europe has historically constituted an invasion funnel from the West into Russia. Similarly, it has constituted an invasion funnel from Russia into Central and Eastern Europe. As an important buffer region made up of small, relatively weak states that are divided from one another by ancient historical animosities, it traditionally has been manipulated and exploited by neighboring great powers for their own ends. Eastern Europe by itself remains incapable of filling the power vacuum that inevitably develops in this region, and it has been the fate of East Central Europe to become the sphere of influence of one of the great powers. If it was not within the sphere of influence of Russia, then it fell within Germany's or that of some German-type state such as Austria. Since World War II, it has become a part of the Soviet sphere, where it functions as the Soviet Union's single most important geographical defense zone.

Hence, it is not likely that the Soviet leaders will permit Eastern Europe to break away in the foreseeable future. As events in Czechoslovakia demonstrated in 1968, they are prepared to intervene, if necessary, to prevent any significant erosion of their Eastern European empire, although the costs in terms of Soviet international prestige may rise with successive interventions.

The Soviet presence in Eastern Europe thus guarantees, at the minimum, a denial of the region to any other great power; currently the pertinent great power is West Germany, because Eastern Europe has traditionally been a sphere of influence of either Germany or Russia. Two of the Soviet leaders' great concerns about West Germany's Ostpolitik, initiated by Chancellor Ludwig Erhard in 1965-66 and extended by Chancellors Kurt Kiesinger and Willy Brandt, were that the policy threatened to loosen the bonds between Eastern Europe and the Soviet Union and that it appeared to represent a bid by West Germany to revive its traditional interest in the area. A policy that served to entice the Eastern European states into developing closer relations with West Germany, it encouraged the autonomous defiance of Romania, particularly in the realm of foreign policy. More importantly, it reinforced those internal developments in Czechoslovakia that might have removed the nation from the Soviet orbit. One reason the Soviet Union intervened in Czechoslovakia in August 1968 was the fear that the West German policy of Ostpolitik, in conjunction with President Lyndon Johnson's policy of "bridge building to

Eastern Europe," would be more successful in eroding Soviet power in Eastern Europe than the frontal, hostile posture that had existed before 1965-66, when Ostpolitik and the bridge-building policy were inaugurated. Although Eastern Europe is vital to Soviet security, the Soviet presence there also constitutes a threat to Western Europe, just as the presence of another great power in the region would constitute a menace to Moscow.

The strategic aspects of the Soviet presence in Eastern Europe can be viewed separately from the ideological and political aspects, since they are not irrevocably interrelated with any specific ideological purpose or political system; but they cannot be separated when measuring the overall liability of Eastern Europe to the Soviet Union. In a psychological sense, Soviet control of Eastern Europe also serves to validate Moscow's credentials as a regional power, as a leader of a group of states, and as a leader of one of the two principal alliance and political systems in the world. It is important to bear in mind that the United States and the Soviet Union are the only two alliance leaders in the world today, and that a certain amount of prestige is derived from that particular role. Furthermore, much of the Soviet Union's prestige in international affairs derives from the fact that it is the leader of a group of states.

Thus, the second general purpose of the Soviet presence in Eastern Europe is essentially political and ideological in character, although the ideological aspect has been assuming an increasingly symbolic context. These ideological and sumbolic purposes are becoming progressively residual but nevertheless continue to be important for the short run, since the ideological element in Soviet behavior has been eroding for many years and probably will continue to do so. The Soviet Union appears to have no real future as the leader of a universal communist movement, because China's emergence as a rival has effectively arrested that role. Before the emergence of China as a rival, the policies of the United States had, in many ways, also blocked the expansion of Soviet or communist power, but in different ways.

In the short run, then, the existence of Eastern Europe as a bloc of communist states modeled on the Soviet system—and the word "communist" is emphasized—continues to validate the Soviet Union's credentials as an ideological and revolutionary power, as well as the residual center of a world revolutionary movement.

Eastern Europe thus is not only an imperialistic extension of the Soviet Union but is also an extension of the Soviet Union's social system; and as the first and most important extension of the Soviet system beyond the borders of the Soviet Union, it represents the residue of Moscow's former ecumenical pretensions. All of the communist states in Eastern Europe came into being under various forms of Soviet sponsorship. They were all cast from the Soviet mold, and in one way or another represented the first step in universalizing the Soviet system. All have been beneficiaries of Soviet protection, as well as victims of Soviet domination. It might be said that while the communist regimes have been the beneficiaries of Soviet protection, the populations have been the victims of Soviet domination.

The communist states of Eastern Europe are, in effect, miniature alter egos of the Soviet Union; and when the Soviet leaders look at Eastern Europe, they find contentment only if it reflects a reasonable facsimile of themselves. The integrity, viability, and even existence of the Soviet system depend upon the maintenance of the communist regimes in Eastern Europe; and thus, for psychological reasons alone, the overthrow of any communist regime in Eastern Europe, even the Albanian, would constitute a threat to the Soviet system. It is important to bear in mind that the Soviet Union does not consider itself to be merely a state; it considers itself as a representative of a particular form of social and economic organization that has universal validity and application. And the Eastern European states are subordinate not simply to Soviet foreign policy; their internal structures are also in some degree subordinate to Soviet will.

The defensive function of the Soviet presence in Eastern Europe has always been recognized as valid by the West, certainly by the United States, and has been justified amply by both history and logic. But the second purpose has concerned the West, particuarly the United States—the function of the Soviet presence in Eastern Europe as a first step in the communization of all Europe. As far as Western Europe and the United States were concerned, of course, the ideological-expansionist aspect of the Soviet presence in Eastern Europe dwarfed all other considerations. In Soviet calculations, however, the defensive and offensive functions of Soviet presence in Eastern Europe remained intricately intertwined and rather equally weighted.

THE IMPACT OF DETENTE

Isolating the political and ideological importance of Eastern Europe to the Soviet Union from its economic and strategic importance artificially sunders relationships that are intimately interconnected and powerfully reinforcing. What takes place in the domain of politics and ideology cannot but influence economic and military considerations, and vice versa. Furthermore, this impact will vary from one country to another in Eastern Europe, depending on each country's specific vulnerabilities to penetrating influences from either China or the United States. While the Soviet regime is overtly concerned principally with the risks of penetrating influences from the West in terms of ideas or political and economic linkages and, to a lesser degree, with influences emanating from China, the greatest danger to the Soviet management of Eastern Europe during a period of detente will be the influences that individual countries of Eastern Europe may have upon one another. Influences from the West can be routinely stigmatized and proscribed as "capitalist," "imperialist," or "decadent," while those from China can, with less credibility and effectiveness, be condemned as "heretical." It would be increasingly difficult, however, to deter mutual contamination within Eastern Europe, as long as the ideas and innovations are derived from a country that has been legitimized as "socialist" by the Soviet regime.

Whether Eastern Europe becomes a liability to the Soviet Union during an era of detente will thus depend upon the degree to which it is vulnerable to noxious external influences and internal developments. These liabilities, however, must be weighed against other, more durable economic and military considerations that may more than justify whatever liabilities are incurred in the political-ideological realm.

Although the United States and West Germany, through a series of treaties and agreements, recently have virtually accepted the territorial, political, and ideological status quo in Eastern Europe and have, de facto if not de jure, recognized the region as a part of the Soviet sphere of influence, and thus off-limits to frontal and overt penetration, Soviet leaders perceive that the danger of "penetration" from the West has not subsided but has, in fact, increased. This point of view is represented by the shrill warnings emanating from Moscow, and echoed in Eastern European capitals, about the dangers of "ideological coexistence" and its condemnation in any form. The detente is not to be extended into the realm of ideas; rather, the ideological struggle is to continue unabated. The Eastern European reception to this call for continuing the ideological battle is mixed, ranging from unsophisticated regurgitation of the orthodox Soviet position to an expression of confident indifference. Even statements from Eastern European capitals that superficially endorse the Soviet position frequently exhibit qualifying nuances and subtle reservations signifying that the possible invasion of Western ideas is not entirely unattractive.

In fact, the Soviet fear on this score is not so much the vigor with which the United States and the West will attempt to ideologically subvert Eastern Europe, nor that indifference, naivete, or negligence will somehow allow noxious ideas to filter through, but, rather, the uneasy and entirely justifiable concern that wide sectors of the Eastern European publics are attracted to these ideas and will willingly import them or revive their local variants even in the absence of exhortations from the West. Thus, one of the real risks that the Soviet leaders perceive is not so much the "export" of ideas as their voluntary and spontaneous "import" and resurrection, which would be particularly difficult to contend with during a period of detente. These differing, even in some respects contrary, expectations were being published in Eastern Europe during the early phases of the current detente process.

The Romanian Party leader Nicolae Ceausescu, for example, appeared to express confident indifference to the possible "penetration" of Western ideas and initially demurred from the Soviet position, a stand he has since reversed:

In our opinion, we should have no fear that the expansion of international relations will involve the danger of the capitalist world exercising an adverse influence upon the nations which have set out along the path of building a new social order. There is an old Romanian saying: "He who is frightened by the wolf will also be afraid of the hare." We have lived in the mountains for a long time and are familiar with wolves. We are not frightened of them, and even less so of hares. We are not afraid of pursuing widespread activities in the field of international cooperation.[1]

In contrast with this position was the Soviet one, which was echoed in East Germany, Poland, Czechoslovakia, Bulgaria, and, to a lesser degree, Hungary, but which found its most explicit and vivid expression in the Polish press:

The climate of international relations necessary for our offensive in favor of a detente may generate trends towards demobilization inside the country (particularly in the ideological sphere); it may contribute to the emergence of illusions about the possibility of permanent and all-embracing agreements between the two systems, about the disappearance of political and social differences between them. It may make for a "softening" of attitudes, a weakening of social vigilance vis-a-vis imperialism, etc. We must reckon with the possibility that this may be accompanied by a temptation to transfer the tactics of compromise to the ideological sphere. We must also reckon with the psychological pressure on certain circles in our country which have ample opportunity to shape public opinion, pressure which will be intensified by the Western apparatus of ideological diversion.[2]

Although in 1971 the Eastern European countries were somewhat critical receptors of the Soviet position, the Soviet and Eastern European positions have since become virtually identical on this issue, at least on the surface. These changes of position, most evident in Romania, Yugoslavia, and Hungary, reflect not so much a belated recognition of the superior wisdom of Moscow as an acute awareness that since 1971 or so the United States has, to all intents and purposes, abandoned Eastern Europe to the Soviet Union and is no longer willing to supply even the psychological umbrella of protection that it unfurled to shield Yugoslavia and Romania after the invasion of Czechoslovakia in 1968. Furthermore, the decreasing usefulness of China as a lever in this connection has contributed to the current Eastern European strategy of avoiding even the appearance of provocation that might be used as a pretext for Moscow's intervention.

Still, the conversion of Eastern Europe into a conduit for the "free flow of ideas," persons, norms, and values from the West to the East remains one of the possible gains of detente for the West, just as the Soviet leaders perceive this process as a potential liability to the "socialist commonwealth" and even the Soviet Union itself. That large sectors of Eastern European publics, including substantial sectors of the elites, are receptive to such a role is recognized in Moscow, Washington, and the capitals of Eastern and Western Europe. Even the Chinese, whose attitude reflects ambivalence on this issue, would seemingly welcome the "free flow of ideas" into Eastern Europe, if for no other purpose than that it would weaken the Soviet grip on the area and simultaneously demonstrate the Soviet revisionism and collusion have undermined socialism in Eastern Europe by creating the conditions rendering them vulnerable to the resurrection and importation of bourgeois ideology.

The liabilities of Eastern Europe to the Soviet Union in the ideological realm during a period of detente can be summarized as follows:

1. So-called "bourgeois" influences, ideas, institutions, and values may be imported or resurrected in Eastern European countries in varying degrees despite measures to block the "penetration" and "export of these ideas.

2. Marginally legitimate norms of socialism in some socialist countries, notably Yugoslavia and Hungary, as well as other innovations that may develop incrementally as a consequence of the "many paths to socialism" doctrine, may proliferate and spill over into other Eastern European states and into the Soviet Union itself. During a period of detente, in the absence of any credible external threat, it would be difficult for the Soviet leaders to intervene in order to arrest or block such developments.

3. The relaxation of international tensions, the institution of further possible arms control measures and force reductions, and the ideological polarization and discontinuities in the world communist movement (as reflected most conspicuously in the Sino-Soviet conflict), can provide the Eastern European countries with the opportunity to disassociate themselves from Soviet univeralist ideological goals while simultaneously aligning themselves more closely with Moscow on diplomatic and security issues. As the officially professed danger from the West subsides, while the Chinese simultaneously step up their attack on Moscow on the ideological front, Eastern European leaders can continue to resist Moscow's demand for a show of ideological unity on the ground that as long as the Chinese and other communist parties have not mended their ideological fences with Moscow, such a show of ideological unity would be hollow and divisive. Thus, by moving closer to Soviet positions on the diplomatic and security fronts, the Eastern European leaders can deprive the Soviet leaders of any pretext to crack down as they continue to resist calls for ideological unity. In this manner, Eastern European states will disassociate themselves from Soviet international ideological goals, and at the same time they will continue to erode the legitimacy of the Soviet Union as a source of ideological leadership, if not orthodoxy.

4. Depending upon the degree to which the developments described above

unfold, the ultimate consequence may be a fundamental transformation of the Soviet-Eastern European relationship with substantive political, as opposed to purely ideological, consequences.

It is at this point that the potential ideological liabilities of Eastern Europe give way to the grave political liabilities that may evolve. Given the current political, strategic and, most important, psychological balance of power between the Soviet Union and the United States, and the general perception of the United States in Moscow and Eastern European capitals that neither the American public nor the American Congress is predisposed to support American military involvement in marginal areas or even to tolerate diplomatic risk-taking as a substitute, one of the few risks that the Soviet Union will not incur is that individual Eastern European states may take advantage of the detente to move away from the Soviet position on foreign policy and military issues or to pry themselves away from Soviet control. The current parameters of the Soviet-American detente effectively preclude these possibilities. Such daring adventurism in Eastern Europe could only be based on false perception that the United States would be actively in support of, or at least receptive to, such developments and, more important, could provide a psychological cover of protection that would deter Soviet intervention to arrest developments of this character.

The Soviet invasion of Czechoslovakia, the course of American foreign policy since then in the direction of lessening international commitments, the general malaise and mood of the American public, Congress's preoccupation with washing America's dirty linen in public, and the general public opposition to future military involvement, have all combined to leave an impact upon both Moscow and the leaders of Eastern Europe. A Harris poll, conducted in December 1974 for the Chicago Council on Foreign Relations and released in March 1975, could only serve to confirm in quantitative terms what the communist leaders in Eastern Europe had earlier discerned intuitively. Only 39 percent of the American public would favor military involvement if Western Europe were invaded. Only 34 percent would favor such action if West Berlin were occupied; the percentage dropped to 32 percent in the event of a Cuban invasion of the Dominican Republic, and plummeted to 27 percent in the event that Israel were being defeated by the Arab states. Of twelve issues of a comparable character, a majority of the public would support the military involvement of the United States only if Canada were attacked.[3]

Is it any wonder, then, that the Eastern European and Soviet leaders have simultaneously arrived at the conclusion that the United States, for the time being at any rate, is in no position to support, encourage, or even welcome attempts on the part of Eastern European states to pry themselves loose from Soviet control?

On the contrary, since 1972, the states of Eastern Europe have fallen all over themselves in moving closer to the Soviet Union on foreign policy and security issues. This has been most evident in Yugoslavia and Romania, the two dissident countries on foreign policy questions. Only barely visible vestiges of Romania's once daring autonomy in foreign policy and security matters are discernible, and even Yugoslavia has moved closer to Moscow on both domestic and foreign policy questions.

Yugoslavia's movement toward Soviet positions, however, is not an unmixed blessing for Moscow; and while it will have undoubted advantages for the Soviet Union, it could also involve substantial liabilities. Although Marshal Tito has cracked down recently on ideological and cultural laxity inside Yugoslavia, most of Yugoslavia's ideological infections are active and flourishing; furthermore, more than two decades of separate, independent communist existence have created psychological attitudes, behavioral patterns, and political habits that cannot be easily eradicated without a widespread and intensive purge, which is not likely under Tito. Hence, the current measures taken by Tito can only have a superficial impact, and may mollify the Soviet leaders sufficiently to risks full acceptance of the Yugoslav regime as a bona fide socialist state without major deficiencies. As Yugoslavia moves closer to the Soviet Union and the states of Eastern Europe, the dangers of contagion will be greater, not less; and the Soviet and Eastern European leaders recognize this risk, the former with anxiety and the latter with mixed emotions.

The greatest liability for Moscow is that Yugoslavia, while moving closer to Soviet positions on foreign and domestic policy, may simultaneously draw some Eastern European states closer to her on other issues. Thus, while the Yugoslavs in 1972 favored the Soviet call for an all-European security conference, their position on the procedures of the conference varied from that of Moscow. Belgrade proposed in 1972 that the European states meet not as "members of blocs" but as "independent and equal countries," which was amplified in the following year with the suggestion that the European states, East and West, move toward the adoption of nonaligned positions:

> Helsinki today is a gateway opening out on a new road. . . . For the first time the problem of European security has been raised as a continental, internal problem of the European nations. . . . It is the first time all European states have had a chance of participating on a footing of equality in the construction of a new European system. . . . The truth is that the inspiration for such radical changes in the European system and in relations between the European nations cannot be found outside the principles of active coexistence and nonalignment. . . . Of all the continents, Europe is numerically the least represented in the nonaligned movement although, objectively speaking, it is searching along [the road leading to] the very principles of non-alignment.[4]

It is no secret that "nonalignment" is an attractive concept for some Eastern European countries. Both Hungary in 1956, and Czechoslovakia in

1968, boldly waved the banner of "nonalignment"; and Romania, during its period of foreign policy autonomy, implicitly flew the same banner behind her repeated calls for the dissolution of all political-ideological and military blocs. Under conditions of detente, it would be difficult indeed for Moscow to arrest Yugoslav-inspired movements in this direction, particularly if NATO simultaneously eroded as a viable military alliance.

But the main political liability for Moscow is not that the Eastern European states may break away from the Soviet orbit, or even that they may conduct autonomous foreign policies, but, rather, that detente may create opportunities for the Eastern European leaders to demand greater autonomy and input into bloc policy. As Eastern European states move closer to Soviet positions in foreign policy, Moscow may imperceptibly move closer to Eastern European domestic positions. This process, too, while not subverting or dissolving the bloc, may result in its basic transformation. Without going into an extensive analysis, and thus omitting the many nuances and subtleties involved in the process of transformation, one could propose that a prolonged period of detente would incur the following potential liabilities for the Soviet Union.

1. With the danger of overt conflict between East and West diminished, increased interaction among the Eastern European states may be expected, even to the extent of forming informal subbloc groupings on various issues. As long as the Soviet connection is not challenged, the process may continue even to the point of transforming the Soviet-Eastern European relationship as a surrogate for sundering it.

2. Similarly, in the absence of an outside threat, Eastern European states may assert greater demands for independent inputs into bloc policy, both on domestic and, to a lesser extent, on foreign policy matters. The parameters of legitimate "socialism" may be stretched, as a consequence of innovations and separate developments, to the point where "socialism" may be defined in terms of empirical-pragmatic evolution rather than predetermined ascriptive criteria.

3. Increased interaction and intrabloc autonomy, however, could erode the bloc as a conflict-containing and conflict-resolving subsystem. Latent antagonisms and grievances of long standing are rife in Eastern Europe, not the least troublesome of which are territorial questions, the most potentially explosive being the Bulgarian claim to Macedonia, the Hungarian claim to at least part of Transylvania, and Polish and Romanian claims against the Soviet Union. The latter are less likely to surface than the claims of the Eastern European states against one another.

Thus, the chief ideological-political liability of Eastern Europe to the Soviet Union during a period of detente will be in the area of bloc management. Although the current strategic and psychological balance of power, together with the Brezhnev Doctrine, virtually assures that the Soviet-Eastern European association will not be ruptured, the Eastern European states have matured sufficiently to the point that, although they have reconciled themselves to remaining under the Soviet roof, they will be inclined to assert themselves more, and hence become less manageable. One should not expect great changes in Eastern Europe in the direction of democratic norms and processes as a result of the transformation of relations in Eastern Europe; rather, one should look for changes of a more modest, if nevertheless important, character.

Eastern European states will use the detente to continue paying greater attention to the needs and interests of domestic constituencies, particularly the nonelites. Emphasis will be placed on improving the conditions of everyday life, not necessarily the expansion of freedom and democratic liberties. Less ideological and political interference in the life of the ordinary citizen will be traded off for, at least initially, more stringent controls over intellectuals and the media. This is likely to mollify the Soviet leaders and induce them to accept the relaxation of controls over ordinary citizens. Eastern European leaders are aware of the deep suspicion that exists between intellectuals and the "masses" in their countries, and adroit manipulation of this distrust can expand and solidify the popular base of local regimes and give them more leverage in dealing with Moscow and other states. If life can be made easier and more bountiful for ordinary citizens, they can be expected to support local regimes as they crack down on intellectuals to appease Moscow and simultaneously strengthen their bargaining position with the Soviet leaders.

THE IMPACT OF THE HELSINKI DECLARATION

In this connection the potential of the Helsinki Agreement as a source of difficulty for the Soviet Union in Eastern Europe is immense, but its actual impact will depend upon the overall strategic balance of power between Washington and Moscow, the course of the Sino-Soviet conflict, and political developments within the Soviet Union itself. Any event, circumstance, or action that diminishes the power, fractures the purpose, or debilitates the will of Moscow will increase the value of the Helsinki Agreement to Eastern Europe. The agreement represents basically a compromise between the United States and the Soviet Union on the basic rules of detente, in which the Soviet Union has traded off lip service to the free flow of ideas and persons in return for a Western recognition of the territorial status quo, not necessarily the political or ideological status quo. The latter rest upon the balance and distribution of power and not upon any agreement; and should that balance change because of Sino-Soviet rivalry, Soviet-American relations, or internal Soviet developments, the political and ideological status quo may change without impairing any boundaries or resulting in territorial alterations. It is important to make these distinctions because many commentators charged the United States with recognixing Soviet control over Eastern Europe.[5] It acknowledged such control by signing the agreement, but this is far from giving legal or formal recognition. In fact, both President Gerald Ford and Secretary of State Henry Kissinger have explicitly denited that the American signature on the Helsinki document recognizes the annexation of the Baltic states or the permanence of Soviet control in Eastern Europe.[6] It does obligate the United States to refrain from using force or supporting the use of force to alter existing de facto boundaries.

In return for American agreement on security and boundary questions, the Soviet Union reluctantly accepted "Basket 3" of the Helsinki Agreement, relating to the free flow of ideas, persons, information, communications, and other humanitarian and cultural concerns. What the Soviet leaders subscribed to in Basket 3 contradicts not only the Breshnev Doctrine and certain key principles of socialist internationalism, but the Soviet constitution itself, and most emphatically Soviet internal practice. To be sure, so far this represents only lip service and the implications for the Soviet Union are only potential. The danger that the Helsinki Agreement might unleash forces in Eastern Europe, however, is much more serious. This may account for the defensive Soviet tone concerning Basket 3, its attempt to downgrade it as a secondary aspect of the agreement, and its indirect disavowal of any intention to give most of its provisions any immediate effect inside the Soviet Union.[7] If only to deter and arrest their possible implementation in Eastern Europe, the Soviet leaders must refuse to give the provisions effect at home, lest a precedent be established for questions) and Leonid Brezhnev explicitly repudiating "bourgeois" interpreta- explicitly disavowing Soviet interpretations of Basket 1 (security and boundary questions) and Leonid Brezhnev explicitly repudiating "bourgeois" interpreta- tions of Basket 3 (humanitarian and information questions).[8]

However Ford and Brezhnev may interpret the Helsinki Agreement, their views must be distinguished from what individual East European states may do in implementing it. The agreement is a European agreement, not a socialist one. The Eastern European states attended and participated in their separate capacities, not as members of a bloc. There is no unified, authoritative communist bloc interpretation of its provisions, although Moscow may attempt to establish one through the Warsaw Pact Organization. Each communist state can interpret the agreement for itself—indeed, East Germany already has on a number of points[9]—and although the Soviet Union may enunciate a "line," it may find it costly to enforce it.

Since the Helsinki Agreement contradicts the Brezhnev Doctrine and many internal practices of the Eastern European states, the latter may abandon or abolish certain internal practices relating to humanitarian and informational concerns by justifying their behavior not as defiance of the Soviet Union but as compliance with the Helsinki Agreement. It should not be bery surprising to see disputes arise between Moscow and some Eastern European states over whether a certain change in policy is in compliance with Helsinki or in defiance of the principles of socialist internationalism, when in fact it may be both. Although many Western critics charged that the Helsinki Agreement might encourage the "Finlandization" of Western Europe, there is the greater possibility that it may encourage the Finlandization of Eastern Europe, much to the chagrin of Moscow. Should the Soviet Union once again resort to intervention to arrest such developments, it would be in direct contravention of the security and boundary provisions of the agreement (of which Moscow was the principal author and supporter), a situation that also adds to Soviet liabilities.

The defensive tone of the Soviet press with respect to the humanitarian and informational provisions of the Helsinki Agreement reflects genuine fears and, perhaps, internal criticism of the concessions made by Moscow.[10] It is noteworthy that American defensiveness about boundaries subsided once President Ford and Secretary Kissinger explicitly disavowed Soviet interpretations. American disavowal of Moscow's interpretations cannot in any way be construed as noncompliance with the Helsinki Agreement; it is only noncompliance with the interpretations that critics like Alexander Solzhenitsyn and Brezhnev gave to the American signature. On the other hand, Soviet disavowals of Western interpretations of Basket 3 represent attempts to avoid compliance, and this accounts for the defensive and self-conscious tone of the Soviet press. Aside from the possibility that Soviet refusal to implement Basket 3 can always stand as a potential excuse for the United States and Western Europe to disavow Basket 1, the Soviet refusal to implement the humanitarian and informational provisions of the Helsinki Agreement exposes Moscow as an open violator of international agreements that she initiated and signed after considerable fanfare and enthusiasm.

Even more critical for Moscow, it would indeed be difficult for her to credibly criticize Eastern European states for taking measures in compliance with the Helsinki Agreement. It is one thing to violate a treaty oneself, and another to force another state to violate an international agreement; yet a third matter is to prevent compliance on the part of another state.

Whatever liabilities develop for the Soviet Union in Eastern Euroee ultimately will be determined by the precise character of the detente relationship between the Soviet Union and the United States, the rivalry with China, and the general role and status of Moscow in the international system. All possible detentes are not born free and equal; and given the strategic paramenters and psychological conditions of the current detente process, including the present American malaise, it is unlikely that Eastern Europe will become a serious liability to the Soviet Union. Should, however, the paramenters of the detente undergo serious change, or should an unforseen internal crisis occur in Moscow, or should the Sino-Soviet conflict take a turn for the worse, the spectrum of liabilities will correspondingly change. The *clausula rebus sic stantibus* is a silent qualifier of all agreements; it always remains in force, and there is no reason to believe that the Helsinki Agreement is immune to its effects.

NOTES

1. *Scinteia*, March 24, 1971.
2. *Wojsko ludowe*, May 5, 1972.
3. Washington *Post*, March 23, 1975, Outlook section, p. B6.
4. *Review of International Affairs* (Belgrade), February 5, 1973, pp. 5-7.
5. See the New York *Times*, July 30, 1975, p. 8, for important excerpts taken from the Helsinki Agreement. For a full English text, see *Conference on Security and Cooperation in Europe. Final Act*, Department of State Publication 8826 (Washington, D.C.: U.S. Government Printing Office, 1975). Soviet exile Alexander Solzhenitsyn was among the severest critics of American adherence to the Helsinki Agreement, which he characterized as a "betrayal of Eastern Europe" that served "to acknowledge its slavery forever." The New York *Times* July 22, 1975. Senator Henry Jackson, on the other hand, while criticizing American adherence to the agreement, correctly emphasized that it "in no way legitimizes Soviet domination" of Eastern Europe. Ibid., July 23, 1975, p. 7.
6. See ibid.
7. The Soviet press published the Helsinki Declaration in full; hence, the Soviet public can easily compare the provisions to which the Soviet leaders actually subscribed and their unilateral, self-serving interpretive attempts to disavow them. For Soviet comments on Basket 3, which deals with human rights, see accounts in the New York *Times*, September 28, 1975, p. 23, and October 2, 1975, p. 7. The avowal of Moscow not to implement these provisions immediately, however, cannot prevent Soviet citizens from raising the applicability of the provisions. Indeed, Brezhnev stated at Helsinki that "the agreements we have reached broaden the possibilities for peoples to influence so-called 'big politics.' " *Pravda*, August 1, 1975. Boris Spassky, the Soviet chess champion, almost immediately invoked a provision of the humanitarian section in order to marry a Frenchwoman, thus confronting the Soviet leaders with an issue. See the New York *Times*, September 9, 1975. More ominously, *Uchitelskaya gazeta* published a letter from a Soviet teacher calling upon the Soviet regime to abolish censorship. She complained that not enough Western films were allowed in the Soviet Union and said: "My opinion is there is no need to forbid anything or to have any such restrictions, for such things stir up an interest in forbidden things." Washington *Post*, August 10, 1975.
8. See the New York *Times*, August 16, 1975, p. 1, for Brezhnev's remarks to a visiting American congressional delegation that suggested that while Basket 1 of the Helsinki Agreement was "of a binding character," Basket 3 "will be fulfilled according to agreement on the part of the states." This suggests that Brezhnev was proposing the view that whereas Basket 1 was immediately applicable, Basket 3 was an enabling set of provisions that requires further specific agreement for execution and fulfillment.
9. See ibid., August 8, 1975, p. 4, for East Germany's interpretation of Baskets 1 and 3. According to this report, the East German Communist party leader, Erich Honecker, said that the Helsinki Agreement "reaffirmed the territorial and political results of World War II and the postwar developments in Europe," whereas its humanitarian provisions were acceptable unless they were designed to undermine the principle of security. Basket 3, he said, provided "a wide field of future bilateral and multilateral arrangements," thus stressing that further action was necessary before the implementation of these provisions.
10. An important article by Georgi Arbatov, "Maneuvers of the Opponents of Detente," *Izvestia*, September 4, 1975, summarized on the "Op-Ed" page of the New York *Times*, October 8, 1975, attempts to impart a unilateral Soviet interpretation to the Helsinki Agreement while noting the difficulties it would create for the Soviet Union. In the process of heatedly, but unconvincingly, denying that Moscow's acceptance of Basket 3 was in trade for the West's acceptance of Basket 1, Arbatov seeks to give a unilateral interpretive gloss to

Basket 3 as he reveals the anxieties of the Soviet leaders over how to handle its impact. As a conspicuous supporter of Moscow's detente "policy," Arbatov broadly hints that Western criticism of the Helsinki Agreement might encourage its Soviet opponents to undermine detente. He charges that Western critics "aim at provoking the socialist countries into a retaliatory campaign that will be sharp enough to unleash a noisy squabble that could spoil the political atmosphere and thus strike a blow against not only what was achieved in Helsinki, but also the process of detente as a whole." With respect to Basket 3, Arbatov states that the Soviet Union fully intends to fulfill its provisions, and highlights those aspects of "information" that will not be allowed free entry, at the same time leaving a wide area for speculation as to Soviet intent:

> Now to discuss the "third basket" in greater detail. As is known, this term is applied to the provisions that deal with the intentions and readiness of states to cooperate in such fields as the development of ties in . . . culture, science, education and information, with contacts between people and the resolution of various humanitarian questions, including family ties, marriages between citizens of different states, etc. In signing the Final Act, the Soviet Union very clearly expressed its intention to fulfill these provisions too (needless to say, on a reciprocal basis and in strict conformity with the spirit and letter of the document). . . . But, judging from many public statements, some people in the West would like to read a quite different meaning into these questions, to make the agreement that has been achieved an instrument for interference in the internal affairs of the socialist countries and for the undermining of the regimes and the social system that exist there. In other words, what we have here is attempts to achieve with the help of detente what it has been impossible to accomplish by armed force or by the forms of pressure that were applied during the "cold war" period. But this is not what is envisaged by detente or by the Final Act signed in Helsinki. On the contrary, one of the principles contained in this document speaks in plain terms of the inadmissibility of interference in the internal affairs of other countries. . . . Naturally, this puts legitimate restrictions on a number of questions that are now being blown up to immense proportions in the Western press. For instance, take the question of freedom of information. The Soviet Union takes seriously the provisions in the Helsinki document on this score and will fulfill them in the forms provided for by the agreement. But if some people regard these provisions as a commitment to open our doors wide to anti-Soviet subversive propaganda, materials that propagate violence and whip up national and racial enmity and pornography, they are profoundly mistaken. The document signed in Helsinki and, indeed, detente in general envisage no such commitment. On the contrary—detente puts on the agenda a quite different question: that of overcoming the legacy of the "cold war" in all spheres, including propaganda activity. This does not mean the cessation of the ideological struggle. There is an objective reason for this struggle, and it will continue in conditions of peaceful coexistence. But the transition to these conditions requires that propaganda activity be confined within a certain framework that envisages the renunciation of slander, the fomenting of hatred and distrust, ideological sabotage and the subversive methods of "psychological warfare." This is in no way at variance with the principle of freedom of speech and the press or with international law.

3

HAS EASTERN EUROPE BECOME A LIABILITY TO THE SOVIET UNION? (II)—THE MILITARY ASPECT

A. Ross Johnson

INTRODUCTION

This chapter addresses the military aspect of the question "Has East Central Europe become a liability to the USSR?" The review of Soviet-Eastern European military relations presented here generally supports the assumption that the Soviet Union has considered Eastern Europe as a military asset. It also suggests that, in the view of Soviet military planners, the Eastern European contribution to Soviet-controlled military capabilities in Europe has shifted from a largely passive role in the 1950s to a much more active one since the early 1960s.

In the period of official Soviet-American detente, Soviet reliance on the Eastern European military contribution to total Warsaw Pact capabilities has further increased, and the significance of that contribution has been elevated by Soviet military discussions that place more credence in the possibility of local European conflict, as distinguished from total nuclear warfare, under conditions of approximate nuclear strategic parity. Nonetheless, the enhanced Eastern European military role in the Warsaw Pact may exacerbate strains in Soviet-Eastern European military relations that could transform some of the Soviet military assets in Eastern Europe into liabilities.

The author has benefited from discussing some of the ideas developed in this chapter at the International Slavic Conference, Banff, Canada, September 1974, and at the Southern California Seminar on Communist Systems, University of California, Los Angeles, December 1974. He is grateful to Lilita Dzirkals and Jeffrey Porro for research assistance.

AN OUTLINE HISTORY OF SOVIET-EASTERN EUROPEAN MILITARY RELATIONS

Stage 1: 1944-47, Consolidation of Power

The national armed forces in Eastern Europe after 1947 were largely "empty shells," small, poorly supplied with often obsolete equipment, and (in most countries) neutralized by occupying Soviet forces.* In the initial postwar years, it was in the interest of both the national communist parties and the Soviet Union that the Eastern European armed forces remain in this emasculated condition. Indeed, in Czechoslovakia, where a relatively strong army emerged from World War II, the Communist party encouraged its dismantling as an institution potentially viable enough to interfere with the later communist seizure of power. A partial exception was Poland, where the Berling Army, formed on Soviet territory during World War II, later became the relatively large nucleus of the new people's army.

Satisfied initially with ensuring that the military command structure was in "neutral" (that is, not anti-communist) hands, the Eastern European communist leaderships concentrated their efforts on placing party activists in key indoctrination and other political control positions within the armed forces—and,.even more important, on gaining control over and then building up the internal security apparatus, including sizable militarized security forces. These militarized security forces, distinct from the regular armed forces and under the control of the interior ministries (and thus the security services), played a pivotal role in backing the Communist party's explicit or implicit threat to employ force to repress "anti-democratic" political forces. Even when internal opposition to communist rule reached the proportions of civil war, as it did in Poland through 1947, the party utilized the militarized security forces, not the regular army, as its instrument of internal repression.

Stage 2: 1948-52, Sovietization as Stalinization

Beginning in 1948, Eastern Europe underwent Stalinization. Domestically, the political systems were forced into the Stalinist Soviet mold; internationally, the Eastern European countries were subordinated to Soviet direction to such an extent that they practically ceased to conduct foreign policies, either with the

---

*Those Eastern European countries later incorporated into the Warsaw Treaty Organization were Bulgaria, Czechoslovakia, East Germany, Hungary, Poland, and Romania. Albania was a member of the Warsaw Pact until 1968, but its participation lapsed after 1960, when it aligned itself with the People's Republic of China in the Sino-Soviet conflict.

outside world or with each other. Each Eastern European state concluded a bilateral mutual defense treaty with the Soviet Union. The national military establishments were immediately affected: command positions were filled with communist and pro-communist officers, usually of "low" social origin and with little or no prior military experience, but with postwar training in Soviet military institutions. The internal organization, training patterns, military doctrine, tactics, and even such matters as uniforms of the Eastern European armed forces were modified to conform to the Soviet model. Each communist party established triple channels of political control over the national armed forces; the command channel secured through the replacement of prewar officers by party loyalists was complemented by extending the networks of the Central-Committee-directed political administration and the security service, each with its own chain of command, to the regimental level or below.

The network of bilateral defense treaties and the dependency of the Eastern European communist parties on Moscow notwithstanding, consolidation of national party control over the respective Eastern European armed forces was for Stalin an inadequate guarantee that they would be fully responsive to Soviet directives. Direct Soviet channels of control were required. The newly appointed Soviet-trained Eastern European commanders were often subordinated to Soviet officers of the respective national origin who had served, sometimes for years, in the Red Army as Soviet citizens and who now formally resumed their original citizenship. This was most evident in Poland, where Soviet Marshal Konstantin Rokossovsky became minister of defense and commander-in-chief in 1949, and the chief of the general staff, commander of the ground forces, heads of all the service branches, and the commanders of all four military districts were likewise former Soviet officers.[1] The practice was almost as widespread in the Hungarian army,[2] and was followed to a lesser extent in the other Eastern European armed forces. Even more important, thousands of Soviet "advisers" were placed within the Eastern European armies, constituting a fourth (in fact, the primary) chain of command. Indeed, by means of this "adviser" system in each Eastern European army, the Soviet high command was in practice able to treat the Eastern European armed forces as branches of the Soviet armed forces. In the Stalinist period, then, an informal but effective, unified Soviet command-and-control system over "integrated" Eastern European armed forces was established, setting a standard to which latter-day Soviet leaders would aspire.

After 1949, conscription was introduced into all the Eastern European armed forces, with the exception of the German Democratic Republic (GDR), where the National People's Army, formally constituted in 1956, introduced conscription only in 1962, after construction of the Berlin Wall had halted massive emigration from East Germany. By 1953 conscription had accumulated a force of some 1.5 million men, organized in roughly sixty-five divisions.[3] Soviet equipment flowed in to replace obsolete World War II armaments. This massive military buildup cannot be explained in domestic Eastern European political terms; although the Stalinist system in Eastern Europe rested importantly on the threat and use of terror and violence, it was the security organs, especially the militarized frontier guards, internal security forces, and the like, rather than the regular armed forces, that were dedicated to this purpose.

Rather, the military buildup of the Eastern European satellites after 1949 was intended to serve Soviet military and foreign policy goals vis-a-vis the West. Air defense forces in Eastern Europe, equipping of which was a Soviet priority, could make an important contribution to the defense of the Soviet heartland against American and British nuclear bombers. Eastern Europe also constituted a staging and buffer zone between the Soviet Union and Western Europe that could be utilized for offensive or defensive Soviet military purposes. In retrospect, the offensive threat of the satellite forces may have been exaggerated in the West, for Stalin could hardly have placed much confidence in the effectiveness or reliability of Eastern European armed forces utilized offensively for an attack on the West. Nonetheless, he may well have intended their buildup as a supplement to that of the Red Army itself, which was designed to alter the local military balance in Europe to the advantage of the Soviet Union. From Stalin's point of view, the combined buildup could have made Western Europe a "hostage" for American nuclear restraint vis-a-vis the Soviet Union and at the same time cast a political shadow over Western Europe that might have hastened its neutralization and eventual incorporation into the Soviet sphere.[4]

Stage 3: 1953-59, Rationalization, Upheaval, and Renationalization

Following Stalin's death, the Soviet leadership sought to mitigate the most extreme forms of forced mobilization and subservience to Soviet control in Eastern Europe, for what had been essentials of the Stalinist interstate system were perceived as Soviet liabilities after the death of the system's personal linchpin. The economic expression of this endeavor in controlled decompression was the "New Course." Economic considerations were cardinal in the Soviet effort to rationalize what was now viewed as Stalin's misallocation of military-related resources in Eastern Europe, which, because it so overstretched the Eastern European economies, had serious destabilizing political ramifications. Thus defense spending was reduced and military manpower cut in Eastern Europe, just as in the Soviet Union, and the Stalinist approach to military mobilization was condemned by Eastern European leaders as primitive and wasteful. Moreover, as Soviet military thought was freed from Stalin's emphasis on traditional "permanent operating factors of war," Eastern European military doctrine was affected in turn. For example, Stalin had resisted doctrinal implications of the technical possibilities for greater mechanization and concentration of ground forces; these were now accepted, and motorized divisions replaced infantry divisions in the Eastern European armed forces. Soviet military doctrine now embraced the realities of the nuclear age; a decade before they acquired nuclear delivery systems from the Soviet Union, the Eastern European armed forces received instruction from the Soviet mentors on nuclear warfare.[5]

The founding in 1955 of the Warsaw Treaty Organization (WTO) as the formal multilateral security alliance of the states within the Soviet orbit had little to do with the process of rationalizing the Soviet and Eastern European military establishments. Instead, creation of the Warsaw Pact was to be explained in political terms. Externally, it was a political response to the incorporation of West Germany in NATO. In internal Soviet bloc terms, it was an effort to establish a multilateral political organization that, together with CEMA and other specialized bloc organizations, could provide an institutionalized substitute for the personalized Stalinist system of Soviet hegemony in Eastern Europe.

Article 5 of the Warsaw Treaty did provide for a joint military command, which was formally established at Moscow in early 1956, yet in military terms the WTO remained a paper organization until the 1960s. Initially it served only one concrete Soviet military purpose: it provided an alternate source of legitimization for deployment of forces in Hungary and Romania after ratification of the Austrian State Treaty in 1955.

But even this military rationale was short-lived. The unrest of 1956 in Eastern Europe led to Soviet military pressure in Poland and Soviet military suppression of the Hungarian Revolution. One consequence was that the Eastern European leaderships became more sensitive to the forms of national sovereignty, in the military as in other realms. Formal renationalization of the Eastern European armed forces, begun in 1953, was completed. In Poland, Marshal Rokossovsky and his fellow former Soviet officers were (with one exception) recalled to the Soviet Union. National military uniforms were rehabilitated. More important, the Soviet government declaration of October 1956 on more equitable relations between the Soviet Union and Eastern Europe (issued just prior to Hungary's renunciation of WTO and the ensuing Soviet military suppression of the Hungarian Revolution) professed a Soviet willingness to review the issue of Soviet troops stationed in Eastern Europe. The declaration pledged that such stationing would occur only with the consent of the state involved. Soviet military suppression of the Hungarian Revolution notwithstanding, in December 1956 the Soviet Union concluded a status-of-forces agreement with Poland specifying the terms of the stationing of Soviet forces in Polish territory and pledging their noninterference in Polish affairs. Similar status-of-forces agreements were concluded with Hungary, Romania, and East Germany in early 1957. In what might be interpreted as a final Soviet gesture to Eastern European national sentiments, perhaps as a specific result of Romanian economic concessions and Chinese support, Moscow acceded to a Romanian request,* advanced even before 1956, and withdrew all Soviet forces from that nation in early 1958.[6]

Stage 4: 1960-68, a New Military Purpose and Institution-Building

After 1957, Khrushchev sought to construct a viable "socialist commonwealth" that would ensure Soviet control over the broad outlines of domestic and foreign policies of the Eastern European states. On the one hand, the Soviet Union would dismantle or mitigate the more onerous forms of direct Soviet control and (in comparison with the Stalinist period) permit room for some domestic autonomy. On the other hand, it would utilize the Council for Mutual Economic Assistance (CEMA) and WTO as institutional mechanisms for ensuring the stability of Soviet hegemony in the region. But little headway was made in translating wish into policy. Indeed, initially after 1957, Khrushchev's presumptive effort to utilize WTO as an organization for Soviet-dominated institution-building in Eastern Europe was not pursued vigorously. Between 1957 and 1961 the WTO's supreme organ, the Political Consultative Committee (PCC), met only three times.

Viewed in this light, the Soviet effort to infuse the Warsaw Pact with military content after 1960 would seem to be explicable not in political, but directly in military terms. Beginning in 1960, Khrushchev sought to initiate a revolution in Soviet military organization and doctrine by emphasizing strategic nuclear missile forces at the expense of the traditional Soviet military strength, ground forces in Europe, and by recasting ground-forces doctrine to emphasize blitzkrief offensives by mobile forces at the expense of traditional Soviet mobilization capabilities. His conception evidently postulated that Soviet ground forces could be reduced more than otherwise would be possible if Eastern European armed forces were to assume a more substantial role in Soviet military planning for Europe. A part of his vision was implemented: the Strategic Rocket Forces were organized in 1960, and the goal of strategic equality with the United States was pursued vigorously. On the other hand, while overall Soviet military forces for conventional conflicts were reduced after 1960, the combination of heightened East-West tension in Europe associated with the Berlin crisis of 1961 and traditionalist institutional opposition within the Soviet military establishment resulted in a practically undiminished level of Soviet ground forces in Eastern Europe.[7]

---

*The Soviet military withdrawal from Romania lends credence to Khrushchev's claim that in this period the Soviet leadership considered withdrawing its forces from Poland and Hungary to mollify Eastern European nationalist resentment and to enhance the Soviet image in Western Europe.

Nonetheless, apparently as a direct consequence of the original Khrushchev vision, the Soviet Union began to improve the military capabilities of the Eastern European armed forces. Following the replacement of Ivan Konev by A.A. Grechko as WTO commander-in-chief in 1960, multilateral training exercises of Warsaw Pact military forces began—in fact, there was a multilateralization of the exercises involving the Group of Soviet Forces in Germany (GSFG) and the East German armed forces organized by Grechko, as GSFG commander, after 1957. While the initial exercises of the early 1960s could be interpreted as largely political demonstrations intended to show Soviet-Eastern European military fraternity, by the mid-1960s they had become serious combat training activities. Moreover, the Eastern European armed forces were now supplied by the Soviet Union with modern T-54 and T-55 tanks, MIG-21 and SU-7 aircraft, and other weapons. By the mid-1960s, some Eastern European armed forces were being armed with, and trained in the use of, delivery vehicles (first of all, ground-to-ground missiles) for nuclear warheads, although the warheads themselves presumably remained under sole Soviet control.[8] Standardization of armaments within the Warsaw Pact was enhanced as Eastern European states abandoned some domestic arms production capabilities; a nascent East German military aircraft industry was abandoned in 1961, and Poland renounced further development of advanced combat aircraft in 1967.[9] These joint combat-training, modernization, and specialization programs seemed to indicate that the Soviet Union now viewed the Eastern European armed forces as an important contribution to Soviet military power that not only extended the Soviet air defense system and constituted a buffer (as they had since Stalin's day), but also would assume an active mechanized ground and air combat role in any military operations in Europe.

It was only after WTO had been infused with this military content that the Soviet Union seriously promoted it as an institutional mechanism to increase political cohesion in the Soviet orbit while seeking to strengthen its military institutions. In the meantime, beginning in 1962, Khrushchev sought to use CEMA for such institution-building purposes, advocating (without success) its transformation into a Soviet-dominated supranational organ that would foster the merger of the Eastern European economies and, in the process, increase the political cohesion of the Soviet bloc. After 1964, Khrushchev's successor's launched an analogous process within WTO. In September 1965, Brezhnev stressed the importance of "further perfecting the Warsaw Treaty Organization" and "the need to set up within the framework of the Treaty a permanent and prompt mechanism for considering pressing problems."[10] Details of the Soviet plan have never been disclosed; the context in which it was proposed suggests that it aimed more at political than at military coordination.

Khrushchev's earlier plans for development of supranational organs in CEMA had led Romania to assert its economic independence from the Soviet Union; this was followed by an explicit assertion of political independence as well. Soviet intentions concerning the Warsaw Pact led Romania to further buttress its political position by asserting its autonomy in military affairs. In late 1964, Romania reduced its term of military conscription from twenty-four to sixteen months, resulting in a cut of 40,000 men from its armed forces. (Analogous reductions by the Soviet Union occurred only in 1967; by the other Eastern European states, thereafter.) In other ways, too, the Romanian leadership sought to reduce what it viewed as an excessive contribution to the collective military strength of the Warsaw Pact and to turn to smaller, more domestically oriented military establishment. Simultaneously, however, it sought to increase its national voice in WTO military affairs and hence to reduce the degree of Soviet contról over Romanian defense. In 1966, Romanian Communist party leader Nicolae Ceausescu obliquely called for the withdrawal of Soviet forces from Eastern Europe. Bucharest evidently subsequently proposed that the position of WTO commander-in-chief (always occupied by a marshal of the Soviet armed forces) rotate—and may have forced a delay in the naming of Ivan Yakubovsky to replace Grechko as WTO commander-in-chief. Romania argued further that Eastern European military expenditures were excessive, brought about a dramatic reduction in the size of the Soviet military liaison mission in Bucharest, claimed at least a consultative voice in matters related to nuclear weapons in the Warsaw Pact, expressed concerns about the Nuclear Non-Proliferation Treaty derived from these sensitivities, refused to permit Warsaw Pact troop maneuvers on Romanian soil, and declined to participate in joint maneuvers involving combat forces in other countries.[11]

Unambiguous as it was, the Romanian deviation alone does not account satisfactorily for the evident lack of progress after 1965 toward the Soviet goal of creating a permanent political coordination mechanism within WTO or for the lack of progress in upgrading WTO military institutions in a manner strengthening Soviet control. That lack of progress would seem to indicate, additionally, uncertainty or division in Moscow and neutrality or support for the Romanian position from some or perhaps all of the remaining Eastern European states. The controversy over the role of WTO as an intrablock political mechanism evidently precipitated previously unarticulated aspirations on the part of other Eastern European countries, besides Romania, for a more equal position in WTO military affairs. Czechoslovak support for some of the Romanian grievances can be documented as early as 1966, when the press voiced only slightly veiled concern about Czechoslovakia's limited participation in Warsaw Pact military organs and its desire for a consultative voice in WTO nuclear affairs.[12] In view of the 1969 changes in WTO military institutions, it seems likely that there was additional support for the "Romanian" position on some issues from other Eastern European countries as well.

In 1968, as a reformist political movement headed by Alexander Dubcek gained ground in Czechoslovakia, dissatisfaction with Soviet domination of the

Czechoslovak armed forces and WTO military institutions was voiced more openly. Czechoslovak military spokesmen criticized submergence of their nation's military doctrine into common, Soviet-dominated WTO doctrine; inequality in decision-making in the WTO's supreme organs; the unequal terms on which Soviet forces were stationed in Eastern European countries; the excessive, Soviet-dictated defense burden on the Czechoslovak economy; and Soviet-determined overemphasis on the size of the Czechoslovak armed forces, to the detriment of their modernization.[13] These military grievances, and especially the bluntness with which they were expressed, were surely an important contributory factor in the Soviet decision to intervene militarily in Czechoslovakia in August 1968 (with East German, Polish, Hungarian, and Bulgarian units joining the Soviet invasion force) in order to halt the "peaceful counterrevolution" that was, in Soviet eyes, threatening to remove the country from the Soviet orbit.

Stage 5: After 1969, Reorganization of the Military Command

In the military sphere, following Soviet suppression of the reformist movement in Czechoslovakia in 1968, it was logical to expect Soviet military and political leaders to have second thoughts about the political reliability of the Eastern European armed forces on which Soviet military planning had placed increasing importance in the 1960s, and, consequently, to place more relative emphasis on Soviet forces in the area. In fact, Soviet military forces in Eastern Europe have so increased that by 1975 there were five more Soviet divisions in the area than in 1967 and the weaponry at the disposal of the thirty-one divisions had been considerably upgraded. This increase in Soviet military strength in Eastern Europe is all the more significant because it has occurred in a period when the main emphasis in Soviet planning for general-purpose forces has been the buildup on the Chinese border.

Nonetheless, despite presumptive doubts about the loyalty of the Czechoslovak armed forces in particular, the Soviet Union has by no means written off the military contribution of the Eastern European armed forces. On the contrary, Eastern European manpower levels have increased slightly since 1967, totaling over 1 million regular military personnel. Significant increases in defense spending devoted primarily to modernization of the armed forces have occurred in the area; defense expenditures have generally increased at the same rate as the increase in national income, with the exceptions of the German Democratic Republic (GDR), where the increase has been much faster, and Czechoslovakia, where it has been somewhat slower. Modernization appears to have been emphasized in the GDR, Hungary and Poland. These and other selected data on Eastern European military capabilities are shown in Table 3.1.

TABLE 3.1

Selected Comparative Data on Soviet and Eastern European Military Capabilities, 1962-75

Country	Population	Total Regular Forces	Combat Aircraft	Internal Security and Border Troops	Total Military Forces	Number of Soviet Divisions[a]	
						Tank	Total
Bulgaria							
1962	7,629,254	120,000	–	40,000	160,000	–	0
1967	8,400,000	154,000	250	20,000	174,000	–	0
1975	8,760,000	152,000	253	20,000	172,000	–	0
Czechoslovakia							
1962	13,581,186	185,000	–	35,000	220,000	–	0
1967	14,500,000	225,000	600	40,000	265,000	–	0
1975	14,570,000	200,000	458	20,000	220,000	2	5
German Democratic Republic							
1962	17,280,000	85,000	–	60,000	145,000	10	20
1967	17,200,000	127,000	300	70,000	197,000	10	20
1975	16,990,000	143,000	330	80,000	233,000	10	20
Hungary							
1962	9,977,870	80,500	–	35,000	115,500	–	4
1967	10,300,000	102,000	140	35,000	137,000	2	4
1975	10,790,000	105,000	108	20,000	125,000	2	4
Poland							
1962	29,527,000	257,000	–	45,000[b]	302,000	–	2
1967	32,000,000	270,000	820	45,000[b]	315,000	1	2
1975	33,580,000	293,000	785	80,000[b]	373,000	1	2
Romania							
1962	18,366,000	222,000	–	60,000	282,000	–	–
1967	19,500,000	173,000	240	50,000	223,000	–	–
1975	21,460,000	171,000	254	45,000	216,000	–	–
Grand total military forces							
1962					1,224,500		26
1967					1,051,000		26
1975					1,339,000		31

[a] A Soviet division roughly equals 9000 men.
[b] Includes armored brigades of territorial army.
Note: All 1962 population data are from 1960.
Source: International Institute for Strategic Studies, The Military Balance, London: the Institute, 1960, 1967-68, 1973-74.

Table 3.2 presents military expenditures. Eastern European armed forces' participation in joint Warsaw Pact exercises has continued, as has their modernization with Soviet-supplied weapons, including T-62 tanks, advanced MIG-21 and (in the case of the GDR) MIG-23 aircraft, and SA-6 ground-to-air missiles.[14] Soviet-influenced specialization of the Eastern European armed forces has also continued; for example, only the Polish armed forces include an airborne division and a sea-landing division.[15] The importance of the Eastern European contribution to Soviet military power is indicated by the estimate that, the increase in Soviet forces in Eastern Europe since 1968 notwithstanding, today the Eastern European armed forces provide 60 percent of the Warsaw Pact divisions and tactical aircraft in the European theater and 50 percent of its in-place divisions and aircraft in the Central Region.[16]

It might have been expected that, following the invasion of Czechoslovakia in 1968, the Brezhnev leadership would return to its 1965 plan for strengthening WTO as a mechanism of Soviet military control in Eastern Europe. It does not appear to have followed such a policy, however—at least not frontally. Six months after the invasion of Czechoslovakia, the PCC met in Budapest to ratify organizational changes in WTO's military institutions. Details of these changes remain sparse; but enough information has been disclosed in Soviet bloc sources to make it clear that they were not the result of a crash Soviet effort after Czechoslovakia to enhance Soviet direction of WTO military affairs through creation of new, Soviet-dominated supranational organs. Rather, the 1969 institutional reforms in the Warsaw Pact were the slightly belated consequence of the post-1965 Eastern European pressure to improve access to, and gain at least a consultative voice in, WTO military affairs. As noted, that drive was spearheaded by Romania and Czechoslovakia, but probably was supported on some issues by other Eastern European states. The pending changes in WTO military organs had been broached as early as 1966; detailed planning evidently was carried out in the fall of 1968.

The formal structure of the WTO military organization incorporating the Budapest institutional changes is outlined in Figure 11.1. First, the Committee of Defense Ministers was formally constituted as the supreme military consultative organ of the alliance; multilateral meetings of the defense ministers had long been common practice. As an example of the kinds of military matters falling within the committee's competence, its March 1971 session was devoted to WTO military infrastructure and command-and-control problems.[17] A Soviet source maintains that the committee ensures "increased collegiality"—that is, a stronger Eastern European voice—in WTO decision-making.[18]

Second, the Joint Command of the WTO armed forces was reconstituted; designated deputy ministers of national defense now replaced the national defense ministers as deputy WTO commanders under the Soviet commander-in-chief, Marshal Ivan Yakubovsky.[19] Third, the Military Council was established as a new body. Although little information is available about its functions,[20]

TABLE 3.2

Selected Data on Eastern European Military Expenditures, 1962-72

| Country | Direct Defense Expenditures | | | | | | Military R & D | | Total Military (Including Regular and Internal Security (thousand men)) |
| | As Percent of | | | Personnel Costs | Operating, Maintenance, and Procurement | Total^a | Estimated Total | As Percent of National Income | |
	National Income	National Product	State Budget		(in local currency, million units)				
Bulgaria									
1962	5	5.8	6	81	177	258	—		160
1967	3.1	3.0	6.1	115	132	247	—		174
1972	3.5		6	132	259	391	—		169
Percentage Changes									
1962) 1967)				42	25	-4			9
1967) 1972)				15	96	58			-3
Czechoslovakia^b									
1962	4.8	4.7	6.7	2,074	6,168	8,242	1,259	0.7	220
1967	4.5	5.7	6.9	2,710	7,446	10,156	2,083	0.9	265
1972	3.8	5.7	6.1	3,128	10,041	13,169	2,575		225
Percentage Changes									
1962) 1967)				31	21	23	65		20
1967) 1972)				15	34	35	24		-15
German Democratic Republic^c									
1962	3.6	3.9	5	472	2,228	2,700	135	0.2	145
1967	3.9	3.7	5	717	2,883	3,600	180	0.2	197
1972	5.2	6.3	7.6	858	5,379	6,237	311		210
Percentage Changes									
1962) 1967)				52	29	33	33		36
1967) 1972)				20	87	73	73		7
Hungary									
1962	3.2	2.5	5.9	1,573	3,340	4,913	—		116
1967	2.7	2.6	5.2	2,004	3,429	5,433	—		137
1972	2.9	3.6	4.1	2,294	7,136	9,430	—		130

Percentage Changes									
1962 ⎫				27	3	11			18
1967 ⎬				14	108	74			−5
1972 ⎭									
Poland[d]									
1962	4.3	3.9	7.4	4,099	14,279	18,378	248	0.06	302
1967	4.4	5.4	8.2	5,046	21,392	26,438	412	0.07	320
1972	4.2		8.9	6,649	32,841	39,490	1,034		353
Percentage Changes									
1962 ⎫				23	50	44	66		6
1967 ⎬				32	53	49	151		10
1972 ⎭									
Romania									
1962	3.2	2.9	5.4	1,457	2,467	3,924	—		282
1967	2.6	3.1	4.1	1,617	3,529	5,146	—		223
1972	2.5	2.7	5.3	1,937	5,773	7,710	—		210
Percentage Changes									
1962 ⎫				11	43	31			−21
1967 ⎬				20	64	50			−6
1972 ⎭									

aTotal equals personnel plus operating, maintenance, and procurement costs.

bData recalculated to exclude nonmilitary security costs.

cData since 1968 recalculated to exclude nonmilitary security costs.

dRobert T. Hinaman and Nancy M. Kling, "Military Spending in Eastern Europe," in U.S. Congress, Joint Economic Committee, *Economic Developments in Countries of Eastern Europe* (Washington, D.C.: U.S. Government Printing Office, 1970), p. 345; assert that internal security expenditures are not included in the defense budget. If this is the case, the Polish numbers must be increased accordingly.

Note: This table assumes (1) that official defense expenditures form a meaningful category embracing all direct military expenditures, except for military research and development costs; and (2) that for a specialized purpose, such as the tracking of relative changes in defense expenditures, an index of defense expenditures in local currencies as a proportion of national income (net material product) according to official Eastern European data is more useful than an index constructed from Western dollar estimates of defense expenditures as a percentage of gross national product.

Sources: Percent of national income, percent of state budget, total defense expenditures, all from official data; percent of gross national product, and totals of military strength, from International Institute for Strategic Studies, *The Military Balance* (London: the Institute, 1960, 1967-68, 1973-74); personnel costs, procurement, operations and maintenance, plus estimated R&D, from Thad P. Alton et al., *Estimates of Military Expenditures in Eastern Europe*, ACDA/E-207, 1973.

Polish and Western sources suggest that it was set up as a consultative organ of the WTO's senior military officers (Soviet and Eastern European) on the pattern of military councils in Soviet military districts; they specify that its composition includes the WTO deputies to the supreme commander (Eastern European deputy ministers of national defense), plus the WTO chief of staff. A Soviet source contrasts the "control" functions of the Military Council with the "advisory" functions of the Committee of Defense Ministers.[21] Fourth, under the Joint Command, the permanent staff of the Joint Armed Forces has been established (evidently for the first time).[22] According to Western accounts, the staff, headed by Soviet General S. M. Shtemenko, now contains Eastern European deputy chiefs of staff at the major-general level, and other officials proportional to manpower and defense budget shares of the individual states.[23] Fifth, a new organ was established at Budapest to coordinate weapons development; details are not available.*

Sixth, a new statute for the Joint Armed Forces was adopted. This was the change in WTO military institutions at Budapest that attracted the greatest Western attention—and was the most misinterpreted. Although details have not been published, announcement of the new statute, coupled with the changes in the command structure and with publication in January 1970 of an article by WTO Chief of Staff Shtemenko,[24] led to speculation that multilateral or even supranational integrated armed forces had been created within the framework of WTO. Article 5 of the Warsaw Treaty had provided for the "assignment" of elements of the national armed forces to the Joint Command; and thereafter the entire East German armed forces, units of the remaining Eastern European armies, and the Soviet groups of forces stationed in Eastern Europe were evidently designated as the Joint Armed Forces and "assigned" to the Joint Command, although the Eastern European forces remained under the command of the national ministers of defense, who were designated deputy WTO supreme commanders.[25] The joint maneuvers of WTO forces carried out in the 1960s evidently involved elements of the Joint Armed Forces. Command authority thus remained in national hands; directives from the WTO commander-in-chief (a Soviet marshal) passed to units through the national ministers of defense who were responsible to their own governments and party leaderships.

Soviet and Eastern European sources agree that the fundamental principles of national control over national armed forces (in peacetime) were not undercut by the Budapest organizational changes.[26] Indeed, it may be speculated that the new system reinforced the principle of national control, since it required a deputy minister of defense to serve as deputy WTO commander-in-chief and to relay directives from the WTO commander-in-chief to the portions of his

---

*In April 1973 a WTO "Convention on Privileges and Immunities" was promulgated, evidently to regulate the position of the Eastern European members of WTO institutions in Moscow.

national armed forces "assigned" to WTO; the deputy minister remained physically in his national ministry of defense; was directly responsible to his minister of defense; and, in Yakubovsky's words,[27] carried out directives of the WTO commander-in-chief in "consultation" with his national political leadership. The new system also gave the Eastern European states a formal position in WTO command institutions more comparable with that of the Soviet Union; all three Soviet commanders-in-chief of WTO had been simultaneously principal deputy ministers of defense of the Soviet Union, and it may be speculated that Eastern Europeans resented subordination of the ministers of defense to a Soviet deputy minister, even for the very limited purposes of the WTO chain of command.[28]

Nevertheless, the crucial question remains: command channels for what? The apparent answer reduces the importance of WTO military bodies, because Soviet military planning evidently assumed that, in case of hostilities in Europe, Eastern European armed forces in the key battle zones, like the groups of Soviet forces stationed in Eastern Europe, would not be commanded through the WTO organization but would be incorporated directly in Soviet fronts commanded by the Soviet general staff through theater or field headquarters. (The possibility is left open that an Eastern European army might establish its own front in a secondary area under overall Soviet command, but without reference to WTO.) This was the command arrangement utilized by the Soviet Union at the end of World War II, the Soviet military planning assumption reflected in the authoritative Soviet military handbook, Marshal Vasiliy Danilovich Sokolovsky's *On Military Strategy* (third edition, 1968).

It was also the pattern followed in the Soviet-led invasion of Czechoslovakia in 1968. In that operation, the WTO military organization commanded by Marshal Yakubovsky was responsible for WTO maneuvers in and around Czechoslovakia through June. However, the Soviet, Hungarian, Polish, East German, and Bulgarian units that constituted the invasion force were mobilized and deployed by various Soviet commands without reference to WTO; and the military intervention itself was directed by the commander of the Soviet ground forces, General Ivan Grigorevich Pavlovsky, operating from a forward headquarters of the Soviet high command.[29] As Malcolm Mackintosh suggests, this pattern relegates the WTO military organization to an analogue of a traditional European war office, with administrative duties for mobilization, training, and equipment but without direct responsibilities for the conduct of military operations.* It makes a greater Eastern European voice in WTO military institutions irrelevant to real military partnership, even a junior one, with the

---

*It may be speculated that abolition of the Soviet Ground Forces Command by Khrushchev in 1964 portended a larger wartime role for WTO institutions, but that reestablishment of the Soviet Ground Forces Command in 1967 and the greater identity subsequently ascribed to WTO institutions, as distinct from the Soviet ministry of defense and

Soviet Union, because the structural accommodation of Eastern European desires for a voice in Soviet bloc military decisions would be set aside'in the event of military hostilities. This subordinate relationship of the Eastern European armed forces is reflected even in peacetime in the organization of air defense (the element of the Eastern European armed forces most crucial to Soviet defense): the Eastern European air defense systems are subordinated to the Soviet commander of the air defense systems, General Pavel Fedorovich Batitsky, whose "second hat" as WTO commander of air defense forces seems to be a formal designation only.[30] Similarly, the Polish and East German Baltic fleets are subordinated (at least in certain respects) to United Fleet Command, headed by the commander of the Soviet Baltic fleet.[31] Nor is there evidence to suggest that the new, post-1968 WTO institutions enhance the WTO's wartime importance.

Key Issues in Soviet-Eastern European Military Relations Today

Soviet Military Hegemony

The fact of Soviet military hegemony in Eastern Europe is beyond question. Apart from the general disparity between the size of the Soviet and the Eastern European military establishments, thirty-one Soviet divisions (over 300,000 men) are stationed in Poland, East Germany, Czechoslovakia, and Hungary. Training and armaments within WTO have been standardized to a considerable extent. Soviet military hegemony in Eastern Europe is legitimized both by the Warsaw Pact and by the supplemental network of bilateral mutual defense and status-of-forces agreements with and among individual Eastern European countries.

Military hegemony in Eastern Europe is evidently regarded in Moscow as essential to the pursuit of Soviet interests in Europe. In the military sphere, Soviet doctrine and organization place increased importance on the role of local military forces, now that the Soviet Union has attained approximate strategic nuclear parity with the United States. In the event of military hostilities in Europe, Soviet military doctrine anticipates a rapid massive offensive to the West, for which a strong military position east of the Elbe remains a prerequisite. Soviet military hegemony in Eastern Europe also ensures that the Soviet Union will enjoy the benefits of a military buffer zone against any hypothetical attack from the West.

general staff, again reduced the potential wartime role of WTO machinery. (The latter process included restricting Yakubovsky's duties as first deputy minister of defense to those of WTO commander-in-chief, in contrast with his predecessors, who simultaneously had other responsibilities within the Soviet ministry of defense.)

Military considerations have induced a gradual bifurcation of WTO since the mid-1960s into northern and southern "tiers." The key political region of Europe, and accordingly the area of primary military confrontation between East and West, is Central Europe, above all the German states. The Balkans are a secondary political, and thus military, area. Consequently, Soviet energies have been concentrated on improving the military capabilities and reliability of the Northern Tier (Poland, East Germany, Czechoslovakia), as the "first strategic echelon,"[32] to the neglect of the other WTO states. This differentiated emphasis is apparent, for example, in the pattern of joint multinational WTO training exercises. Of the forty-six exercises held between 1961 and 1974, thirty-eight were held in the Northern Tier.[33]

In political terms Soviet military hegemony in Eastern Europe remains the ultimate guarantor of Soviet domination of the area, as demonstrated on numerous occasions since 1945. The Soviet military intervention in Czechoslovakia in 1968 should have laid to rest recurring doubts in the West about a continuing "internal policing role" of Soviet forces in Eastern Europe. The lesson of that invasion for Eastern Europe as a whole is that the Soviet Union remains determined to prevent unacceptable kinds of autonomous national policies in Eastern Europe and is capable of utilizing its military forces to buttress political measures to that end. But does this also guarantee that Eastern Europe cannot become a liability to the Soviet Union?

The Warsaw Pact as a Quasi Alliance

If military and intrablock political considerations motivate the Soviet Union to maintain its military hegemony in Eastern Europe, the WTO in its military countenance is, nevertheless, an alliance of sorts. Military withdrawal from WTO by an Eastern European country, on the pattern of the military disengagement of France and Greece from NATO, clearly remains unacceptable to the Soviet Union, which, judging by its behavior as recently as 1968, is prepared to use military force to prevent that action. Moscow, nonetheless, continues to tolerate perpetuation of the Romanian military deviation within WTO, presumably because the Romanian leadership has been careful to avoid crossing the threshold separating autonomy from anti-Soviet heresy. Although Romania's secondary position in the Balkans evidently has increased its room to maneuver in military as in other matters (permitting it to follow autonomous policies that on geostrategic ground would be unacceptable to the Soviet Union in Poland, for example), the extent of the post-1968 Romanian military deviation has nevertheless been surprising. Fearing in August 1968 that the Soviet military intervention in Czechoslovakia might be extended to Romania itself, the Romanian party leadership under Ceausescu has since then emphatically reasserted the principle of undiluted national control over Romanian armed forces and has continued the effort, begun in 1967, of building up a domestic arms industry. Romania also has adopted (at least in principle) attributes of the Yugoslav system of total national defense, including organization of a substantial Patriotic Guard of militia; it has consulted regularly and ostentatiously with Chinese, Yugoslav, and, more recently, Western military leaders. Moreover, in an unprecedented excursion by a WTO member outside the WTO for armaments, Romania has entered into arrangements with Yugoslavia for coproduction of a jet fighter-trainer.[34]

In 1974, as Romania adopted a somewhat more self-assertive policy of autonomy vis-a-vis Moscow, it returned to the offensive in seeking a greater national voice in WTO affairs. Obviously Romanian-inspired Westerern news reports refloated the 1967 Romanian proposal that the position of WTO commander-in-chief should rotate among the member countries; these reports accused the Soviets (not necessarily accurately) of attempting to introduce a tighter Soviet-controlled military command structure at the April 1974 PCC meeting and revived the 1970 Romanian complaint that the Soviet Union was demanding extraterritorial transit routes across Romania in order to be able to periodically deploy its forces to Bulgaria.[35]

The Romanian case has been the only dramatic demonstration since 1968 of Eastern European determination to pursue a national military policy. In general, however, Soviet suppression of the Czechoslovak reform movement in 1968, while restating Moscow's claim to decide unilaterally the content of socialist orthodoxy in Eastern Europe, has not resulted in a Soviet effort to enforce Stalinist-like conformity. Differences of views continue to be displayed among Soviet bloc states on issues ranging from permissible forms of relations with the West to the proper role of CEMA. There also are indications that different perspectives on military issues continue to exist within WTO.

As a first example, there is the evident Soviet desire for Eastern European military solidarity with the Soviet Union within WTO, if only for symbolic and political demonstration purposes in its military confrontation with China. At the Budapest meeting of the PCC in early 1969, held in the wake of the Ussuri clash between Soviet and Chinese forces, Moscow evidently tried, and failed, to obtain declaratory backing for its position from the Eastern Europeans. Similarly, in 1970 Soviet claims (keyed to the fifteenth anniversary of WTO) that WTO obligations should extend to Asia as well as Europe were likewise conspicuously ignored in Eastern Europe. Some Eastern European spokesmen have gone out of their way to declare that their WTO obligations do not apply in the event of a Sino-Soviet conflict.[36]

As a second example, implicit polemics continue between Soviet and Eastern European military writers on whether there is jusification for national Eastern European military doctrines distinct from Soviet-directed, "unified" Warsaw Pact doctrine. The former Polish chief of staff and other Polish military commentators offer a clear statement of one Eastern European position; they stress the importance of the participation of all WTO member-states in working out unified alliance doctrine, and define a national Polish military doctrine as a supplement to WTO doctrine that determines, primarily, the role of Poland's Territorial Army.[37]

As a third example, there has been some public reflection of presumed reservations among Eastern European party and military leaderships about the reliability and automatic extension of the Soviet nuclear shield to Eastern Europe as the Soviet Union more fully embraces the possibility of limited conflict in Europe. During the Czechoslovak "Spring" of 1968, a Czech commentator articulated fears that "[Eastern European] countries of the Pact would become a theater of war, without sufficient guarantees of nuclear defense."[38] Further, Poland's demonstrated concern with the dangers of tactical nuclear conflict in Europe, while originally derived from fear that the traditional German enemy might gain control over nuclear weapons, in recent years may be more explicable in these intra-alliance terms.[39]

As a final example, Eastern European complaints about "burden-sharing* support the natural suspicions that there are differences between the Soviet Union and Eastern European countries (and among the latter) over "offsetting" the stationing costs of Soviet forces in Eastern Europe, over the terms of trade of Soviet weapons, and over the "fair share" of each in total WTO defense expenditures. The defense "burden" ranges from 5.5 percent of national income in East Germany to 2.5 percent in Romania; no information is available on Eastern European "offset" payments or costs of Soviet weapons (but see Table 3.2 for a compilation of available data on Eastern European defense expenditures).

Has the Soviet Union made progress since 1968 in transforming WTO into a military organization that, by allowing the Eastern Europeans a greater voice in decision-making, constitutes a multilateral institution that is both Soviet-dominated and viable? Such an organization could be harnessed to the general Soviet effort to create an institutional structure in Eastern Europe ensuring both stability and responsiveness to Soviet directives. It may be argued, on the one hand, that the Eastern European officer corps—composed of men of modest social origin, trained in the Soviet Union and/or under Soviet auspices, and commanding increasingly professional and modern military establishments through military alliances with the Soviet Union—have a special stake in close relations with Moscow that will enhance Soviet prospects of success in this institution-building endeavor. The continuing modernization of Eastern European armed forces with Soviet weapons, including tactical nuclear delivery systems, supports this argument; so do the major roles assigned to these forces in Soviet military preparedness and the post-1969 organizational changes in the

*Raised by Czechoslovakia and Romania in the mid-1960s, as described, and voiced to the present author during a trip to Eastern Europe in 1972.

Warsaw Pact improving Eastern European access to and participation in WTO command organs.

But how much is enough? In making some concessions to its Eastern European allies, has Moscow accommodated them with prospects in accordance with their long-term satisfaction? Or has the Soviet Union simply introduced measures that will further increase expectations or promote dissatisfaction among the Eastern European military elites? It must be doubted whether Moscow is ready and able to grant the Eastern European military establishments the status of junior military partners that this newly found and mounting sense of professionalism may demand. A number of factors would seem to diminish the chances of such "more equal" status (entailing, for example, multinational staffing of second-level command positions, on the NATO pattern): traditional Soviet military secrecy; the national pride of a growing superpower; the arrogance of Soviet officers who will not grant that the Eastern Europeans may have found better solutions for such military tasks as training; continued transfer of new Soviet weapons to the Middle East before they enter the inventories of WTO allies; continued Soviet concern about the stability and loyalty of the Eastern European countries and the resultant reality of a Soviet internal policing role in Eastern Europe; and above all the irrelevance of WTO to Soviet planning for eventual military operations in Europe. Nor can the military aspect of WTO be divorced from its political role; in political terms it remains what Roman Kolkowicz has called an "entangling alliance," with intra-alliance coercive functions binding the Eastern European states to the Soviet Union. If, indeed, segments of the Eastern European military elites become dissatisfied on professional grounds with their status vis-a-vis the Soviet Union, then one should expect the future development "from below," on professional institutional grounds, of national sentiments within the Eastern European military establishments that would reinforce the more familiar autonomous military sentiments developing on national-political grounds "from above," as manifested in Czechoslovakia and Romania.

CONCLUSION

Judgments about the outcome of the conflicting currents of solidarity and strain in Soviet-Eastern European military relations in specific future circumstances will require not only accurate appraisal of the general state of relations between the Soviet Union and its Eastern European client-allies, but also more understanding than exists at present of the composition, motivations, and attitudes of the national Eastern European military establishments. For the present, far from having become a military liability to the Soviet Union, Eastern Europe is a military asset that has appreciated in recent years and shows every sign of continuing to increase in value. Yet the greater importance of the Eastern

European military establishments and their concomitant professionalization may give rise to distinct national outlooks and heightened expectations that could in time devalue its present asset status for the Soviets. Whether this happens will depend in part on the answer to the perennial but still cardinal questions in Soviet-Eastern European relations: Will the Soviet Union prove able in the next decade to accept a broader definition of socialist orthodoxy in Eastern Europe? Will Moscow allow somewhat greater scope for the expression of Eastern European national aspirations that could change the Soviet-Eastern European relationship into one of long-term solidarity? On both counts—prospects for changes in the functional, interelite military relationship and the changes in the intrabloc political relationship that would satisfy Eastern European aspirations—there are strong grounds for pessimism.

NOTES

1. B. H. Liddell Hart, *The Soviet Army* (London: Weidenfeld and Nicolson, 1956).

2. A useful, in part eyewitness, account of the Sovietization of the Hungarian armed forces is in Istvan Szent-Miklosy, *Political Trends in the Hungarian Army*, RM-1948 (Santa Monica, California: Rand Corporation, 1957).

3. Thomas W. Wolfe, *Soviet Power and Europe, 1945-1970* (Baltimore: Johns Hopkins Press, 1970), p. 43.

4. Ibid., p. 34.

5. Ministry of National Defense, *Materialy do studowania wojska i sztuki wojennej* (Warsaw: the Ministry, 1967), p. 184.

6. Robin A. Remington, *The Warsaw Pact: Case Studies in Communist Conflict Resolution* (Cambridge, Mass. and London: M.I.T. Press, 1969), pp. 59-65; Nikita Khrushchev, *Khrushchev Remembers: The Last Testament*, Strobe Talbott, ed. (Boston: Little, Brown and Co., 1974), pp. 225-29.

7. Wolfe, op.cit.,pp. 128-216.

8. Ibid., p. 151.

9. *Wehr und Wirtschaft* no. 6 (1971): 274.

10. *Pravda*, September 16, 1965; *Tass*, September 29, 1965.

11. Fritz Ermarth, *Internationalism, Security, and Legitimacy: The Challenge to Soviet Interests in East Europe, 1964-1968*, RM-5909-PR (Santa Monica, California: Rand Corporation, 1969), pp. 33-40; Joseph J. Baritz, "The Warsaw Pact and the Kremlin's European Strategy," *Bulletin for the Study of the USSR*, May 1970, pp. 15-28; Michael Dsizmas, *Der Warschauer Pakt* (Bern: Verlag SOI, 1972), pp. 113-20.

12. *Mezinarodni politika* no. 7 (1966).

13. Remington, op. cit., pp. 101-03; Robert W. Dean, "The Political Consolidation of the Czechoslovak Army," *Radio Free Europe Research (REFR)*, Czechoslovakia BR/14, April 29, 1971; Roman Kolkowicz, "The Warsaw Pact: Entangling Alliance," *Survey* no. 70/71 Winter/Spring 1969.

14. *Aviation Weekly and Space Technology*, March 19, 1973; *Die Welt*, June 13, 1974.

15. Malcolm Mackintosh, "The Warsaw Pact Today," *Survival*, May-June 1974, pp. 122-26; International Institute for Strategic Studies, *The Military Balance* (London: the Institute, 1973-74).

16. Thomas W. Wolfe, *Soviet Military Capabilities and Intentions in Europe*, P-6188 (Santa Monica, California: Rand Corporation, 1974).

17. A. Ratnikov, *Krasnaia zvezda*, March 24, 1971.

18. A. S. Bakhov, *Organizatsiia Varshavskogo dogovora* (Moscow: Nauka, 1971), p. 90.

19. Marian Jurek and Edward Skrzypkowski, *Uklad Warszawski* (Warsaw: Ministry of National Defense, 1970), p. 53. The respective deputy commanders have been identified by *Neues Deutschland*, November 19, 1974, as Gen. Molczyk (Poland); Gen. Niculescu (Romania); Gen. Rusov (Czechoslovakia); Gen. Kessler (GDR); Gen. Smerdzhief (Bulgaria); and Gen. Czeni (Hungary).

20. Mackintosh, op. cit.

21. Jurek and Skrzypkowski, op. cit., p. 54; A. Staroverov, in *Kommunist Voruzhenikh sil*, September 1970.

22. *Obrana lidu*, November 22, 1969, reported that earlier the staff had been constituted on an ad hoc basis to support individual joint maneuvers.

23. Mackintosh, op. cit.; Csizmas, op. cit., p. 25.

24. *Krasnaia zvezda*, January 24, 1970, in Remington, op. cit., document 11.

25. Jurek and Skrzypkowski, op. cit., pp. 54-55.

26. Ibid., p. 63; *Sovremennye problemy razoruzheniia* (1970): 271; Ceausescu to the State Council and Council of Ministers, *Scinteia*, April 11, 1969.

27. Interview with Ivan Yakubovsky, *Smena*, February 3, 1970.

28. Interview with Polish Chief of Staff Cocha, PAP in English, May 13, 1970.

29. Malcolm Mackintosh, "The Evolution of the Warsaw Pact," *Adelphi Papers* no. 58 (June 1969): 11-15; Mackintosh, "The Warsaw Pact Today."

30. Mackintosh, "The Warsaw Pact Today."

31. Csizmas, op. cit., p. 29; GDR Defense Minister Heinz Hoffman, lecture of January 20, 1969, in Heinz Hoffman. *Sozialistische Landesverteidigung*, 2 vols., II (Berlin: Deutscher Militarverlag, 1971), pp. 790-805.

32. Heinz Hoffman, *Neues Deutschland*, April 22, 1965.

33. Wolfe, *Soviet Power*, pp. 478-80, updated from media reports.

34. See Remington, op. cit., p. 130; "Law on National Defense" (1973); *Aviation Space and Technology Weekly*, March 6 and August 22, 1972.

35. For instance, Reuters dispatch from Bucharest, July 31, 1974.

36. Remington, op. cit.; Jurek and Skrzypkowski, op. cit., p. 73 (who note, however, that such assistance might be extended on a bilateral basis).

37. For instance, Julian Lider, *Armie ludowe* (Warsaw, Ministry of National Defense, 1969), p. 377; interview with former Chief of Staff Cocha, *Polityka*, May 5, 1973; Henryk Michalski, articles on Polish military doctrine, *Wojsko ludowe* (June, July, August 1972).

38. *Rude Pravo*, March 6, 1968.

39. Ryszard Frelek, "Nuclear Weapons and European Security: A Polish Perspective," in J. J. Holst, ed., *Security, Order, and the Bomb* (Oslo: Universitetsforlayet, 1972).

4

HAS EASTERN EUROPE BECOME A LIABILITY TO THE SOVIET UNION? (III)—THE ECONOMIC ASPECT
Paul Marer

INTRODUCTION

From the point of view of analyzing the question of whether Eastern Europe has become an economic liability to the Soviet Union, the timing of this issue could not be more auspicious. It was revealed in early 1975 that the Soviets reneged on a 1970 agreement to keep unchanged until January 1976 the prices of basic commodities, such as oil, that they supply to Eastern Europe. The change has become necessary primarily, they argue, to mitigate the large and growing losses they suffer in trade with Eastern Europe.

In a study for the U.S. Congressional Joint Economic Committee completed in 1974, I presented evidence suggesting that during the postwar period, Eastern Europe has metamorphosed from a Soviet economic asset, much exploited under Stalin, into, on balance,[1] a net economic liability. In 1974 one could only speculate on what the Soviets were going to do about this problem, but since then the broad outlines of the solution have begun to emerge.

The first sections of this chapter summarize my previous study and incorporate the results of other studies that have become available since then. The major new contribution is a reconstruction, analysis, and interpretation of recent developments in Soviet-Eastern European economic relations, with a brief look ahead to what these relations might be like during the remainder of the 1970s.

Support of the International Development Research Center of Indiana University during the preparation of this chapter is gratefully acknowledged.

SUMMARY AND A FRAMEWORK FOR ANALYSIS

The most significant general factor in the relations between the Soviet Union and the countries of Eastern Europe—Bulgaria, Czechoslovakia, East Germany, Hungary, Poland and Romania—is the large disparity between the population, territory, resource endowment, and military power of the Soviet Union and those of Eastern Europe, individually and collectively. Given these differences and given Soviet policy, intrabloc relations involving the Soviet Union are inevitably asymmetrical. They are, in the most general terms, marked by the dominance of a superpower and the dependence of six relatively small client states. (Yugoslavia is excluded from the study because its relationship with the Soviet Union since the Stalin-Tito break has differed in substance from that of the European members of CEMA.)

Any such relationship of asymmetrical interdependence offers opportunities for the strong to take advantage of the weak. In the political-military sphere, discussed in Chapters 2 and 3 of this book, the Eastern European nations have certainly been subordinated to the Soviet Union. An interesting question is, therefore, whether the Soviet Union has also asserted its power to dominate the Eastern European countries economically. Has the Soviet Union exploited its political-military position for its own economic advantage?

The logic of the situation would seem to support an affirmative answer, as do the well-documented cases of economic coercion by the Soviets under Stalin. Recent research, however, reveals some rather surprising evidence on this matter. It shows that the economic relationship between the Soviet Union and Eastern Europe after Stalin has changed substantially, so much so that it is no longer to the advantage of the dominant power in all respects. Evidence indicates that there is a net cost to the Soviet Union that is measurable, large, and, up to January 1, 1975 (when the Soviet Union renegotiated the terms upon which it trades with the rest of CEMA), had been increasing.* Since the mid-1960s or so, the costs to the Soviets have been so substantial that they have constituted a significant pressure for some type of economic disengagement from Eastern Europe, a pressure counterbalanced by the political costs to the Soviets that would result from any fundamental change in the degree or terms of their involvement.

This paradoxical relation between the political and economic aspects of the Soviet-Eastern European relationship has been noted by a few observers, among them David Granick, J. Michael Montias, and John Hardt.[2] Based on the author's own work and on recent scholarship by others, a systematic

---

*CEMA includes the Soviet Union, the six Eastern European countries, Mongolia, and Cuba.

compilation of evidence (on a subject on which accurate information is admittedly very difficult to obtain) reveals three different phases of Soviet-Eastern European economic relations.

First, before Stalin's death in 1953, the Soviet Union's political domination of Eastern Europe was accompanied by conventional types of economic extraction. The size of the uncompensated flow of resources from Eastern Europe to the Soviet Union was approximately equivalent to the flow of resources from the United States to Western Europe under the Marshall Plan—roughly on the order of $14 billion.

Second, since the mid-1950s the Soviet Union has not obtained uncompensated resource transfers from Eastern Europe. In fact, until the end of 1974, the Soviet Union had been paying an increasingly steep price for the continued dependence of the Eastern European countries. This net cost was reflected in adverse and deteriorating terms of trade. One form of that disadvantage was, and remains, a highly unfavorable commodity composition of trade. Large energy and raw material exports to Eastern Europe force the Soviet Union to forego larger purchases of machinery and other commodities from Western countries that Eastern European countries are unable to supply.

Third, early in 1975 the Soviet Union renegotiated intra-CEMA foreign trade prices, which were supposed to remain fixed from January 1971 until December 1975, substantially to its advantage, retroactive to January 1, 1975. The justification for discarding the old agreement is that no one could have foreseen the dramatic changes in world market prices and supply conditions that had occurred during the last few years. These new agreements reduce substantially, but do not eliminate, the economic disadvantage to the Soviets.

The finding that for quite some time the Soviet Union has not, on balance, been benefiting from its economic involvement in Eastern Europe fails to accord with the distribution of political power within the bloc. It also runs counter to the logic one would expect to find on the basis of supply and demand considerations within CEMA. At prevailing CEMA prices there are within the bloc acute shortages of primary products and large surpluses of manufactures, particularly machinery, much of it not modern. Within the bloc, the Soviet Union is the only net supplier of primary products and the principal net importer of machinery and other manufactures. Thus, the commodity composition of trade should reinforce the strong potential bargaining power inherent in its superpower status.

The paradox can be explained by considering the economic and political costs and benefits of intrabloc relations as interacting factors and joint products. A framework for explaining how a power-oriented nation can use commercial policy to advance its ends was developed three decades ago by Albert Hirschman. In this view, foreign trade has two principal effects upon the power position of an imperialist country. First, economic gains from trade increase the economic power of the dominant country—the supply effect. Second, foreign trade becomes a direct source of power if other countries become economically dependent on the dominant country and thus provide it with an instrument of coercion—the influence effect. The power to interrupt or redefine commercial relations with any country is the root cause of the influence that the dominant country acquires over other nations.[3]

The influence effect requires that the dependence of the trade partners be greater than that of the dominant power. In such a situation, dependent countries will likely grant the dominant country certain economic, political, and military advantages in order to maintain stable trade relations. Such dependency is enhanced to the extent that the smaller countries cannot dispense with trade with the dominant country, or replace it as a market and source of supply. In the case of CEMA the larger difficulties lie with the smaller countries, because their ability to divert trade is limited by the fact that much of what they export is produced to Soviet specifications, with quality often not up to world market standards. This dependence on the Soviet Union for both imports and exports was created during the early postwar period.

In addition to creating exclusive complementarities, there are also price considerations. Hirschman argues:

> If by some preferential treatment A induces B to produce a commodity for export, A becomes B's only market, and the dependence of B upon A thus created may well be worth to A the economic cost involved in not buying in the cheapest market. In general, any attempt to drive the prices of exports from trading partners above world prices [or the prices of imports to trading partners below world prices] ... will fit in with the policy of increasing their dependence.[4]

I do not wish to argue that after Stalin the Soviet Union deliberately set out to grant subsidies to its allies in CEMA in order to enhance its power position in Eastern Europe. Rather, I would argue that when a combination of circumstances resulted in increased but economically unfavorable dependence, it found itself constrained to alter the situation in any fundamental way by the political-military imperative of having to maintain its influence in the region without exercising brute political or military force, except as a last resort.

From a game-theoretic point of view, one must also consider that an assessment of Soviet power vis-a-vis Eastern Europe must take into account Soviet opportunity costs—the political cost of using its power over CEMA for economic gain—and the cost to Eastern Europe of noncompliance with Soviet demands.[5]

CAPITAL TRANSFERS, 1945-60

The probable Soviet military objectives in Eastern Europe during the first postwar decade were to deny the area to Germany (whose reemergence was a potential long-term threat) and, later, to potentially hostile Western powers; the political objective was to ensure that individual countries would not be controlled by governments hostile to the Soviet Union; and the economic objective was to use the resources of the area for Soviet reconstruction and industrialization by means of reparations and other forms of economic extraction.[6] Reparations-type deliveries by the former enemy countries of East Germany, Hungary, Bulgaria, and Romania must of course be viewed in the light of the destruction inflicted on the Soviet Union during the war.

I have constructed a cumulative balance sheet of (a) reparations and other forms of subvention transfers from Eastern Europe to the Soviet Union and (b) Soviet foreign aid to these countries. The year 1960 was chosen as a dividing line, probably the last year by which transfers related to the war were settled. Until 1955 resources flowed primarily from Eastern Europe to the Soviet Union. In the second half of the 1950s, there was a reverse flow that can be viewed as a partial compensation for earlier extractions. Thus, it is proper to discuss both flows in the same context. The frequency and importance of subvention- and aid-type transfers have diminished considerably since 1960.

In this balance sheet no account is taken of several types of transfers, potential or foregone, conditioned by dependence on the Soviet Union. These include the sacrifice of not accepting, on Soviet insistence, Marshall Plan aid; the aid that Eastern Europe has been obliged to provide to other socialist countries and to the Third World; the net value of blueprints and licenses exchanged free of charge; the subsidies that might be involved in a cumulative, interest-free balance-of-payments surplus; and the implicit subsidies that may result from discriminatory noncommercial exchange rates used in settling invisible transactions.

Omitting the details of calculation and tabulation of results, only the balance sheet of Eastern European subventions and Soviet aid is presented.* Eastern European subventions and Soviet aid flows during 1945-60 are brought to a common denominator by calculating their grant equivalent, which measures the unilateral transfer component of each transaction.[7]

---

*For additional details, see source cited in note 1. The balance sheet excludes Albania and Yugoslavia, the former because information on Soviet aid is not available and because the benefits it received from the Soviet Union under Stalin would have to be balanced against losses due to Soviet economic pressure after 1960, which is outside the scope of this analysis, and Yugoslavia, because one would have to quantify the cost of Stalin's economic blockade and other pressures, which again is beyond our scope. See R. Freedman, *Economic Warfare in the Communist Bloc* (New York: Praeger, 1970).

Subvention

On balance, we found that the cumulative grant equivalent of Eastern Europe's estimated sacrifice during 1945-60 was $23.2 billion and the corresponding gain to the Soviet Union, $19.2 billion. The gain is less than the sacrifice because dismantled Eastern European plants and machinery were not always reassembled in the Soviet Union. These figures do not include uranium shipped by Czechoslovakia and Hungary and the maintenance of Soviet troops in Hungary and Romania, for which no estimates are known to the author, and do not take account of unfavorable prices on commercial exports during the early postwar years, except on Polish coal. The largest burden by far was shouldered by East Germany: its $19.5 billion sacrifice represents almost seven-eighths of the Eastern European total, although its share would be reduced somewhat if estimates of comparable completeness were available for the other countries. The next largest burden was on Romania ($1.7 billion), then Hungary ($1.3 billion) and Poland ($626 million). Among the former enemy countries, Bulgaria apparently received preferential treatment, at least relative to that of other countries.

Soviet Aid

The grant equivalent of Soviet economic assistance to Eastern Europe was estimated in two versions: one that excludes reparations cancellations, and one that includes this item at full value (the approach followed by CEMA sources).*

On balance, we find that the cumulative grant equivalent of Soviet aid during 1945-60 was $2.6 billion, excluding reparations cancellations, and $9.4 billion including this item. According to the first version, all countries benefited, in amounts ranging from $16 million for Czechoslovakia to $842 million for Poland, with the composition of aid varying from country to country. According to the second version, more than two-thirds of the aid benefited East Germany, because the Soviet Union claims to have lightened the country's repatriations burden by almost $7 billion.

---

*The grant equivalent of loans to Eastern Europe has been calculated by assuming, following Horvath (pp. 2-6), that all Soviet loans were for twelve years, at 2.5 percent interest, with a two-year grace period, a 10 percent opportunity rate of discount, fully delivered, and that aid-tying represented a 10 percent cost to the recipient as compared with aid that could have been spent freely on the world market.

Balance of Aid and Subvention

If reparations cancellations are excluded, the six Eastern European countries have provided, on balance, approximately $20 billion subvention to the Soviet Union (corresponding gain to the Soviet Union, about $17 billion). If reparations cancellations are included, the net subvention estimate declines to below $14 billion (with the corresponding gain about $3 billion less). The size of this flow of resources from Eastern Europe to the Soviet Union is of the same order of magnitude as the flow of resources from the United States to Western Europe under the Marshall Plan, which amounted to about $14 billion. The distribution of this large subvention has been most uneven, with East Germany accounting for more than nine-tenths of the total. Significant amounts were also provided by Romania and Hungary, whereas Bulgaria, Czechoslovakia, and Poland are shown to have been net beneficiaries in small amounts.

It cannot be emphasized enough that these figures should be interpreted with a great deal of caution, not only because of the roughness of the component estimates but also because the above calculations take account of only some of the most highly visible capital transfer items. Taken in conjunction with other, difficult-to-quantify evidence on postwar Soviet-Eastern European economic relations, it is clear that during at least the first postwar decade Eastern Europe was not a liability, but a significant asset, to the Soviet Union.[8]

TERMS OF TRADE: 1955-74

The technique of intra-CEMA price determination has been shrouded in secrecy. Prices are said to be based on the world market because such prices represent alternative opportunities to CEMA buyers and sellers and also because, given arbitrary domestic prices, CEMA countries have been unable to find an alternative to world prices acceptable to all members. There is no question, however, that considerable bargaining does take place on prices, if for no other reason than that "world market price" is too ambiguous a concept to serve even as a starting point. Furthermore, world prices are said to be adjusted to eliminate the influence of speculation and monopoly and to take into account CEMA demand and supply.

CEMA literature offers only limited insight into how world prices are translated into CEMA prices. The only definite point is that since 1958, certain formal principles have been agreed upon as to which historical period's prices should be used as a base.* For 1971-75 an average of 1966-70 world prices was used, with some exceptions and modifications.

---

*During 1945-50, prices were reportedly based, at least formally, on current capitalist world market prices. The period 1951-53 was the era of "stop prices," when

It is important to note in connection with interpreting empirical studies of CEMA foreign trade prices that individual commodity prices and quantities traded are determined not by single buyers and sellers in relative isolation from the prices of other commodities, as in the West, but by government agencies that bargain over a whole range of export and import prices at once. Bargaining power in such a situation may be exerted through prices (obtaining high prices for exports and paying low prices for imports) and also through quantities (supplying small or zero quantities of goods whose prices are disadvantageous and forcing the trade partner to supply specified kinds of goods in specified quantities if prices are advantageous). It is for this reason that if a Western observer finds, say, the price of a particular commodity high or low relative to current world prices, this may be because the CEMA price has remained fixed while the world price has changed or, alternatively, because the price that is "out of line" may be compensated by offsetting deviations in the prices of other export and import items.

As to the benefits or "gains" from trade, it is useful to distinguish between short-term and long-term considerations. The issue with respect to gains in the short term is whether CEMA countries trade according to their short-run comparative advantage, that is, whether they specialize in a way that makes good economic sense, given their relative labor, capital, and natural resource endowments. A substantial part of CEMA trade within the bloc probably is not according to this criterion because domestic costs are now fully known as a result of inadequacies in their system of determining prices, but also because as long as price ratios in intra-CEMA trade are different from those on the world market—which is very much the case—there are unrealized gains from further trade (that is, from opening up the bloc as a whole). There appear to be such

---

negotiators used prices agreed upon prior to this period in order to avoid the the distorting influence of inflation due to the Korean war. During 1954-57, selected "stop prices" were adjusted to eliminate the greatest discrepancies between these and current world prices. A situation existed whereby "stop prices," their adjusted versions, and current world market prices for new trade products existed side by side, causing frictions that came more and more to the open, rather than remaining repressed, as under Stalin.

The ninth session of CEMA (Bucharest, June 1958) adopted comprehensive new rules that (1) introduced average 1957-58 world market prices, with exceptions that were not clearly defined; (2) fixed prices for several years, except for new and improved products, whose prices would be currently negotiated; (3) allowed certain references as acceptable documentation of world prices in bilateral negotiations; and (4) introduced the principle of "half-freight" charge, that is, half of the hypothetical charge is added to the world market price in order to establish the documented negotiating base price. Prices continued to be determined bilaterally; the new element was the multilateral agreement on rules to be followed in bilateral negotiations.

By the early 1960s, CEMA prices had deviated from current world market prices; and an agreement was reached during the mid-1960s that introduced a new 1960-64 world-market price base, implemented during 1966-67 in several stages.

large unrealized gains, suggested in the first instance by the extremely high proportions of total trade conducted with CEMA partners. Members of CEMA give each other "an excessively large preferentiality"; that is, they voluntarily channel a portion of their trade to bloc partners even when more profitable opportunities are available on the world market.[9] Evidence presented below indicates that this type of cost tends to fall disproportionately heavily on the Soviet Union, so this is a liability for the Soviets.

With respect to the long term, gains from trade are foregone if the preferential or "sheltered" CEMA market absorbs poor-quality goods and obsolete equipment for a long time, thereby reducing the incentive to innovate and produce "for the market" and causing the exporter to fall more and more behind its competitors. This is the cost that appears to fall disproportionately heavily on the smaller and relatively more advanced CEMA countries: East Germany, Czechoslovakia, and Hungary. The importer of shoddy goods and equipment loses productivity, yet is often unable to resist buying such goods if its own producers are dependent upon the same CEMA suppliers for their export market. This is why in a bilateral, state-trading framework, terms of trade cannot be divorced from the commodity composition of trade. But now let us summarize some of the principal findings on prices and the terms of trade involving price considerations only.

Statistical information on CEMA prices before 1955 is scarce and episodic. What there is suggests strongly that the Soviet Union under Stalin used every type of chicanery in the book to obtain favorable prices; there is documented evidence in the case of low prices for Hungarian and Romanian reparations goods, Polish coal, and Czech uranium. Circumstantial evidence is also offered by the Stalinist purges of senior communist leaders in Bulgaria (Traicho Kostov in 1949) and in Czechoslovakia (Rudolf Slansky and Eugene Loebl in 1952), who during their trials were charged with having asked too high, and offered too low, prices in trade negotiations with the Soviet Union and with trying to maintain commercial secrecy during the negotiations.

Numerous other cases and episodes are listed in the specialized literature.[10] Lack of systematic, published data makes it very difficult, however, to quantify the extent of price discrimination by the Soviet Union during this early period, so we must stay with the vague conclusion that, until 1953 at least, prices were almost certainly heavily slanted in favor of the Soviet Union.

The post-Stalin period was one of upheavals, retrenchment by the Soviet Union, and a movement toward putting many aspects of intrabloc commercial relations on a more stable and equitable basis. Covering the period since the mid-1950s, statistical evidence and interpretive studies suggest the following:[11]

1. Until about 1972, before world inflation became such a serious problem, prices in intra-CEMA transactions were, on the average, substantially higher than world market prices. During 1958-64, the gap between CEMA and world price levels is estimated to have been about 20 percent, ranging between

20 and 40 percent for major groups of manufactures and between 0 and 20 percent for groups of primary products. Between 1965 and 1972 the price-level gap narrowed, but the differences between manufactures and primary products persisted. Since the Soviet Union was already a net exporter of primary products and a net importer of manufactures, intra-CEMA prices have not been particularly advantageous from its point of view.

2. With respect to the movement of prices over time, the price adjustments in 1958 and in 1965-67 reduced prices on balance, particularly those of raw materials and industrial consumer goods, bringing them closer to actual world prices. Since the Soviet Union is the largest supplier of raw materials to the rest of CEMA (absolutely as well as in terms of percentage of trade volume), these adjustments led to a deterioration (roughly 20 percent) in Soviet (net barter) terms of trade with CEMA between 1957 and 1970. During the same period, the terms of trade of Czechoslovakia, East Germany, and Hungary with all socialist countries as a group improved. This finding does not imply anything about the level or equity of Soviet-CEMA prices during the mid-1950s. The point is that the Soviet Unions's export prices have fallen relative to import prices, so that gains from trade are now relatively lower, and its losses relatively higher, than they were during the mid-1950s.

3. The actual distribution of gains and losses in Soviet-CEMA trade in 1960 and 1970 was estimated by two Western scholars. Under ordinary circumstances, when two nations engage in trade, both partners are expected to benefit, even though the distribution of gains may not be equal. Defining gains from trade as the ratio of the estimated resource costs of exports to the potential resource cost of full import substitution, Edward Hewett found that trading with CEMA actually results in a loss for the Soviet Union. That is, by these calculations, in 1960 it cost the Soviet Union 38 percent more resources to export to CEMA than it would have cost to substitute domestic production for imports from CEMA. In contrast, all CEMA countries except Romania were able to save anywhere from 3 to about 30 percent of the resources they would have had to expend had they been forced to produce domestically the commodities imported from the Soviet Union (Romania "lost" 19 percent).

By 1970, both CEMA foreign trade prices and the commodity structure of Soviet-CEMA trade had changed. Assuming that only prices changed (that the commodity composition in 1970 remained the same as it was in 1960), Hewett calculates that the Soviet loss on trade with CEMA increased to 67 percent. This is because fuels and ores have had to be extracted in increasingly remote regions of Asia, with production and transport costs to Eastern Europe rising. The actual loss was only 28 percent because of changes in the structure of trade: by 1970 a larger proportion of Soviet exports to CEMA was composed of machinery than a decade earlier. Despite changes in the commodity composition, CEMA countries had increased their gains from trading with the Soviet Union by 1970 as compared with 1960 (gains for Poland remained about the same).[1][2]

4. Somewhat similar results were obtained by C. H. McMillan with a different methodology. Using the so-called Leontieff method, he calculated the capital, labor, and natural resource requirements of a typical basket of Soviet exports and import replacements. He found that in 1959 (the only year for which he was able to perform these calculations) Soviet exports contained absolutely greater amounts of labor, capital, and natural resources than those of import substitutes of equivalent value. McMillan determined that the overall losses had originated in trade with the more developed CEMA partners: East Germany, Czechoslovakia, Poland, and Hungary. That is, Soviet exports to these countries used more labor, capital, and natural resources than would have been required to produce the manufactured goods that make up the bulk of Soviet imports from them.[13]

Because of data problems and the simplifying assumptions that had to be made, the results should be interpreted only as broad trends rather than as precise measurements. Although Hewett's and McMillan's calculations do confirm that intra-CEMA trading prices tend to overvalue machinery relative to primary products, and are consistent with what is claimed by the Russians and generally acknowledged by the Eastern Europeans, we must not accept with full certainty that Soviet export and import decisions are so poor that they result in a large net transfer of resources to their trade partners in CEMA. For example, we have no information on the volume and price of military equipment shipped from the Soviet Union to Eastern Europe (scattered evidence suggests that the prices charged are on the high side), which could influence not only the magnitude, but perhaps also the direction, of these results.

THE COMMODITY COMPOSITION OF TRADE

During the first postwar decade the Soviet Union was instrumental in forcing the development of high-cost industrial branches in Eastern Europe, probably for several interrelated reasons.[14] First, the Soviets probably did believe that their own pattern of industrialization was ideologically correct and did have universal applicability for the new socialist states. Second, this pattern also had the beneficial political effect of limiting the Eastern European states' interaction with one another, at least more than regional specialization would have, thereby heightening each state's dependence on the Soviet Union. Third, this dependence was beneficial to the Soviet Union as a means of supplementing its requirements for investment goods from the less industrialized East European countries during the Western embargo. As the embargo was relaxed, the more developed Eastern European trade partners gradually fell behind Western technological standards. As a consequence of Eastern Europe's development strategy, poor endowment of natural resources, and wasteful use of materials, net import needs of energy and raw materials grew rapidly during the 1960s. The smaller countries absorbed an increasing share of their total output of primary products domestically and redirected some raw material exports to the West. The Soviet Union became a large supplier of their needs, to the extent of about $2.5 billion worth of raw materials and energy by 1970, importing mainly machinery and equipment (about $3 billion) and industrial consumer goods (about $1.5 billion).[15]

The Soviet Union also exports machinery, equipment, and turnkey plants to its CEMA partners; in fact, since 1970 it has increased the sale of these goods more rapidly than the export of primary products. Almost 80 percent of Soviet engineering exports are purchased by the socialist countries, mainly by its European CEMA partners.

There are alternative interpretations as to which Soviet trade policy is giving rise to these trade patterns. To some extent the commodity composition has been shaped by Eastern Europe's development strategy and resource endowment. Moreover, the Soviets clearly wish to be self-sufficient in high-technology products and probably need the Eastern European markets to take advantage of economies of scale.

With respect to Soviet imports from Eastern Europe, Steven Rosefielde argues that the Soviet Union has a strong and rational interest in buying consumer goods (whose import in 1973 from CEMA exceeded $2 billion); these purchases serve the Soviet interest by augmenting domestic stocks of consumer goods in order to satisfy growing consumer demands, paid for by a relatively abundant supply of natural resources.[16]

Clearly, there is merit to the argument that the Soviets need large quantities of consumer goods as well as machinery and equipment. However, if the former could be produced with less resources at home than it takes to pay for them via exports, as suggested by McMillan, and if exports currently going to CEMA could be exchanged on the world market for higher-quality goods and on much more favorable terms, then Soviet interest in importing manufactures from Eastern Europe becomes less clear. The Soviet Union is the main market—some say the dumping ground—for the consumer goods exports of socialist countries. Bulgaria supplies 69 percent of its exported consumer goods to the Soviet Union, Poland 52 percent, East Germany 43 percent, Hungary 41 percent, Romania 39 percent, and Czechoslovakia 38 percent. The Soviets complain regularly about the poor quality of these wares.*

---

*For example, "Regrettably, there is much evidence that the Socialist countries . . . supply low-quality consumer goods, including clothes, knitwear, footwear, fabrics, leather-wear, and furniture. . . . There are also latent defects . . . the assortment of goods does not always satisfy the Soviet people's needs, since modern fashions and models are sometimes disregarded . . . suppliers sometimes violate contracts by shipping goods which neither meet the contractual terms nor correspond to the selected samples." V. Zoloyev, "Soviet Foreign Trade in the First Half of the Decisive Year," *Foreign Trade* (Moscow), November 1974.

Dissatisfaction with the commodity composition of Soviet trade with Eastern Europe relates, however, to more than just quality problems. Since the mid-1960s the Soviet Union has been complaining that the exchange of raw materials for poor-quality manufactures is disadvantageous because it limits its ability to import technology and other goods from the West and involves a net export of embodied capital.

THE PROBLEM ASSUMES A NEW DIMENSION: 1972-75

During 1972-75 a series of events and unusual circumstances occurred whose combined effect was to exacerbate the tension related to economic issues between the Soviet Union and its CEMA partners.

First, the Soviet Union had been facing, and continues to face, a declining rate of growth of national product, attributable not only to cumbersome planning and the problems of bureaucracy and poor managerial incentives, but also to a substantial slowdown in the rate of growth in the labor force (due to demographic factors) and capital stock (as an increased proportion of new capital replaces rather than adds to the existing stock). Under these circumstances, acceleration of economic growth requires a more rapid improvement in productivity, which, in the view of the current leadership, requires increased Western capital and know-how. These imports must be paid for, currently or as credits are repaid, largely with Soviet energy and raw materials. The more these earners of convertible currency are exported to CEMA partners rather than to the West, the more Eastern Europe is viewed by the Soviets as an economic liability.

A somewhat more sophisticated argument, not necessarily in conflict with the above, is made by Steven Rosefielde. He argues that a principal objective of Soviet planners during the early 1970s was, and will be, to provide more consumer goods. Considering that labor productivities in the light and food industries are very much lower than in the heavy industries, to further this objective largely with a domestic effort would mean a diversion of capital from capital-intensive to labor-intensive sectors, leading inescapably to a falling rate of growth of national product. Confronted with this dilemma, the Soviets will want to purchase more machinery from the West and, to save hard currency, much more industrial consumer goods from Eastern Europe. To pay for Western machinery, the Soviets need to reorient some hard-currency-earning exports from Eastern Europe to the West, and to push their machinery, produced relatively more efficiently, in the East.[17] Still another way to help achieve these objectives, we might add, is to substantially improve the terms of trade with Eastern Europe.

Many Western observers interpret Soviet interest in pursuing detente—under which Russia presumably would give political concessions in exchange for Western, particularly American, technology and credits—in the light of these economic realities facing the Soviet Union. As the conclusion of a recent empirical study, J. M. Montias suggests that while it is too early to trace the impact of American-Soviet detente on intra- and extra-CEMA trade, to the extent that the volume of Soviet exports of raw materials to the West will have to expand for increased machinery imports from the United States, they may have to be switched away from CEMA consumers:

> The Soviet Union might then no longer be in a position to act as the all-purpose purveyor of raw material inputs for the industries of Eastern Europe and as the never-satiated outlet for their manu-factures. Since the willingness of the Soviet Union to perform these twin roles has provided the bond that has kept COMECON [CEMA] from disintegrating ... this new direction may cause [Eastern European countries] considerable hardship.[18]

The second set of recent events of consequence for Soviet-Eastern European economic relations was the poor harvests of 1972 and 1975 that forced the Soviet Union to purchase large quantities of agricultural products in the West—close to $3 billion worth during 1972-73, and probably close to that amount again in 1975. Such huge and unplanned purchases contribute to large trade deficits with hard-currency countries. The larger the Soviet hard-currency deficits, the greater the opportunity cost—economic liability—of supplying CEMA countries with commodities that could be sold readily for hard currency in the West.

Third, since the early 1970s world market prices of energy and raw materials have increased rapidly, with the prices of some commodities, such as oil and gold, soaring spectacularly. Paradoxically, this probably had both a positive and a negative effect on Soviet willingness to continue to supply energy and raw materials to Eastern Europe at fixed prices. The positive effect would be due to the dramatic improvement the price increases had brought in Soviet balance of payment with the West in 1974, thereby lessening the pressure to redirect exports from CEMA to the West. The negative effect, probably much more important, is that rising world market prices increase the opportunity costs to the Soviets of supplying Eastern Europe with growing quantities of commodities at fixed pre-1970 prices.

More than any other commodity, oil illustrates some of the key issues in Soviet-Eastern European relations: the dilemma of the Soviet Union, some of the current problems, and the anxiety concerning the future source and cost of this vital commodity in Eastern Europe. In 1974 the Soviet Union exported approximately 60 million tons of crude oil and petroleum products to the five

European members of CEMA (Romania did not purchase oil from the Soviet Union) at the price agreed upon in 1970 and based on world prices of the late 1960s—that is, at approximately $16 to $20 per ton (depending upon the mix of crude and oil products and transportation charges, which vary slightly from country to country), for a total revenue of $1.0 to $1.2 billion. During the same year the Soviets sold approximately 40 million tons of oil in the West at the average world market price of about $70 per ton, for a total revenue of about $2.8 billion. If we make the extreme and politically unrealistic assumption that the Soviets could have sold an additional 60 million tons of oil to the West, we find that they could have earned $3 billion more, thereby increasing their hard-currency revenues ($7.5 billion in 1974) by 40 percent. The other side of the coin, of course, is how much more the five CEMA countries would have had to pay, had they been obligated to buy oil at current world market prices.*

THE SOVIET RESPONSE

Compensatory Actions Taken Before 1975

Soviet leaders' concern about prestige, and their vital interest in maintaining political stability in Eastern Europe, surely have been two of the reasons for their not moving precipitously in reneging on the specified-quantity, fixed-price, medium-term trade agreements signed in 1970. But even before 1975, the Soviets had taken five compensatory actions for what they view as the economic liability of supplying Eastern Europe with cheap energy and raw materials.

1. They moved toward "commodity bilateralism"—a network of tied exports and imports—under which machinery imports are increasingly linked to machinery exports.

2. They obtained special-purpose credits from Eastern Europe for developing new energy and raw material sources in the Soviet Union, on the basis that some of the resulting output will be used to supply Eastern Europe. The commodity realization of these credits need not be limited to the type of resources required directly for, say, the oil fields, but can include machinery and consumer goods acceptable to the Soviets. Since 1960 Czechoslovakia, for example, has participated in at least seven large projects in the Soviet Union, involving credits well in excess of $1 billion. The principal issues of contention

---

*The actual opportunity cost to the Soviets (or gain to CEMA) may be higher or lower than $3 billion, depending upon the availability, quality, and price of goods that the Russians could have bought with the money in the West versus what they actually bought in the East. Taking into account the better availability and quality of Western goods would increase the opportunity costs; the fact that the Soviets bought from Eastern Europe at pre-1970 prices tends to decrease the opportunity cost.

relate to the type of machinery and manufactures acceptable to the the Soviets and to the low, subsidized interest rate customary in CEMA, usually 2 percent.*

3. They agreed to deliver additional quantities of "hard goods" over and above those specified in earlier agreements, but in some cases only in exchange for convertible currency or against goods that first had to be purchased for convertible currency. For example, the Soviet Union agreed to deliver 760,000 tons of crude oil to Hungary during 1975, in addition to the 6 million tons previously contracted, in exchange for an equivalent value of goods Hungary would "purchase on third markets."[19]

4. They pressured CEMA partners to improve the quality, modernity, and Western-import content of their regular exports to the Soviet Union: "We shall under no circumstances be customers for an assortment of goods which cannot be sold on other markets. The goods [supplied to us] must be of first quality and ... a proportion of them must consist of products made from import materials or under foreign license."[20]

5. They directed the Eastern European countries to buy an increasing share of the additional quantities of some scarce commodities from non-Soviet, preferably Middle Eastern and African, sources.

Refusal to be Bound by the Rules:
Price Revisions in 1975

By 1974 both the Soviet Union and the Eastern European countries found themselves in a difficult situation. The former found it more and more costly to adhere to the 1970 agreements under which increased quantities of energy and raw materials were to be supplied during 1971-75 at fixed (average 1966-70) world market prices; the latter became uncertain about the size of the adjustment burden that they would soon be required to carry. Essentially, the Eastern European countries needed to know how much more exports will they have to give up, to the Soviet Union and to the world at large, to secure their energy needs and raw material supplies. If a much larger volume of exports becomes necessary to finance a given basket of imports, this will adversely affect living standards, which could lead to popular resentment, ultimately requiring repressive measures and possibly a need for Soviet intervention.

---

*Until the energy crisis demonstrated vividly to the Eastern Europeans the serious-ness of their predicament, they reportedly were dragging their feet on these investment projects. During and since 1974 a good number of them have been signed, some even with Romanian participation. More generally, the Soviets have been getting improved coopera-tion concerning "socialist integration" (which, in addition to its economic aspects, stands as a watchword for maintaining Soviet political hegemony in Eastern Europe) as the smaller countries contemplate the escalating cost of noncompliance with Soviet demands.

Thus, the logic of the situation, confirmed by reports from Eastern Europe, suggests that the strongest trump card Eastern European leaders have had when negotiating on these matters was an appeal to Soviet interest in maintaining political stability in Eastern Europe. In recent years much of the region's political stability could be traced to improved living standards (*vide* the situation in Poland since 1970), which paradoxically, have risen much faster and further—at least in East Germany, Czechoslovakia, Hungary, and Poland—than in the Soviet Union.

For quite some time proposals had been made within CEMA on how to improve the intra-CEMA price determination and supply systems, but each country has been proposing formulas that would maximize its economic gain or at least minimize its new economic burden. Since, for this reason, the experts could not agree, the basic decision on adjustment and burden-sharing had to be made by the top Soviet leadership, with a careful eye on the political consequences of their actions.

As best as can be reconstructed, this is what happened. There is circumstantial evidence that Soviet leaders chose Hungary as the first country with which to renegotiate prices.[21] The agreement, revealed with unusual speed, detail, and frankness in the February 23, 1975, issue of the Hungarian party daily *Nepszabadsag*, has the following main provisions:

1. The price to be paid by Hungary for Soviet crude oil in 1975 is 37 rubles (approximately $49) per metric ton, 2.3 times the 1974 price but still only about half the peak world market prices in effect at the end of 1974.*

2. Selected price changes were introduced effective January 1, 1975, taking the average of 1972-74 world prices as an initial negotiating base. The 1975 price adjustments will affect 56 percent of Hungary's import and 63 percent of its export trade with the Soviet Union.

3. In an unusual move, the Hungarian article revealed enough information to permit calculation of projected 1975 changes in Hungarian-Soviet (net barter) terms of trade:

> The average price level of Hungarian imports of raw materials and energy will increase by 52 percent and that of imported machinery and equipment by 3.3 percent.... The price level of Hungarian exports of machinery and equipment will rise by 15 percent, that of agricultural products by 28 percent, and that of light industrial products by 19 percent.

A preliminary calculation suggests that the net result will be an increased burden of over $100 million in 1975.

---

*Since then oil prices on the world market have declined somewhat, so that Hungary now pays about two-thirds of what it would cost to import oil from the Middle East or North Africa.

4. With respect to the financing of this deficit, Soviet posture has been one of accommodation. Specifically, the Soviet Union allowed Hungary to apply its 1974 trade surplus of 36 million rubles (approximately $47 million) toward reducing its projected 1975 deficit. This would be standard procedure in the West but is an unusual move in CEMA, where currencies are not convertible and deficits customarily must be settled with additional shipments. Further offsets are to come from applying toward the deficit the previously scheduled 1975 delivery of Hungarian investment goods for the development of Soviet energy and raw material sectors. Of greatest significance is the Soviet Union's readiness to grant Hungary a series of ten-year loans at low rates of interest to help finance deficits that still remain. Such credits will help alleviate the immediate adverse effects on Hungarian living standards of unfavorable price changes in Hungarian-Soviet trade.

5. With respect to supply quantities, it was revealed that during 1975 the Soviet Union was willing to deliver oil and certain raw materials over and above those scheduled earlier, to be paid for in part, apparently, by convertible currency. The linked announcement of prices and quantities suggests that the Soviet Union withheld contracting for additional amounts pending settlement of the price issue.

With respect to the other Eastern European countries, it was subsequently revealed that other "CEMA countries also proceeded from 1972-74 world market prices when concluding their agreements on 1975 prices." For all Eastern European countries the initial price adjustments presumably will be selective except for the price of crude oil, which in 1975 appeared to be uniformly 37 rubles (with some variations due to transport costs). At the time of writing no details comparable with those for Hungary have become available to permit a rough estimate of the price change's impact. The increase in Eastern Europe's oil bill to the Soviets alone, due to price changes only, will be well in excess of $1 billion, which represents about 15 percent of Eastern Europe's total 1973 exports to the Soviet Union.*

In a move of major significance, the method of determining intra-CEMA prices after 1975 also was changed. Beginning with 1976, the old system of maintaining fixed prices for several years will be replaced by a moving average price base. Each year's prices will be based on the average world market prices

---

*Calculated on the assumption that in 1975 the Soviets shipped to Eastern Europe about 65 million tons of crude oil and products and charged 37 rubles ($49), versus the old price of 16 rubles ($21). It is important to note that the nominal revaluation of the CEMA currencies vis-a-vis the American dollar increases the dollar, but not the ruble, value of intra-CEMA trade. Thus, when calculating the dollar equivalent of the burden of price changes in CEMA from one year to another, the same ruble/dollar exchange must be used for the old and for the new price.

for five years immediately preceding the year to which the newly calculated prices apply. Thus, prices in 1976 will be established across the board on the basis of average world prices of 1971-75, in 1977 on the basis of average prices in 1972-76, and so on. The decision on the new uniform system of determining intra-CEMA foreign trade prices after 1976 was formally agreed upon at the CEMA Executive Committee meeting held in Moscow on January 21-23, 1975.[22]

The Impact of Price Changes:
A Preliminary Assessment

There appears to be a somewhat paradoxical situation with respect to Soviet-Eastern European prices. In 1975 a substantial share of trade (at least for Hungary) was to be traded at 1972-74 world prices, and in 1976 at 1971-75 world prices. The prices of energy and raw materials skyrocketed in 1973 and 1974; the trend in 1975 was for prices to retreat, with indications that world price levels for energy and raw materials would be lower than in 1974. Thus, CEMA prices based on 1972-74 world prices would capture most of the impact of the dramatic recent world price rise (two out of three of the worst inflation years), whereas prices based on 1971-75 world prices would incorporate only three out of five of the bad inflation years (two out of five for some commodities). It is conceivable, therefore, that after a sharp rise in 1975 CEMA prices would level off in 1976, and rise again thereafter. To be sure, the magnitude and the direction of year-to-year price changes will be determined by factors yet unknown or unrevealed, including the proportion of Soviet-Eastern European trade affected by the "selected" 1975 price adjustments, the commodity composition of that trade, how intra-CEMA prices of manufactures (for which the price range is much greater than for energy and primary products) will be adjusted, and how world market prices will move.

Just before it became known that the 1975 price adjustments would be based on 1972-74 world prices, some quick calculations were performed by Harry Trend to estimate the impact of price changes in CEMA.[23] On the assumption that in 1975 the Soviets would uniformly charge 37 rubles for oil and that 1970-74 world prices would be applied to all exports of energy, raw materials, and semimanufactures (no price change for finished products), it was estimated that if in 1975 the Soviets delivered the same goods to the six CEMA partners as in 1973, the value would be higher by one-third, or 2.5 billion rubles ($3.3 billion).

Taking into account that the physical volume of goods imported from the Soviet Union is greater in 1975 than in 1973 (which increases Eastern Europe's adjustment burden), that 1972-74 prices are being applied (which also increases the adjustment burden), but that only a portion of 1975 trade is subject to price

TABLE 4.1

Energy, Raw Materials, and Semifinished Goods Imported by
Eastern European Countries from the Soviet Union in 1973:
Differences Between Actual 1973 and Hypothetical
1975 Values

Country	Absolute Difference (million Devisa rubles)	Percent of 1975 Total Imports from USSR
Czechoslovakia	542	40.0
Hungary	362	37.1
Poland	528	36.5
East Germany	629	33.9
Bulgaria	393	32.0
Romania	95	18.3
Total Eastern Europe	2,549	34.5

Sources: Harry Trend, "Some Effects of COMECON's Revised Price System," RAD Background Report, February 20, 1975; International Trade Information Management System, International Development Research Center, Indiana University.

revisions (which decreases the burden), the results nevertheless provide a rough estimate of the price change impact. Of particular interest is the estimated distribution of the adjustment burden among the importing countries, shown in Table 4.1.

Considering only imports from the Soviet Union, without the effect of price adjustments on Eastern Europe's exports to the Soviet Union, relatively the highest adjustment burden falls on Czechoslovakia and Hungary, and the lowest on Romania, which does not import oil from the Soviet Union. Considering the export side, Poland is in a relatively favorable position, primarily because of coal: the Soviet Union is its largest customer by far, importing about one-fourth (some 10 million tons) of total Polish coal exports. For all other countries something like half of the increased cost of imports might be covered by increased prices on their exports to the Soviet Union.

CONCLUSIONS

Not all information and data are in yet; but on the basis of preliminary evidence, one may conclude that the Soviet response to the rising cost of supplying energy and raw materials to Eastern Europe—at relatively low prices and in exchange for manufactures, many of them not modern—can be characterized as prudent. The Soviets have chosen what appears to be a middle ground between a "sock it to them" approach, which could have had dangerous political consequences in Eastern Europe, and a "do nothing" approach, which would have been economically and politically unacceptable in the Soviet Union.

The new, much more flexible, moving-average-market-price-base method of determining intra-CEMA prices has important advantages over the old, more rigid system, under which prices remained fixed for a long time. First, the gradual adjustment gives the Eastern European countries time to adjust to the current world market price situation: for the time being, adjusted prices of energy and raw materials will be lower, on the average, than current world market prices. At the same time, moving the base each year avoids the repetition of either exporter or importer being locked into extremely unfavorable prices for a long time, should rapid inflation, or massive price change of any kind, continue. This more flexible method of determining prices will help to ensure that intra-CEMA prices will remain closer to world market prices, which in turn should help to improve the rationality of economic decisions, either domestic or trade-oriented. Adjusting prices only once a year will provide a degree of stability essential for planning. Finally, more flexible intra-CEMA prices are, on balance, more compatible with comprehensive domestic economic reforms than foreign trade prices with socialist partners remaining fixed for five years.

A wise man once said, "If you want to know a man's character, divide an inheritance with him." By their recent actions the Soviets have revealed, if not their character, at least their views about the trade-off between decisions that would benefit them economically but could trigger events portending substantial political costs, versus those that would yield smaller economic gain but would minimize political costs. This revealed preference is the basis on which to predict that the present Soviet leadership will continue to exercise prudence in negotiating the quantities to be traded under the next (1976-80) Five-Year Plan. That is, they probably will maintain the current levels of energy and raw material exports to CEMA and may even supply a portion of Eastern Europe's increased energy and raw material requirements.

Turning to the question of whether Eastern Europe has become an economic liability to the Soviet Union, the answer, looking at the current and near-term future situation, is yes. But the perspective on this question might well be different if one considers the economic and political costs and benefits of intra-bloc relations as interacting factors and joint products. While the Soviet Union might find it economically attractive to diminish its direct economic links with CEMA partners, it certainly also views their increased economic dependence on the Soviet Union and the subsidies it provides as an asset—political influence levers—because the Eastern European countries must continuously weigh the economic cost of noncompliance with Soviet political demands.

NOTES

1. Paul Marer, "Soviet Economic Policy in Eastern Europe," in U.S. Congress, Joint Economic Committee, *Reorientation and Commercial Relations of the Economies of Eastern Europe* (Washington, D.C.: U.S. Government Printing Office, 1974), pp. 135-63.

2. David Granick, "Economic Relations with the USSR,' in N. J. G. Pounds and N. Spulber, eds., *Resources and Planning in Eastern Europe* (Bloomington: Indiana University Publications, 1957), pp. 129-48; J. Michael Montias, "Obstacles to the Economic Integration of Eastern Europe," *Studies in Comparative Communism*, nos. 3 and 4 (1969): 38-60; and John P. Hardt, "East European Economic Development: Two Decades of Interrelationships and Interactions with the Soviet Union," in *Economic Development in Countries of Eastern Europe*, a compendium of papers submitted to the Subcommittee on Foreign Economic Policy of the Joint Economic Committee, U.S. Congress (Washington, D.C.: U.S. Government Printing Office, 1970).

3. Albert O. Hirschman, *National Power and the Structure of Foreign Trade* (Berkeley: University of California Press, 1945).

4. Ibid., pp. 31-32.

5. The game-theoretic approach to the exercise of power is discussed by John Harsanyi, "Measurement of Social Power," in Martin Shubik, ed., *Game Theory and Related Approaches to Social Behavior* (New York: John Wiley and Sons, 1964).

6. Zbigniew K. Brzezinski, *The Soviet Bloc: Unity and Conflict* (New York: Praeger, 1961), pp. 4-5.

7. The application of this approach to intrabloc transactions was pioneered by Janos Horvath in his "Grant Elements in Intra-Bloc Aid Programs," *ASTE Bulletin* 13, no. 3 (Fall 1971): 1-17. My estimates and assumptions in some cases differ from those of Horvath.

8. For much useful information on this period, see Frederic L. Pryor, *The Communist Foreign Trade System* (Cambridge, Mass.: M.I.T. Press, 1963).

9. Franklyn D. Holzman, "Soviet Foreign Trade Pricing and the Question of Discrimination," *Review of Economics and Statistics* 44 (May 1962): 146; and Robert W. Campbell, "Some Issues in Soviet Energy Policy for the Seventies," in U.S. Congress, Joint Economic Committee, *Soviet Economic Perspectives for the Seventies* (Washington, D.C.: U.S. Government Printing Office, 1973), pp. 15-16.

10. Eugene Loebl, *Sentenced and Tried* (London: Elek Books Ltd., 1969); Pryor, op. cit.; P. J. D. Wiles, *Communist International Economics* (New York: Praeger, 1969); J. Wszelaki, *Communist Economic Strategy: The Role of East Central Europe* (New York: National Planning Association, 1959).

11. In addition to my own calculations, these findings are based on studies by CEMA economists—the most informative ones are Sandor Ausch, *A KGST-egyuttmukodes helyzete, mechanizmusa, tavlatai* (CEMA cooperation, situation, mechanism and perspectives) (Budapest: Kozgazdasagi es Jogi Konyvkiado, 1969); and Adam Marton, "Price Developments in Hungary's Foreign Trade: 1949-70," Working Paper no. 10 (Bloomington: International Development Research Center, Indiana University—and on Western calculations; the most comprehensive is Edward A. Hewett, "Foreign Trade Prices in the Council for Mutual Economic Assistance" (Ph.D. dissertation, University of Michigan, 1971). All are discussed in Paul Marer, *Postwar Pricing and Price Patterns in Socialist Foreign Trade* (Bloomington: International Development Research Center, Indiana University, 1972).

12. Edward A. Hewett, "Prices and Resource Allocation in Intra-CEMA Trade," paper prepared for Conference on the Consistency and Efficiency of the Socialist Price System, University of Toronto, March 8-9, 1974.

13. C. H. McMillan, "Factor Proportions and the Structure of Soviet Foreign Trade," *ACES Bulletin* 15, no. 1 (Spring 1973).

14. For a discussion of evidence on this matter, see Marer, "Soviet Economic Policy in Eastern Europe."

15. Paul Marer, *Soviet and East European Foreign Trade, 1946-1969: Statistical Compendium and Guide* (Bloomington: Indiana University Press, 1972). More recent data can be found in the computerized Soviet-East European files of the International Trade Information Management System (ITIMS) maintained at the International Development Research Center of Indiana University.

16. Steven Rosefielde, "Revealed Policy Preference and the Commodity Structure of Soviet International Trade," unpublished ms.

17. Steven Rosefielde, "The Changing Pattern of Economic Interests Within the COMECON: The Impact of Factor Substitution and Detente," paper presented at the International Conference of Slavists, Banff, Canada, September 1974.

18. J. M. Montias, "The Structure of COMECON Trade and Prospects for East-West Trade," in U.S. Congress, Joint Economic Committee, *Reorientation . . .*, pp. 662-81.

19. *Nepszabadsag* (Budapest), February 23, 1975.

20. I. Semyonov, in Czechoslovak daily *Svoboda*, September 13, 1972.

21. New York *Times*, January 28, 1975, p. 3, and *East-West Markets*, January 13, 1975. Possible reasons for choosing Hungary first are the following: it has been a large creditor to the Soviet Union during the last few years (its trade surplus partly the result, according to some reports, of an inadequate volume of machinery purchases by Hungarian enterprise managers under the new flexibility allowed them since the 1968 comprehensive economic reforms); the country's extreme dependence on Soviet energy sources and raw materials; and the intended psychological effect on other CEMA members, and in the West, since Hungary is neither a Soviet puppet nor a pesky adversary. That is, coming to terms with Hungary first might give more an appearance of genuine bargaining rather than imposition of Soviet conditions than if the first announcement of a price rise came from, say, Bulgaria or Czechoslovakia.

Four important meetings are said to have been held by Hungarian and Soviet officials during the last three months of 1974. The Russians reportedly pressed to make any price increase retroactive to 1974, while the Hungarians are said to have stood firmly against this. The issues evidently were resolved or finalized during the last week of December in Budapest, at a meeting with a Soviet delegation headed by N. Baibakov, chairman of the State Planning Committee, and N. Patolichev, minister of foreign trade.

22. *Nepszabadsag*, February 23, 1975. For the date of the Executive Committee meetings, see Business International, *East Europe Report*, February 7, 1975. Agreement on the new 1975 oil price and on the new system of price determination has been confirmed in the official press reports of the other Eastern European countries. See *Zacie gospodarcze* (Poland), February 16, 1975; *Neues Deutschland* (East Germany), February 18, 1975.

23. Harry Trend, "Some Effects of COMECON's Revised Price System," Radio Free Europe Background Report, February 20, 1975.

5

CHINA'S EMERGING ROLE
IN EASTERN EUROPE

Robin Remington

INTRODUCTION

East Central Europe is Moscow's backyard. Geography and politics combined to make the area a natural arena of Russian concern long before there was a Soviet Union, and the revolution of 1917 did nothing to change that foreign policy priority. The Soviet Union continued, and continues, attempts to consolidate East Central Europe as a Soviet sphere of influence.

Conversely, there is no "natural" Chinese-Eastern European connection. Peking's relationship to these countries has been a function of ideological, organizational considerations flowing from their membership in what today has become a multiply defined "socialist commonwealth." Moreover, the interaction is symbiotically tangled in the ongoing Sino-Soviet schism. There is no Chinese role in Eastern Europe separate from Peking's relations with Moscow; no bilateral East Central European relationship with China has developed that is not a part of China's political stand vis-a-vis the Soviet Union. In short, the links that tie China to Eastern Europe form not a line but a triangle.

Political analysis is always based on a series of implicit or explicit assumptions about the units involved. For our purposes, this chapter assumes the following:

1. That Chinese-Eastern European relations are primarily a reflection of the ideological-political systems involved; that is, the most important fact about that relationship is that communist countries are involved.

My writing benefited from the research assistance of Rada Vlajinac. I am also grateful to Peter R. Prifti of the M.I.T. Center for International Studies, both for his checking of the Albanian Press and for his helpful comments on the most recent aspects of Chinese-Albanian relations.

2. That members of what George Modelski has called "the Communist system" do share "an ensemble of norms, standards and values which is . . . common to party members" and separates them "from non-members: 'reactionaries', 'capitalists', 'imperialists', and the like. This culture is embodied in its own prolific literature, has its own distinct language and symbols, its own history and its own heroes, villains, and martyrs, and its own special ritual behavior."[1]

3. That, as Alfred Meyer put it, "throughout the European communist world the societal base is tending to reassert its sovereignty over the political super-structure; the native political cultures are regaining some influence; the political systems are forced to adjust themselves to their several political cultures and social structures."[2]

4. That this process of domestic adjustment has had a series of foreign policy consequences both for individual East Central European nations and for Soviet ability to achieve Moscow's objectives within the region as a whole.

5. That the Chinese alternative has been influencing Eastern European political options since the mid-1950s in ways that today set boundaries on policy of the 1970s in both Peking and Eastern European capitals.

To understand the dynamics of this relationship, it is necessary to recall briefly how it developed.

HISTORICAL OVERVIEW, 1956-65

Whether or not the Chinese overstated their importance during the crises of 1956, when they claimed credit for the Soviet decisions to tolerate the outcome of the Polish October rather than intervene militarily, and to use troops to end the Hungarian "counterrevolution,"[3] Peking was actively involved. Indeed, the first explanation of these events appeared in the form of a long Chinese article reprinted in the Soviet press, followed almost immediately by a Chinese version of the differences between the two crises.[4] Thus began the period Zbigniew Brzezinski has characterized as the Maoist effort to reconstruct a center.[5] Whether Peking was more concerned with strengthening the center or with exploring the limits of Chinese influence on Soviet decisions regarding policy direction within the communist world is academic. The answer could easily be "both," for in 1956 these goals were in no way mutually exclusive. The importance of Eastern Europe for either objective is more relevant.

Late in 1956 and early in 1957, Chinese Premier Chou En-lai made a trip through several Eastern European countries, preaching unity. According to the later Chinese version, he also criticized Soviet leaders for failing to consult with other parties before denouncing Stalin at the Twentieth Congress of the Communist Party of the Soviet Union in February 1956.[6] As events of 1957-58 made even more explicit, the Chinese wanted Soviet leadership of the camp for tactical reasons. They also wanted a voice in how such "leadership" would be exercised—which, in retrospect, one might consider, at a minimum, "veto power," with the maximum goal including positive inputs on what was and was not ideologically/organizationally acceptable.

1957 was Nikita Khrushchev's time of troubles. Challenged by the "anti-party" group, retaining his position by virtue of frantic domestic maneuvering, he sacrificed his special relationship with Yugoslavia under pressure from Peking at the Moscow 1957 meeting of ruling communist parties. This is not to say he did not have reason to be annoyed with Belgrade's interpretation of the Soviet-Yugoslav rapproachement of 1955-56, or that Khrushchev would not have wanted some "tightening" of visible Soviet control. Given both his subsequent policy and the amount of effort that he had already invested in rehabilitating the Yugoslavs, however, it is doubtful that he would have gone so far without insistence from Peking. Mao had succeeded in temporarily isolating Yugoslav revisionism.

Meanwhile, China's perception of its Eastern European possibilities began to expand along Romanian lines. There is scant evidence, and not even much speculation, as to who was courting whom. Tentative Romanian feelers for Chinese support on ideological formulations have been documented as early as 1954.[7] Then quietly, certainly without attracting Western attention at this time, Peking became a factor in Bucharest's efforts to maneuver Soviet troops out of Romania. Success of these efforts provided an indispensable base for subsequent Romanian foreign policy deviations from "jointly coordinated" initiatives by other members of the Warsaw Pact. In April 1958, a high-level Romanian delegation went to China. Although the general purpose of this visit remained cloudy, its consequence, in communist jargon was, "no accident." In Peking the head of the delegation, Premier Chivu Stoica, spoke warmly of Chinese troop withdrawal from North Korea.[8] Then, in the joint statement of April 8, both Chinese and Romanian parties openly called for diminution of military blocs in Europe and Asia, as well as withdrawal of armed forces from "military bases on foreign territory".[9] The statement made no distinction between imperialist and socialist forces, and did not refer to the socialist camp headed by the Soviet Union.

Officially the Soviets paid no attention to these contacts, yet the Romanian delegation returned via Moscow. It was met at the airport by top Soviet leaders, although there were no reports on the content of subsequent discussions. Timing and previous Soviet inattention to Romanian attempts to negotiate troop withdrawal indicate that, well before the West began to suspect it, Bucharest was manipulating Soviet desire to contain Chinese influence in Eastern Europe in order to further Romanian national goals.[10] The Warsaw Pact PCC was informed in May 1958 that Bucharest had agreed to a Moscow-proposed withdrawal of Soviet forces stationed in Romania under the Warsaw Treaty.[11]

Not all Chinese-Eastern European contacts in 1958 had such visible results, but the volume of exchange increased markedly. During 1958 an estimated 108 Chinese delegations visited Eastern European capitals, and 150 Eastern European delegations went to Peking.[12] This was in a context of wide Eastern European media coverage of Chinese internal developments that in itself carried implications for ideological innovations in other communist countries. The "Hundred Flowers" period of 1957, the "Great Leap Forward," and the reorganization of China into "people's communes" excited interest in Eastern Europe. This spreading of Peking's influence into an area Moscow had long held as a "natural" Soviet preserve undoubtedly combined with the undesirable implications of the implicit Chinese challenge in the claim that the road to communism might be best traveled via people's communes. All of this undoubtedly contributed to Soviet lack of enthusiasm for the Great Leap Forward.

Poland, for example, had mistakenly construed the brief blooming of the "Hundred Flowers" of Chinese willingness "to support our efforts aimed in the direction outlined in October."[13] That agreeing to a Polish desired degree of diversity was about the last thing likely, given internal Chinese developments or even Peking's preferences for collective appearances (if not reality) in the communist world, is politically almost beside the point. The degree to which Eastern European hopes focused on a Chinese alternative to Soviet hegemony was important whether or not those were false hopes.

By 1960 the Sino-Soviet dispute, as yet a nonissue to Western analysts of communist affairs, was a fact of life in interparty relations. This conflict involved Eastern Europe in more than one dimension.

First, Eastern European forums served as a staging ground from which the cards of what was initially a cautious, esoteric game were gingerly played. At the February 1960 meeting of the Warsaw Pact's PCC, the Chinese observer's speech provided a militant contrast to the moderate tone of the official declaration. In late June, at the Romanian Party Congress, hostilities broke into open, bitter debate between Krushchev and the head of the Chinese delegation, P'eng Chen. The Soviet leader not only attacked the Chinese but reportedly issued a long letter to other parties, detailing Peking's ideological shortcomings and restating Moscow's positions.[14] Compared with later pronouncements, the Chinese reply was a model of moderation.[15] Nonetheless, it showed little willingness to recant or even to retreat. The meeting ended with differences unresolved and Eastern European party leaders increasingly aware of the dispute in which they were, willing or unwilling, about to become deeply involved.

Second, both Moscow and Peking had reasons for wanting to keep awareness of their differences within communist circles. Therefore, following the first phase of esoterically communicated disagreement came a period of surrogate struggle during which the Soviets attacked Albania, meaning China, and the Chinese retaliated with polemics against the Yugoslavs, meaning the Soviets. This shadowboxing continued until the Twenty-Second Congress of the Communist Party of the Soviet Union in 1961, when Kruschev's angry outburst against Tirana brought open objection from Chou En-lai on the procedural issue that disputes between fraternal parties should not be handled "by public, one-sided censure; that showing one's differences . . . in face of the enemy cannot be regarded as a serious Marxist-Leninist attitude."[16] The head of the Chinese delegation proceeded to make the magnitude of Sino-Soviet "differences" symbolically clear by putting a wreath with an inscription to Stalin as "the Great Marxist-Leninist" on the dead dictator's tomb and walking out of the congress. Thus, by 1961 Albania had split with Moscow and politically had become an island of Chinese influence in the Balkans. This in turn moved the Soviets almost automatically closer to that past renegade but traditional Albanian bete noire, Tito's Yugoslavia, thereby completing the cycle in part begun by a Soviet softening on the issue of whether revision (Yugoslavia) or dogmatism (China and Albania) was the "main danger" to the international communist movement. Eastern Europe had moved from being a platform where Sino-Soviet clashes took place to providing Balkan surrogates as the dispute escalated. Soon these nations assumed a third role—that of participant-observers whose support was sought by both Moscow and Peking.

Romanian cleverness in maximizing the opportunities provided by the dispute is well known. Moreover, Bucharest's natural sympathy for Chinese opposition to the scope and method of de-Stalinization was reinforced by the dynamics of events. As Soviet control in Eastern Europe suffered the shocks of Poland and Hungary in 1956, the falling away of Albania, and potential further ideological undermining from China, Moscow attempted to compensate by strengthening joint institutions as organizational instruments of Soviet influence. Concretely, this meant emphasis on integration and "socialist division of labor" within CEMA. Nothing could have been more directly threatening to Romania's hard-won achievements in socialist industrialization.[17] For, despite major successes in establishing some industrial infrastructure, Romania remained predominantly agricultural; it had a natural base both for food and for valuable raw materials in any economically rational division of labor starting at the present level of development.

Not surprisingly, Khrushchev's interpretation of the direction to be taken by the world socialist system at the present stage (one in which he considered "conditions" had "ripened for raising economic and political cooperation to a new and higher level") was not echoed by Romanian party leader Gheorghe Gheorghiu-Dej or even a minor Romanian functionary. Khrushchev had committed the political blunder of being unambiguous about an unpalatable end goal. He was blunt:

The task is to do everything to consolidate the national economy of each [county], broaden its relations and gradually advance towards that single worldwide organism embracing the system as a whole that Lenin's genius foresaw.

With the emergence of socialism beyond the boundaries of a single country, its economic laws found much greater room for action and their operation became more and more complex.

For example, the law of planned proportional development operating on the scale of the system as a whole calls for planning and definite proportions both in each of the socialist countries taken separately and on the scale of the entire commonwealth.[18]

It would have taken much less sophisticated politicians than the Romanian leadership not to see the implications for their country's future economic development. Despite evident Eastern European hesitation, the Soviet leader pushed ahead, demanding "bolder steps toward the establishment of a single planning body for all countries."[19]

Scant progress was made at the seventeenth CEMA session in December 1962; and by the summer of 1963 the Romanians had visibly moved out of line, one step closer to the Chinese.[20] As the Sino-Soviet dispute intensified, the important of Romanian resistance to economic integration apparently faded in the Soviet perspective. Moscow wanted support for an international communist conference to expel or at least condemn Peking. Bucharest first stalled, then maneuvered itself into the position of go-between.

Predictably, bilateral Sino-Romanian meetings did not resolve matters to Soviet satisfaction or, perhaps, to Bucharest's. At that moment Moscow seems to have been more willing than Peking to suspend polemics. Nonetheless the Romanian endeavors delayed for two months the publication of Soviet ideologist M. A. Suslov's "February Report," a violent attack on the Chinese that explicitly renewed Soviet pressure for an international communist conference. When the attempted mediation collapsed under the combined weight of the fury of the Chinese "Comment on the Soviet Open Letter," published March 31, and Suslov's call for collective action against Peking, the Romanians documented their own reflections on the process. This remarkable statement amounted to a public declaration of neutrality that made clear Bucharest's objections to international communist conferences called to refereee interparty differences. It did not hesitate to draw pointed historical analogies on the danger of misusing communist organizations taken from both the time of the Comintern's "wrong methods, interference in the domestic affairs of Communist parties [that] went as far as the removal and replacing of leading party cadres ..." and the Cominform's pressure tactics against Yugoslavia.[21]

There was no public Soviet response. A brief period of cool relations thawed with the Romanian visit to Moscow in May; then, after the fall of Khrushchev in October 1964, Brezhnev and Aleksei Kosygin evidently wished to mend fences by treating Soviet-Romanian tensions as a personality conflict with their "hare-brained" predecessor. As we now know, such efforts met with limited success. By this time Bucharest had a vested interest in "correct" socialist relations with all disputants. Moscow continued to press for condemnation of the Chinese, while Peking continued to encourage Romanian neutrality in hopes of "tilting" a second Balkan country into the Chinese camp.

Indeed, there is some evidence that in the early 1960s, Chinese aspirations for winning away the more Stalinist of Moscow's Eastern European allies extended beyond the Balkans to East Germany. German leader Ulbricht did not become a disciple of Maoism, yet given the circumstances of his fall in May 1971, it is not completely farfetched to speculate that ideologically the East Germans were tempted, or at a minimum sympathetic, toward the Chinese.[22] In any case, politically and economically the flirtation was too expensive to continue at a time when the only real sphere of East German influence was the extent to which the German Democratic Republic controlled—indirectly, if not directly—the policy of at least the other Eastern European members of the Warsaw Pact toward the "other Germany," the German Federal Republic. Therefore, as the lines were drawn, Ulbricht stepped in behind the Soviets, along with Poland, Hungary, Czechoslovakia, and Bulgaria. Reportedly Chinese attempts to retain at least a foot in the door via offers of trade benefits were curtly refused.[23]

Peking's efforts to penetrate Eastern Europe were not limited to trade, aid, and more traditional political maneuvering. In 1965 a "Communist Party of Poland" in opposition to the "Gomulka clique's betrayal of Marxism-Leninism" appears to have been formed by Kazimierz Mijal, a former minister and a Central Committee member of the Polish United Workers party who fled to Albania, where he continued to broadcast his call for the Poles to overthrow Gomulka in support of a "pure Marxist-Leninist regime".[24] Mijal also visited Peking. This dabbling with extremist factions came to little, but it did exist as one end of a spectrum of techniques by which the Chinese tried to compete with—or, at a minimum, loosen—Soviet control over Eastern Europe.

CHINA AND CZECHOSLOVAKIA, AND THE CONSEQUENCES OF 1968

From the Chinese point of view, the events of 1968 left their Eastern European policy in a shambles. Before the "allied socialist" invasion of Czechoslovakia, Peking's Eastern European priorities had a kind of ideological-political symmetry. Albania came first in terms of resources and support, for, in intra-communist parlance, Tirana functioned as a Chinese "running dog" in Eastern Europe, a role that was not a disadvantage in the eyes of the Albanian leadership. As Albanian party leader Enver Hoxha was fond of pointing out, two million Albanians plus eight hundred million Chinese added up to considerably more political clout than that Balkan David would have been able to muster in the face of the Soviet Goliath on its own. Romania was an ally of sorts (at least to the extent of neutrality in intraparty conflict), certainly worth economic and moral support whenever Soviet pressure threatened to shake Ceausescu's ability to maneuver independently. Yugoslav revistionists were as bad as or worse than the Soviets, their only saving grace being that size and lack of resources limited Belgrade's ability to corrupt. Brezhnev and Company had followed in the unspeakable, anti-Marxist-Leninist path of Khrushchev, a fact demonstrated as much by the growth of Czech reformer and party leader Alexander Dubcek's dangerous deviations as by anything else.

Logically one might assume that Peking's approach to Czechoslovakia in 1968 would follow the lines of Chinese advice during the Hungarian crisis of 1956. No single convert could be allowed to slip from the path of socialism. From this perspective the use of Soviet troops to prevent undermining of Czechoslovakia by counterrevolutionary forces from within would have been seen as a regrettable necessity or even a first sign that Brezhnev was beginning to face up to Soviet responsibility for maintaining minimum ideological standards among communist states of East Central Europe.

In life, logic and politics seldom mix. Or, to be more precise, the logic of politics is intrinsically illogical in any classical meaning of the word. All of the above notwithstanding, the invasion of Czechoslovakia in August 1968 sharply worsened Sino-Soviet hostilities. Chinese verbal violence against the Soviets escalated to new heights. According to Peking's analysis:

This act of naked armed intervention has brought to the full the grisly fascist features of the Soviet revisionist renegade clique, fully revealed its extreme weakness, and proclaimed the total bankruptcy of Soviet modern revisionism. . . .

The Soviet revisionist renegade clique also claims that its action was taken for the "unbreakable solidarity" of the "fraternal countries" and in "the interests of the security of the states of the socialist community." In that miserable mishmash of your revisionist bloc, where is your "unbreakable solidarity"? It is clearly a case of each trying to cheat each other and each going his own way. You do not really want to build any "socialist community". What you really want is to found a colonial empire with the Soviet revisionist clique as the overlord, and to redivide the world in collaboration with U.S. imperialism. . . .[25]

Politically, the invasion of Czechoslovakia brought China back into Eastern Europe with sudden, if temporary, force. Except for dabbling in the Balkans, Chinese-Eastern European contacts had become almost nonexistent.

After the rebuffs of the early 1960s and before the intervention, Peking appeared to accept this deterioration as inevitable. Blatant interference in Czechoslovak domestic affairs, however, reactivated Chinese political initiatives toward the region. The intervention offered new possibilities for playing on Eastern European hopes and fears, and simultaneously was a threat direct to the Chinese leadership's sense of physical security.

First, Peking may have thought that the Soviet act was so repressive as to give even those Eastern European countries that took part second thoughts about the utility of shoring up a Chinese alternative to Soviet dominance. Hungarian party leader Janos Kadar, for example, had shown less than his share of enthusiasm for the joint venture.[26] Moreover, the Romanians flatly condemned the invasion as a violation of socialist norms.[27] The Albanians took the occasion to denounce the Warsaw Pact as a treaty of slavery and, somewhat tardily, formally withdrew from that organization.[28]

Second, China had even more direct reasons for concern. Soviet invasion of China was unlikely, but at that time it certainly was not unthinkable. If Moscow was willing to ignore not only world public opinion, but the strong feelings within the international communist movement as well, in order to reestablish a more acceptable brand of socialism in Czechoslovakia, Soviet leadership might begin to reassess military means for getting rid of the openly anti-Soviet regime in Peking. Militarily, the intervention had operated like clockwork, effectively demonstrating the well-oiled Soviet military machine. China was not Czechoslovakia, but the ex post facto justification of Moscow's use of force against the Dubcek government was not country-specific.

Generally referred to as a doctrine of "limited sovereignty" in the East, the Brezhnev Doctrine, as it became known to Western analysts, justified the entry of Soviet troops into Czechoslovakia on the ground that within the socialist commonwealth, "sovereignty" must be viewed as a class rather than a national attribute: that is, Moscow reserved to itself the right to use military means whenever developments within any socialist country might damage either its own socialism or the basic interests of other socialist countries.[29] If this reasoning applied to the "Prague Spring," it could easily be extended, in the Soviet view, to Chinese-style Marxism-Leninism. Moscow's line of argument could easily be that not only was socialism in China (not to mention Albania) at stake, but also that corrupting Chinese influence endangered the ideological purity of other communist states and parties.

Peking did not wait to see what the Kremlin's next move would be. Within a few days after Soviet troops occupied Czechoslovakia, Chinese radio broadcasts in Czech, Slovak, Romanian, and Polish relayed the Chinese interpretation of these events to Eastern European audiences via transmitters in Albania.

Perhaps the most important break with past policy was the sudden move toward "normalization" of China's relations with Yugoslavia. Propaganda attacks against Tito's revisionism virtually ceased; and even Albania's polemics against its arch enemy took on a remarkably gentle tone, considering that as recently as July 1968, the Albanian press had been blasting Yugoslavia as a "mirror of degeneration and failure. . . ."[30] By October, as the coincidence of Belgrade-Peking interest in united struggle against the Brezhnev Doctrine[31] become more evident, Yugoslav officials in Prague were invited to the nineteenth anniversary of the founding of the People's Republic of China. This symbolic feeler soon expanded into concrete negotiations on trade and credit between the two countries, a move accompanied by a Chinese suggestion that cultural exchanges be resumed.

Cautious Yugoslav responses paralleled deteriorating Soviet-Yugoslav relations. As the 1969 Moscow Conference of the World Communist Parties drew near, Chinese desire for Yugoslav support intensified. Yugoslav concern not to repeat its unpleasant experiences with the international communist conferences of 1957 and 1960, reinforced by Tito's own worries as to Moscow's military intentions, made China a palatable, if not ideal, ally. Criticism of Peking and Tirana disappeared from Yugoslav media, replaced by Chinese and Albanian polemics against the Soviet Union. Moscow grumbled about this collusion[32] to little avail, for it was an almost inevitable spin-off of Soviet policies toward China and Eastern Europe.

Once Moscow gave up its admittedly unequal battle of competing for the hearts and minds of Czechs and Slovaks against Dubcek's "socialism with a human face" and decided to use troops to force the Czechoslovak Community Party back in line, what we may loosely consider Soviet hard-liners at least temporarily had the upper hand. The military success, despite its accompanying political fiasco, strengthened the arguments of those favoring force over persuasion, of those more prone to think in terms of military solutions. Since the damage both to East-West relations and the fabric of international communist considerations had already been done, those arguing for "toughing it out" had no visible opposition. After all, it was humiliating enough to have been maneuvered into returning Dubcek and the other kidnapped Czechoslovak leaders to Prague. Thus Moscow resorted (as have other major powers throughout history) to randomly brandishing "a big stick." This tactic was most apparent (and dangerous) on the Sino-Soviet border.

SABER-RATTLING ON THE BORDER: SINO-SOVIET "WAR PSYCHOSIS" OF 1969-70

Like Janus, the Soviet Union faces in two directions, and its borders have historically proved scant protection from attack. Thus Soviet leaders form their policy against the nightmare possibility of a two-front war. Such worries intensified in 1969 with NATO statements that the intervention in Czechoslovakia had changed the European balance of power and with China's violent response to the nature of the "Czechoslovak solution." The border between the Soviet Union and China is one of the longest in the world, amounting to a 4,000 mile headache in Moscow.

As post-intervention tensions mounted in 1969, the two countries moved rapidly from verbal militancy to armed clashes along that border, which were most publicized at the time of the Damansky-Chen Pao Island battle in the Ussuri River.[33] Official accounts have muddied the issue to such an extent that who fired the first shot is, and most likely will remain, an academic mystery. Neither Moscow nor Peking had the slightest interest in concealing the incident, in part because it provided both sides with considerable propaganda.

Certainly, both the Chinese and the Soviets had reasons that might have touched off the actual conflict. The "Brezhnev Doctrine" had escalated China's fears of an actual Soviet strike against Chinese nuclear capabilities. In such circumstances, a limited demonstration of Peking's will to resist any military pressures might well have been considered essential. It also served to solidify Chinese national sentiment against an increasingly real external enemy. Conversely, Moscow may have decided that prior to the June Moscow conference, proof of Chinese aggressive, militaristic, and expansionistic ambitions would aid in rallying reluctant supporters to the Soviet position. Just as likely is the often forgotten possibility that a frightened soldier on the border shot first, thought later, and either was never found or was ignored because both sides decided to utilize the event to political advantage.

Questions of who was to blame in such cases are much less important than political consequences. Hence it is interesting that although the conflict was an exercise in military self-restraint, the attending propaganda tirades skyrocketed.[34] Public demonstrations in both Peking and Moscow gave the impression that the citizens of both countries were being prepared for war. In August clashes again erupted in Singkiang, this time accompanied by only slightly veiled insinuations that Soviet preventive action against Chinese atomic installations was among Moscow's contingency plans.[35] Even if such threats were designed primarily to force Peking into unwelcome border talks, they led to a spiral of speculation that the once unimaginable war between Russia and China had become a frightening possibility.

In any event Eastern Europe did not have the luxury of being uninvolved. As early as 1967, and certainly by the time of open border fighting in 1969, there were indications that the Soviets were trying to expand Eastern European obligations under the Warsaw Treaty Organization (WTO) to the Soviet Union's Asian border. As improvement in Soviet-German relations paralleled escalating Sino-Soviet violence in 1970, pressure increased for some kind of collective defense to the east. Despite the clear limitation of WTO responsibilities to Europe, by September there were rumors that air force units from Poland, Hungary, and Bulgaria had been transferred to Soviet Central Asia, within striking distance of China.[36] There is also reason to believe that Soviet desire for "fraternal solidarity" from the Eastern European members of WTO met with a general lack of enthusiasm and with a Romanian unwillingness to cooperate.

According to one report, Bucharest first blocked a Soviet-sponsored move to have China declared an aggressor in the Ussuri clash at the March 1969 meeting of the WTO.[37] It then rejected the suggestion of symbolic Eastern European military detachments on the Sino-Soviet border.[38] In light of the history of Romania's studied neutrality in the dispute, such a position was to be expected. Poland's apparent ambivalence was considerably more out of character. First, if the reports that Polish units did in fact make a token appearance on the Soviet-Chinese border are correct, clearly "some forces" at the highest levels in Warsaw felt it necessary to comply—with or without enthusiasm.[39] On the other hand, by 1970 either those involved were having second thoughts or a split had surfaced within the Polish leadership over that nation's responsibility for trying to deflect the wind from the east. Otherwise it is almost impossible to explain a curious small book quietly published under the auspices of the Polish Ministry of Defense, a major purpose of which seems to have been reiterating the fact that military obligations under the Warsaw Pact did not extend beyond Europe.[40] However, its interpretation of alliance responsibilities was cautiously couched in assurances that bilaterally Eastern European countries must continue to think in terms of one for all and all for one, no matter at what border aggression took place.

Sino-Soviet border talks became a classic example of one step forward, two steps back. By winter they had broken down completely. Moscow increasingly complained of Peking's "war psychosis" and saber-rattling.[41] Seen in the context of stepped-up references to the common socialist duty of mutual defense in case of aggression,[42] these accusations could not have been reassuring either to the Chinese or to the Eastern Europeans attempting to retain some vestige of neutrality.

China responded with a monumental attack that bluntly put the Brezhnev theory of limited sovereignty into the category of "imperialist ravings:"

> ... the "theoretical basis" for military intervention in or military occupation of a number of East European countries and the Mongolian People's Republic. The "international dictatorship" you refer to simply means the subjection of other countries to the new Tsar's rule and enslavement.[43]

This in turn led not only to Soviet polemics that reached new heights in personal vilification of Mao, who was blamed for complicity in the death of his eldest son (reportedly for the young man's rejection of his father's "pseudoscientific junk,") but also to an ominous institutionalization of the Brezhnev Doctrine in the Soviet-Czechoslovak Treaty of May 1970.[44] Only the external motivation provided by American invasion of Cambodia broke the deadlock, bringing the

Soviet first deputy minister of foreign affairs back to Peking to resume the border negotiations.

Romanian policy most visibly felt the pinch. There was no doubt that Bucharest was under considerable pressure to model its own long-delayed, still unsigned treaty of mutual assistance to fit the Soviet-Czechoslovak example. Throughout May the deteriorating Sino-Soviet relations and stepped-up Soviet concern for integration within CEMA and WTO was back in gear. Moreover, Bucharest's bargaining position sharply worsened with bad luck in the form of natural disaster, the catastrophic floods for which the Romanians reportedly received four times more relief from Washington than from Moscow.[45]

Close contact with China continued. In June the former Romanian defense minister, Emil Bodnaras, made a friendship visit to Peking, during whcih he held cordial conversations with Mao, toasted "everlasting" Romanian-Chinese friendship, and reminded all interested parties of Romanian adherence to principles of "sovereignty, independence, equality, and noninterference in internal affairs . . . of [the right] of every country to determine their own development free from any foreign interference".[46]

It was a reminder designed to echo in Moscow. Bodnaras also thanked his hosts for China's generous flood relief, which, according to Western estimates amounted to $25 million. Then, in line with the traditional Romanian art of balancing, the Soviet-Romanian Friendship Treaty was renewed after a two-year delay. Rather than reflecting the Soviet-Czechoslovak agreement signed in May, it was modeled much along the lines of Moscow's 1967 friendship treaties with Hungary and Bulgaria. This agreement was as important for what it did not say as for what it did. For example, there was no reference to collective obligations of socialist countries to come to the defense of socialist achievements. On the question of foreign policy coordination, both parties agreed to "consult." They did not go on to say, as they had in earlier treaties, that they would act on the basis of that consultation so as to reach accord or, as the Czechoslovaks had conceded in May, "to proceed from their common standpoint." The treaty, however, did extend beyond Europe, specifying that in case the Soviet Union were subject to attack "by any state or group of states," Romania was bound to enter the fray.[47]

This implied a commitment against China that, in Moscow's interpretation, must have been seen as a victory over willful Romanian neutrality in the face of strong Soviet vested interest. Bucharest stressed a broader interpretation of its obligations, with continual references to Romanian military coooperation with all socialist countries. After signing the treaty, Romanian Defense Minister Ion Ionita again went on an Asian tour. Reaching Peking via North Korea, he reiterated Romania's faithfulness to WTO in case of "aggression in Europe."[48]

In short, the Romanians had come to China to assure the Chinese that treaty or no treaty, Bucharest would reserve the right to decide who had attacked whom in any future Sino-Soviet confrontation. In response, the

Chinese pledged that their Romanian comrades could be assured that "we are always your reliable friends when you struggle against foreign aggression, control, and intervention."[49] Such a promise might have little military utility, in view of the logistics involved. As a joint Chinese-Romanian symbolic rejection of the Brezhnev Doctrine, it did have political value. Furthermore, by 1970 Chinese political, moral, and military support for Romania had acquired an important economic component.

THE ECONOMICS OF CHINESE-EASTERN EUROPEAN RELATIONS

Foreign trade, like war, is a form of politics. Although in 1970 Chinese trade with the Soviet Union had dwindled to $47 million, the general pattern vis-a-vis East Central Europe had been one of steady increase. In fact, Chinese trade with that area doubled between 1965 and 1970, a strong indication that Peking's political interests had been reactivated. The following trade statistics are more than an academic curiosity.

Given the political situation, the small amount of Chinese-Soviet trade and the fact that Peking was virtually supporting Albania should not surprise anyone. The increase in Chinese-Romanian aid was substantial, particularly since it had dropped by $3 million between 1968 and 1969. The unanticipated jump, only later recognized as politically significant, came in Chinese-East German trade, which grew by $15 million, compared with a $2 million drop the year before. There was also a less radical increase with Poland, while Czechoslovak-Chinese trade declined.

TABLE 5.1

Chinese Foreign Trade with Selected Socialist Countries, 1969-70 (million U.S. dollars)

	1969	1970
Soviet Union	55	45
Albania	115	115
Romania	81	108
East Germany	63	78
Poland	41	50
Czechoslovakia	59	56

Source: A. H. Usack and R. E. Batsavage, "The International Trade of the People's Republic of China," in The People's Republic of China: An Economic Assessment, a compendium of papers submitted to the Joint Economic Committee, Congress of the United States (Washington, D.C.: U.S. Government Printing Office, 1972), p. 351.

Against the background of Moscow's differences with East Germany over the pace and nature of "inner German relations," a crucial part of the detente package,[50] these figures add substance to the speculation that Ulbricht's failure to ritualistically attack the Chinese at the Twenty-Fourth Congress of the Communist Party of the Soviet Union, in March 1971, was an index of the East German leader's alienation from the demands that "jointly coordinated" foreign policy was putting on East German national interest as he understood it. Less than one month later, Ulbricht resigned and was replaced by Erich Honecker as first secretary of the East German Communist party. Most likely the Soviets were not uninvolved bystanders in the switch that reshuffled what had appeared to be the most stable of Eastern European leaderships.

Despite its deceptive appearance as the smoothest of transitions, Ulbricht's fall began another cycle of intense, submerged maneuvering in the Balkans. Moscow attempted to regain control. Peking competed for influence, and the Eastern Europeans sought to retain as much autonomy as possible.

In Yugoslavia, rumors that the Soviets were putting on pressure for a naval base at Split or Pula added to nervousness created by the claims of Croatian emigre leader Dr. Branko Jelic that Moscow was financing Croat separatists.[51] True or not, the claim maximized psychological tension on the Yugoslav government. Belgrade had little reason to believe the Soviets would hesitate to aid Croatian and/or Macedonian terrorists as a part of a systematic campaign to weaken the internal fiber of Yugoslavia and thus make it more difficult for that maverick socialist state to resist being pulled back into the fold after Tito either died or became too weak to rule.

In June, Yugoslav Foreign Minister Mirko Tepavac went to China.[52] His trip was more symbolic than substantive, for Belgrade had little common ground with Peking beyond fear of Soviet intervention. Anything beyond verbal support in case of actual confrontation would be extremely difficult to manage. As Chou En-lai subsequently made quite explicit, "distant waters cannot quench fire."[53] His caution did not signal disinterest. Chinese-Yugoslav trade climbed steadily from less than $2 million in 1969 to $7 million in 1970 and about $20 million in 1971. This was in addition to an agreement on the use of the Yugoslav port of Rijeka for transit of goods in Sino-Eastern European trade.

As for Romania, the Chinese-Romanian trade agreement for 1972-75, signed in February 1971, was the first of such a long term with an Eastern European country since the 1950s. Chinese loans to Romania, as of the fall of 1971, were being estimated at $200 or $300 million, no doubt a profitable result aided by Ceausescu's personal visit to China in June, virtually at the same time the Yugoslav delegation was touring.[54]

Also, despite Chou En-lai's warning against relying on Chinese assistance to turn the tide in the event of actual confrontation, the prolonged visit of a high-level military delegation of Albania and Romania in August-September 1971 was a firm sign that Peking retained active concern for the fate of its

Balkan allies and had no intention of withdrawing from those troubled waters. Soviet annoyance notwithstanding, China appeared not only to have retained but also to have expanded its role in East Central European political and economic affairs. If that process is to be slowed, the brake may be applied in Washington, not Moscow.

IMPACT OF AMERICAN-CHINESE RAPPROCHEMENT

With the establishment of correct relations between China and the United States in 1972, the great-power triangle was to become one of the most important facts of international political life. Sino-Soviet hostilities aside, China was on its way back to becoming an accepted member of the family of nations. The blood-feuding nature of that community is anything but ideal; yet, in my view, it is correct that potentially the level of violence declines with normalization of relations. When states have normal contact, trade, cultural exchanges, and channels for diffusing conflicts of interest, such normalization has not historically prevented war; it has perhaps made war less frequent. In any case, the touch of realism in American foreign policy shown by admitting the necessity for recognizing the existence of 800 million Chinese was encouraging.

Eastern Europe had its part in weaving one strand of the new relationship. For years the only city in the world where Peking and Washington were officially on speaking terms was Warsaw. Subsequently, Romania appears to have expanded—one might go so far as to say exchanged—its go-between activities in the Sino-Soviet context for a similar position on delicate questions as the United States and China moved gingerly closer to one another. This did not, of course, improve the climate of Soviet-Romanian affairs.

For the most part, however, the pattern of Chinese-Eastern European relations remained unchanged by Peking's new global position. Rather, the smaller Sino-Soviet-Eastern European triangle and inter-communist considerations continued to dominate, with the exception of Albania.

Tirana showed no initial sign of an inability to absorb the new situation. Yet for the Hoxha regime—still violently hostile to Moscow, isolated and ideologically fanatical—to see China fall from the path of revolutionary purity had unpleasant implications.[55] One must recall that the Soviet-Albanian break occurred largely because the Soviets moved toward what at that time had been enemy number one in Tirana—the renegade Yugoslavia. Now Albania was seeing China, its most important ally and supplier of the bulk of Albania's needs, move toward rapprochement with American "imperialists" who, in Albanian policy, had been portrayed as partners with Moscow, representing almost equally evil demon twins in the drama of international politics. Perhaps most important, the fabric of Albanian domestic political control was so closely interlaced with these foreign policy stereotypes that Hoxha genuinely could not afford to follow Peking's lead.

Therefore Albanian hostility continued unabated toward both Moscow and Washington. Tirana made it quite clear that with limited exceptions for Albanian-Americans, it wanted no part of normal relations with the United States, which remained high on Tirana's list of "international hooligans." This did not visibly change the special nature of Chinese-Albanian relations. China had a long-standing commitment much more important to its image in the communist world than an extra ounce of ego satisfaction that might come from instant Albanian imitation.

The problem is, rather, that over time both continued Albanian violence in polemicizing against the United States and Tirana's usefulness in an intra-communist context has begun to change subtly. As Peking has become less attractive to the most fanatic "Marxist-Leninist" splinter groups, these disciples of revolutionary purity have begun to turn to Albania. Congresses that might once have been held in Peking have taken place in Albania (for example, the Italian (M-L) Communist Party Congress at Parma, January 5-7, 1973). From the Chinese point of view, such activities are undoubtedly a minor but annoying challenge to the example that China is currently setting as a self-proclaimed guardian of international communist ideological purity. If the Chinese have not read events that way, indirect criticism of Peking's flirtation with the United States by means of Albanian attacks on other "revisionist" parties has made the point:

> The path to the complete destruction of modern revisionism is by way of contacts and talks with opposition revisions, under the pretext of waging common struggle against imperialism and Soviet Social-imperialism. . . . One cannot have contacts with some revisionists because they have differences with certain other revisionists.[56]

On the surface all remains friendly, yet that telltale indicator, foreign trade, has begun to waver for the first time since the early 1960s. Despite the strong Chinese participation in the celebration of the thirtieth anniversay of Albania's liberation in 1974, by the spring of 1975 there was still no agreement for funding Albania's next Five-Year Plan. The delay was most likely political, for a high-level Chinese economic delegation spent seven weeks in Albania, then returned to Peking in January without signing an agreement. The delegation had been received by Albanian Premier (recently also appointed to head the Ministry of Defense) Mehmet Shehu on arrival. No Albanian leader of equal importance saw them off, although on both occasions the group was dined and wined by the head of the Albanian State Planning Commission.[57] Evidently trying to resolve this delicate question, Tirana subsequently sent a high-level economic delegation, headed by Politburo member and First Deputy President of the State Planning Commission Adil Carcani, to China.[58] It is unlikely that Hoxha would send such a delegation without reasonable assurance that the desired economic agreement could be successfully negotiated.

Even if, as is likely, Peking continues to foot a large part of the bill for Tirana's sixth Five-Year Plan, some changes are certain, at least partly because it seems less and less possible that China's rapprochement with the United States is a passing fancy. Nor will that "normalization" of Chinese-American relations become easily acceptable to the current Albanian regime. Whether the long-range impact will be on the Albanian-Chinese level of political-economic intimacy or on the Albanian leadership itself is unclear. For all concerned at this stage, any Albanian-Chinese differences are best kept low-key. The history of such intra-communist disputes, however, reveals a tendency to escalate.

CONCLUSIONS

In retrospect, the Chinese objectives in Eastern Europe, referred to by Vernon Aspaturian in Chapter 2 of this volume, have met with limited success. Peking certainly has not deprived Moscow of either Eastern European human and natural resources or of ideological support. If Chinese-Albanian friendship indeed represented a "fantasy model" of future Chinese-Eastern European relations, that fantasy is becoming less and less an ideal reality, thereby decreasing the likelihood that either Peking or other Eastern European countries would be interested in moving toward a similar intimacy.

Nonetheless Chinese trade has become more important to Eastern European economies, and the region has become more difficult to mobilize for the Soviet Union's anti-Chinese organizational maneuvers.[59] On balance, it will be the inertia of past commitments and the dynamics of Sino-Soviet conflict that will continue to determine China's role in East Central Europe in the near future. In the long run, to paraphrase Winston Churchill, Mao will be dead. What that will mean for Chinese policy, domestic as well as foreign, is impossible to measure. Nor is it useful to try to second-guess how Tito's death will shape Chinese-Yugoslav relations. One thing is clear: for those Eastern European nations increasingly tied to Soviet energy resources (the price of which is going up) and unable to pay world prices, China does not provide a real economic or political alternative.

NOTES

1. George Modelski, *The Communist International System* (Princeton: Center for International Studies, 1960), p. 45.

2. Alfred G. Meyer, "The Comparative Study of Communist Political Systems," in Frederic J. Fleron, Jr., ed., *Communist Studies and the Social Sciences* (Chicago: Rand McNally, 1969), p. 194.

3. "The Origin and Development of the Differences Between the Leadership of the CPSU and Ourselves—Comment on the Open Letter of the Central Committee of the CPSU (1)," *People's Daily* and *Red Flag,* September 6, 1963, which is document 10 in William E. Griffith, ed., *The Sino-Soviet Rift* (Cambridge, Mass.: M.I.T. Press, 1964), p. 395.

4. *Pravda,* November 4 and 5, 1956.

5. Zbigniew K. Brzezinski, *The Soviet Bloc,* rev. ed. (Cambridge, Mass.: Harvard University Press, 1971), p. 271.

6. "The Origin and Development . . .," in Griffith, ed., op. cit., p. 393.

7. *Scinteia,* February 14, August 1, and August 23, 1954; analysis in Stephen Fischer-Galati, *The New Rumania; from People's Democracy to Socialist Republic* (Cambridge, Mass.: M.I.T. Press, 1967), p. 50.

8. *Survey of China Mainland Press* (SCMP) 1748 (April 10, 1958): 38.

9. Ibid., 1750 (April 14, 1958): 44. For analysis see Fischer-Galati, op. cit., pp. 70-71.

10. For a more detailed discussion, see Robin Alison Remington, *The Warsaw Pact: Case Studies in Communist Conflict Resolution* (Cambridge, Mass.: M.I.T. Press, 1971), Ch. 5, pp. 56 ff.

11. *Pravda,* May 27, 1958.

12. Hemen Ray, "China's Initiatives in Eastern Europe," *Current Scene; Developments in Mainland China* 7, no. 23 (December 1, 1959): 2.

13. *Zycie Warszawy,* April 23, 1957; quoted by Brzezinski, op. cit., p. 297.

14. See William E. Griffith, *Albania and the Sino-Soviet Rift* (Cambridge, Mass.: M.I.T. Press, 1963), pp. 41-45.

15. *Peking Review* 3, no. 26 (June 28, 1960): 4-6.

16. Ibid., 4, no. 43 (October 27, 1961): 9.

17. For detailed analysis see John Michael Montias, *Economic Development of Communist Rumania* (Cambridge, Mass.: M.I.T. Press, 1967); Michael Kaser, *COMECON: Integration Problems of the Planned Economies* (London: Oxford University Press, 1965); J. F. Brown, "Rumania out of Line," *Survey* 49 (October 1963); as well as the third article in Philippe Ben's series "La Roumanie entre Moscou et Pekin," entitled "Comecon, homme malade de l'Europe de l'Est," *Le Monde,* December 3, 1963.

18. "Vital Questions of Development of the World Socialist System," *Kommunist* 12 (August 1962), as translated in *World Marxist Review* 5, no. 9 September 1962).

19. *Pravda,* November 20, 1962.

20. For example, a three-column summary of the Chinese "Proposal Concerning the General Line of the International Communist Movement" appeared in the Romanian press, but not in the Soviet and other Eastern European media. *Times* (London), June 24, 1963.

21. "Statement on the Stand of the Rumanian Workers' Party Concerning the Problems of the International Communist Movement," complete English text in William E. Griffith, *Sino-Soviet Relations 1964-1965* (Cambridge, Mass.: M.I.T. Press, 1967), pp. 269-96.

22. See Hemen Ray, "Peking and Pankow—China's Engagement in Osteuropa und das Verhaltnis zur DDR," *Europa Archiv* no. 16 (1963): 621-28.

23. Ray, "China's Initiatives in Eastern Europe," p. 11.

24. *Zeri i popullit,* December 5, 1968. According to a Polish source in London, Mijal had been conducting Polish-language broadcasts from Albania. *Dziennik Polski,* September 8, 1966.

25. "Total Bankruptcy of Soviet Modern Revisionism," *Peking Review* 11, no. 34 (August 23, 1968). For an early interpretation see "Asia and the Crisis in Czechoslovakia,"

Asian Analyst (September 1968): 10-12; and M. Kamil Dziewanowski, "China and East Europe," *Survey* 77 (Autumn 1970): 59-74.

26. For analysis of his last-minute attempts at reconciliation, see Richard Lowenthal, "The Sparrow in the Cage," *Problems of Communism* 17, no. 6 (November-December 1968): 20-22.

27. Official Romanian communique on the military occupation of Czechoslovakia, *Scinteia,* August 22, 1968.

28. *Zeri i popullit,* August 23, 1968. For a detailed study of the legal implications of this act, see John N. Washburn, "The Current Legal Status of Warsaw Pact Membership," *International Lawyer* 5, no. 1 (January 1971): 129-34.

29. First put forward by S. Kovalev in "Sovereignty and the Internationalist Obligations of Socialist Countries," *Pravda,* September 26, 1968.

30. *Zeri i popullit,* July 6, 1968. For an analysis of the post-invasion change of line in Tirana, see Peter R. Prifti, "Albania," in Adam Bromke and Teresa Rakowska-Harmstone, eds., *The Communist States in Disarray,* 1965-1971 (Minneapolis: University of Minnesota Press, 1972), pp. 215-18.

31. Michael M. Milenkovitch, "Soviet-Yugoslav Relations and the Brezhnev Doctrine," *Studies for a New Central Europe* 5 (1968-1969): 112-21.

32. See *Izvestia,* March 30, 1969, for complaints that these reprints in the Yugoslav press were intended to create distrust of Soviet foreign policy.

33. For a detailed account of this skirmish, see C. Hinton, "Conflict on the Ussuri; Clash of Nationalisms," *Problems of Communism* 20 (January-April 1971): 45-68.

34. John W. Strong, "The Sino-Soviet Dispute," in Bromke and Rakowska-Harmstone, ed., op. cit., pp. 37 ff.

35. *Izvestia,* September 11, 1969, and *Krasnaya zvezda,* January 21, 1970; for Western analysis, see Washington *Post,* September 11 and 17, 1969, and January 9, 1970.

36. Don Cook reporting from Berlin, New York *Post,* September 13, 1969.

37. Whether or not Anatole Shub's analysis is correct in detail with respect to the March PCC meeting—Washington *Post,* March 18 and 19, 1969— the fact remains that none of the documents published by its participants so much as mentioned China. *Pravda,* March 18, 1969.

38. See Thomas W. Wolfe, *Soviet Power and Europe, 1945-1960* (Baltimore: Johns Hopkins Press, 1970), pp. 497-98.

39. During his April visit to the Soviet Union, Polish Defense Minister Wojciech Jaruzelski strongly attacked the Chinese and seems to have said that each socialist state should "make its contribution" in defending against danger from the East. *Zolnierz wolnosci,* April 23, 1969. Quoted by Wolfe, op. cit., p. 498.

40. Marian Jurek and Edward Skrzpokowski, *Ulad Warszawski* (Warsaw: Ministerstwa Obrony Narodowej, 1970).

41. For the charge that China was building a military road to the Soviet border, see *Krasnaya Zvezda,* March 31, 1970.

42. Col. S. Lukonin in *Pravda,* March 7, 1970. Also see I. Alexandrov, a pseudonym for one of the most active polemicists against the Dubcek regime in 1968, *Pravda,* March 19, 1970.

43. "Leninism or Social Imperialism?" *Peking Review* 13, no. 17 (April 24, 1970): 10.

44. *Pravda,* May 7, 1970; *Current Digest of the Soviet Press* 22, no. 18 (June 2, 1970): 5-6.

45. Romanian ambassador to the United States, quoted by New York *Times,* June 13, 1970, p. 3.

46 *Peking Review* 13, no. 25 (June 19, 1970): 10.

47. *Pravda,* July 8, 1970. English text in Remington, op. cit., pp. 242-45.

48. New China News Agency broadcast in English, July 31, 1970.

49. New China News Agency domestic broadcast in Chinese, July 20, 1970. See also *Peking Review* 13, no. 31 (July 31, 1970): 20.

50. Remington, op. cit., pp. 134 ff.

51. *Hrvatska drzava*, February/March 1971; reported by *Times* (London), April 19, 1971.

52. *Borba*, June 5, 1971. He was in China June 9-15, 1971.

53. Interview given Yugoslav correspondent of *Vjesnik*, August 28, 1971.

54. *Peking Review* 14, no. 23 (June 4, 1971): 4. For joint Sino-Romanian communique, ibid., no. 24 (June 11, 1971): 8.

55. For the best and most detailed analysis of these events, see Peter R. Prifti, "Sino-Soviet Relations and the 'Problem' Parties: Albania and the Sino-Soviet Conflict," *Studies in Comparative Communism* 6, no. 3 (Autumn 1973): 241-67.

56. *Zeri i popullit*, February 13, 1972. Quoted from Prifti, op. cit., p. 157.

57. *Zeri i popullit*, December 7, 1974, and January 25, 1975.

58. Ibid., June 12, 1975.

59. Radio Free Europe, "Survey of East European Developments, April-June 1974," July 17, 1974 (mimeo).

6

YUGOSLAVIA, ALBANIA, AND EASTERN EUROPE
Trond Gilberg

INTRODUCTION: A HISTORICAL OVERVIEW

It has become somewhat of a commonplace that the "Soviet bloc" no longer really exists, and that the socialist countries of Eastern Europe are becoming semiautonomous states within the new and complex relationships of the "Socialist Commonwealth" and the international communist movement. In this context, Yugoslavia and Albania represent the most clear-cut deviations from the Soviet model for interstate relations among socialist countries. Within this model, Yugoslavia in many ways represents a "right-wing deviation," and Albania is the prime example of "left-wing deviation," as defined in the Kremlin. Both countries have had considerable influence on the more orthodox countries in the area; and at the present time, with the continuing erosion of Soviet hegemony in Eastern Europe, this influence is becoming even more pervasive.

Yugoslavia has exercised a powerful influence on the countries of Eastern Europe since the establishment of communist regimes after World War II. In his early drives for socialization of the economy and a full-scale social revolution, Tito became the most orthodox leader outside the Soviet Union; and Belgrade considered the Yugoslav road a possible path for the other fledgling communist regimes in the area, especially since Tito was faithfully following in Stalin's footsteps toward socialism and communism. After the break between Moscow and Belgrade in 1948, Yugoslav influence in Eastern Europe was seemingly eradicated; all the satellite regimes were mobilized for a ferocious witch-hunt against domestic Titoists and foreign agents, and a political and economic boycott against Yugoslavia was instituted and carried out with great vigor. Tito, in his quest for national and personal survival, turned increasingly to the West for military and economic assistance, and in the domestic political and economic fields he effected major changes that ultimately established Yugoslavia as a unique political and socioeconomic system.[1]

The reorganization of the Yugoslav economy, the establishment of workers' councils with a considerable amount of decision-making power and local autonomy, and the reorganization of the Communist party as a decentralized "league of communists" had profound effects on the cultural scene as well. Yugoslavia became a relatively liberal country in which considerable criticism of political elites was tolerated. Questions of Marxist-Leninist theory were extensively debated in the press and in the universities, and new avenues of political thought were explored. All in all, Yugoslavia represented a sharp and intriguing comtrast with the politically and economically centralized communist systems in the rest of the area.[2]

With the end of the Stalin era and the move toward de-Stalinization in the Soviet Union, the influence of Yugoslavia increased sharply in all of the satellites. Many of the ideas advocated and implemented by Tito were now discussed openly in Moscow, including a possible rearrangement of the investment structure in the economy to emphasize the long-neglected field of consumer goods production, and the possibility of peaceful coexistence with capitalism. But the most important effect was the existence of Yugoslavia as a possible alternative to the terror and the political mobilization of the Stalinist era. The populations of Eastern Europe, tired after the political and economic deprivations of the past five or six years, yearned for a life that would be a little freer, a little more comfortable materially and spiritually. Without Stalin's watchful supervision, more and more elite figures joined the masses of Eastern Europeans in looking to Belgrade as an alternative.[3]

The emergence of Yugoslavia as a potential alternative to the Stalinist model was vastly enhanced by the discredited Stalinists, the men who had risen to the top of the political pyramid through anti-Titoist purges. They had terrorized their populations and had minimal popular suppert, their source of power being Stalin. In the post-Stalin era, they were Stalinists without their source of inspiration. Their opponents, accused and imprisoned as "nationalists," "domesticists," and "Titoists," utilized the opportunity produced by the power vacuum in the Kremlin to settle some old scores; and Tito grasped the opportunity to hint broadly that there were all sorts of "national roads" to socialism and communism, of which the Yugoslav example might be particularly worthwhile.[4]

The power vacuum engendered by Stalin's death and the stirrings of anti-Stalinist feelings in many of the countries of the area were important factors in enhancing the Yugoslav influence in Eastern Europe, but the most important development was the Soviet quest for improved relations with Belgrade. For several years, starting almost immediately after the first power struggle (which resulted in Laurenti Beria's ouster in 1953), the Kremlin sought to mend the many fences that had been erected around Yugoslavia. In this process, Khrushchev had to make considerable concessions to Tito, including the grudging admission that the Yugoslav road was a valid one, given the special circumstances of that country. This admission, produced largely by Khrushchev's need for external allies in his bid for domestic power, came close to establishing the principle of "national communism"—a very costly development for the Soviet Union, a trend against which the leaders in the Kremlin have been struggling ever since.[5]

The Yugoslav impact on post-Stalin Eastern Europe was most dramatic in Poland and Hungary in the short run, and in Czechoslovakia in the longer run; but other countries, notably Romania, were also strongly influenced by Belgrade. This influence was of two kinds, direct intervention and indirect example. First, Tito directly intervened in several major political crises that beset the Soviet bloc in the aftermath of Stalin's death. This was certainly the case in Hungary, where the old dictator Matyas Rakosi was removed from his dual control of state and party in 1953, and from his party bastion in 1956. The man who increasingly came to the fore in Hungary in this period was Imre Nagy, a moderate who had strong ties with Tito and whose position the latter strongly supported during three years of vicious infighting for political power in Hungary. Tito let it be known that one of the concessions he would definitely extract for a more friendly dialogue with Moscow was the ouster of Rakosi. Yugoslav pressure thus had an important impact in this case.[6]

During the summer and early fall of 1956, when the power foundation of the regime of Rakosi and his successor, Erno Gero, eroded, Tito's direct involvement in Hungarian matters became a major factor in the move toward open rebellion, although the Yugoslav leader certainly harbored serious misgivings about a development that eventually reduced the local communist party to impotence in the face of the nationalist storm. Thus, Tito endorsed many of the Hungarian demands for increased autonomy from the Soviet Union. On this basis he condemned the first Soviet invasion, but the total destruction of communist power in Budapest and in much of the country led him to support the second Soviet show of military strength as a necessary evil.[7]

In Poland, Titoism was an important factor in bringing Wladyslaw Gomulka to power in 1956. The direct influence here is somewhat harder to establish than was the case in Hungary; Gomulka respected Tito as a spokesman of national roads to socialism and communism; but the former was a staunch Marxist who had serious misgivings about the Yugoslav experiment of political and economic decentralization, and this skepticism reduced the influence that Belgrade could exert in Poland. On the other hand, Tito's insistence on a moderate Soviet policy in Poland was of considerable importance, and helped set the stage for a major political change in Warsaw without direct Soviet intervention.[8]

The indirect effect of Yugoslavia on Poland and Hungary was perhaps even more important. Yugoslavia represented the ultimate in national deviation from the Soviet model, and Belgrade's political and economic practices were examples of what could be accomplished in a system where some of the fundamentals of

Marxism-Leninism had been put into practice in a highly original manner. The reformers in Warsaw and Budapest looked to Belgrade as a living example of the possibilities inherent in a flexible, nationally oriented application of the Marxist-Leninist fundamentals. With this outlook, Poland and Hungary were launched, however cautiously, on a road of national development that would remove the possibility of a reestablishment of total Soviet hegemony in Eastern Europe.

Yugoslavia's policies had a major impact on other countries in Eastern Europe as well. Tito's emphasis on national roads to socialism and communism found a receptive ear in Bucharest, where Gheorghe Gheorghiu-Dej, once considered a Stalinist par excellence, began a process of steering Romania away from its heavy dependence on the Soviet Union and onto a path of nationalism that would ultimately make Romania the chief maverick among the erstwhile satellites, at least in foreign policy. By 1964 this development had gone so far that the Romanian Politburo produced a celebrated "declaration of independence," in which Bucharest stated its complete adherence to the principle of separate roads to socialism and communism, coupled with a forceful denunciation of big-power interference in the domestic affairs of any state.[9] The ideas of Tito concerning national autonomy had been decisively accepted by Gheorghiu-Dej, with a dash of Romanian nationalism added. The stage was set for a period of close cooperation between Romania and Yugoslavia, a relationship that has blossomed since Nicolae Ceausescu assumed leadership of the Romanian party.

Other countries in Eastern Europe were decisively influenced by Belgrade's policies as well, but the reaction to this influence differed markedly from that of Poland, Hungary, and Romania. East Germany, struggling to establish a nation inside the borders of the Soviet occupation zone, viewed any deviation from the Soviet example as anathema; and Tito never became acceptable to Walter Ulbricht, even after the former's partial vindication by Khrushchev in 1955. Since the mid-1950s East Germany and Yugoslavia have often been at opposite ends of the poltical spectrum in such fields as ideological control, the organization and administration of the economy, and the position to be accorded the Soviet Union in the world communist movement.

Even Ulbricht's demise as an obstacle to detente in Europe did not significantly change the situation; his successor, Erich Honecker, personifies the pro-Soviet *apparatchik* in Eastern Europe, a vanishing breed in many of the other countries in the area.[10]

In Czechoslovakia, the leading political figures also received the rehabilitation of Tito with considerable misgivings. The anti-Titoist purges had been at their bloodiest in Czechoslovakia; and Antonin Novotny, head of the Communist party, had made his way to the political pinnacle as a staunch Stalinist whose attacks on Tito and Yugoslavia matched those of Rakosi in Hungary, both in frequency and in ferocity. Strict economic centralization, ideological control, and heavy dependence on the Soviet Union in ideological and foreign policy matters remained the essential features of Czechoslovakia until 1968.

By 1963, the strict centralization of the Czechoslovak economy had produced stagnation; the growth rate was in fact negative, and labor productivity remained distressingly low. A series of economic reforms had profound effects on Czechoslovakia, not only in the economic system but in political and social matters as well. In a tightly controlled system, relaxation in one area is bound to have repercussions elsewhere; and the period 1963-68 saw a remarkable liberalization in the cultural field, a process that eventually engulfed the communist party itself and thus set the stage for the ill-fated experiment of "socialism with a human face."[11]

During the five-year period preceding the "Prague Spring," the Yugoslav influence in Czechoslovakia was pervasive. First of all, Tito publicly supported the trends toward liberalization; and during the tense summer of 1968 he made a show of solidarity with Alexander Dubcek (as did Nicolae Ceausescu).[12] Second, Yugoslavia was perceived by many Czech and Slovak intellectuals, labor leaders, and party apparatchiks as the most prestigious example of the principle of national roads to socialism and communism, a path upon which Czechoslovakia then seemed irrevocably launched.[13] For Moscow, the vociferous endorsement of the Dubcek experiment by Belgrade represented yet another compelling reason for reaffirming the limits of "national deviation" in Eastern Europe.

The Yugoslav influence on East Germany was mostly negative (or negatively perceived), but Bulgaria represented an even more extreme case of rejection of the dangerous ideas emanating from Belgrade. Bulgaria had always been one of the most servile satellites, and this position was not changed after the leadership reshuffle that propelled Todor Zhivkov to the political top in the mid-1950s. Sofia continued to erect and maintain strong barriers against Yugoslav influence, and the idological animosity was enhanced by the old national struggle between Yugoslavs and Bulgarians over Macedonia.[14] It is symptomatic that when domestic political opposition made a bid for power in Bulgaria in 1965, it was an ultra-leftist wing that acted, not a revisionist, Belgrade-inspired group. Tito's influence in this Balkan nation remains unimportant.[15]

While Yugoslavia had considerable direct and indirect influence in most of the countries of Eastern Europe in 1955-60, Albania remained a relatively unimportant source of inspiration or influence. The country was too small and too backward to represent a model of interest to the other countries in the area. Ideologically, Tirana was extremely orthodox, a relic of the kind of Stalinism that was now decried everywhere in the area, even in the Soviet Union. Albania therefore represented little of value or importance to any other political leadership in the area.

The advent of the 1960s drastically changed the situation of Albania in this respect (see Chapter 5). When the Chinese delegation walked out of the meeting of communist parties at Bucharest in 1960, followed by the Albanians, it became clear to everyone that a major rift had taken place in the once monolithic camp. From then on, Albania acquired added importance in Eastern

Europe, first as a fierce critic of Soviet "revisionism" and as a spokesman for China; second, as a country that became a possible informal partner for countries wanting to utilize the Sino-Soviet split to enhance their own semi-independence from Moscow. The impact of Albania and Yugoslavia on Eastern Europe in the 1960s and 1970s therefore can be measured only within the context of major Soviet policies, the Albanian and Yugoslav reactions to these policies, and the response to this interaction by the other states in the area.

DETENTE AND THE SOVIET QUEST FOR HEGEMONY: THE YUGOSLAV AND ALBANIAN REACTIONS

The main elements of the Soviet quest for detente in Europe and in the world are well known, and need no major elaboration. In a sense the Soviet leadership has attempted to gain economic advantage by obtaining access to Western credits and technology. Politically, detente has been intended to establish Western recognition of Soviet hegemony in Eastern Europe, thus freeing Moscow's energies for the more pressing problem of relations with the recalcitrant Chinese. Ideologically, detente has been meant to enhance Moscow's ability to control Eastern Europe, again giving the Brezhnev regime more possibilities in meeting the challenge from Peking.[16] In order to further its military and political goals vis-a-vis the United States and Western and Eastern Europe, the Kremlin successfully sponsored the Conference on European Security and Cooperation; for the reestablishment of Soviet hegemony in ideological matters, Moscow has been emphasizing the need for a new world conference of communist parties (although it has been careful to let demands for such a conference "originate" with others, such as the West German Communist party).[17]

Yugoslavia and Albania have reacted to the Soviet-sponsored detente in Europe and elsewhere in diametrically opposite ways. For Belgrade, the moderate signals emanating from Moscow have been interpreted as a final vindication of Tito's policy of maintaining good relations with both East and West. There is more than a little smugness in the many political commentaries by Yugoslav leaders and foreign policy analysts when this subject is raised; the implicit and sometimes explicit comment is that the Kremlin and the other capitals of Eastern Europe have finally seen the light, and thus have vindicated the Yugoslav detente policy, which has existed for a quarter of a century.[18]

It is natural that the Yugoslavs should take such an attitude. Belgrade stands to profit considerably from expanded relations between East and West in Europe. Specifically, detente has provided Yugoslavia with increased opportunities for trade with both sides, and its overheated economy has been somewhat stabilized through a series of credit agreements with West Germany, France, the United States, and Great Britain; even Hungary has extended a modest credit to

Belgrade. Massive Soviet credits so far remain primarily in Moscow banks because of political and economic restrictions on their use that so far have been unacceptable to Tito.[19] Clearly, such close economic relations with both sides would have been impossible in a harsher political climate in Europe.

In addition to credits and loans, Yugoslavia has also been able to establish a series of joint economic ventures with Western firms and with several Eastern European governments. In the latter category is the agreement to construct an oil pipeline from the Yugoslav coast through Hungary into Czechoslovakia. This tripartite agreement with two of Moscow's staunchest allies and one-time ferocious critics of Titoism would certainly not have been possible without Moscow's policy of detente and improved relations with Belgrade.[20]

In the political field, Belgrade's endorsement of detente has been less enthusiastic. The Yugoslav political leadership has continued to maintain its staunch support of state sovereignty and the right of each country to determine its own internal and external affairs. Detente is perceived as a valuable setting for the exercise of such sovereignty, but it must not turn into a bilateral agreement between Washington and Moscow that would sanction the existence of "blocs" and spheres of interest.[21] For Yugoslavia, such an agreement, however informal, would spell trouble, in that it might lead to closer integration of the political and economic systems of the rest of Eastern Europe, thus possibly establishing new barriers against anyone who would not go along, notably Yugoslavia.

The Albanian reaction to detente has been predictably negative. Tirana has interpreted detente as a deal between the United States and the Soviet Union to carve up the world among themselves. The Albanians characterize the United States as "imperialist" and the Soviet Union as "revisionist-expansionist," and charge both powers with identical dreams of world domination, against which all progressive and peace-loving forces must struggle with determination and perseverance.[22] Albania is therefore negative on both economic cooperation and political and military detente in a general sense; each country has the right to establish whatever ties it wishes, as long as it does not result in "capitulation" to "reactionary forces." It follows, then, that Tirana has echoed Belgrade's concern · over possible agreements between the two global powers that would in any way reduce the sovereignty and independence of smaller and medium-sized countries. In fact, Albanian leader Enver Hoxha and others have repeatedly castigated all dealings between "progressive" forces and capitalism on a political basis, an attitude that has sometimes been considered an indirect criticism of Albania's mentor China after her establishment of political ties with the United States.[23] This position has not prevented Albania from expanding its political ties with selected Eastern European countries, notably Yugoslavia and Romania, and there is also increased economic trade with a number of Western European countries. There apparently are no bilateral economic exchanges with the Soviet Union; none has been listed in Soviet foreign trade statistics, and Tirana is adamant that there is no such exchange.

The Soviet quest for a final ideological reckoning with the Chinese Communist Party (CCP) through an international conference of communist parties (which would presumably "read Peking out" of the movement) has met with considerable resistance from the Yugoslavs and the Albanians.

The Yugoslav view was perhaps most forcefully stated by Belgrade's delegate to the Warsaw preparatory meeting of communist parties, held in the fall of 1974. The main arguments used were familiar ones: Consultations among communist leaders are always useful as long as they are carried out in the spirit of fraternal relations; due respect for national sovereignty and a national road to socialism and communism; noninterference in domestic affairs; and due respect for national peculiarities. The Yugoslav delegate further demanded that no world communist conference be empowered to exclude any party; in fact, Belgrade specifically rejected the idea that China and the CCP could be subjected to any kind of sanction, either at such a meeting or in any other way. He stated that he found the early convening of the communist parties of the world "rather unlikely."[24]

The Yugoslav position at the Warsaw meeting was merely the dramatic enunciation of long-standing principles within the international movement, and Belgrade has continued to issue similar statements. Despite Tito's attempts to maintain good relations with Moscow during the last few years, Belgrade has never given in on any question of principle in the field of relations among communist parties.[25]

The Albanian position remained adamant in this field as well. Tirana utilized the numerous requests from the pro-Moscow parties for a new world conference as a starting point for a new round of denunciations directed at Moscow's alleged big-power chauvinism and imperialism. The Moscow-inspired call for a new world conference was seen as another example of Soviet imperialism; a conference of presumed "fraternal parties" would become a forum in which the socialist chauvinists would simply attempt to obtain the full blessing of other parties for their policy of subjugation of progressive parties, in this case the CCP and the Albanian Workers' Party. Such machinations were roundly castigated; and Tirana indirectly criticized those parties that had issued the call for the conference, notably the East German, Czechoslovak, Bulgarian, and Hungarian parties. The sharpest attacks were, of course, reserved for the Communist Party of the Soviet Union (CPSU).[26]

The isolationism of Tirana was accentuated by the fact that the Albanian party also castigated the move toward expanded relations with non-communist parties and movements on the left in Western Europe, notably the social democrats and the trade unions. For the Albanian party, most of the "progressive" forces in Western Europe, now wooed by local communists, represented reaction in a clever disguise. Tirana's insistence on the one correct way, coupled with the heavy emphasis on national sovereignty, gave the Albanian argument a somewhat unreal air at a time when virtually every other communist party in Europe was busily expanding its relations across former bloc delineations. At times it appeared that Enver Hoxha was administering a scolding to the CCP for its lack of vigilance in ideological matters, just as Tirana had indirectly criticized Peking for its expanded ties with the United States and other Western countries. Such stridence fell on barren ground in the rest of Eastern Europe.*

While Albania emphasized its isolationism, the Yugoslav party leadership expanded its attack on the hegemonistic ideas behind the proposed conference into an eloquent plea for increased interaction among all communist parties and progressive movements, on the basis of independence and full recognition of each party's uniqueness and right to a national road to socialism and communism. Tito expanded this message into a series of meetings with important communist party leaders from Western Europe, including the French and the Italians. Belgrade also played host to a number of delegations from the smaller Western European countries.[27]

Economic and political detente with the West and an ideological offensive against China have become two of the basic characteristics of Soviet foreign policy in the 1970s. Another very important policy is the massive attempt to achieve political, economic, and military integration of Eastern Europe in a Moscow-led bloc. While the parameters of national political deviation appear to have been decisively stated by the Brezhnev Doctrine, the move toward more positive integration has been conducted principally through CEMA and WTO, a move extensively documented elsewhere.[28]

Albania and Yugoslavia provided little direct input and guidance for the other Eastern European states on the questions of economic and political-military integration in CEMA and WTO. Neither country is a member of those organizations, and their policies therefore could have no direct impact on the attitudes of these multistate bodies. Both Belgrade and Tirana continued to resist real efforts of integration in principle, however, their arguments centering on the familiar themes of national sovereignty and the mutual advantage of economic and military cooperation. Both countries expanded their economic relations with the members of CEMA, but this was part of a set of bilateral trade agreements and cannot be seen as economic integration per se.

In military cooperation, the threatening echo of the Brezhnev Doctrine continued to ring ominously in the ears of the Yugoslav and Albanian leaders. Ever since the 1968 invasion of Czechoslovakia, the concept of military

---

*Even the Romanians emphasized their support for the principle of cooperation, as stated by Nicolae Ceausescu in interviews with *Die Presse* (Vienna), March 23, 1974, and *Guardian* (Manchester), April 9, 1974.

integration had meant the possible, indeed the likely, use of WTO to cloak Soviet military intervention in any socialist state in Eastern Europe whose policies were considered unsatisfactory in Moscow. In the face of such direct danger, both Yugoslavia and Alabania moved decisively to strengthen their defenses, in order to deter invasion by "big power imperialism." The direct source of such imperialism was seldom mentioned in Yugoslavia; but the Albanians, true to form, had no qualms about identifying Moscow as their most immediate enemy.[29] Both countries built up their defenses, bolstered the technical arsenal of their armed forces, and passed laws and decrees designed to enhance their defense potential. Yugoslavia enacted a law that made resistance against military intervention a duty for all citizens, even for individuals or groups not formally enrolled in military formations.* In Albania, the military became more and more involved in the social, political, economic, and educational life of the country; increased military training in the schools and in factories was instituted, and a number of books extolled guerrilla warfare in South Vietnam and elsewhere.[30] The message was clear in both countries: A militarily superior invading force would be met by total people's war, which would defeat even the best-equipped army. In Yugoslavia, this commitment had a definite ring of authority to it, given Tito's experience in guerrilla warfare in World War II against a militarily superior German army.

THE EASTERN EUROPEAN REACTION TO YUGOSLAV AND ALBANIAN POLICIES IN THE 1970s

During the early 1970s, the impact of Yugoslav and Albanian policies on the other countries of Eastern Europe was considerable. With the decline of Soviet influence in the area, each country had to face the need of reacting to the signals emitted from Belgrade and Tirana; these responses were quite varied, further reflecting the increasing foreign policy heterogeneity of the area.

In matters pertaining to detente, the Yugoslav and Albanian positions have influenced the foreign policies of the other socialist states in the area, both directly and indirectly. First of all, the very existence of a Yugoslavia that is recognized as a legitimate state with which communist regimes may establish friendly relations has resulted in vastly expanded bilateral relations between all the socialist states and Belgrade.† The indirect influence of Yugoslav and

---

*This law served as a model for a similar Romanian law, passed in 1973.

†An example of this expansion can be provided by a list of direct contacts between Tito and communist leaders, including Brezhnev's visit to Belgrade in 1971; Aleksei Kosygin's trip to Yugoslavia in 1973; and repeated consultations with Romania's Ceausescu, Czechoslovak Foreign Minister Bohuslav Chnoupek in early 1973, and Gustav Husak later that year. Tito also visited the Soviet Union and Hungary in this period.

Albanian positions on detente has been more pervasive and important. Belgrade and Tirana have articulated positions that have been utilized by other countries to further their foreign policy goals, and there has been a lineup of countries on the Yugoslav side on the question of expanded contact with the West and on the issue of the sovereignty of each individual country (which precludes "bloc" solutions, either in the West or in Eastern Europe). Some of the countries in the area have utilized the Yugoslav position as something against which one could rally.

The Albanian position on both issues has been such that nobody has endorsed Tirana's entirely negative attitude on expanded relations with the "capitalists," but the East German leadership has on occasion voiced its fear of increased East-West contacts in terms quite similar to the Albanian position.* Similarly, no one has denounced detente as a big-power plot to destroy small or medium-size states with the virulence customary in Tirana, but some states have adopted elements of the Albanian argument to reinforce their own policy position.

Among the Eastern European countries, Albania, Yugoslavia, and Romania have consistently emphasized the need to safeguard state sovereignty and cooperation among small and medium-size states in a period of big-power detente; Albania is willing to cooperate only with "genuine" socialist states, while Yugoslavia and Romania have emphasized such cooperation across ideological borders.[31] East Germany, Poland, Czechoslovakia, Hungary, and Bulgaria have paid much less attention to the argument over individual state sovereignty and have emphasized the need for foreign policy coordination and reliance on the Soviet Union within the "Socialist Commonwealth."†

On the issue of expanded economic ties with Western Europe and the United States, the alignment of states for or against the Yugoslav position is somewhat different. The most enthusiastic supporters of expanded economic relations with the West during the 1970s have been Romania and Poland. Romania has recently altered its foreign investment laws to allow a much larger share of foreign capital in joint economic ventures, and Nicolae Ceausescu negotiated a considerable expansion of economic relations with the United States during his trip to Washington in the fall of 1973.[32] Strong Romanian ties exist (and have been expanded) with France, Great Britain, and especially West Germany.‡ Poland under Edward Gierek has relied very heavily on credit from

---

*The hard-line position of Ulbricht's successor Erich Honecker at least indirectly reflects such views. For a thorough exposition of his views, see Honecker's speech to the Socialist Unity Party of Germany (SED) Congress, printed in *Neues Deutschland*, May 4, 1971.

†This attitude has been reflected both in individual country press commentaries and speeches and in the position adopted by these states at CEMA and WTO meetings.

‡West Germany has spearheaded Western "penetration" of Romania, and the RCP leadership has continuously emphasized the importance of these ties (see Ceausescu in *Scinteia*, July 20, 1972).

the West in order to maintain rapid development by means of economic modern-ization, increased productivity through import of Western technology, and a steep increase in the standard of living, which appear to be necessary conditions for the continued viability of the post-Gomulka regime.[33] There is no sign that the pace of Polish economic intereaction with the West is slackening.

Since 1968, when the New Economic Mechanism (NEM) was introduced in full force in Hungary, the economic relations between Budapest and Western countries have also proliferated. Several economic ventures have been established with Western credit, and Hungary's recent membership in GATT has further facilitated such interaction.[34] Since the early 1970s, Czechoslovakia and Bulgaria have followed suit by expanding economic ties with capitalist states. Thus, Czechoslovakia, after years of wrangling, settled its relations with the United States by signing an agreement on reimbursement for confiscated Ameri-can property; and in 1974 the Prague and Bonn governments finally agreed to a formula annulling the Munich Agreement of 1938. Shortly thereafter, West Germany established formal diplomatic relations with Prague, Budapest, and Sofia, and economic relations gathered momentum.* Even Bulgaria, whose econ-omy is very closely integrated into the Soviet development plans, adopted the stance that expanded trade with the West was both permissible and beneficial in a period of general detente. During 1974, two high-level Bulgarian delegations traveled to the United States, and economic relations with Western Europe were also expanded.[35]

East Germany, on the other hand, tended to soft-pedal the Eastern Euro-pean rush to make bilateral economic arrangements with the West. It had long enjoyed a privileged position within the socialist bloc as a major supplier of sophisticated technology and know-how to the fraternal countries; increased Eastern European reliance on the West in this field could only undermine its advantageous position. Besides, East Germany enjoyed a special economic rela-tionship with West Germany and, through it, with the Common Market; and the Honecker leadership perceived no particular need to expand economic coopera-tion with the West for the bloc as a whole. East Germany was also worried about the political ramifications of such expanded economic interaction; the policy of *Abgrenzung* (sharp political delineation between the two German states) might be seriously undermined as a result of such expanded ties.[36] The caution signs from Honecker nevertheless had a minimal effect on the other socialist states, which moved to take advantage of the economic detente while it was still possible.

---

*An example of such enlarged trade relations was the agreement between Bonn and Sofia to expand economic relations, achieved during Foreign Minister Walter Scheel's visit to the Bulgarian capital in early 1974.

In the field of economic relations with the West, then, the Yugoslav influence on the foreign policies of the Eastern European socialist states was primarily indirect, in that a time-honored policy of Belgrade's became the standard approach for almost all the other communist regimes in the area. The Yugoslav example was of considerable importance, in that it helped focus attention on the many economic advantages of active economic interaction with the West; but the other socialist states grasped the implications of detente primarily in order to further their self-interest. The largely negative Albanian attitude to increased economic interaction had no appreciable effect on any other state, except that it tended to further isolate Tirana from the other states in the area.

In the political field Romania became the most vocal supporter of Tito's policies, and Nicolae Ceausescu added a few elements of his own in Bucharest's definitions of detente, security and military power blocs. The Romanians steadfastly refused to accept any bloc solution to European security. Bucharest's delegates resisted any indication that decisions adopted at the security conference in Helsinki or at the reduction-of-forces talks in Vienna could in any way become binding on participants. Furthermore, the Romanian delegates repeatedly and pointedly demanded a rotation of the chairmanship of both conferences, veto rights in all conference votes, and a larger voice for small and medium-size states in the negotiations.[37]

Through two years of considerable activity in both Helsinki and Vienna, the Romanian position became clear. First, the most important principle of international relations is the reciprocal recognition of national sovereignty as the cornerstone of all foreign policy. No regional or international agreement can be established that will in any way, however minor, infringe upon national sovereignty. Second, there must be a clear-cut delineation between foreign relations among states and the internal politics of each state. Noninterference in domestic affairs is another fundamental and indispensable principle of international relations. Third, relations among states must be based on mutual advantage and reciprocity; states cannot, and should not be expected to, accept any form of exploitation by another state, be it economic, political, or ideological. Fourth, since international relations today are dominated by big powers, small and medium-size powers, no matter what their internal political life and system, must be given a bigger voice in Europe and in the world. Romania is willing and anxious to cooperate with all states, without regard to social and political systems, although relations with socialist states are of a special nature (which nevertheless will not allow for any breach of the principle of national sovereignty and noninterference in domestic affairs).[38]

This policy is part of the traditional Romanian emphasis on national sovereignty, which was enunciated in the 1950s and formally established by the "Romanian declaration of independence" in 1964.[39] Despite pressures from the Soviet Union and the more "orthodox" Eastern European states to modify or discard this policy, Nicolae Ceausescu expanded it during the last decade. His delegates' stand in the debates of the Helsinki security conference and the Vienna reduction-of-forces talks thus represent a policy more than fifteen years old—a remarkable monument to the relative deterioration of Soviet influence in Eastern Europe.

The Yugoslav and Romanian positions on security and disarmament met with considerable misgivings in Moscow and elsewhere in the "socialist commonwealth." Soviet displeasure with the outspoken independence of Bucharest was not direct, however; the Kremlin preferred to let others make their views known, clearly with Soviet approval and most likely upon the invitation of Moscow. Thus, Polish delegates at Helsinki and Vienna, as well as the Polish press, voiced repeated concern over foreign policy positions that could only weaken the solidarity of the socialist states; and there were many references to "unnecessary harping" on national sovereignty concerning this question.[40] The Poles pointed out that proletarian internationalism precluded exploitation of one state by another, and that relations among socialist states were by definition of such a nature that all such states, no matter what their size or military-economic capabilities, would be treated as equal; why, then, such Romanian emphasis on the obvious? Implicit in this argument was a hint that perhaps Bucharest did not follow proper socialist guidelines in its foreign policy; this was a rather ominous point, but the commentaries from Warsaw tactfully avoided any real elaboration on this issue.[41]

The Hungarians, on the other hand, were less circumspect. Traditional rivalry between Budapest and Bucharest had surfaced on numerous occasions in the 1960s and 1970s, notably during the spring and summer of 1971, when Zoltan Komocsin, a member of the Hungarian Politburo, criticized Romanian foreign policy and delivered a blast at Ceausescu's policies toward the sizable Hungarian minority in Romania.[42] Since 1971, the continuation of Bucharest's maverick foreign policies, coupled with close Hungarian-Soviet relations, have created considerable friction between Hungary and Romania despite official friendship meetings and expanded economic relations. The Romanian stand at Helsinki and Vienna was characterized by the Hungarian press as dangerous, detrimental to socialist solidarity, and possibly playing into the hands of the "capitalist powers."[43] Even after Hungary was unceremoniously relegated to observer rather than participant status at the Vienna talks (a move clearly designed to strengthen the Soviet bargaining position vis-a-vis the United States), the Hungarians swallowed their bitterness at the peremptory Soviet move, which had been undertaken without prior consultation with Budapest, and the Kadar regime and its controlled press continued to emphasize socialist solidarity while criticizing the Romanian position.[44]

Similar, but less strident, voices were heard in Czechoslovak and Bulgarian commentary as well. In both cases socialist solidarity and a common front against imperialism were stressed, and there were warnings against excessive emphasis on relations across ideological frontiers. Both Prague and Sofia went to some length to sound conciliatory in general terms, however, and there was a scrupulous avoidance of direct criticism of the Romanian position by actual naming of names. It was nevertheless clear that Romania's views were considered out of tune; and this evaluation also pertained to the Yugoslav position, since Bucharest and Belgrade had cooperated closely on the formulation and execution of foreign policy for more than a decade.*

As indicated above, the Albanian position on general detente, as exemplified by the Helsinki security conference and the Vienna talks, was so consistently negative and anti-Soviet (as well as anti-American) that no country in Eastern Europe could afford to be too closely associated with it. Even Yugoslavia and Romania were careful not to endorse any part of the Albanian position. It should nevertheless be pointed out that there is a certain degree of congruence between the Albanian emphasis on national sovereignty and Tirana's distrust of American-Soviet detente, on the one hand, and the consistent emphasis by its two Balkan neighbors on independence, noninterference in domestic affairs, relations with other states on the basis of mutual advantage, and the need for greater cooperation among small and medium-size states, regardless of social and political system, on the other. This congruence was certainly noticed and appreciated in Tirana, where the Hoxha regime moved to reinforce its friendly relations with Bucharest and significantly improved its ties with Belgrade.[45]

East Germany's policy toward general detente reflected the fundamental dilemma in its situation. More than any other state in Eastern Europe, it was beholden to the Soviet Union for its very existence, a fact that demanded a close coordination of the foreign policies of the two countries. At the same time, East Germany must attempt to establish an identity of its own, separate from that of West Germany, which had been widely accepted as the international representative of the German nation. In East Germany's estimation, only a sharp delineation or *Abgrenzung* vis-a-vis West Germany could safeguard the nation-building effort so strenuously carried out, especially since 1961, when the Berlin Wall was erected. Under such circumstances, the Soviet-sponsored detente in Europe, as exemplified in the Helsinki conference and the Vienna talks, might become detrimental to the need for *Abgrenzung*.[46]

The Honecker regime attempted to solve this dilemma by cautiously supporting the Soviet position in both forums, and the East German press dutifully criticized the position of "some states" (Yugoslavia and Romania) that unduly emphasized national goals at the expense of international solidarity. These attacks were nevertheless rather mild and did not approach the Polish, Czechoslovak, or Bulgarian coverage in either depth or virulence. One might wonder if

---

*Such close cooperation has now been institutionalized at levels below that of the top party leaders.

perhaps the East German leadership secretly admired the autonomous position of Bucharest and Belgrade, although it seems clear that if East Germany had possessed a similar independence in foreign affairs, it might have been utilized to stall the process of detente or at least slow it down, rather than to enhance cross-bloc dialogue, as was emphasized in Romania and Bulgaria.

As usual the East Germans scarcely honored the Albanian position by even outlining it.

INCREASING BILATERAL RELATIONS IN EASTERN EUROPE

Despite the considerable diversity among the Eastern European socialist states on detente, the Helsinki conference, and the Vienna talks, the first years of the 1970s saw a considerable upswing in bilateral political relations, much like the expansion in the economic field. Virtually every country sent high-level delegations to every other country, the years 1972 and 1973 being extremely busy in this respect.[47]

As a result of such expanded bilateral ties, several old problems were settled or at least pushed into the background; and it can be said generally that most of the states in the area enjoyed better relations with almost all the others than had hitherto been the case. The close relationship between East Germany and Poland was further expanded in this period, and the joint communique issued after the 1974 Gierek-Honecker meeting had elements of a "special relationship" in both economic and political terms.[48] Similarly, close ties existed between Warsaw and Prague, and several visits and cooperative economic ventures since the early 1970s have strengthened this relationship.[49] Czechoslovakia moved decisively to mend its record of animosity in relations with Tito, and Gustav Husak's visit to the Yugoslav capital in 1973 seemed to help dissipate much of the mutual distrust that had lingered after the invasion of Czechoslovakia in 1968.* Hungary enjoyed continued good relations with all the countries in the area, with the possible exception of Romania, whose maverick foreign policy position joined with the old issue of the Hungarian minority in Transylvania to keep some distance between the two capitals. Hungarian-Romanian relations were nevertheless better than in 1971, when they reached somewhat of a nadir.

Nicolae Ceausescu continued his whirlwind diplomacy in the 1970s, with a view toward establishing closer ties with the West, the developing countries, and the Middle Eastern states while bringing Romania out of the relative isolation in

---

*Tito and Ceausescu both condemned the invasion in very strong language, and both Yugoslavia and Romania mobilized troops and border guards as a precautionary measure.

which it had found itself in Eastern Europe during the latter half of the 1960s. The dynamic and charismatic president was largely successful in this endeavor. In Eastern Europe, Bucharest's relations with East Germany and Poland have improved markedly; in the latter case, there seems to have been a marked up- swing in both economic and political contacts, and the tone of these relations is much warmer.* Czechoslovakia, in its moves to erase the stigma of the 1968 invasion and the "normalization" that followed, also drew somewhat closer to Romania. Both Husak and Ceausescu apparently have decided that the past should be forgotten, so that better relations can be enjoyed now and in the future. The widely divergent positions of the two countries on many of the broader foreign policy issues have not hindered this considerable improve- ment.[50]

The most important elements of Romanian policy toward Eastern Europe can be found in its emphasis on special relationships among the states in the Balkans and the Aegean, regardless of socioeconomic and political systems. Ceausescu has repeatedly called for greater economic and political cooperation in this area, and Romania has moved to improve its relations with Bulgaria and Greece. Although Bulgaria has been somewhat reluctant to accede to a special relationship (clearly because of Soviet doubts about such a scheme), the bilat- eral ties between Bucharest and Sofia have been strengthened considerably since the early 1970s through a series of meetings between Ceausescu and Bulgarian leader Todor Zhivkov.[51] Yugoslav-Romanian relations remain extremely close, and the presidents of the two countries meet regularly for consultations and foreign policy coordination (Tito and Ceausescu have met more than a dozen times since the latter came to power in 1965). This is indeed a very special rela- tionship, as witnessed by the close correlation of the two sets of foreign policy outputs in most crucial fields.

REACTIONS TO THE PROPOSED CONFERENCE
OF COMMUNIST PARTIES

The Eastern European reaction to the Albanian and Yugoslav positions on the proposed international conference followed predictable lines. The most ardent supporters of the Yugoslav position were the Romanians. Ceausescu and his col- leagues repeatedly emphasized that any international conference of communist parties could not become a forum for castigation of any party; and resolutions

---

This improvement is conceivably due to Bucharest's attempts to show interest in CEMA and WTO activities (such as joint military map exercises between Soviet and Romanian staffs in 1973).

adopted at such a meeting could only be advisory, unless the conference was run on the basis of unanimity. Having so far followed the Yugoslav position quite closely, the Romanian Communist Party (RCP) launched a few important ideas of its own. In the face of the increased threat from imperialism and the danger of war, the Romanians called for all communist parties to establish the closest possible cooperation among themselves and, if possible, to expand such cooperation to other "progressive" forces. In fact, Ceausescu transferred the call for cooperation of small and medium-size states into an appeal for similarly close relations between the communist parties of such states, a clear indication that Bucharest tended to get away from the closed circle of ruling communist parties clustered around their mentor, the CPSU. Furthermore, in conformity with Ceausescu's attempts to expand Romania's relations with the developing countries, the RCP made clear overtures to improve its relations with many of the nationalist movements and parties in Asia, Africa, and Latin America. Here, then, was another example of the dynamic, multifaceted foreign policy emanating from Bucharest at a time when Moscow was attempting to draw the former bloc closer together in international, "proletarian" solidarity.[52]

In the other Eastern European states, the proposal for another world conference won routine approval, but only after a significant period of waiting and informal consultation. Throughout 1973 and 1974, the Polish, East German, Hungarian, and Bulgarian parties approved the idea, a position formally reflected at the Warsaw meeting in the fall of 1974. There were a few nuances in views expressed: the Hungarians were perhaps sharpest in their attacks on the Chinese party and, by implication, also criticized the Romanians; the Bulgarian Communist Party (BCP) became the most ardent supporter of the early convening of a world conference, and Todor Zhivkov, the BCP leader, engaged in much travel diplomacy to bring about an early settlement of the date for the massive gathering.* In general, the pro-Moscow parties, which had endorsed the Soviet positions on general East-West detente, the Helsinki conference, the Vienna talks, and economic and political-military integration in CEMA and WTO, also lined up with the Soviets on the issue of the world communist conference. In this field, as well as in the other areas under examination, Belgrade, Tirana, and Bucharest provided the deviations from the rule.

REACTIONS TO ECONOMIC AND MILITARY INTEGRATION

Predictably, Romania was the only formal member of both CEMA and WTO that followed the Yugoslav lead in resisting economic and military

---

*In October 1973, for example, Todor Zhivkov went to Vienna, Prague, Moscow, Warsaw, Havana, and several Far Eastern countries.

integration under Soviet auspices in both words and deeds. In fact, Romania's celebrated 1964 "declaration of independence" stemmed largely from Nikita Krushchev's attempts to turn CEMA into a truly integrated economic organization, in which the more developed countries (notably East Germany, Czechoslovakia, and, to some extent, Hungary and Poland) would become the chief suppliers of machinery and advanced technology, while the less developed countries, notably Romania, would specialize in agricultural production and the development of the fuels and raw materials industries.[53] The Romanian regime under Gheorghiu-Dej roundly rejected this idea, and the Ceausescu position has become even more strongly nationalistic in this area. Romania has gone ahead with one of the most ambitious industrialization programs in all of Eastern Europe, with an investment level exceeding that of any other socialist state in that part of the world.[54] Romania also has been markedly reticent about participating in many of the cooperative ventures undertaken by CEMA, only recently agreeing to join in the financing of several joint production facilities to be established in the Soviet Union.[55] There has been a conscious attempt by the Ceausescu regime to diversify Romanian foreign trade and to reduce the country's dependence on the Eastern European states; and Ceausescu has traveled to Africa, the Middle East, and Latin America in search of raw materials for the advancing Romanian industries and export markets for the finished goods turned out by the new factories built since World War II.* Expanded trade with the West and a heavy reliance on financial credit from the Common Market have further reduced Soviet and CEMA influence in the Romanian economy. Despite recent developments toward a somewhat closer relationship with CEMA members, Romania remains a maverick in this field as well.

Just as Romania's reluctance to participate in the many multilateral integrative efforts of WTO and CEMA was predictable in view of that country's general foreign policy, it followed logically that the other member states of the two organizations would endorse such efforts enthusiastically. Gierek's Poland, anxious to prove its reliability as a close ally, has been one of the strongest supporters of closer economic, military, and ideological integration while pursuing its quest for increased Western credits and trade.[56] Czechoslovakia, until recently laboring under the stigma of the invasion and the establishment of an orthodox regime that has engaged in widespread purges (an image that has hampered relations with the West), has strongly supported both economic and military integration as a guarantee of Czechoslovak economic security and also as a safeguard against Western influence on a disaffected population. Hungary's considerable economic progress during the 1960s and 1970s has been due to a

---

*This was clearly a major reason for Ceausescu's visit to Latin America, extensively reported in *Scinteia* and other Romanian papers, in August 1973.

confluence of several factors, chief of which are internal economic reforms and Soviet tolerance of such policies as long as Budapest remains firmly within the Soviet sphere of influence. Enthusiastic endorsement of the Soviet-sponsored multilateral organizations is one way in which Moscow can be reassured of Hungary's policies, a situation safeguarding the continuation of internal reform. Bulgaria, the long-standing loyalist par excellence in Eastern Europe in relations with the Soviet Union, has strongly supported cooperative moves and has integrated a substantial part of its production facilities with Soviet trusts and factories, in a communist form of multilateral corporations.[57]

In the military and security fields, the four reliable supporters of Soviet policy-making have performed predictably by endorsing continued and unquestioned Soviet leadership, including the control over the command structure of WTO. Participation in joint maneuvers is a frequent occurrence; and 'the standardization of weapons systems, uniforms, and strategic and tactical doctrine continues. As shown above, these four countries provided unquestioning support for the Soviet position at the Helsinki conference and the Vienna talks—even Hungary, whose initial views were unceremoniously shunted aside by the Kremlin during the Vienna talks on member or observer status for Budapest. But even with such a close correlation between the Soviet Union and its most faithful allies in Eastern Europe, it is clear that the countries in that area are no longer mere satellites, but junior participants in a continuing dialogue, in which mutual advantage and reciprocity increasingly constitute the most important concepts and principles of interaction, even in CEMA and other bodies.

East Germany, once the most vocal advocate of regional integration in all fields, has had some reservations lately. It clearly has been apprehensive lest the multilateral organizations in Eastern Europe become important vehicles for the imposition of Soviet foreign policy goals that could be detrimental to it. This outlook has occasionally resulted in East German unwillingness to take the lead in integrationist efforts; and there have also been attempts in the East German press to lecture the less highly developed fraternal countries on effective management, better production techniques, and even the correct interpretation of Marx—to the considerable annoyance of the recipients of such advice.[58] East German views in this field represent an interesting insight into the problems facing the most highly developed socialist economy when it is forced into close reliance on relatively underdeveloped systems, especially the Balkan members of the "Socialist Commonwealth."[59] Despite such manifestations of occasional hesitance to follow the Soviet quest for integration, East Germany remains too dependent upon the Kremlin, both politically and economically, to produce any startlingly new or unsettling initiatives apart from sponsorship of Soviet policies. It is no Romania, Yugoslavia, or Albania; and its policies in all fields will undoubtedly continue to reflect strong Soviet influence for many years to come.

CONCLUSIONS

The foreign policies of Eastern Europe are the product of myriad factors and their innumerable interactions and combinations. In the totality of this multifaceted system of influence, Albania and Yugoslavia play only a limited part. As indicated above, the direct influence of these two countries upon the foreign policies of the socialist states in the area is much less than their indirect effect. During the Stalinist period, the existence of a maverick state run by a "renegade" Communist party was indeed a dangerous force; Titoism might (and did) provide an alternative to the dreary uniformity of the Eastern European political systems at the time. Now it seems that everybody, including the Soviet Union itself, has begun to engage in expanded relations with the West; and the Yugoslav experience is no longer of such danger to any of the centralized systems in this area. Furthermore, the relative political and economic liberalization that has characterized Yugoslavia since the 1950s has now spread (although in smaller measure) into many of the other socialist countries. With such a development, what, precisely, is the influence of Yugoslavia in Eastern Europe?

First of all, Yugoslavia and its Communist party staunchly support national sovereignty and the right of every party in the international communist movement to determine its own ideological path to the common goal of socialism and communism. This emphasis has set certain limitations on the Soviet quest for coordination of Communist party policies and the need for clear lines of demarcation between those who belong and those who must be removed from the family of "progressive parties," notably the Chinese. Furthermore, the Yugoslav position on this question has become a rallying point for many of the Western European communist parties in their efforts to escape Moscow's domination. Finally, the principles of sovereignty enunciated in Belgrade have served to lend support to the policies of that troublesom maverick, Romania, thus further weakening Soviet influence in Eastern Europe.

Second, Yugoslavia's insistence on the rights of all states to full sovereignty and a foreign policy based on noninterference in domestic affairs, mutual advantage, and reciprocity acts as a powerful hindrance to Moscow's attempts to coordinate, integrate, and control the basic foreign policies emanating from all socialist capitals. Belgrade is not alone in this position, of course; Bucharest has made its position on these topics clear, and the so-called "axis Bucharest-Belgrade" has created no end of trouble for the Soviet Union. It is in considerable measure the policy of Tito and Ceausescu that has reduced the recent moves by the Kremlin to stricter control in Eastern Europe to a rather frustrating game.

Third, Yugoslavia is of great importance as a symbol of Soviet fallibility in Eastern Europe. Since the early 1950s Belgrade has emphasized national sovereignty and independence as well as polycentrism. Now virtually every party in the area adheres to the same principles; and even the Soviet Union has been forced to accept them, at least in theory. This constant reminder of Soviet mistakes has further reduced Moscow's influence in Western Europe and else-where. For a power that claims to be the leader of a universal movement, this reminder is certainly a bitter pill to swallow; and the taste becomes doubly sour when once-staunch satellites such as Romania blithely pick up the Yugoslav views and expand upon them, thus effecting a considerable expansion of their own autonomy and a corresponding lessening of Moscow's influence.

By contrast, the Albanian influence in the foreign policies of Eastern Europe has been limited. Tirana has served as a reminder of China's influence, and the vitriolic Albanian attacks against the Soviet Union have constituted a considerable nuisance. But the other socialist states of the area have clearly per-ceived the impossibility of joining Albania's camp; such a move would almost certainly bring in the Red Army. If one wants to deviate from the Soviet path, it is far better to deviate toward "revisionism;" in that direction there is no danger of ending up on the side of Moscow's lone competitor for the crown of "leader of the world communist movement." Thus Albania has become primar-ily a symbol against which the communist-dominated regimes of Eastern Europe could rally. There is little indication that Tirana will soon escape from this unenviable position.

At the mid-point of the 1970s, both the United States and the Soviet Union are confronted with massive problems of foreign policy. The United States, slowly recuperating from the devastating experience of Vietnam and the domestic turmoil of Watergate, has been beset by the multiple problems of rampant inflation throughout the noncommunist world, an explosive situation in the Middle East, and a considerable weakening of the economic and military power of its closest allies. Such a combination of factors would seem to provide the Soviet Union with unparalleled opportunities for expanded influence in the ongoing game of regional and global politics. But despite such unprecedented opportunities, the Kremlin has been unable to make significant inroads in Western Europe in terms of influence. The principal reason for this relative failure is the restiveness in the socialist states of Eastern Europe. Nationalism, expanded foreign policy autonomy for some of the states in the area, and increasing diversification as the modernization process continues from the Elbe to the Black Sea will provide the Soviet Union with numerous problems in the years to come. The conclusion of CSCE, with the formal Western acceptance of the existing socioeconomic and political realities in Eastern Europe, probably will not decisively reduce the trend toward increasing nationalism and autonomy among the states of the area.

NOTES

1. Zbigniew K. Brzezinski, *The Soviet Bloc* (Cambridge, Mass.: Harvard University Press, 1971), pp. 185-210.

2. For instance, M. George Zaninovich, "The Yugoslav Variation on Marx," in Wayne S. Vucinich, ed., *Contemporary Yugoslavia: Twenty Years of Socialist Experiment* (Berkeley: University of California Press, 1969), pp. 285-316.

3. Brzezinski, op. cit., esp. pp. 155-85.

4. Vernon V. Aspaturian, "East European Relations with the U.S.S.R.," in Peter A. Toma, ed., *The Changing Face of Communism in Eastern Europe* (Tucson: University of Arizona Press, 1970), pp. 281-311.

5. Brzezinski, loc. cit.

6. See, for example, J. M. Mackintosh, *Strategy and Tactics of Soviet Foreign Policy* (London: Oxford University Press, 1963), pp. 150-91.

7. Brzezinski, op. cit., pp. 120-30.

8. Ibid., pp. 230-68.

9. Stephen Fischer-Galati, *Twentieth Century Rumania* (New York: Columbia University Press, 1970), pp. 159-83.

10. See Heinz Lippmann, *Honecker: Portrat eines Nachfolgers* (Cologne; Verlag Wissenschaft und Politik, 1971).

11. A great many books have been produced on this topic in recent years, two of the more informative being Tad Szulc, *Czechoslovakia Since World War II* (New York: Viking Press, 1971); and Vladimir V. Kusin, *Political Groupings in the Czechoslovak Reform Movement* (London: Macmillan, 1972).

12. Szulc, op. cit., pp. 377-435.

13. Ibid., pp. 305-77.

14. Stephen E. Palmer, Jr., and Robert R. King, *Yugoslav Communism and the Macedonian Question* (Hamden, Conn.: Archon Books, 1971).

15. For a good overview of politics in Bulgaria since World War II, see J. F. Brown, *Bulgaria Under Communist Rule* (New York: Praeger Publishers, 1970).

16. Vernon V. Aspaturian, "Moscow's Options in a Changing World," *Problems of Communism* 21, no. 4 (July-August 1972): 1-21.

17. Ibid.

18. See, for example, *Borba*, July 10, 1971; also, such views were implicit in Tito's foreign policy interview with *Vjesnik*, February 23, 1973.

19. For a commentary on this problem, see *Vjesnik*, May 24, 1973.

20. A report on this pipeline was published in New York *Times*, February 23, 1974.

21. Tito made this point in one of his frequent foreign policy interviews in recent years, *Vjesnik*, October 8, 1972.

22. A very detailed discussion of Albanian foreign policy views was provided by Enver Hoxha in a major speech on Independence Day, 1972, in *Zeri i popullit*, November 29, 1972.

23. Ibid., February 27, 1972.

24. The Yugoslav position can be found in Devin Devlin, *Radio Free Europe Research*, RAD Background Report/5, Eastern Europe, January 17, 1975: 9-19.

25. For Tito's position in 1972 and 1973, see *Vjesnik*, October 8, 1972, and February 23, 1973.

26. *Zeri i popullit*, October 14, 1974.

27. This principle was strongly defended in long articles in *Borba*, January 4-7, 1973.

28. Aspaturian, op. cit.

29. See, for example, editorial in *Zeri i popullit*, July 15, 1972.

30. For discussion of Albanian education, see an article in ibid., June 23, 1971.

31. For a statement of the Romanian position, see Nicolae Ceausescu's speech to the National Conference of the Romanian Communist party, July 1972, in *Scinteia*, July 20, 1972.

32. The Ceausescu visit to the United States was extensively reported in *Scinteia* and other papers during the first two weeks of December 1973.

33. See a detailed analysis and future forecasts (up to 1980) of Polish foreign trade, in *Rynki zagraniczne*, September 9, 1972.

34. For a discussion of Hungary's trade with the West, see "Hungary's Economic Relations with the West," *Radio Free Europe Research* East-West/4 (March 12, 1973): esp. 5-7.

35. For an analysis of Bulgarian foreign policy, see F. Stephen Larrabee, "Bulgarien in der Aussenpolitik—Bundnispartner oder Satellit Moskaus?," *Osteuropa* (August 1972): 608-18.

36. See Honecker's speech to the 1971 SED Congress, in *Neues Deutschland*, May 4, 1971, in which this position is strongly implied.

37. This view was strongly emphasized by Gheorghe Macovescu, Romanian foreign minister, in an interview with *Le monde diplomatique*, January 5, 1973.

38. The most thorough general exposition of the basic principles of Romanian for foreign policy was given by Nicolae Ceausescu at the 1972 RCP party conference, printed in *Scinteia*, July 20, 1972.

39. See, for example, Stephen Fischer-Galati, "The Socialist Republic of Rumania," in Toma, op. cit., pp. 13-39.

40. *Trybuna ludu*, for example, devoted dozens of pages of speeches and commentary to the Helsinki conference on European security in July 1973.

41. Ibid.

42. This criticism was met in a series of articles in *Scinteia* and other Romanian papers throughout the fall of 1971—for instance, October 3, 1971.

43. See, for example, indirect criticism of Romania (through criticism of China) in *Tarsadalmi szemle*, December 1973.

44. Ibid. and also in numerous statements in CEMA and WTO meetings.

45. An article in *Rilindja* (Prishtina), December 22, 1971, outlined some of the new economic agreements with Yugoslavia. Since then, relations have been further expanded, in both economic and political terms.

46. See Honecker statement in *Neues Deutschland*, May 4, 1971, and January 2, 1974.

47. A further evidence of expanded relations can be found in the many new friendship treaties signed during 1972 and 1973 (Bulgaria-Hungary, reported in *Rabotnichesko delo*, June 29, 1972; Bulgaria-Poland, reported in ibid., November 12, 1972; and East Germany-Poland, reported in *Trybuna ludu*, January 14, 1973).

48. *Trybuna ludu*, June 9, 1974.

49. For a review of such ventures in the economic field, see ibid., August 18, 1972.

50. For the Romanian view of the improvement of relations between the two countries, see *Scinteia*, March 7 and 8, 1973 (reporting on Ceausescu's visit to Prague).

51. For the Romanian view, see Ceausescu in *Scinteia*, July 20, 1972; the Bulgarian view is well expressed in a German translation of a major speech by Bulgarian party leader Zhivkov, which appeared in *Suddeutsche Zeitung*, April 23, 1971.

52. See Ceausescu's views in *Die Presse*, March 23, 1974.

53. Fischer-Galati, "The Socialist Republic of Romania," pp. 24-31.

54. See the projections for the period 1972-1990, in Ceausescu's speech to the 1972 party conference, *Scinteia*, July 20, 1972.

55. For details on investment in Romania through the CEMA Investment Bank, see *Die Wirtschaft* (East Berlin), October 11, 1972.

56. For a Polish analysis of this "move to the west" that has centered on relations with the Federal Republic of Germany, see *Polityka* (Warsaw), March 29 and 30, 1974.

57. See, for example, Bogoslav Dobrin, *Bulgarian Economic Development Since World War II* (New York: Praeger Publishers, 1973), pp. 88-119.

58. See, for example, Gunter Mittag, in *Neues Deutschland*, December 7, 1972.

59. Ibid.

THE UNITED STATES: "PEACEFUL ENGAGEMENT" REVISITED

Bennett Kovrig

INTRODUCTION: BETWEEN IDEALISM AND PRAGMATISM

The historical experience of the United States in its dealings with East Central Europe is one of disappointed idealism and modestly rewarded pragmatism.* Official policy has vacillated between activism and benign neglect, but at its core one finds the constant factor of revisionism—of dissatisfaction with the political status quo of the region in both its indigenous and its hegemonic dimensions. Traditional American hostility to European imperialism prompted sympathy for the nineteenth-century nationalistic movements that challenged the rule of Berlin, Vienna, Moscow, and Constantinople. Five of President Woodrow Wilson's Fourteen Points explicitly urged self-determination for the various national groups of East Central Europe and, however imperfectly implemented at Versailles, produced approximately the present configuration of states. The lure of the power vacuum created by this fragmentation proved irresistible for German, then Soviet hegemonic ambitions, eliciting new variations of American revisionism on the theme of national self-determination. The proclamation of war aims in the Atlantic Charter indicated the continuing American aspiration—inaccurately interpreted by many as a commitment—to restore sovereignty to the Eastern Europeans. Finally, in the early years of the cold war, American policy again took a revisionist turn, most forcefully—and, again, misleadingly—expressed in the liberation rhetoric of the Dulles era.

These high points of revisionism—1918, 1941, and 1952—were all followed by periods of disappointment and compromise that testified to the largely

---

*For the sake of verbal economy, the term East Central Europe is employed here for the post-World War II period to designate Bulgaria, Czechoslovakia, East Germany, Hungary, Poland, and Romania; in normal use it also includes Albania and Yugoslavia.

ideological substance (rounded out by marginal strategic and economic interests) of the policies and the limited leverage available to the United States for altering essentially European shifts in imperial power. Indeed, at no time did the United States deploy its military might with the principal aim of restoring independence to East Central Europe. That goal was seen, rather, as a desirable, but ultimately expendable, by-product of bolstering the Western European democracies against aggression and, in more recent times, of coming to terms with the age of nuclear deterrence.

The substance and limitations of American interest in self-determination for East Central Europe can be traced through statements of policy-makers that indicate, allowing for variations in emphasis, a continuing and almost teleological faith in the achievement of that goal with little, if any, American intervention. As early as September 1943, President Franklin Roosevelt speculated privately that ten or twenty years of European influences might mitigate the inevitable Soviet hegemony over the area. In advocating containment, notably in his famous "X" article of 1947, George Kennan advised the West to "wait for the internal weaknesses of Soviet power, combined with frustration in the external field, to moderate Soviet ambitions and behavior." In a 1952 article elaborating the policy of liberation, John Foster Dulles confidently predicted that "within two, five or 10 years substantial parts of the captive world can peacefully regain national independence." And in a dispassionate style consonant with his advocacy of detente, Secretary of State Henry Kissinger observed in 1974 that "if we remain cautious enough to prevent the imposition of Communist hegemony, then I believe that transformations of the Communist societies are inevitable."[1]

Such professions of faith in the ultimate triumph of Western defensive endurance over Soviet imperialism and of liberal democratic traditions over Marxism-Leninism compensated for an absence of will and power to achieve the emancipation of East Central Europe from hegemony. The test of that emancipation was progressively diluted as policy-makers came to terms with the immutability of Soviet dominance over the region. The Atlantic Charter enjoined respect for "the right of all peoples to choose the form of government under which they will live."[2] By the time of Yalta, this had been qualified to exclude regimes with any hint of "Sovietphobia." In the early 1950s the operative objective became Titoism (national communist regimes), an admittedly evolutionary stage palatable to both Dean Acheson and Dulles, but one that soon proved equally unattainable. The decade following the Hungarian revolution saw further weakening of the test to any demonstration of voluntarism that might indicate polycentric tendencies within the Soviet sphere. A succession of policies and slogans—containment, liberation, peaceful engagement, bridge-building—reflected deepening fatalism regarding the prospect of emancipation and encompassed a series of operational tactics designed to affect the rate of change. These tactics, ranging from trade embargoes, psychological warfare, and denunciations at the United Nations to economic aid, cultural exchanges, and selective normalization of commercial and diplomatic relations, were at best anodyne, and at worst counterproductive, in terms of the respective degree of emancipation that they sought. Exhortative propaganda was hardly sufficient to stem the Soviet invasion of Hungary. The low profile of bridge-building did not assuage Soviet fears about the direction of liberalization in Czechoslovakia in 1968. Neither threat nor cajolery, it seemed, could alter the determination of Soviet leaders to control the political future of East Central Europe.[3]

Protracted stalemate over what often seemed an area of marginal importance to the United States finally produced the abandonment of even verbally active revisionism. The purposes of this essay are to assess the place of East Central Europe in the broad span of American foreign policy in the early 1970s; to adumbrate concurrent developments in the Soviet sphere; and to examine the balance of interests and alternative strategies in the era of detente.

FROM BRIDGE-BUILDING TO DETENTE

The main features of current American policy concerning East Central Europe can be traced back to the mid-1960s, when the strategies of peaceful engagement and its semantic variant, bridge-building, emerged as Washington's response to the deadlock in East-West relations. Designed for the long haul, the new approach abandoned the monolithic view and removed the status of East Central Europe from the sphere of American-Soviet negotiations, the latter in tacit recognition that ritualistic raising of the question as an alleged test of Soviet goodwill had only exacerbated superpower relations without gaining any tangible benefits. Instead, the United States adopted a low-key policy of gradually normalizing relations with the Eastern European regimes, with the professed goal of encouraging diversity and tendencies toward disengagement and neutrality and a spiritual, if not political, reintegration of the Eastern Europeans into the European community of nations. Pluralistic and liberalizing tendencies, notably in Poland, Hungary, and Romania, encouraged American policy-makers in the belief that, as Dean Rusk observed in 1964, "one can begin to think of liberation through change and through the reappearance of historic ties."[4] Indeed, for a time it appeared that the principal obstacle to this evolution lay not in the intractability of the communist regimes but in the reluctance of Congress and the American public to abandon the image of the satellites as undifferentiated, servile appendages of Moscow. President Lyndon Johnson's proposed East-West Trade Relations Act, promoted as a profitable way to exploit polycentric tendencies, did not even reach the floor of Congress; and the WTO invasion of Czechoslovakia in August 1968 only rekindled popular hostility toward the Soviet Union and its allies.

That invasion also served to remind the advocates of peaceful engagement of the limits of Soviet tolerance, and accordingly the Nixon administration endorsed its predecessor's approach with ever more cautious references to accommodating "whatever pace and extent of normalization these countries are willing to sustain."[5] Official allusions to East Central Europe were laced with reassurances that the United States would not seek to undermine the Soviets' "legitimate security interests" or to alter the domestic political and economic structures of the individual states. Their sovereignty was assumed, and the contentious historical issues of self-determination and the sources of legitimacy of the various regimes studiously avoided in the new era of detente diplomacy. Notwithstanding the occasional public disapprobation of the Brezhnev Doctrine of limited sovereignty—a superfluous reminder of established practice—the Nixon administration in effect recognized the status of East Central Europe de jure as well as de facto, and abandoned all pretense at revisionism.

This realistic acceptance of an apparently irreversible fait accompli was one precondition for the American-Soviet rapprochement that has been mafested in the successive SALT agreements, the 1972 Moscow declaration of principles, the Final Act of the CSCE, and the ongoing Mutual Force Reductions talks in Vienna. That rapprochement subsumed the definition of detente as progress toward a stable peace and implied recognition that stability in Europe meant inviolability of the Soviet sphere. As far as concrete policy toward East Central Europe was concerned, detente brought the final ratification of the political consequences of World War II and the normalization of diplomatic and commercial relations, both eagerly sought by the Soviet bloc and now virtually concluded. The West German treaties with the Soviet Union and Poland and resumption of dialogue with East Germany, the upgrading of diplomatic relations with the other Eastern European states, the quadripartite agreement on the status of West Berlin, and the American recognition of East Germany eliminated the issues of German reunification and alleged West German revanchism. The Nixon and Ford administrations' staunch advocacy of the trade bill authorizing the president to end trade discrimination against the Soviet bloc was another major affirmative gesture of detente. It is a tribute to the political skills of the Nixon-Kissinger team, as well as an indication of the altered public mood, that rapprochement progressed with little domestic opposition apart from the controversy over the emigration of Soviet Jews.

In the midst of these advances only one official American statement dealt exclusively with East Central Europe, an address by Deputy Secretary of State Kenneth Rush in April 1973.[6] American policy, said Rush, is

> . . . to engage the countries of Eastern Europe in an expanding set of close and individual relationships with ourselves and with their neighbors to the west. We intend to pursue our policy of engagement diligently and prudently. We will not seek to force the pace. We do seek to encourage a process we believe to be advantageous to world peace.

He cited three guiding principles. First, the United States would "deal with each country of Eastern Europe as an independent sovereign state entitled to be free of all outside interference," and the Moscow agreement was cited as indicating a joint American-Soviet undertaking on this score. A second basic principle was to "create a continuing economic relationship with the countries of Eastern Europe by expanding our trade and by encouraging their growing receptivity to foreign investment." Third, "it is fully as important for us to promote a deepening of political and economic relations between the countries of Eastern and Western Europe as it is to develop Eastern European ties with us." The record shows some progress in all of these spheres.

One indication of the development of bilateral relations is the frequency of high-level contacts. Richard Nixon became the first American president to visit a WTO capital other than Moscow when he passed through Bucharest in August 1969, an initiative apparently intended to signify approval of Romania's critical stance over the invasion of Czechoslovakia and its generally unorthodox foreign policy. President Nicolae Ceausescu returned the visit in October 1970, and in July 1972 Secretary of State William Rogers signed a consular convention in Bucharest. A subsequent visit by Ceausescu to the United States, in December 1973, produced a joint statement on friendly relations and an undertaking to foster economic, industrial, and technical cooperation.

President Nixon was welcomed in Warsaw on his return voyage from Moscow in April 1972, and a consular convention was signed. On the occasion of the return visit of the Polish party leader, Edward Gierek, in October 1974, a potpourri of agreements testified to the intention of the two governments to intensify relations. Gierek came seeking an expansion of trade (Poland being the one WTO member presently enjoying most-favored-nation status), industrial cooperation deals using American credits and Polish production facilities, and a further rescheduling of Poland's $280 million debt (which dates back to the grain purchases of the late 1950s). Two joint statements on friendly relations and the development of economic, industrial, and technical cooperation, and seven agreements ranging from a tax convention to cooperation on environmental protection, issued from the visit.

Relations with Hungary's Kadar regime were long hampered by memories of the bloody repression of the 1956 revolt and began to ease only in 1962-63, when an amnesty for political prisoners was announced. The presence of Cardinal Joszef Mindszenty in the American embassy, where he had taken refuge after the revolution, remained another stumbling block until his departure into exile at the pope's request in September 1971. The pace of normalization picked up with Rogers' visit in July 1972, coinciding with agreements on consular facilities and scientific cooperation, and with the settlement of outstanding American property rights, signed during Deputy Premier Peter Valyi's sojourn in Washington in March 1973. On the latter occasion the official American communique indicated that the most-favored-nation status sought by the Hungarians depended only on congressional approval. The last unresolved and largely symbolic problem in American-Hungarian relations is custody of the crown of St. Stephen, which has been in the United States since the end of World War II.

There has been less bilateral progress with the other three Eastern European countries. Relations with the Husak regime in Czechoslovakia are still in the "purgatory" phase, as was once the case with Kadar, but it seems only a matter of time before the outstanding financial issues of American-held Czech gold and American property rights are settled. A consular convention was signed with Moscow's most orthodox ally, Bulgaria, in April 1974. The diplomatic recognition of East Germany in September 1974 ended a quarter-century of professed American interest in the reunification of Germany, the pursuit of which had been linked to Bonn's sensibilities and had become redundant with the onset of Ostpolitik.

For much of the postwar period the United States, and to a lesser extent its allies, resorted to economic weapons, such as discriminatory tariffs and selective embargoes, to express their displeasure and, it was hoped, to hinder the development of military technology in the East. By the mid-1950s the Western Europeans began to reestablish their traditional commercial links with East Central Europe; but in the United States, domestic opposition retarded the elimination of a weapon that on all counts had been futile and—in the eyes of many American businessmen who saw their European counterparts invade the market—costly. Between 1961 and 1972, American exports to East Central Europe (including Albania, Bulgaria, Czechoslovakia, East Germany, Hungary, Poland and Romania) rose from $87 million to $267 million, and imports from $57 million to $223 million, with Poland taking the lion's share. This steady but unspectacular growth was hampered by several factors: the limited appeal of Eastern European exports for the American market; discriminatory tariffs against all except Poland, and the consequent inaccessibility of Export-Import Bank credits; and, to a rapidly diminishing extent, the list of goods under the strategic embargo. At the same time, the relatively poor performance of the Soviet and Eastern European economies induced the regimes to seek Western technology and know-how, a quest that became one of the principal incentives for detente with the United States. Romania, Poland, and Hungary have been most assiduous and innovative in their pursuit of Western trade and technology, offering Western firms coproduction ventures and minority shares in new enterprises.* The Hungarians have even floated loans on the Eurodollar and North American money markets. The Soviet attitude could be summed up in the perhaps   apocryphal advice "Make the best deals, but don't fall in love."[7]

---

*For example, Control Data Corp. has a 45 percent interest in a new Romanian enterprise, and Siemens AG of West Germany a 49 percent share in a Hungarian joint company.

The powers to liberalize trade, finally granted by Congress in December 1974, fell short of what President Johnson had sought in the mid-1960s, for the Jackson Amendment prohibits trade favors or credits to any communist country that imposes unreasonable hindrance on the emigration of its citizens. This qualification was ill-received in the target states and, indeed, prompted Moscow to abrogate the 1972 American-Soviet trade agreement in January 1975. Congress did acquiesce in mid-1975 to the granting of most-favored-nation status to Romania after hearing testimony that the Ceausescu regime had allowed a modest acceleration in emigration. The Ford administration had evidently calculated that Romania's voluntaristic forays in diplomacy, notably at the CSCE talks, deserved to be rewarded.* Although East Central Europe (as distinct from the Soviet Union) has little potential for becoming a major market or source for American trade, there appears to be no objective reason for maintaining discriminatory tariffs and withholding the technology and expertise that the Eastern Europeans crave. Nor, on the other hand, can the United States expect to derive significant leverage from trade liberalization, for neither the Soviet Union nor, in consequence, the Eastern European regimes will make significant concessions in return.[8]

The third principle noted by Rush, the encouragement of closer relations between the two European camps, relates to a major shift in American attitudes that has been under way at least since the mid-1960s. Whereas at the height of the Cold War the United States stood as the principal revisionist power vis-a-vis East Central Europe, with the Western Europeans offering only halfhearted support, by the mid-1960s the pace of Western European involvement quickened as the French and West German governments launched their own versions of peaceful engagement. The Gaullist vision of a reconciled and independent Europe lacked practical substance, and never recovered from the disillusioning blow of the invasion of Czechoslovakia; but the German variant, Ostpolitik, played a key role in easing tensions and facilitated the revival of Germany's historical commercial influence in the East. Thus Henry Kissinger's view, written in 1968, that "the major initiatives to improve relations between Western and Eastern Europe should originate in Europe, with the United States in a reserve position," reflected an accomplished fact as well as the emerging American preference to uncouple the Eastern European question from superpower negotiations.[9] There were some early apprehensions in Washington that Bonn's initiatives might go too far, and President Nixon stressed that the Western allies had "a responsibility to consult together in sufficient depth to ensure that our efforts are complementary and that our priorities and broad purposes are essentially the same."[10] However, by 1974 Ostpolitik had achieved an apparently

---

*In a remarkable departure from Eastern European practice, the Romanian chief of staff, General Ion Coman, met with his American counterpart at Washington in March 1975 and reportedly discussed the possibility of purchasing American armaments. *Time*, August 18, 1975, p. 22.

terminal degree of normalization and the new West German chancellor, Helmut Schmidt, could insist with no fear of contradiction that his current policies went no further than the American understanding of detente.[11]

THE SOVIET SPHERE

In the first of the three guiding principles listed by Rush, the United States proclaimed its intention to conduct bilateral relations with the Eastern European regimes on the assumptions that the latter were sovereign and "entitled" to act as free agents. The former merely acknowledges current international legal practice, which bases recognition on effective control and at least a semblance of independence without probing too deeply into domestic legitimacy and hegemonic or other constraints on a state's freedom of action. The latter assumption, on the other hand, is more an aspiration than a statement of fact, for even the most optimistic proponents of detente would hesitate to argue that the Brezhnev Doctrine of limited sovereignty has been nullified by the subsequent Nixon-Brezhnev agreement on principles of noninterference and respect for national sovereignty. Such professions of good intentions have never withstood the call of higher national interest; and the Soviet Union's past conduct, its negotiating stance in the European security conference and the force-reduction talks, and its current policies in East Central Europe are more reliable indicators of the constraints on Eastern European sovereignty.

The motivation for the aggressive Soviet pursuit of detente since 1971 has been the subject of endless speculation focusing on factors such as domestic economic problems, fears of China, the achievement of strategic parity with the United States, and the (desirable) disintegration of the Western alliance in Europe. A further factor, as Marshall Shulman has argued, is the desire to consolidate the Soviet position in Eastern Europe:

> The persistence of nationalism and the social and political effects of advancing industrialization combine to make this area one of unrest and potential disturbances, and the Soviet problem of control is likely to be made more difficult by the increasing contacts of the West with the states of Eastern Europe. The Soviet Union seeks assurance that there will be no exacerbation of these difficulties from the West and no interference in the event of trouble.[12]

Thus, for the Soviet Union detente has brought tangible benefits in Bonn's treaties with the East (and adherence to the nuclear nonproliferation treaty), the agreement on West Berlin's separate status, the West's recognition of East Germany, and the Nixon-Brezhnev agreement, all of which signify Western acquiescence in the Eastern European status quo.

The American and Western rationalization of these apparently asymmetrical aspects of detente has been somewhat ambivalent. On the one hand, it has been argued that the abandonment of overt revisionism and the formal recognition of the geopolitical division of Europe were not political or strategic concessions, but an essentially gratuitous accommodation of the Soviet Union's obsessive insecurity regarding its sphere of influence. On the other hand, these steps toward normalization have been defended as necessary preconditions for a more tolerant climate in which the Eastern Europeans could evolve toward greater autonomy and domestic diversity.

Any evaluation of trends in East Central Europe depends on the application of necessarily subjective criteria, whether those of the Soviet leadership, the individual regimes, the various national and subnational interest groups and strata, American or Western European policy-makers, or simply of the individual observer; and it is dangerous to assume congruence among any of these perspectives. All of the Eastern European communist parties have committed themselves to develop a national basis of legitimacy within the limits of Soviet tolerance. Popular support for the regimes derives in large measure from perception of these external constraints and assessments of the individual party's inclination to maximize its independence. All ruling parties have been the agents of a historically inevitable process of modernization, and it is of only academic interest to speculate whether less revolutionary and costly methods might have achieved equal benefits.[13] What is clear is that since the death of Stalin, a degree of diversity in experimentation with the Soviet model has materialized that, punctuated by setbacks and fraught with constant uncertainty regarding the vagaries of Moscow's permissiveness, remains in evidence to this day.

In Czechoslovakia, a spirit of economic and political innovation flourished briefly in 1967-68 until, defeated by its own momentum, it engendered a degree of pluralism and free expression unacceptable to the Kremlin. The forcible restoration of orthodoxy under Husak required lasting repressive measures and induced such profound popular despair that the Czechoslovak party, which in the immediate postwar period enjoyed the most substantial electoral support in East Central Europe, remains near the nadir of its legitimacy. The Romanian party's strategy, initiated in the early 1960s, was to legitimize its rule by professing a voluntaristic foreign policy calculated to appeal to domestic nationalism. The withdrawal of Soviet forces from Romanian soil, the successful challenge of the more unpalatable integrative goals of CEMA, a cautious ambivalence regarding the Sino-Soviet schism, rapid expansion of diplomatic and commercial contacts with the West, and overt opposition to the invasion of Czechoslovakia were the more apparent outcomes of this strategy. At the same time, domestic policy remained inflexible and Ceausescu's rule is the closest contemporary approximation of Stalin's cult of personality. Romania's assertion at the CSCE of the sovereign equality of nations regardless of alliance links again struck a discordant note in the Soviet bloc chorus, but more recently Ceausescu felt impelled to pledge publicly that Romania would improve relations and overcome differences with Moscow and strengthen its ties with other members of WTO.[14]

It is the Kadar regime in Hungary that, considering its inauspicious beginnings, surpassed most domestic and Western expectations in its pursuit of legitimacy and efficacy. By the early 1960s, after concluding the collectivization of agriculture, the party felt confident enough to cease its persecution of the 1956 counterrevolutionaries and proceeded to launch a program of economic reform that partially decentralized planning, introduced a limited market mechanism, and resulted in impressive economic growth. This "new economic mechanism" was accompanied by a tolerance in the cultural sphere that is approximated only in Poland, and by a foreign policy stance of steadfast loyalty to Moscow. However, by 1974 there appeared clear signs of retrenchment in both the economic and the cultural spheres. In Poland, the deviant factors of the Roman Catholic Church involvement in political and cultural life and of private farming remain, and the Gierek regime has managed to mitigate the economic problems that led to the December 1970 riots. As for the Honecker regime in East Germany, its success in spurring economic growth through refinements of a still highly centralized command model and in gaining international recognition has enhanced popular perceptions of distinct nationhood and has had a positive effect on its domestic legitimacy.

Without relinquishing their monopoly of political power, the several Eastern European parties have thus followed diverse paths in the general direction of economic efficiency and a more tolerable modus vivendi with their constituents. The police repression of Stalinist times still recurs in cases of extreme deviance, as in Czechoslovakia after 1968; but it has largely receded from public consciousness, and methods of control are now more subtle: three left-wing Hungarian intellectuals, detained briefly in October 1974 on charges of antisocialist agitation, were first threatened with banishment to the West, then allowed (on unspecified conditions) to remain in Hungary. Cultural russification, a prominent feature of the 1950s, has been abandoned as counterproductive in its arousal of nationalistic resentment. Restrictions on travel to the West have been eased, notably in Poland and Hungary, least in East Germany. All the regimes are eagerly seeking trade concessions and hard-currency tourism from the West.

At the same time, it must be noted that the most active phase of detente diplomacy since 1971 has coincided with a progressive retrenchment in the East that induces doubt about the future prospects of autonomous change in the individual states. While it would be erroneous to attribute all policy shifts by the Eastern European parties to Soviet interference or alterations in the international system, the areawide campaign against Western influences, technocratic secularization, ideological relativism, potentially anti-Soviet nationalism, and embourgeoisement at the expense of the doctrinal leading role of the working class is too well-orchestrated not to lead one to the conclusion that Moscow is proceeding to consolidate its sphere against the alleged erosive effects of detente. Decompression in East Central Europe has undergone reversals before—in Hungary after 1956, in Poland after 1957, in Czechoslovakia after August

1968—but there is no reliable predictive formula for ascertaining the limits, short of the obvious indivisibility of party power and of the WTO.

Finally, in this brief survey of legitimacy and change in East Central Europe one must confront the issues of public interest and popular opinion. If it could be demonstrated that communist rule over nations with little experience of liberal democracy (except in Czechoslovakia) has created a viable, responsive, and popularly based modernizing political system that offers no threat to its neighbors, then the case for American revisionism, even in as innocuous a guise as peaceful engagement, would lose much of its validity. Nuclear deterrence has reduced the region's significance as a potential springboard for westward aggression, and the satellite armies are an unreliable element in the calculations of both NATO and WTO strategists, although the withdrawal of Soviet forces to Soviet territory remains a goal worth pursuing in the interests of Western European security and Eastern European morale. Beyond this, does the traditional rationale of revisionism, the restoration of self-determination, remain relevant today?

The limited popular appeal of communism prior to the revolutionary accession to power of the parties between 1945 and 1948 (party support in relatively free elections ranged from 16.9 percent in Hungary in November 1945 to 36 percent in Czechoslovakia in May 1946) can offer only faint guidance. The dramatic erosion of communist support and the proliferation of non-communist parties during the Hungarian revolution of 1956, and the pluralistic tendencies that were unleashed during the spring of 1968 in Prague indicate at least that the Leninist principle of democratic centralism did not, in its application, strike many Eastern Europeans as the optimal political system. The variations on the Soviet economic model and the accompanying social benefits have sunk deeper roots. It is doubtful that the salaried employee of an efficient collective farm would readily revert to an independent but relatively insecure farming existence, or that a majority of Eastern Europeans would welcome the return to private ownership of large industries; but the persistence of otherwise repressed entrepreneurial ambitions and skills is evident in those mechanisms, notably the Hungarian, that provide a few outlets.

On balance, communism as an operational political model has failed to convert the Eastern European masses, not least because it did not live up to its own ideals, as some "new left" dissidents now openly charge, much to the ruling parties' embarrassment. Like many in the West, the Eastern Europeans have come to love the welfare state and subsidized culture. They are embracing consumerism with a vengeance and show patriotic pride in secular achievements for which the party claims ultimate credit. However, only force majeure has reconciled them temporarily to official obfuscation and censorship, to the stupefying barrage of party propaganda, to the secrecy of political decision-making and leadership selection, to the petty bureaucratism inherited from earlier regimes but aggravated by party norms, to a standard of living that, despite all advances, is far behind that of much of Western Europe, and to the intrusion of party control into virtually all spheres of human activity.

Sociological surveys tend to show widespread political apathy and the declining perceived relevance of the messianic, revolutionary party in the technocratic age. As one observer notes, "the Party's successes in modernizing the region have turned its young only further westwards," while relative economic and technological backwardness is widely attributed to the inefficiencies of communist and Soviet rule.[15] An opinion poll conducted among an allegedly representative sample of Eastern European travelers in Western Europe presented alternatives that understandably are not raised in communist surveys. A freely elected democratic regime was preferred by 68 percent of the respondents, while 25 percent opted for a liberalized version of the present system; 87 percent favored joining the Common Market, and 83 percent preferred participation in a politically united Europe.[16] While this study confirmed other indications that the majority of Eastern Europeans prefer structured pluralism to one-party rule masquerading as consensus politics, one must distinguish between aspirations and the capability to adopt liberal democracy, to which habits acquired under a succession of authoritarian regimes are ill-suited. As one young Hungarian writer observed:

> It's true, we can't expect to have democracy until international alignments change. But meanwhile, how about changing what we have inside the country, and in people's minds? So we can have democracy when the chance arises. What we have at the moment is more or less a socialist reproduction of what there was before the war. Instead of feudal capitalism, we have feudal socialism. And inside people's heads too, a feudal mentality, of either ordering others about or waiting to be ordered about. If there's going to be change, that's where it'll have to start. . . .[17]

A further indicator of the perceived degree of self-determination is popular attitudes toward the Soviet Union, which is officially and unrelentingly depicted as liberator, ideological fountainhead, defender, and inestimable economic partner. By all accounts the most pervasive bond linking these nations traditionally divided by imperial manipulation and nationalistic passions is a devastating resentment of Soviet hegemony. Least evident in Bulgaria, most openly flaunted in Poland, this amalgam of hatred, fear, and feelings of cultural (and material) superiority must send chills down the spines of the men in the Kremlin and influence their operational definition of detente. Meanwhile, their client regimes in East Central Europe are left facing the daily dilemma of pursuing modernization without deviating from an amorphous orthodoxy, and of the twin specters of silent or open rebellion at home and swift retribution from Moscow.

ALTERNATIVE STRATEGIES AND DETENTE

For the United States, East Central Europe remains a target in search of a policy. One measure of the ephemeral nature of peaceful engagement is the difficulty of assessing its impact on the area. Certainly it has fulfilled the Eastern European regimes' desire for formal recognition and the abandonment of overt American revisionism, and for somewhat less discriminatory trade practices, although on the last count they are much more worried by the European Economic Community's protectionism than by the remnants of American discrimination. However, their political status and economic development were hardly dependent on this progressive normalization of relations, which was therefore acquiesced in by the United States without any bargaining beyond some minor property settlements. If Washington's purpose had been simply to relinquish the outdated punitive tactics of the Cold War and regularize official relations, then peaceful engagement has indeed been a success. But the original rationale of peaceful engagement surpassed mere acceptance of the status quo and of relations that the Eastern European regimes considered sufficiently free of the threat of ideological contamination. It subsumed the old evolutionary strategy of gradually undermining the legitimacy and efficacy of Soviet hegemony and of preparing the Eastern Europeans for alternative political choices, and in this sphere peaceful engagement has been a signal failure. No wonder, then, that American policy-makers have become progressively ambivalent and evasive about the issue of self-determination.

American interests, ideological as well as strategic, would be best served by a democratic East Central Europe, not aligned with the Soviet Union, harmonious in its regional relations, and free to enter into confederal arrangements on a European scale. This scenario would restore a certain balance of power on the continent and satisfy both American ideology and indigenous aspirations for self-determination. It also is patently unrealistic. The next-best scenario would be a set of national communist states with a high degree of authentic domestic legitimacy, aligned with Moscow but subject to only a modest degree of subordination and free of Soviet military presence, and enjoying untrammeled commercial and cultural interaction with the West. Regrettably this, too, appears fanciful at present. Finally, the most prudent projection serving American interests would be an East Central Europe still under the strictures of the Brezhnev Doctrine but with a reduced Soviet military presence, expanding commercial relations with the West, and fewer restrictions on communications—a scenario that sporadically, and on a low level of priority, seems to inform current Western detente diplomacy. The tentativeness of this last approach is defended more often in negative than in positive terms. In Kissinger's words:

> [If] . . . we look for final results before we agree to any results, then we would be reviving the doctrines of liberation and massive retaliation of the 1950s. And we would do so at a time when Soviet physical power and influence on the world are greater than a quarter

century ago when those policies were devised and failed. The futility
of such a course is as certain as its danger.[18]

The subordination of American interest in the disengagement and self-
determination of East Central Europe to the higher stakes of stabilizing superpower competition and to activism in more salient crisis areas, such as the
Middle East, reflects the Kissinger-Nixon Realpolitik that also reversed the old
China policy. The challenge of our time, observed Kissinger, is to reconcile the
reality of competition with the imperative of coexistence.[19] In the European
theater that challenge has been met by a sequence of symbolic gestures, culminating in the 1975 ceremonial CSCE Summit, that sanctify division and (at
least for the West) transform active competition into a passive spectator sport of
historical speculation. The short-term results are characterized by an ambiguity
that is fascinating a growing army of scholars, pundits, and assorted observers.
and that has been analyzed most perceptively in Pierre Hassner's writings:

> The essential attribute of this state is neither force nor cooperation
> but the constant influence of societies upon one another within the
> framework of a competition whose goals are less and less tangible,
> whose means are less and less direct, whose consequences are less
> and less calculable, precisely because they involve activities rather
> than strategies and because these activities affect what societies *are*
> as much as what they *do*.[20]

Political, social, and economic tensions and contradictions characterize both
sides of the contemporary European equation. In the West, they are accommodated with difficulty by the relatively open and flexible nature of the political
systems, but in the East the picture of authoritarian regimes attempting to
modernize while maintaining closed societies is not one that inspires confidence
about the prospects of a frozen status quo or of peaceful change. The asymmetries of East-West interaction only aggravate such doubts.

The confirmation of the status quo by joint fiat of the superpowers dis-
mays Europeans of both camps, who see in it their political eclipse. It will
dismay even more those who perceive the asymmetrical features of this ostensibly conservative condominium. The CSCE, which got under way in 1972 and
was concluded in mid-1975, has touched on the most salient contentious issues
in its quest for a set of principles governing relations among the participating
states (including all of Europe except Albania, the United States, and Canada).*
The principal themes in "Basket I" have been security and the sanctity of existing frontiers, with the Soviet Union and its allies demanding a perhaps redundant

---

*For more details on the talks and the CSCE Summit, held in July-August 1975 in
Helsinki, see Chapter 9 in this volume.

affirmation of the permanence of the territorial status quo resulting from World War II and the Western powers insisting on the possibility of peaceful change and on certain confidence-building measures in the military field, such as forewarning and observation of military maneuvers. Expectations that the Final Act's formalized consensus on these issues will significantly enhance the security of Western Europe and offer a modest deterrent to future applications of the Brezhnev Doctrine are understandable if also ahistorical. Even less encouraging is the desultory pace, bordering on paralysis, of the concurrent Vienna talks between selected members of the two alliances on mutual force reductions—talks that are taking place against a background of Soviet accretions of military might in East Central Europe and the Mediterranean and of flagging Western determination to maintain even the existing, relatively low levels of NATO strength. To dismiss this growing military asymmetry on the grounds that American guarantees and military power are adequate compensation is to ignore the insidious psychological impact of a proximate and irresistible military power.

Even if one excludes the military component from the East-West equation in Europe and assumes an authentic compact between the superpowers to eschew change by force, there remains the question of how genuinely the two sides are committed to respect the political status quo. It is a question that begs for an answer, and that answer is the already hoary concept of Finlandization. On the Soviet side, insistence that the Soviet model in East Central Europe will be preserved at all costs is combined with candid reminders that the international class war will be pursued within the context of peaceful coexistence. In operational terms this means consolidation of the Soviet sphere, the subversion of nonaligned neighbors, the disengagement of conventional American strength from Europe, and the progressive and piecemeal political penetration of Western Europe. Reports of Soviet connivance in the subversive activities of "Stalinist" dissidents, uncovered by Yugoslav authorities in September 1974, and of Soviet aid to the minority Portuguese Communist party in its drive for monopoly power suggest that beyond the Soviet bloc the status quo is less than inviolable. Lord Chalfont's account of long-range Soviet plans, drawn from conversations with the Czech defector General Jan Sejna and examination of WTO documents that he brought out, encompasses the drive for clear military superiority, the debilitation of NATO, and the total demoralization of the West, and reinforces the impression of asymmetry in detente.[21]

Finlandization, observed one journalist, is to the Western Europeans a nightmare, to the Eastern Europeans a dream.[22] That is where another asymmetry arises, for the United States and its allies are, by a combination of purpose and neglect, inclined to shatter the dream. In their pursuit of normalization at the expense of revisionism, American policy-makers have gone full circle. At the height of the Cold War, American policy was to ignore and ostracize the Eastern European regimes while exhorting their oppressed subjects to retain hope of eventual liberation. Today, the policy is to pursue cordial relations with the regimes and ignore the peoples. The distinction between governors and governed is denied by all states inwardly but, legalistic pretense to the contrary, liberally applied outwardly. Indeed, it is a distinction prominently featured in communist rationalizations for pursuing the class struggle in the midst of detente. It would therefore seem entirely in keeping with the logic of the Soviet conception of detente, with past promises, and with current interests for the United States to simultaneously conduct a prudent policy of detente with the Eastern European regimes and of active entente with the Eastern European masses who, as was suggested earlier, still yearn for eventual self-determination without entertaining illusions about the immediate prospects of release from hegemony.

What might be the practical significance of such a twofold approach? To begin with, we can note that "a positive objective for Western countries in dealing with the East cannot be the overthrow of communist regimes and the breakup of the Warsaw Pact, but it can and should be the encouragement of as much autonomy as possible for East European states within that alliance and, even more, of individuals and groups within their respective societies."[23] Peaceful engagement extended new lines of communication and certain facilities for diversification of trade relations to the communist regimes. However, a mood of ideological uncertainty arising from the Vietnam debacle, the appeal of an ostensibly nonideological balance-of-power diplomacy, and the immediacy of crises ranging from the Middle East conflict to the energy shortage and economic recession have all conspired to undermine the American dedication to the war of ideas.

Yet the reality and primary importance of that struggle should be obvious to all whose understanding of detente goes beyond SALT and the pursuit of lucrative commercial deals with the East. At the CSCE and in its Eastern European policies the Soviet Union has shown that above all else it fears the impact of Western ideas, of pluralistic modes of political behavior and intellectual inquiry. Negotiations on "Basket II," covering such items as trade policy, technology, environment, and transport progressed relatively smoothly, for they involve areas of undisputed state control. Far more contentious has been "Basket III," in the context of which the Western participants have advanced proposals for facilitating travel, the reunion of families, and generally an unrestricted interchange of ideas and information. The last issue is at the core of the incompatibility between "closed" and "open" societies, and WTO members have insisted on reference to a state's right to protect its own laws and customs in order to justify their protective isolation. The anodyne text of the Final Act indicates that the haggling had a largely face-saving outcome in the semantic synthesis of antagonistic principles. It does not erase the doubt expressed by the Canadian secretary of state for external affairs that for some detente might signify "the mere replacement of opposing armed camps of steel with closed camps of the mind."[24] In their purely humanitarian aspects the agreements may alleviate some problems, but the whole cultural-information package is clearly regarded as secondary by Brezhnev, whose pursuit of CSCE was motivated by a desire for a personal diplomatic triumph ostensibly projecting the Soviet Union as the principal advocate of peace and security. Brezhnev's assertion that the ideological struggle will intensify to become an even sharper confrontation between the two societies, and tacit Soviet admissions that the Final Act has not invalidated the cryptohegemonic dictates of "socialist internationalism," are more accurate reflections of political reality, which will be one of tragic asymmetry if it sets a passive and permeable West against an active and impermeable East.

It is a mark of the insecurity felt by Soviet bloc leaders that they are anticipating detente to have disintegrative consequences and are pursuing an intensive campaign to shore up ideological dikes in East Central Europe. Their mass media have concentrated their fire on the dangers of creeping Westernization, on the ideological contamination transmitted by tourists and foreign media. Dutiful endorsements of East-West cultural cooperation are invariably accompanied by warnings about the unshakable supremacy of Marxism-Leninism and the impossibility of compromise and convergence, let alone surrender, in the ideological realm. Dissident or nonconformist intellectuals are silenced by methods that range from the Soviet practice of commitment to psychiatric clinics to the more subtle pressures prevalent in East Central Europe. The parties' mobilizing agents, especially youth organizations, are being reinvigorated. The communist regimes reserve their harshest strictures for Radio Free Europe and Radio Liberty, and would like nothing better than a convention arising from CSCE that would silence them permanently. Jamming, immensely expensive in terms of energy consumed, and of limited effectiveness, is currently resorted to by Bulgaria, Poland, and Czechoslovakia as well as the Soviet Union. The Soviets, looking well into the future, have submitted a draft UN resolution prohibiting satellite-relay television between countries when it is construed by the recipient as unwarranted interference with or as prejudicial to international peace.[25]

The Eastern European regimes have more or less willingly followed Moscow's lead in applying this regional *Abgrenzungspolitik*, although history and geography make it more unpopular and physically less feasible than is the case in the Soviet Union. Western cultural influences are deeply rooted throughout the region, and are outweighed by Soviet influence only in Bulgaria. Access to Western plays, literature, films, and, at least in the border areas of East Germany, Czechoslovakia, and Hungary, to Western television, is a legacy of the more tolerant cultural policies pursued in some measure by all the regimes in the 1960s and could be revoked only at great cost to the parties' popular legitimacy. The ruling parties of course never abdicated their function as ideological and cultural watchdogs, but they are now facing the difficult task of halting and even reversing liberalizing trends while preaching the benefits of detente to their constituents and to the West.[26]

Apart from tactical pressures in the final drafting phase of the CSCE, when largely because of its own sense of urgency the Soviet Union made certain textual concessions, American policy on the "free flow of ideas" has been deliberately subdued. In his statement on detente before the Senate Foreign Relations Committee in September 1974, Secretary of State Kissinger avoided any reference to "Basket III" but averred that "we must know what can and cannot be achieved in changing human conditions in the East" and that to combine detente with increasing pressure on the Soviets would be disastrous.[27] The abandonment of overt revisionism has had a debilitating impact on American information programs aimed at the East. Radio Free Europe (RFE), which claims an audience of 30 million in East Central Europe, is barely surviving amid intensified communist attacks and lagging Western support. Established in 1951 with the purpose of inciting the Eastern Europeans to actively prepare for liberation, after the Hungarian revolution and the humiliating eclipse of rollback, the Munich-based RFE became a relatively innocuous alternative source of news, commentary, and popular music while remaining a valuable listening post for Eastern European developments. With the onset of detente it came under fire, notably from Senator J. William Fulbright, for being a CIA-financed relic of the Cold War; and since 1972 it has been supported (along with Radio Liberty) by annual congressional appropriations administered by the Board for International Broadcasting, established in 1973. Despite declining revenues and drastic staff reductions, RFE has not yet cut its broadcast hours; and even the New York *Times* was moved to editorialize that the station's function of continuing international debate over the airwaves was not inconsistent with detente.[28]

The official outlet of the United States Information Agency, the Voice of America (VOA), appears to have been even more effectively muzzled by the administration line on detente. In response to intramural and public criticism that the VOA was overly cautious not to offend communist governments, the director declared: "Detente has changed what we do in USIA. Our program managers must be sensitive to U.S. policy as enunciated by the President and the Secretary of State. That policy is that we do not interfere in the internal affairs of other countries. We're not in the business of trying to provoke revolutions and uprisings."[29] For various reasons the Western European broadcasting services are ill-suited to take the lead in communicating with the East. The British are objective and competent but financially constrained, while the West Germans are effective vis-a-vis East Germany but, for historical reasons, somewhat suspect elsewhere; the French broadcasting service to Eastern Europe had, until its recent suspension, tended to reflect de Gaulle's fulsome courtship of the official East.[30] A diminished perception of threat, wide pools of ideological relativism, and acute economic problems all contribute to Western European inertia in this sphere.

Two hypothetical rationales can be surmised for the scaling down and neutralization of American propaganda and information activities regarding East Central Europe: that they are counterproductive, or that they are superfluous. The first might signify that on balance these operations impede progress in more critical areas of negotiation between the superpowers. To test this assumption conclusively, one would have to be privy to the secrets of the mighty; but it is difficult to conceive of an overt American objective, such as the stabilization of the arms race, whose achievement would have been dependent on the unilateral renunciation of direct and constructive communication with the Eastern European peoples. Neither can one find evidence that the normalization of American relations with the Eastern European regimes in the diplomatic and commercial spheres was ever contingent on such renunciation. That would have been an implausible bargain, considering the relatively greater interest of the Eastern Europeans in normalization. Aggressive prosecution of the war of ideas also would be dysfunctional if it induced more repressive policies in the target country, but the current campaign of ideological consolidation has coincided precisely with a low point in Western revisionism. Propaganda is of course counterproductive when, as in the early 1950s, it incites rebellion with implied and unfounded promises of aid; but the crusading cadences of liberation have long ago left the airwaves, and it is disingenuous to argue that the only alternative to the current dilution of information activities is a return to the sword-rattling excesses of the Cold War. Finally, a fear of retaliation can lead to perceptions of dysfunctionality. Since the Soviet Union has repeatedly reaffirmed its dedication to active pursuit of the international class struggle, any threatened retaliation would necessarily be so disproportionate as to be incredible.

The second set of hypotheses revolves around superfluity. This migtht mean that Eastern Europeans perceive no need for alternative, extraterritorial sources of information, and that from the American perspective they are already Western-oriented and politically well informed. Even a cursory survey will demonstrate the falsity of the first proposition. In the most liberal of Eastern European systems, the limitations of the mass media have created an atmosphere of almost obsessive speculation often characterized by conspiratorial theories and fanciful assessments of the implications for East Central Europe of external political and diplomatic developments. For example, many Eastern Europeans were convinced (and encouraged by their media to believe) that the Watergate affair was part of a right-wing plot to discredit Nixon's detente policy, and could not be simply the prosecution of White House misdemeanors. Prior to the recent consolidation campaign, the illusion that a prime Western objective in detente was the mitigation of Soviet dominance also enjoyed wide currency. Appreciation of intrabloc events also suffers from inadequate reporting. The

Soviet-led invasion of Czechoslovakia is frequently attributed, even by generally well-informed Eastern Europeans, to the Dubcek regime's alleged inclination to renounce WTO.

Such misconceptions, whether inspired by propaganda or resulting from uninformed speculation, are as dysfunctional for the Eastern Europeans and for the West as is the political apathy induced by isolation and impotence. It would seem, therefore, that the ambiguities and uncertainties of detente necessitate more than ever a sustained dialogue with the peoples of East Central Europe, parallel but not subordinated to official normalization. The goal should be the progressive liberation of minds, not a futile crusade to alter foreseeably immutable geopolitical realities. The Eastern Europeans must be approached neither as ideologically hostile masses (one probably could find more convinced if inexperienced Marxists in the West) nor as societies fully prepared to reconcile the requisites of modernization with the free play of multiparty contestation. Their need is for objective and comprehensive information about both the West and the Soviet sphere, and for analysis informed by sound liberal democratic principles as well as by the dictates of realism and prudence. Such analysis will endorse patriotism and minority rights without inflaming nationalism, and also will credit the regimes' modernizing efforts and need to accommodate Moscow without condoning their political shortcomings. These guidelines are neither novel nor revolutionary. They have for many years inspired the principal agents of Western communication with the East; and their application has already induced palpable, although apparently not irreversible, improvements in the performance of the Eastern media. Nevertheless, RFE's commissioned surveys show that a majority of Eastern Europeans continue to listen to Western boradcasts (primarily RFE), which they regard as more reliable sources of information on foreign and domestic events than their home services.

In institutional terms, the need is for a rededication of American efforts to the battle of ideas, the sustenance or revival of RFE and VOA involvement in the political education and emancipation of the Eastern Europeans, for hard bargaining to achieve free travel, free access to the more orthodox Western media, the establishment or expansion of American information offices, and effective application of new communications technology. The informational spin-offs of conventional commercial and cultural exchanges—visible, for example, in the adoption of American marketing techniques and in the proliferation of Western-style pop music groups—are tangible but incidental and, in the aggregate, insufficient.

In recent years there has materialized a certain neo-functionalist view asserting the inescapable effect of technological and economic imperatives. In a 1974 interview, Dr. Kissinger predicted that "the combination of industrial necessity plus the fact that a complicated society cannot be run by direction and must have a certain amount of consensus will begin to permeate even totalitarian regimes," adding that "the pressure of this realization on Communist systems is going to bring about a transformation apart from any conscious policy the United States pursues, so long as there is not a constant foreign danger that can be invoked to impose regimentation."[31] The secularizing impact on political life of the expanding Eastern European technocracies is undeniable but, as in the West, it is political structures and values that ultimately determine whether such phenomena serve humanistic or Orwellian futures. Similarly, Kissinger's assertion that the Soviet Union and its allies "have come closer to acknowledging the reality of an interdependent world economy" implies rather prematurely that scarcity transcends ideological incompatibility and is more likely to induce cooperation than competition.[32] Any analogy between the ideological homogeneity of the early nineteenth-century European balance-of-power system and current perceptions of economic interdependence is tenuous at best. It is one thing to profess faith in the ultimate triumph of peace and humanism by way of global functional accommodation, and another to let the faith rule policy. Statesmen may feel the future in their bones, as Kissinger once observed, but is it necessarily the same future?

Far from resolving the uncertainties of the future, the Helsinki Summit momentarily revived the old debate on the fate of East Central Europe. Alexander Solzhenitsyn's hyperbolic characterization of American acquiescence in the Final Act as "the betrayal of Eastern Europe" and President Gerald Ford's initial snub of the Russian emigre writer served to galvanize politicians and pundits into a belated reappraisal of detente and of the symbolic balance sheet of CSCE. The Final Act itself offered little cause for alarm. The inviolability of frontiers was qualified by the possibility of peaceful change. Affirmations of the right of all peoples to determine their internal political status without outside interference (including specifically the right to neutrality) could hardly be challenged on their intrinsic validity. But a general understanding, not discouraged in official circles, that such professions of good intentions did not alter the Soviet Union's determination to preserve its hegemonic sphere by all means necessary raised doubts in some minds about the wisdom of President Ford's signing such a fraudulent document.[33] The Western view that the CSCE was at best the inoffensive reaffirmation of unexceptionable and unenforceable principles of civilized international intercourse was strengthened by evidence that American acquiescence formed part of the bargain of detente diplomacy, for, as one of Dr. Kissinger's aides put it, "we sold it for the German-Soviet treaty, we sold it for the Berlin agreement, and we sold it again for the opening of the MBFR."[34]

Admittedly, the more independent-minded Eastern European regimes feared that the Helsinki Final Act would in some subtle, symbolic way facilitate even greater Soviet constraints on their freedom of action. The fruitless quest by Romania and Yugoslavia for firmer guarantees against outside intervention and for a permanent body to monitor the implementation of the Final Act sorely tried Moscow's patience. President Ford's visits to Warsaw before, and to

Bucharest and Belgrade after, the Summit were sought-after demonstrations of American interest and presumably also were designed to persuade the American public that Eastern Europe was not, as Charles Gati put it, the "forgotten region." To conclude on a more positive note, the CSCE's hortatory provisions for expanded contacts and functional cooperation hold opportunities for both Eastern Europeans and the West that should be explored and tested before the final verdict on the Final Act.

The preservation of the tangible benefits of detente between the pitfalls of relapse into rigid hostility and passive drift into ideological disarmament is a task of immense complexity. If American statesmen still recognize the reality of a political struggle, be it cold war or hot peace, that their Soviet counterparts have never ceased to profess openly, then they cannot afford to let the managers of closed societies dictate the conditions of engagement. There are many other dim dimensions of American policy that cannot be neglected: the maintenance of strategic and tactical military parity; the coordinated pursuit of Western political stability, economic welfare, and credible collective defense; and the preservation of nonaligned countries such as Finland, Yugoslavia, and Austria. In the context of detente, East Central Europe is less a barometer of Soviet intentions—they seem only too consistent—than a test of American leadership, purpose, and endurance. It would be the supreme historical irony if the West rested the defense of its civilization on nuclear parity and ideological disarmament. Without a revival of political will, peaceful engagement and detente may turn out to have been the hollow victory of hope over experience.

NOTES

1. Robert I. Gannon, *The Cardinal Spellman Story* (New York: Doubleday, 1962), p. 222; George F. Kennan, *Memoirs, 1925-1950* (Boston: Little, Brown and Co., 1967), p. 356; John Foster Dulles, "A Policy of Boldness," *Life*, May 19, 1952, p. 157; interview with James Reston, New York *Times*, October 13, 1974, p. 35.

2. *Department of State Bulletin* 5, August 16, 1941, p. 125.

3. For a more extensive account and analysis of these policies and issues, see Bennett Kovrig, *The Myth of Liberation: East-Central Europe in U.S. Diplomacy and Politics since 1941* (Baltimore: Johns Hopkins Press, 1973).

4. *Department of State Bulletin* 51, October 5, 1964, p. 465.

5. "U.S. Foreign Policy for the 1970's: A New Strategy for Peace," report by President Nixon to Congress, February 18, 1970.

6. *Department of State Bulletin* 68, April 30, 1973, pp. 533-38.

7. Quoted by John Newhouse, "The United States and Western Europe," in Henry Owen, ed., *The Next Phase in Foreign Policy* (Washington, D.C.: Brookings Institution, 1973), p. 41.

8. This argument is elaborated in Alec Nove, "Can We Buy Detente?," New York *Times Magazine*, October 13, 1974, pp. 34, 89-93.

9. Henry A. Kissinger, *American Foreign Policy* (New York: Norton, 1969), p. 76.

10. Nixon, op. cit., quoted in Alan M. Jones, Jr., "Nixon and the World," in Alan M. Jones, Jr., ed., *U.S. Foreign Policy in a Changing World: The Nixon Administration, 1969-1973* (New York: McKay, 1973), p. 22.

11. New York *Times*, July 18, 1974.

12. Marshall D. Shulman, "Toward a Western Philosophy of Coexistence," *Foreign Affairs* 52, no. 1 (October 1973): 46.

13. See Charles Gati, "East Central Europe: Touchstone for Detente," *Journal of International Affairs* 28, no. 2 (1974): 162-63. A conceptual analysis and case studies of modernization can be found in Charles Gati, ed., *The Politics of Modernization in Eastern Europe: Testing the Soviet Model* (New York: Praeger, 1974).

14. *Globe and Mail* (Toronto), November 26, 1974.

15. Paul Neuberg, *The Hero's Children: The Post-War Generation in Eastern Europe* (London: Morrow, 1972), p. 340.

16. See Radio Free Europe, Audience and Public Opinion Research Department, *Radio Freee Europe in the 1970s* (Munich: RFE, 1974).

17. Quoted in Neuburg, op. cit., p. 321.

18. United States Information Service (Ottawa), *Official Text*, September 19, 1974.

19. Ibid.

20. Pierre Hassner, "Europe: Old Conflicts, New Rules,"*Orbis* 17, no. 3 (Fall 1973): 897; also see Hassner's *Europe in the Age of Negotiation*, "The Washington Papers" I, 8 (Beverly Hills and London: Sage Publications, 1973).

21. Times of London Service, *Globe and Mail* (Toronto), July 30, 1975.

22. C. L. Sulzberger, New York *Times*, July 25, 1973.

23. Hassner, "Europe: Old Conflicts, New Rules," p. 911.

24. Secretary of State for External Affairs Allan J. MacEachen, September 6, 1974; External Affairs Canada, *Statements and Speeches*, no. 74/10.

25. See Maurice Latey, "Broadcasting to Eastern Europe," *Survey* 19, no. 3 (1973): 106-09. Alexander Solzhenitsyn's comments on this issue in his Nobel Prize Lecture are noteworthy: "This information blockage between the different parts of our planet is a deadly peril. Modern science is aware that information blockage leads to entropy and total collapse. Information blockage makes a mockery of international agreements and treaties; within the jammed zone it is no problem at all to reinterpret a treaty, and even simpler to suppress it as if it never had been (something that Orwell understood very well); within the jammed zone live not so much earth-dwellers as an expeditionary force from Mars: they haven't a clue about how the rest of the earth lives and are perfextly ready to trample it underfoot in the sacred certainty that they are 'liberating' it." Quoted in Leopold Labecz, "Shadows over Helsinki," *Encounter* 40, no. 6, June 1973, p. 81.

26. See Labedz, op. cit., pp. 82-88.

27. U.S.I.S., op. cit.

28. New York *Times*, July 16, 1973, p. 28.

29. James Keogh, quoted in *Time*, December 16, 1974, p. 58.

30. See Latey, op. cit., pp. 110-12.

31. Interview with James Reston, New York *Times*, October 13, 1974, p. 35.

32. U.S.I.S., op. cit.

33. See, for instance, "Jerry, Don't Go," *Wall Street Journal*, July 25, 1975, p. 14.

34. Helmut Sonnenfeldt, quoted in *Time*, August 4, 1975, p. 22.

8

**OSTPOLITIK
AND EASTERN EUROPE**
Andrew Gyorgy

INTRODUCTION

As Western historians and poltical scientists have viewed the evolution of Ostpolitik since the early 1960s, three main objectives seemed to have emerged as its dominant themes:

1. Ospolitik attempted to improve the international political status and prestige of the Federal Republic of Germany (FRG) and gradually transform its worldwide image along more favorable and acceptable lines, not only vis-a-vis East Central Europe but also toward the uncommitted nations of the Third World.

2. A secondary, but highly relevant, objective was to open slightly the long-closed door to the German Democratic Republic (GDR), and thus exert some moderating influence on the ideological and political character of the other Germany.

3. It clearly has been one of the long-term goals of Ostpolitik to restore and reestablish West German influence in both the northern and southern tiers of East Central Europe, thus obliterating the lasting, adverse (and ever disastrous) legacy of the Nazis' Third Reich period.

This chapter examines these three objectives and measures the achievements of Ostpolitik against the original expectations of successive West German

---

*The author is grateful to Prof. Charles Gati for suggesting an inquiry into the principal objectives of Ostpolitik.

political regimes. Ancillary issues of importance are queries as to how leaders of the FRG, particularly Chancellors Kurt Kiesinger, Willy Brandt, and Helmut Schmidt, envisaged the implementation of their objectives; whether they foresaw the immense difficulties involved; and what their subsequent perceptions were concerning the success or failure of Ostpolitik. Our substantive concern then centers on three perspectives: the historic background of Ostpolitik; current developments in FRG-East Central European relationships; and a view of long-term prospects, placing Ostpolitik into the broader, continent-wide dimension of European peace-and-security considerations.[1]

An interesting and complex historic argument has been raging in recent years concerning the origins and earliest beginnings of the more recent rounds of Ostpolitik. A number of scholars place the date of initiation in 1963, when the end of the Adenauer era of Cold War militancy toward Soviet and Eastern European communism yielded to the more pliable and conciliatory regime of Chancellor Ludwig Erhard. Clearly, the few feeble overtures made by the Erhard government later came to fruition under the auspices of the Kiesinger-Brandt coalition.

Actually, the truly historic aspects of Ostpolitik predate by many decades the currently known and practiced diplomatic efforts of the FRG. Leaving aside the 1933-45 disasters of Hitlerism, one could go back to the revolutionary year of 1848 and to the intellectually exciting, economically oriented, and geopolitically well-conceived theories of Friedrich List and Karl Ritter (not to mention the later works of the political geographer Friedrich Ratzel), which embodied some of the principal motivations and aspirations of Imperial Germany's early Ost policies. The slogans of the last three decades of Germany's nineteenth-century Eastern diplomacy were clear and unambiguous indeed: "Drang nach Osten" and "Berlin to Bagdad" were aggressive geopolitical milestones automatically implying that the "German road to the East" led directly through and over the prostrate and victimized bodies of some of the newly emerging nations of East Central Europe.

For purposes of an up-to-date analysis, we are compelled to ignore the revolutionary 1848 backdrop, the imperial "flexing of muscles" era of Bismarck and William II, the vacillating and insignificant Weimar Republic, and the multidimensional tragedies of the Nazi period. Even World War II and the postwar era of four-power divisions and Cold War antagonisms can be treated peripherally from our perspective. In effect, to understand and appreciate the current and future rounds of Ostpolitik, one ought to move up all the way to 1966, when a major, programmatic address by Chancellor Kiesinger launched the first phase of today's Ostpolitik.

THE KIESINGER-BRANDT "GROSSE KOALITION" PERIOD, 1966-69

On December 1, 1966, Kurt Georg Kiesinger as chancellor, and Willy Brandt as his foreign minister, outlined in detail a reinvogorated East Central European policy for the Bonn government. Ostpolitik had a two-pronged objective in accomplish West Germany's first "peaceful engagement in Eastern Europe since the end of World War II:

First, it aimed at the resumption of formal diplomatic relations with as many Eastern European countries as were willing to exchange ambassadors with Bonn.

Second, it set in motion broadly based, generous economic aid, trade, and loan programs for Eastern European countries, offering in particular hard-currency, long-term, and low-interest credit arrangements for industrialization and for the execution of the various "New Economic Mechanisms" (or Plans) announced by several of these countries in 1966-68.

In the diplomatic realm, Ostpolitik proved to be instantly successful. Romania and the Federal Republic extended diplomatic recognition to each other on February 1, 1967, and Belgrade and Bonn did likewise a year later. If Soviet occupation had not intervened, Czechoslovakia would have been next, with Hungary also following suit. In view of the Czech developments (see Chapter 2), further acts of mutual diplomatic recognition were delayed until 1973.

Economically, there was also substantial accomplishment. Four West German trade missions were established in the countries where most intensive commercial ties materialized. Budapest, Sofia, Bucharest, and Warsaw were chosen as the principal sites of these missions as early as 1963-64; Prague was not included until August 1967. Dozens of "economic counselors" represented West Germany in each major mission, often carrying out ambitious duties extending into the political sphere. Although for two or three years Bonn's diplomatic offensive was deadlocked by the Czech events of 1968 and the economic campaign slowed down, there was a well-attended West German businessmen's conference at Prague in mid-February 1969. Also, even though in terms of official statistics Hungarian-West German trade in 1968 was somewhat below its 1967 total volume, a large Hungarian trade mission was negotiating in 1969-70 at Cologne and Bonn for a two- to five-year resumption and enlargement of West German-Hungarian export-import trade and tourist relations.

This ambitious phase of Ostpolitik was forced to decelerate considerably after August 1968. One of the principal motivating factors in the final Soviet decision to invade Czechoslovakia must have been the fear of West German resurgence. Czechoslovakia and Hungary appeared to be the main losers in this tactical retreat of the West Germans under inexorable pressure from the Soviet

Union. However, the polycentric economic impact of Bonn's aid and trade programs was already obvious; a cleverly and tactfully planned West German Ostpolitik did contribute to the weakening of the Eastern European power position of the Soviet Union and, more specifically, of its economic alliance system. This appears to be the likeliest trend for the second half of the 1970s, too, even if the fear of a resurgent Germany and, more directly, the latent Eastern European suspicions of Ostpolitik, tend to counterbalance the intensity of cooperation with the Federal Republic. Economically, Bonn looms large on the Eastern European horizon; its disruptive effect on CEMA is already a matter of historic record. It is also clear that economic and military matters do not parallel each other; despite the manifold and tangible economic advantages of closer cooperation with Bonn, in the short run the specific fear of the Federal Republic is bound to cement together the northern tier of WTO: The Poles and East Germans in close alliance with the Soviet Union, and the Czechs as silent and benumbed bystanders still under military occupation. However, the promise of fruitful trade cooperation with Bonn, even if combined with an anxiety over the "colossus again" complex, is bound to complicate the Soviet Union's blueprint for future Danubian-Balkan cooperation.

It is important to stress that "nonaligned" Yugoslavia and "semialigned" Romania have been useful and likely partners in the West Germans' peaceful "Drang nach Osten." While there has been renewed political caution on both sides since the invasion of August 1968, three important sets of relationships show positive and vigorous trends for a more, rather than less, bilateral relationship. These are, in order of significance, trade (lively, mutually beneficial, and offsetting CEMA problems), tourism (more obvious on the Dalmation coast than on the Black Sea, but nevertheless amounting to an annual mass invasion by hard-currency-carrying West German tourists), and a cultural rapprochement based on exchanges of scholars, students, and artists.

THE 1968 INVASION OF CZECHOSLOVAKIA AND OSTPOLITIK

To place the military and political occupation of Czechoslovakia in its proper historic perspective, both the salient events of August 1968 and the preceding January-July period must be briefly reviewed. The "Brezhnev Doctrine" invasion occurred during the night of August 20-21, 1968, when the Soviet Union and four other communist armies (those of Poland, East Germany, Hungary, and Bulgaria) suddenly moved into Czechoslovakia. Approximately 500,000 communist troops, largely Soviet, speedily effected a total military occupation of their "fellow socialist" nation. Subsequently all but the Soviet armed forces gradually withdrew. In the mid-1970s, approximately 60,000 Soviet troops were still deployed in the occupied country.

The dramatic events of August signaled the climax of a political, cultural, and social process that had begun in January 1968. Early that month a vigorous, young, and relatively liberal Slovak Communist party functionary, Alexander Dubcek, replaced the aging and unpopular Stalinist first secretary of the Czech Communist party, Antonin Novotny. In March, Novotny also lost the presidency of the Republic, yielding it under great political pressure to a well-liked military figure, Major General Ludvik Svoboda. The new leadership became the nation-wide symbol of liberalization and "internal relaxation," promising primarily the introduction of significant reform measures: the abolition of all press, radio, and television censorship; the encouragement of dissent within the party and government; unrestricted literary freedom for artists, poets, and writers; and free travel to the West for all Czechoslovak citizens.

These projected reforms not only exhilarated Czech public opinion but also accelerated the already obvious trends of anti-Soviet feelings and Czecho-solovak nationalism. Critics of Czech communism openly advocated pro-Western economic and political policies while denouncing the past twenty years of Soviet-imposed terrorism and Stalinist rigidity. In May-June 1968, public state-ments in the country questioned the wisdom of the "guiding role" of the Com-munist party and called for a Western-oriented multiparty system. Simulta-neously several policy moves indicated a growing rapprochement between the coalition government of the GFR and the new Dubcek regime, promising a full resumption of diplomatic relations between the two countries as well as signifi-cant trade, credit, and loan agreements.

July and August 1968 were months of protracted negotiations and dis-cussions between Dubcek and the Soviet leaders, who were increasingly con-cerned that the Czech Communist party was losing internal control and that the country was somehow going to withdraw from the Soviets' vital "sphere of in-fluence" zone in Eastern Europe. Shortly before the precipitate military invasion (between August 10 and 18), friendly warnings were delivered to the Czech leadership by President Tito of Yugoslavia and Nicolae Ceausescu of Romania, while less friendly messages were conveyed through Walter Ulbricht of East Germany and Janos Kadar of Hungary. These warnings obviously were rejected by the Czech party and government elite, which quietly but successfully con-tinued on the road to internal liberalization and a pro-Western realignment of major foreign policies. Following the failure of the Ulbricht ultimatum, the Brezhnev-Kosygin leadership team must have drawn the conclusion that unless a radical military intervention drastically changed the course of Czechoslovak events, this key Eastern European country, with its 14 million people and unique geopolitical position, would be lost to the Soviet Union and its two prin-cipal alliance systems, WTO and CEMA.

The aftermath of the invasion can be summed up in the following major characteristics. Although militarily well planned and, in technical terms, superb-ly executed, the invasion itself must have been a last-minute political decision by the Soviet leadership; it certainly had no political blueprint and only a minimal degree of advance planning. Retroactively, the Soviets anxiously attempted to use WTO as a justification for their military act. As in Hungary in 1956, they stressed that their troops were "invited" by certain local authorities worried about the "counterrevolution." An agreement also was forced on the Czech government in late August 1968, calling for the "temporary" stationing of WTO troops on Czech soil and for a series of political restrictions under the general heading of a "normalization" of the situation. In exchange, the Soviet leaders promised that there would be no direct interference in Czech domestic affairs, a promise that was immediately violated and became the basis of lengthy wrangling between occupier and occupied.

It also is clear in retrospect that the Soviet Union misunderstood the widespread popularity of the Dubcek regime as well as the unusual role that was to be played by the aging military hero, President Svoboda, who stood up with resolute determination against the Soviet leaders—even in the face of the Soviet abduction of several key Czech party and government officials. At Svoboda's insistence, Dubcek and his colleagues were released from their Soviet prison, brought to Moscow for a dramatic confrontation between Czechs and Soviets on August 26, and later conditionally returned to Prague. For at least August 1968-April 1969, the invading WTO forces were not prepared to face the show of striking unity of the Czechoslovak people and their moral determination to resist in the face of truly overwhelming odds. The initial absence of collaborators or quislings in the occupied country was an amazing and novel pattern, unlike the 1956 developments in Hungary, which produced overnight a pro-Soviet government led by Janos Kadar.

The future of the Dubcek-Svoboda regime thus depended on, and was at first determined by, the inability of the Soviets and their fellow invaders to find a "cooperative" government as a replacement for the nationalistic and liberal leadership of Alexander Dubcek. Finally, the replacement of Dubcek by Gustav Husak in late April 1969 created an increasingly collaborationist government that emerged as a relatively long-range solution to the Soviet problem.

The case of Czechoslovakia undoubtedly has restricted the freer aura of previous polycentrism and severely limited the scope and assertiveness of nationalism in Eastern Europe. It has considerably upset the tenuous balance of such opposing elemental forces as the impact of a communist ideology versus indigenous waves of political patriotism. As a prototype of direct intervention by a large power in the domestic affairs of a small nation, it is bound in the long run to impair the attractiveness of Marxism-Leninism and to accentuate the primacy of national considerations for the smaller countries of East Central Europe.

On the whole, the WTO invasion of Czechoslovakia was a disastrous blow to West German efforts at bridge-building. After August 1968 and until early 1974, major economic transactions between Bonn and Prague had been halted; and cultural and tourist-trade connections reached a new low. Simultaneously a great debate was carried on in several Eastern European capitals and in Bonn concerning the relative significance of Ostpolitik in the Soviet decision to invade in 1968. For example, West German diplomats and Hungarian officials in Budapest felt that it was a low-priority concern for the Soviets but served as a convenient excuse. On the other hand, West German and Polish diplomats in Washington were convinced of its crucial importance, feeling that the very success of Willy Brandt's policies alerted the Soviets to dangers threatening their sphere of influence in Eastern Europe. Thus the invasion served to prevent, or at least considerably slow down, the next few and carefully projected rounds of Bonn's Ostpolitik.[2]

THE BRANDT-SCHEEL ERA, 1969-74

The September 28, 1969, federal elections were significant in terms of bringing into power Willy Brandt's Social Democratic party (SPD) in coalition with the Free Democrats (FDP). Brandt served as chancellor in the new coalition, while the foreign minister's post had been assigned to Walter Scheel, parliamentary leader of the FDP. Despite such major political changes, however, West Germany's Ostpolitik was not modified after the elections and seemed to be moving along the lines described earlier. If anything, the change in the chancellorship from Kiesinger to Brandt was likely to improve the image of this newest Ostpolitik in the public opinion of the Eastern European countries.

The Brandt-Scheel government promptly and energetically set out to offset the major slowdown of FRG efforts following the 1968 Czech invasion. The resumption of Ostpolitik late in 1969 asserted itself along four parallel levels in a carefully synchronized chronological sequence: first, negotiations were taken up directly with the Soviet Union, then with Poland, then in multilateral and sensitive discussions on the "Berlin question," and finally with East Germany.

In its direct negotiations with the Soviet Union, the Brandt-Scheel government paid careful attention to the "step-by-step" or "stage-by-stage" aspect of improving relations with the dominant superpower in the East. An important area in Bonn's negotiations with the Soviet Union was related to the general timing of world political events. For example, the election of a new president of the Federal Republic, to be held in West Berlin, was scheduled for March 5, 1969. Reiterating its view that West Berlin was a territorial part of the GDR, the East German government attempted to persuade the Soviet Union to prevent this election from taking place. Ulbricht, however, failed in this endeavor. From a current perspective it appears that the Soviets were not interested in sacrificing their policy of "peaceful coexistence" in Central Europe for the sake of East German tactical gains in the controversial Berlin issue. Rather, they were more interested in three aspects of their foreign policy that could be adversely affected by a breakdown in relations over the embattled city of West Berlin: continuation of the dialogue with West Germany that might lead to West Germany's ratification of the Nuclear Non-Proliferation Treaty; a desire not to further jeopardize the SALT talks, which had been suspended as a result of the Czechoslovak invasion; and a desire to keep their western flank secure, in view of the deterioration in Sino-Soviet relations. The Federal Republic's signature on the Non-Proliferation Treaty in November 1969 signaled to the Soviet Union that it was ready for serious negotiations on a bilateral treaty concerning the renunciation of force. This was a further step that could accelerate the Soviets' much-sought goal of convening CSCE.

Negotiations with the Soviet government picked up momentum in 1970. Apparently the most significant part of these discussions was a thirty-six-hour dialogue between Gromyko and Brandt over an eight-week period in which all problems were raised. The result was the West German-Soviet treaty signed at Moscow in August 1970. This treaty centered on two points: a declaration not to use force against each other and an acknowledgment of the geopolitical realities as they had existed de facto and, it was hoped, would continue to exist for some time to come.

More important than the words themselves, for the West Germans this treaty paved the way for negotiations on the other three levels: with Poland, with East Germany, and on the Berlin issue. Poland apparently was given the green light to begin bilateral negotiations with West Germany when Secretary-General Wladyslaw Gomulka, in a speech on May 17, 1969, invited Bonn to open talks, with a view to improving relations between the two nations. Bonn responded to that invitation with an acceptance note dated November 25, 1969. The December 1969 WTO meetings further confirmed these overtures. At that time the considered judgment of expert observers was that the Poles did not have carte blanche in dealing with the West Germans, but that their negotiations probably would be confined to an attempt to secure recognition of the Oder-Neisse boundary line, to recognize East Germany as part of any agreement, and to obtain long-term German economic credits of up to 2 billion Deutsche marks as a basis for increasing trade with the West.

West German-Polish talks were held in abeyance while negotiations with the Soviet Union were in progress. Initial reports from Poland by Western reporters emphasized the old German-Polish animosities and suspicions. The logical implication was that pressure for negotiations with the West Germans came from Polish technocrats. FRG Foreign Minister Walter Scheel and Polish Foreign Minister Stefan Jedrychowski, who were the primary negotiators, announced bilateral acceptance of a new treaty on November 17, 1970, and signed it on December 7, 1970.

For the FRG the pact maintained the overall momentum of Ostpolitik. For the Poles it meant primarily a recognition of the Oder-Neisse boundary line, confirming in Paragraph 2 of Article I the "inviolability of their existing frontiers, now and in the future," and mutually pledging "to respect unreservedly their territorial integrity"; it also meant later progress toward an all-

European security conference.* For both West Germany and Poland the treaty meant a giant step taken toward a normalization of relations, both diplomatic and commercial. As Bonn and Warsaw announced their agreement, prepatory talks between the FRG and Czechoslovakia were also being publicized.

---

*The full text of this brief but momentous pact between Poland and West Germany is reproduced here from New York *Times,* November 21, 1970, p. 11.

> The Polish People's Republic and the Federal Republic of Germany, CONSIDERING that more than 25 years have passed since the termination of World War II, of which Poland was the first victim and which brought grave sufferings upon the peoples of Europe, MINDFUL that during that time in both countries a new generation has grown up which must be secured a peaceful future, DESIROUS of creating lasting bases for peaceful coexistence and development of normal and good relations between them, AIMING at consolidation of peace and security in Europe, AWARE that the inviolability of the frontiers and respect for the territorial integrity and sovereignty of all states in Europe within their present frontiers are the basic condition of peace, HAVE AGREED AS FOLLOWS:
>
> ARTICLE I. 1. The Polish People's Republic and the Federal Republic of Germany unanimously affirm that the existing border line, the course of which was established in Chapter IX of the decisions of the Potsdam Conference of 2 August 1945 as from the Baltic Sea immediately West of Swinoujscie (Swinemunde) and thence along the Oder River to the confluence of the Lusatian Neisse River and along the Lusatian Neisse to the Czechoslovak frontier constitutes the western state frontier of the Polish People's Republic. 2. They confirm the inviolability of their existing frontiers, now and in the future, and mutually pledge to respect unreservedly their territorial integrity. 3. They declare that they have no territorial claims against one another nor shall they advance such claims in the future.
>
> ARTICLE II. 1. The Polish People's Republic and the Federal Republic of Germany shall be guided in their mutual relations as well as in matters concerning the safeguarding of European and world security by the purposes and principles set out in the Charter of the United Nations.
>
> 2. Accordingly, in conformity with Articles 1 and 2 of the Charter of the United Nations, they shall settle all their disputes exclusively by peaceful means, and in questions of European and international security as well as in their mutual relations they shall refrain from the threat of force or the use of force.
>
> ARTICLE III. 1. The Polish People's Republic and the Federal Republic of Germany shall undertake further steps aimed at full normalization and all-round development of their mutual relations, the lasting basis of which shall be the present treaty. 2. They agree that the expansion of their cooperation in the fields of economic, scientific, scientific-technical, cultural and other relations is in their common interest.
>
> ARTICLE IV. The present treaty does not affect bilateral or multilateral international agreements previously concluded by the parties or concerning them.
>
> ARTICLE V. The present treaty is subject to ratification and shall come into force on the date of exchange of the instruments of ratification, which will take place in Bonn.
>
> In witness whereof the plenipotentiaries of the contracting parties have signed this treaty.
>
> The present treaty was drawn up in Warsaw in two copies, each in the Polish and German languages, both texts being equally authentic.

The third level of negotiations in Ostpolitik was carried out with East Germany. As a result of the Soviet Union's newly emerging concern for detente and Westpolitik orientation, it is clear in retrospect that Soviet diplomats urged the GDR government to engage in talks with the West Germans, while the Federal Republic's aims were to prevent a further deepening of the gulf between the FRG and GDR, to reverse the trend if possible, and to secure guarantees on Berlin. The negotiations with the GDR have proved to be the most critical for the eventual success of Ostpolitik. Brandt accepted Willy Stoph's offer, and the two met at Erfurt in March 1970 to open the first talks between the heads of the two Germanies.

After securing ratification of the nonaggression treaties with the Soviet Union and Poland, Brandt turned his attention to reaching an agreement with the East Germans. Once again it was Egon Bahr, newly named minister for special tasks, who conducted the negotiations. After long and often frustrating talks, the two sides eventually came to terms. During the last week of December 1972 Bahr traveled to East Berlin for the historic signing of the basic treaty between the FRG and the GDR (the treaty had been initialed on November 8, 1972), providing for mutual diplomatic relations between the two states. The treaty opened the way for international acceptance of the GDR. In the forty-three days before the treaty was signed, fifteen new countries, led by Pakistan, accorded recognition to the East German regime, bringing the total number of nations recognizing the GDR at that time to forty-nine.

Actually the basic treaty was a legal compromise: the two Germanies still would not deal with each other as "foreign," and would exchange plenipotentiaries, not ambassadors. Implied in the treaty, at least from the West Germans' point of view, was the acceptance of Brandt's "two states within one nation" concept. Critics warned that the GDR's full participation in world diplomacy would seal the fate of Germany as a divided nation. Brandt insisted that increased cooperation between East and West Germany would serve to hold the two German states together until the ultimate goal of reunification might be realistically accomplished.

Nevertheless, most observers agreed that with the signing of the basic treaty, the East Germans had finally received the recognition that they had so long desired. The basic treaty embodied a trade-off of mutual recognition for practical improvements and increased human contacts. Article VII declared the readiness of both Germanies to "regulate practical and humanitarian questions." Shortly after the signing of the treaty, the GDR began to open its borders to the West. It released more than 3,000 political prisoners, permitted more than 300 children to rejoin their parents in the West, and granted some 2,500 permits to East German women so they could marry their West German sweethearts.

The FRG and the GDR agreed to disagree about the question of "one German nation." This reflected their different perspectives about detente and the meaning of the treaty itself. The West Germans viewed detente as a dynamic ideological development, and the treaty was considered merely one of several dimensions in the transformation process of East-West relations, an expression of existing and evolving political changes. The East Germans, on the other hand, held a static conception of detente; they saw the treaty primarily as a de jure codification of a de facto political and social status quo. For them the treaty represented the underwriting of the final separation of the two Germanies. While moving toward a position of limited cooperation and human contacts, the Socialist Unity Party of Germany (SED) leaders forcefully rejected the West German view that the treaty, if fully implemented, would help to retain the common national bond. Brandt's doctrine of "two states within one German nation" and Honecker's *Abgrenzung* principle* were compatible enough to allow limited cooperation, but contradictory and sharply in conflict about the central issue of the ultimate relationship between the two states and the role they were destined to play in continental European developments. Although the basic treaty was not a clear-cut victory for either side, it at least promised the GDR a speedy recognition by the international community of nations, including admission to the United Nations in September 1973.

The most recent wave of diplomatic moves linked to Ostpolitik was carried out quietly, unobtrusively, and with relatively little fanfare. It was, in a sense, an expected follow-up to prior Ostpolitik agreements. The crucial time frame was compressed into the period June 1973-April 1974. The sequence of bilateral diplomatic treaties and agreements involved Czechoslovakia first, then Hungary, and finally, in the spring of 1974, Bulgaria. These diplomatic steps had been carefully prepared: Ambassador-designates had been waiting in their respective capitals, and agenda details had been anticipated several years earlier. The various economic aspects also had loomed large in this picture since these were the very capitals—Budapest, Prague, and Sofia—in which the FRG's economic missions had been the most active ever since the early and middle 1960s. Thus, as one might expect, economic considerations eventually paved the way for the full-fledged political and diplomatic phases of Ostpolitik.

It would be impossible to discuss here in detail such complex ramifications of Ostpolitik's third and last stage as, for example, Prague's claim of the ab initio rejection of the Munich Agreement of 1938 as the price of any bilateral

---

*The policy of "demarcation," or *Abgrenzung,* was described by its initiator, SED First Secretary Erich Honecker, as one in which the GDR embarked on a course of "separate" national development that would diametrically distinguish it from the national status of the Federal Republic. "Demarcation" thus implies "the SED's formal, and frequently proclaimed, renunciation of an all-German solution to national development." For a useful analysis of this point see John Starrels, "Nationalism in The German Democratic Republic," in *Canadian Review of Studies in Nationalism* 2, no. 1 (Fall 1974): 23-35, esp. 31.

agreement with the FRG. It must be stressed, however, that the general improvement in East-West relations and Chancellor Brandt's relatively successful Prague
visit in 1973 helped to remove the Czechoslovak roadblock from the path of
Ostpolitik. In the astute observation of Robert W. Dean: "Bonn's settlements
with Moscow, Warsaw, and East Berlin, and its declared willingness to establish
normal ties with Hungary and Bulgaria have left Prague as the Warsaw Pact's
odd man out, and have probably generated sufficient pressures to change its
inflexible attitude."[3]

The new West German chancellor, Helmut Schmidt, has been described
as an American-style politician. He earned his nickname "Schmidt-Schnauze"
(Schmidt the Lip) from his reputation as a rough-and-tumble fighter. Schmidt
apportioned his cabinet in almost the same ratio as Brandt: eleven Social Democrats and four Free Democrats. The most significant change in his government
has been the departure of Free Democrat chief Walter Scheel as foreign minister.
Scheel was replaced by another Free Democrat, Hans Dietrich Genscher.
Although Schmidt and Genscher are expected to continue Brandt's Ostpolitik,
it undoubtedly will be pursued with less fervor and ideological exuberance.
Genscher, a refugee from Halle, East Germany in 1952, is less trusting of the
Eastern European regimes than Brandt or Scheel had been. Schmidt has long
been opposed to granting easy credits to the communist regimes of Eastern
Europe. In his first policy speech to the Bundestag, he pledged a firm partnership with the United States, stating: "The security of Western Europe remains
for the foreseeable future dependent on the presence of the United States in
Europe." Schmidt, a vigorous NATO advocate, has already taken a harder
position toward the East than Brandt did. He has focused his attention on Berlin
and the GDR, and less on the other nations of Eastern Europe. Schmidt
promises to lead his party (SPD) in the direction the Christian Democrats have
been "suggesting" for years. In a speech in June 1974 Schmidt forcefully stated:

> By its treaty policy, especially by concluding the Treaty on the Basis
> of Relations [basic treaty] between the Federal Republic of Ger-
> many and the German Democratic Republic, the Social-Liberal
> coalition has opened up a practical road for a policy of attaining
> good-neighborly relations in Germany. Despite all the difficulties
> and setbacks, we shall not slacken in our effort to improve mutual
> relations. We abide by our view that the relations between the
> Federal Republic and the GDR are of a special nature.[4]

ECONOMIC ASPECTS OF OSTPOLITIK AND
THE EUROPEAN ECONOMIC COMMUNITY

The European Economic Community (EEC), a nine-member complex
presenting a case study of exceptional capitalist prosperity and skillful organiza-

tional accomplishment, has exerted a pervasive impact on a majority of the East Central European nations as well as on the uneasy neutrals poised on the EEC periphery, particularly Austria and Finland. With Great Britain's inclusion as a principal member and the demises of Charles de Gaulle and Georges Pompidou, who ruthlessly applied restrictive and discriminatory tactics against all outsiders, the lure of EEC was further intensified for the 135 million people of East Central Europe. The *Grosses Wirtschaftswunder* (great economic miracle) of the West has acted as a magnetic field for the CEMA members of the socialist commonwealth. For such geopolitically suitable countries as Yugoslavia or Czechoslovakia, future (even associate) membership in the EEC would loom as a highly desirable expectation. In that sense Ostpolitik may well be considered an essential and thinly camouflaged bridge between an involuntary Eastern-oriented commercial alliance system, and a wholly voluntary and prosperous Western set of economic treaty arrangements.

As long as the Soviet Union's largely negative attitude toward EEC continues,* the economic aspects of Ostpolitik are bound to suffer from the Soviet Union's "guilt by association" identification of West German policies with Common Market diplomacy. Thus a Soviet-inspired "plague on both your houses!" attitude may well serve as a brake on such economically exuberant and essentially Western-oriented countries as Poland, Czechoslovakia, and Hungary in terms of being equally anti-West German and anti-Western European. Austria has already been pressured against membership in the EEC by the Soviet Union, and the Soviets will also manage to keep Finland out of that organization. Nevertheless, the magic attraction of the "Inner Nine" is bound to generate further divisive forces within East Central Europe, in the direction of generally

---

*It is important to note that since the early 1970s the Soviet leaders' attitude toward EEC has shown a perceptible change. The Soviet Union now grudgingly accepts the economic existence of EEC as a fact of international life, and seems to tolerate, if not to encourage, the increasing scope of commercial activities between its own CEMA and the West's EEC. While the Soviet leadership used to be totally opposed to any form of recognition of EEC (either diplomatic or economic), this hard-line view vis-a-vis Western Europe's "Inner Nine" began to change slowly after Brezhnev's historic Tbilisi, Georgia, speech to the trade unions, delivered on March 20, 1972, and reported in detail in *Pravda* of March 21, 1972, pp. 1-3. The key passage of his remarks—brief but momentous—was contained in the following statement:

The Soviet Union by no means ignores the existing situation in Western Europe, including the existence of an economic grouping of capitalist countries such as the Common Market. We are carefully observing the activity of the Common Market and its evolution. Our relations with the participants in this grouping will, needless to say, depend on the extent to which they recognize the realities obtaining in the socialist part of Europe, particularly the interests of the member-countries of the Council for Mutual Economic Aid. We are for equality in economic relations and against discrimination.

weakening the economic infrastructure of the entire region. Thus the EEC-East Central Europe-Ostpolitik relationship is a tenuous composite of pluses and minuses: the "plus" of an economically hyperactive FRG Ostpolitik is balanced by the "minus" of a Soviet displeasure of the overall Western European economic penetration of East Central Europe. For every policy or move denoting Western acceleration we may well witness a comparable Eastern countermove of economic barrier-building under the seven-nation "Socialist" aegis of CEMA.

THE "GERMAN QUESTION"

The "German question" is inextricably interwoven with the general course and socioeconomic processes of Ostpolitik. Here we can focus on only a few of the more salient aspects of the widely and profoundly differing ideological and policy situations of the two Germanies. The crucial problem of the continuing existence of the two German states must be viewed as the most basic fact influencing the nature of Germany and, in broader terms, of the entire European continent. The chances for unification are minimal in the foreseeable future. The longer the division is maintained, the more rigid will be the lines of separation arbitrarily dividing East from West in Germany.

The growth of East German nationalism has received relatively little scholarly attention because of the usual assumption that the GDR served simply as a Soviet occupation zone. However, since the early 1970s several sociological studies have pointed out that East Germany had been attempting to create its own national image since approximately 1952, when the "two Germanies" doctrine began to officially replace the policy of German unification under communist auspices.

The GDR's nascent nationalism is based on the stabilization of its political, economic, and social life, and on a rapidly accelerating academic and managerial interest in the country's politics and economics. It is characterized, above all, by a firmly antagonistic posture toward Bonn. As the most common expression of East German nationalism, the anti-West German orientation is not a startling development by itself. Its most surprising aspect, however, is the degree of popular identification that

> . . . one finds among citizens of the GDR with their government and with the new society which is emerging. Young people particularly express approval for the German Democratic Republic, and ask accusingly why the West refuses to recognize it. "It is our state, after all," many say, "and by refusing to deal with it you are really hurting us." Identification with Bonn has lost its appeal, for the Berlin Wall makes it abundantly clear where life must be spent.[5]

The Berlin issue is inextricably interwoven with the separate nationalism of the two Germanies and the gloomy perspective of the Eastern Europeans as they view the divided and walled city. Berlin, whether East or West, cannot be separated from the Soviet role in Eastern Europe or from the broader problem of a direct East-West confrontation. The two Berlins are the focal points of several conflicting ideological forces: an East German sense of nascent nationalism; a specifically West Berlin nationalism expressed in both the localized nationalism and the continued support of the Bonn government, which places a great deal of symbolic emphasis on the need to maintain a free West Berlin and is engaged in highly sensitive negotiations both with the Soviet Union and the East German regime concerning a future easing of tensions; and the resolve of Western Europe, NATO, and the United States to stand fast in West Berlin.

On the whole, the "German question" has had a negative impact on Ostpolitik if the purpose of such "eastern policies" is to promote the eventual reunification of the two Germanies. The anti-reunification school has lately acquired important exponents in both the Federal Republic and the United States. This broadly shared East-West perspective can generally be buttressed by three clearly articulated points of view:

1. Many East Central Europeans are firmly convinced that the sudden reunification of 75 million Germans (combining both West and East) would be nothing short of an eventual catastrophe for the rest of Europe. This view is repeatedly expressed by Europeans ranging from northern France to southern Greece, also including (understandably) the Dutch, Danes and Norwegians.

2. After thirty years the profound division of the two Germanies has created two diametrically opposed and separated countries based on totally different ideologies and economic and social developments. Instead of the existence of "two states" in one nation, we see here the contrasting spectacle of two separate nations.

3. The fearful legacy of Hitler's Third Reich cannot be easily forgiven or forgotten. The horrible memories of 1933-45 not only linger on, but pervade Eastern Europe as a historic force exacerbating the lines of division. Anti-German feelings are widespread in Western Europe, but bitter memories of military oppression, Nazi brutality, and genocide are most pronounced in Czechoslovakia, Poland, and, of course, the Soviet Union. While more than thirty years may seem to be a long time, it is not quite long enough to forget or forgive the incredible wartime record of the Third Reich. This fear of Germany and of specific German policies forcefully persists in most of Eastern Europe.

PROSPECTS AND EXPECTATIONS

At the beginning of this chapter we raised three key questions in an a attempt to place the Brandt era of Ostpolitik in its proper perspective. Now it is time to formulate a few tentative answers.

As to the first query, whether Ostpolitik raised the international political status of the Federal Republic of Germany, the reply must be positive. Clearly, the energetic and ambitious sequence of moves and diplomacies designed to create "openings to the East" represented a significant improvement in prestige and goodwill in the post-World War II era of West Germany's evolution. Prior to being caught in a series of domestic crises, Chancellor Brandt accomplished a set of near-miracles in restoring West Germany's tarnished position in the Soviet Union and among the nations of East Central Europe.

As for the second question, involving an opening of the door as well as a moderation of the character of the German Democratic Republic, the answer must rest on a "mixed bag" of variables. Although the basic treaty between the two Germanies seemed to have resolved the most glaring differences and disputes between the antagonists, it left several important loopholes both in the legal-constitutional interpretation of the treaty texts and in the continuing status of West Berlin, still a most unenviable enclave and continually harassed by a very unfriendly GDR monitoring of its access routes. Despite the more than a decade of Ostpolitik, the beleaguered city of West Berlin maintains its highly sensitive Cold War characteristics. It is a constant irritant in the relations of the two Germanies and contributes, on a continuing basis, to ideological and political misunderstandings between the FRG and the GDR.

The third question, the issue of restoring West German influence in Eastern Europe, also must elicit a carefully qualified and balanced answer. On the whole, the recognition and acceptance of the FRG has varied sharply from country to country; and apparently the original expectations of the Brandt regime have been fulfilled in only one dimension, the economic and trade penetration of East Central Europe. In cultural, political, and diplomatic terms, and even more so in the diverse ideological interrelationships, the West German position is not only vulnerable (especially in the "northern tier" countries) but still quite tenuous (in the "southern" and "southeastern" or Balkan tier), as compared and contrasted with the all-pervasive and truly ubiquitous "sphere of influence" or status of the dominant Soviet Union. If Brandt and Scheel ultimately envisaged a drastic transformation and upgrading of West Germany's political influence in East Central Europe, they either misjudged the strength and flexibility of the Soviets' ideological and institutional umbrella as well as the effects of thirty years of Soviet communist control, or they simply did not foresee the difficulties implicit in any restructuring of the overall triangular relationships of West Germany-East Germany-Soviet Union.*

---

*A great deal will depend on the course of relations between East and West Germany. Unless they improve in the near future, and unless Ulbricht's successor, Erich Honecker, ceases to react hysterically to "Eastern" initiatives by Bonn, the Federal Republic will find it increasingly difficult to probe more deeply into Eastern Europe. The

Whatever the vagaries of these complex interconnections, Ostpolitik cannot be dismissed or lightly regarded for the balance of this century. Its impact, and particularly former Chancellor Brandt's unique imprint on its formulation and execution, will be of lasting significance not only for the "socialist commonwealth" nations of East Central Europe but also for the peace and security of Europe.

The recent rounds of Ostpolitik suggest certain successful techniques of operations, on the one hand, and areas of underachievement and minimal accomplishments, on the other. Whenever the FRG's Eastern European political campaign was carried out in a low-key, quiet, underpublicized, and diplomatically well-prepared manner, it managed to overcome, or at least temporarily minimize, even such historic obstacles as the Poles' traditional hatred of Germans and the Soviet people's bitter World War II memories of Nazi cruelty. Thus, at its best, Ostpolitik was able to find a suitable modus vivendi among several strong antagonists who for centuries had been divided by historically irreconcilable forces and motivations.

On the other hand, whenever the designers of Ostpolitik pushed too hard and too fast, their campaign either failed (in an atmosphere of mutual recrimination) or was forced to decelerate considerably. The years 1969-71 formed such a transition of "suspended animation," and it was not until early 1972 that Ostpolitik took off again under the patient prodding of Willy Brandt.

Another salient feature of Ostpolitik has been its highly personalized diplomacy. While Chancellor Kurt Kiesinger, deeply suspected by Eastern Europeans because of his earlier Nazi connections, was a distinctly unpopular manager and orchestrator of "eastern policy," Willy Brandt, for both personal and professional reasons, was effective and richly deserving of the Nobel Peace Prize. At the present time, Chancellor Helmut Schmidt rates a cautious "maybe." During his tenure Ostpolitik had to yield to serious economic problems on the domestic front and, in foreign policy, to preoccupations with the United States, NATO, EEC, and the West. Similar cyclic fluctuations disqualified Gomulka and Ulbricht, or at least sharply limited their effectiveness, while their successors, Gierek and Honecker, have been more successful in the treaty-making and ratifying phases of their own Westpolitik.

In the long run, the implicit message of Ostpolitik is an admirably constructive one. The peoples of East Central Europe clearly are yearning for peace,

---

GDR's protests usually have triggered increased Soviet pressure on the other nation-states of East Central Europe. In such an atmosphere there is little prospect for a viable Ostpolitik. Bonn may not be able to negotiate effectively and directly with Budapest, Prague, or Warsaw in the long run if active displeasure voiced by the GDR leadership may bring about a Moscow veto, or at least a considerable slowdown, of East European diplomatic and political efforts.

security, and stability. In all likelihood, the composite and tragic results of Hitlerism and Stalinism did have an impact on these nations, and one might hope that the old adage first applied to the Bourbon dynasty of France—that it neither learned nor forgot anything from the lessons of past history—will not be applicable in the future of East Central Europe. Even if Ostpolitik cannot be considered a major ideological beacon, it is at least an economic and political milestone for this part of the world. A "revolution of rising expectations" is sweeping through these eight nations, and some are insisting, in an ever-rising crescendo, on giving priority to economic values and considerations rather than suffering a national psychosis that forces them to relive an angry and frustrating political past.

NOTES

1. Of the mushrooming literature on Ostpolitik, particularly as related to the current detente and the "German question," the following items are particularly noteworthy: Willy Brandt, *A Peace Policy for Europe*, (New York: Holt, Rinehart and Winston, 1969), and "Germany's *Westpolitik*," *Foreign Affairs* 50, no. 3 (April 1972): 416-26; Charles Gati, "East Central Europe: Touchstone for Detente," *Journal of International Affairs* 28, no. 2 (1974): 158-74; Walter F. Hahn, "Nuclear Proliferation," *Strategic Review* (Winter 1975): 16-14; Jan S. Prybyla, "Oligopole et reforme economique: Le cas hongrois," *Revue de l'Est* 5, no. 3 (July 1974): 115-31; and the Stanley Foundation, *Conference Report on the 15th Strategy for Peace Conference* (Warrenton, Va.: the Foundation, 1974), esp. pp. 10-19.

2. The following books are among the leading studies of the 1968 events in Czechoslovakia and their international ramifications: E. Czerwinski, and J. Piekalkiewicz, eds. *The Soviet Invasion of Czechoslovakia: Its Effects on Eastern Europe* (New York: Praeger, 1972); G. Golan, *The Czechoslovak Reform Movement* (New York: Cambridge University Press, 1971), and *Reform Rule in Czechoslovakia: The Dubcek Era 1968-9* (New York: Cambridge University Press, 1973); B. Jancar, *Czechoslovakia and the Absolute Monopoly of Power* (New York: Praeger, 1971); V. Kusin, *The Intellectual Origins of the Prague Spring* (New York: Cambridge University Press, 1971); R. Littell, ed., *The Czech Black Book* (New York: Praeger, 1968); I. Switak, *The Czechoslovak Experiment 1968-9* (New York: Columbia University Press, 1971); T. Szulc, *Czechoslovakia Since World War II* (New York: Viking, 1970); O. Ulc, *Politics in Czechoslovakia* (San Francisco: W. H. Freeman, 1974); P. Windsor and A. Roberts, *Czechoslovakia 1968: Reform, Repression and Resistance* (New York: Columbia University Press, 1969); and I. Zartman, ed., *Czechoslovakia: Intervention and Impact*. (New York: New York University Press, 1970).

3. See Robert W. Dean, "Bonn-Prague Relations: the politics of reconciliation," *The World Today* 29 (April 1973): 149-95, esp. 159. Also see Dietrich Moller, "Die Verstandigung zwischen Bonn und Prag," *Aussenpolitik* 24 (1973): 333-46.

4. See Helmut Schmidt, "Government Policy," *Vital Speeches* (July 1, 1974): 548.

5. See Jean Edward Smith, "Limitations of Political Persuasion; the German Democratic Republic and Soviet Policy in Central Europe," a summary of a paper presented to the American Political Science Association, New York, September 10, 1966. Smith also analyzes the East Germans' growing revulsion against Bonn's claim to represent all of Germany and to speak in the name of the citizens of the GDR. A less biased and more

restrained view of East Germany's nationalism is presented by Welles Hangen, "New Perspectives Behind the Wall," *Foreign Affairs* 45, no. 1, (October 1966): 135-47. Also see the comprehensive summary by John Starrels, "Nationalism in the German Democratic Republic," *Canadian Review of Studies in Nationalism* 2, no. 1 (Fall 1974): 23-35.

9

CSCE, MFR,
AND EASTERN EUROPE
Lawrence T. Caldwell

INTRODUCTION

The summit meeting in Helsinki from July 29 to August 1, 1975, brought together thirty-five heads of government from Europe, Canada, and the United States to sign documents that ended nearly three years of negotiations and possibly also marked the conclusion of a definable period in postwar politics. The signing of the 100-page Final Act of the Conference on Security and Cooperation in Europe (CSCE) may also help break the conceptual and procedural logjam that has tied up the Conference on Mutual (and Balanced) Force Reductions—M(B)FR or MFR—in Vienna.*

The fates of these two conferences have been complexly intertwined since late 1969, when the policies that have come loosely to be called "detente" received their contemporary form. Analysis of how these two conferences have affected East Central Europe presents two separate kinds of difficulties. First, the time frame poses substantial problems. We are too close to the conclusion of CSCE to be very confident of our historical judgments, and that qualification is multiplied in the case of MFR, whose story is still unfolding. Second, the conferences have arisen out of, and contribute to, the larger process of detente, through which relationships are changing between the socialist states of Europe and the pluralist-democratic states of Europe and North America.

---

*This chapter uses MFR, although the original NATO designation was mutual and balanced force reductions—M(B)FR. President Nixon dropped the reference to "balanced" in the documents of his 1973 Summit with Leonid Brezhnev, and the official title is "mutual reduction of forces and armaments and associated measures in Central Europe."

The analysis of CSCE and MFR cannot be separated from assessment of detente generally. In this broader sense, then, the process now under way involves a mutual gamble that, if the participants can avoid catastrophe and permit the natural evolution of those historical forces to which they have given impetus, will take generations to assess. By this gamble each side assumes that the peaceful resolution of their competition will be favorable to it.

These broad historical and international questions of time frame and detente aside, there are more specific difficulties with analyzing these two conferences in terms of their effects on East Central Europe.

PROBLEMS OF INTERPRETATION

All great diplomatic events succeed in part by obfuscation. Real conflicts of interest must be adjusted among participating states; and when adjustment is difficult or impossible, conflicts often are relegated to obscure and sometimes directly conflicting language. The document of CSCE is a patchwork of such adjustments, nonadjustments, and downright contradictions. For example, a central conflict between the Soviet Union's consistent efforts to obtain recognition of the "inviolability" of national frontiers and the German Federal Republic's desire for acceptance of the principle that frontiers might be changed by "peaceful" means was accommodated simply by placing both formulas in the final document.[1] Thus a conflict that had nearly precluded any meeting at all, and the presumed "resolution" of which in April and the summer of 1974 had gained West German and Western support for moving toward a final summit, finally was resolved by agreeing not to resolve it at all.[2]

But these international conflicts of interests are not the only ones that have affected CSCE and MFR. Within the major countries, various elements of the bureaucracies have attended to separate considerations under negotiation, and these bureaucratic conflicts have required resolution by internal political processes. Thus, in the Soviet Union different sections of the Communist party Secretariat and the government apparatus had to be brought into the staff preparations for the work of Committee Two (trade) and Committee Three (cultural contacts) of CSCE, and their assessment of and support for the conference as a whole differed.[3] The ministry of foreign trade may well have been enthusiastic in its support of the prospects for the work of Committee Two to facilitate trade and easier access to Western technology.* But the

---

*It is rare that leading Soviet officials will comment directly on matters of detail concerning international negotiations, but a great deal can be inferred from the public pronouncements of trade officials. The speeches of Nikolai Patolichev, Soviet minister of foreign trade, have been consistently supportive of expanded trade and the CSCE's likely contribution to it. For example, *Pravda,* December 27, 1973.

international department of the party Secretariat probably had as its object, at a minimum, containing the work of Committee Three, which it saw as an invitation to ideological subversion by imperialism.* Similarly, some members of the Arms Control and Disarmament Agency and the Pentagon in Washington had differences over the objectives of MFR. Furthermore, at times the executive branch of the American government seemed to use the idea of force reductions as a weapon against the Congress, or at least those elements of it who supported Senator Mike Mansfield's resolutions to reduce the number of American troops in Europe or Senator Sam Nunn's resolutions to restructure the forces there.†

Analysis of the effects of CSCE and MFR on Eastern Europe is affected by one further problem. The impact of any outcome for these conferences has been diminished by subsequent shifts of emphasis in international politics since these negotiations were first linked in the late 1960s.[4] The issues addressed in Helsinki (CSCE) and in Vienna (MFR) have since diminished in significance because Europe has seemed, particularly in comparison with Southeast Asia and the Middle East, a region of relative stability—at least until oil producers increased petroleum prices during the winter of 1973-74.

Just as the geographic focus of the international system has shifted from the arena of these negotiations, so too the general trend toward emphasis on economic considerations—particularly access to raw materials, the press of population on food and other resources, the quality of global environment— has tended to bypass their central thrust. More and more the new focuses of international politics have emphasized the similarity of European states— as consuming nations, as nations dedicated to quantitative indicators of economic growth, as nations of relative prosperity. Thus, this second shift

---

*In contrast, Vladimir Zagladin and Vladimir Shaposhnikov, members of the international department of the Central Committee Secretariat, have been much less enthusiastic; see, for example, "The European Public and Peace in Europe," *Kommunist* no. 16 (August 1972).

†Senator Mike Mansfield introduced "sense of the Senate" resolutions from 1967 to 1970 that had as their purpose reducing American forces in Europe. in 1970 the Nixon administration launched a strong counterattack. See the "debate" between Mansfield and Elliott Richardson, then with the Department of Defense, New York *Times*, December 4, 1970, p. 11; January 24, 1970, p. 8. President Nixon sent a statement to the NATO Council meeting the following December. New York *Times*, December 4, 1970, p. 1. But the biggest drama came in May 1971, after Mansfield had amended the bill to extend the Selective Service System with a demand that the number of American troops in Europe be halved by the end of the year. It failed by a vote of 61-63. Ibid., May 11 and 12, 1972, p. 9; May 20, p. 1. For the Jackson-Nunn amendment to the Defense Authorization Bill for fiscal 1974, see U.S. Congress, *Congressional Record*, September 15, 1973, pp. S17621-22, and Ad Hoc Sub-committee of the Committee on Armed Services, *U.S. Military Commitments to Europe* (Washington, D.C.: U.S. Government Printing Office, 1974).

in the definition of the salient issues of international politics has given both CSCE and MFR a slightly archaic tone. In their concerns for rather narrow definitions of military security and their attention to issues of freedom and ideology, they have a ring of the past.

Thus three sets of difficulties confront any analysis of the impact of CSCE and MFR on East Central Europe. Analysis will be affected by conflicting national and bureaucratic interests. Furthermore, any analysis must be placed in the perspective of generally reduced significance for both conferences due to geographical and definitional shifts in the focus of international politics.

A FRAMEWORK FOR ANALYSIS

The three problems complicate interpretation, but do not render it impossible. Two sets of questions will give form to the analysis.

The Political Dimension: Conservation or Transformation

Evaluation of the effects of CSCE and MFR on Eastern Europe depends on a basic question: Is the objective of the process to which these conferences contribute one of conserving the political status quo or of transforming it? In its essence this first question requires that all participants decide between promoting change or stability in the political order.

Conflict over the answer to this question underlies the debate over detente in the United States, and a parallel debate exists within the Soviet Union. At one level on the American side, the controversy revolves around the judgment of whether to recognize political reality, to accept the Eastern European status quo, which it is not within American capacity to change, or to refuse the extension of any additional legitimization to the status quo even if there is precious little one can do about it. Alexander Solzhenitsyn has been particularly eloquent in condemning participation in any agreements that seem to acknowledge the status quo of Eastern Europe, because he and those who share his views see the practice of communism there as morally corrupt and compromise with it as a morally corrupting act. Furthermore, this argument goes, extension of any legitimization to the status quo undercuts those courageous people who have protested the system's moral corruption, as have the Hungarian freedom fighters and Czechoslovak reformers who attempted to create a more humane political order.[5]

Although the debate has not been nearly as explicit in the Soviet Union, there have been parallel warnings about detente's corrupting socialism by its validation of contacts with imperialism. Especially concern over the issue of "freer movement" led to substantial campaigns among the socialist states to contain the ideological effects of increased movement of ideas and people between the two political and economic systems.[6]

At another level, conflict over the issue of conservation or transformation rests on both sides' assumption that change in the other side is desirable, and the controversy is over appropriate means to bring about change. Secretary of State Henry Kissinger and his supporters in the United States maintain that transformation of communism is better accomplished by its natural evolution, that a relaxation of tensions will undercut the rationales by which "hardliners" justify harsh social repression and economic priority for high military investment.* On the communist side, too, there is disagreement over whether frontal opposition unifies NATO and the imperialists or whether detente creates the conditions favorable to "progressive" political forces in capitalist society.[7] Thus, at this second level, a strategy of recognizing the status quo, of conserving it, seems the best means to accomplish its transformation.

The Security Dimension: Bipolarity or Multipolarity?

A second basic question is in some ways inseparable from the first. Is the geopolitical focus of CSCE and MFR to be bipolar or multipolar? Obviously both, but the emphasis on one conceptualization or the other can have important effects on analysis. Security questions relate primarily to military confrontation between East and West—between NATO and WTO or between the Soviet Union and the United States. In this sense the bipolar framework simply describes reality.

There is also a multipolar dimension to the threat against which nations are attempting to organize a European security system. It has remained implicit in much of CSCE and MFR, but has exerted great influence nonetheless. Yugoslavia and Romania have taken the lead in inserting into the CSCE document language that can be interpreted to preclude such exercises of the "Brezhnev Doctrine" as the invasion of Czechoslovakia in 1968. In fact, much of the Romanian behavior in the conference can be understood to have been particularly concerned with threats to security outside the bipolar context. In this sense, the multipolar conceptualization implies diversity within political-economic-military blocs.

There is still another multipolar feature of CSCE and MFR. Even the most thoroughgoing bipolar assumptions of the Cold War have always sanctioned

---

*Secretary Kissinger's most elaborate discussion of his position came before the Senate Foreign Relations Committee on September 19, 1974.

encouraging diversity in the other bloc. The assumption that threats to security came exclusively from the other side made logical a policy that encouraged multipolarity in it on the parallel assumption that a divided enemy was weaker than a united one.

Thus evaluation of the security accomplishments of CSCE and MFR depends not only on one's perspective regarding the fundamental bipolarity of military power in Europe but also on two kinds of multipolar perspectives—the possibility that threats to security originate from several sources and not only from the bipolar adversary, and the persistent conception that security for one side in the bipolar model of European military power is increased by promoting diversity, or multipolarity, in the other side.

THE IMPACT OF CSCE AND MFR ON EASTERN EUROPE

There has been a persistent bias in Western Europe and the United States that these two conferences were distinguished roughly according to the political content of CSCE and the security content of MFR. In less flattering terms, skeptics in NATO remained convinced to the end that CSCE was largely devoid of substantive content in security terms and that WTO had successfully avoided serious negotiations on European security by detaching the linkage between MFR and CSCE. Although the enthusuasm for the Helsinki Summit seemed a bit manufactured among most NATO delegates, both NATO's acceptance of the detachment of CSCE from MFR in 1972 and its agreement to the Final Act of the former signified the emerging consensus that both conferences were part of a larger process of detente, on which security ultimately depended and the momentum of which had become a kind of shared interest among the major powers. This recognition represented a larger conception of security than had the earlier insistence that CSCE lacked substantive content. Conditions had changed during the progress of diplomacy from 1969 to 1975.

On the surface, Soviet and WTO policy seemed consistently conservationist, protective of a status quo thought in the West to be distinctly favorable to the East, particularly in military terms. In one sense the Helsinki Summit did represent the successful multilateralization of that legitimacy previously achieved for the socialist regimes of Eastern Europe by bilateral diplomacy, and the reported of emotion of Leonid Brezhnev as he signed the document no doubt reflected a genuine sense of achievement. After all, his generation of Soviet leaders had struggled for most of their political lives to secure recognition of the "reality" that had emerged from World War II and remains both a symbol of their own legitimacy and the primary justification for their own exercise of political power. Conversely, American and Western policy seemed thoroughly transformationist. It promoted adjustment in the military balance and advanced a series of items covered under "freer movement" that all had as their aim the alteration of some features in the political regimes in Eastern Europe and the Soviet Union.

But this picture is not entirely satisfactory. The WTO was at least induced to agree to some potentially transforming "confidence-building" measures. The Soviet Union also was consistently transformationist on economic questions in Committee Two of CSCE and endorsed the notion of national subceilings in MFR, possibly as a means of encouraging dissent in NATO as well as a device for putting a lid on West German military forces. Similarly, WTO policy seemed to be cast primarily in a bipolar framework for CSCE and MFR by seeking to limit the mischief these negotiations might cause in Eastern Europe, although Romania and Yugoslavia exercised active diplomacy to gain national security from threats within the socialist bloc.

Both NATO and the WTO have used the conferences to probe for and promote diversity within the other bloc. This multipolar framework has combined with the effort on both sides to rally their own allies behind common positions, and especially NATO seems to have had success in achieving this end.

CSCE

CSCE, then, produced a variety of successes and failures for each participant and group of participants. Whether these successes or failures have any real meaning still provokes controversy, and for this reason four CSCE issues in particular should be carefully examined.

Freer Movement of People and Ideas

The issue that seemed most pregnant with the transformationist and multipolar biases of NATO was the desire to promote "freer movement of people and ideas." This idea originated, officially, at the NATO Council meeting in December 1971. From the beginning it represented an attempt by NATO to get "talking points." As the conference itself became less easy to deny after the agreements on Berlin in late 1971, it seemed important to deflate the obvious initiative for CSCE that rested entirely with WTO and the Soviet Union. Something was needed to mitigate the appearance that the conference was "theirs." Or, at the very least, if the conference could no longer be denied, some price for the incipient Soviet diplomatic success might be exacted. Thus, "freer movement" served both to gain some CSCE initiative for NATO and to reduce the appearance of CSCE's being a solely ritualistic conference. The way the Soviet and Eastern European press reacted to Politburo member Mikhail Suslov's and Leonid Brezhnev's speeches in June 1972 indicated the success of these NATO purposes.[8]

In the end, the Final Act of CSCE included four general categories of specific measures "to facilitate freer movement and contacts": to facilitate reunification of families divided in different participating states; to "examine favorably . . . requests for exit or entry permits from persons who have decided to marry a citizen from another participating state"; to promote travel among the states; and to "facilitate the freer and wider dissemination of information of all kinds."[9] Whether any of the specific provisions will alter actual conditions is difficult to predict. One hopes; but the language does not, and could not, compel. It is replete with hedging terms—"to simplify" procedures, "will examine," "intend to promote," and "express their intention."

One curious result suggested a "victory" of a procedural sort. Brezhnev's speech in December 1972 had set the limit beyond which discussion in the Soviet Union on the "freer movement" question could not go: exchanges of people and ideas could not infringe on the sovereignty of states.[10] This formulation became a ritual in Soviet writing on the subject and provoked sharp disagreement during the early phases of the conference, when the issues were being defined. In fact, in the spring of 1973 it seemed that CSCE might not take place at all because of Soviet insistence that any mention of "freer movement" be closely qualified by a phrase respecting the laws and customs of participating states. With the exception of the paragraph on contacts and meetings among religious faiths, which is qualified by reference to "practicing within the constitutional framework of participating states," the references to freer movememnt are not specifically encumbered by qualifications that they be exercised in conformity with national sovereignty and custom. Rather, the Western preference for leaving any such reference to the opening section of general principles carried the day. But, again, the "victory" will be symbolic unless each participating state has the will to alter conditions unilaterally. The phrases themselves allow wide interpretation and do not bind the signatories to any specific actions.

Still, the document does give citizens in the Soviet Union and Eastern Europe an important quasi-legal text. Especially since the Soviets did assiduously publish the full document, it may prove useful in educating some citizens and in bolstering the struggle of others for legality. We know from the testimony of dissidents and emigres that gaining knowledge of one's rights in the Soviet Union is not easy, and that to know them does have occasional value in the monotonous struggle with lower levels of the bureaucracy, if not in the more dramatic struggle with higher levels of the "competent organs."

Thus, the most promising feature of CSCE in terms of potential for transformation may have only marginal value. Even that, however, depends on incremental changes over time: on the prospect that regimes more secure within their borders and more legitimate in their own exercise of political power might show more tolerance for the conditions of life taken for granted in pluralist societies; on the continued brave demand of their own citizens that such conditions are the minimum they will accept even in a communist system; and on an assumption that the system itself need not be threatened by a more open access to competing ideas.

Romania's Program

Probably the most delicate diplomacy of CSCE was conducted by the Romanian delegation. The key phrases inserted in the document at Romanian insistence merit careful examination. In addition to general references to sovereignty, territorial integrity, and freedom to "choose and develop [each nation's] political, social, economic and cultural system," four other references are of interest:

> They also have the right to belong to or not to belong to international organizations . . . including the right to be or not to be a party to treaties of alliance; they also have the right to neutrality.
>
> No consideration may be invoked to serve to warrant resort to the threat or use of force. . . .
>
> The participating states will likewise refrain from making each other the object of military occupation or other direct or indirect measures of forces. . . .
>
> The participating states will refrain from any intervention, direct or indirect, individual or collective, in the internal or external affairs falling within the domestic jurisdiction of another participating state, regardless of their mutual relations.[11]

The implicit subject was very clearly the "Brezhnev Doctrine," and the Czechoslovakian and Hungarian interventions by WTO. Explicit inclusion of the "right to be or not to be a party to treaties of alliance" was emphasized by the prohibition that "no consideration may be invoked" to merit threat or use of force, obviously a reference to WTO. Intervention is prohibited "regardless of their mutual relations," as is occupation under the guise of fulfilling treaty obligations. These references are as explicit in prohibiting exercise of the "Brezhnev Doctrine" as might reasonably have been expected. Romania not only took the lead in urging these references against the "use of threat" of force, but also pushed for a follow-on mechanism to the conference that would have "teeth."[12] This latter objective of course was designed to provide participants with a mechanism for continued collective influence in Europe, and not simply as a means of policing the agreements.

There was no doubt some satisfaction with the Romanian efforts in terms of Western transformationist and multipolar objectives, but these efforts were simply additional manifestations of independence in foreign policy that Bucharest had demonstrated for over a decade. Romania profited simply from having the conference as a forum from which to articulate its view, and in so doing demonstrated the diversity that exists in Eastern Europe. Whether that demonstration or the language of the text will further encourage polycentric tendencies in Eastern Europe depends on myriad domestic and international political conditions over which the conference could exercise only marginal influence.

Economic Measures

Elaboration of statements about economic and technical cooperation was left to Committee Two, which did not contain the elements of contro-versy found in Committees One and Three. All sides recognized that trade was mutually advantageous, that economic costs and benefits could be denominated more easily than political ones, and that the limits of what a multilateral declaration could do were very real. The most controversial issue, the most-favored-nation treatment, was dispatched by the statement: "The participating states recognize the beneficial effects which can result for the development of trade from the application of most-favored-nation treat-ment."[13] Thus the Soviet Union and its Eastern European partners in CEMA recognized that they culd not get through CSCE what they had not achieved bilaterally. The West, on the other hand, did obtain references to the need for promoting "publications and dissemination of economic and commercial information at regular intervals and as quickly as possible." Furthermore, no doubt there was some benefit just in the process of discussion on this issue, for it emphasized the limits that secrecy of information had placed, and continued to place, on trade. Thus, both the process and the document probably served limited transformation purposes, but in this case both sides were agreed that progressive transformation was the goal; incremental expansion of trade within the clear limits of their "different levels of economic development" constituted the desired end.

Confidence-Building Measures

The most difficult issues for CSCE, from the viewpoint of its contribution to transformation of the European security environment (as understood in narrower, more strictly military terms), were the proposals generally grouped under confidence-building measures, or CBM's, as they came to be called. The British had taken the lead in pushing for these; and as NATO's enthusiasm increased, its insistence hardened. It was one of the real achievements of CSCE, from the point of view of NATO, that its solidarity on this issue held, despite only lukewarm and intermittent American support. CBM's served a political purpose, countering WTO's interest in encouraging NATO diversity. On this issue the sides seemed to operate mostly in a bipolar framework, WTO and NATO. Notification of troop movement also was important as a sanction against the kinds of intervention exercised in Czechoslovakia and Hungary, and its inclusion in the final document reinforced the Romanian efforts to prohibit the use or threat of force within alliances. Thus CBM's worked both to transform the status quo in real terms and to promote modest diversity or multipolarity.

CBM's threatened to stall the conference during its last months. Two issues seemed most difficult: the size of troop movement to be included and the geographical zone within which notification would be required. On the former issue differences were substantial late in the negotiations. The West had proposed notification of all movements as large as a division (or 12,000 men), and the Soviets preferred notification only of movements the size of a corps (60,000 men). WTO, moreover, proposed notification of movements within 100 kilometers of a participating state's border and NATO preferred 700 kilometers.[14] Real progress was achieved only after Secretary of State Kissinger and Foreign Minister Andrei Gromyko met in Geneva on May 19 and May 20.[15] The result was compromise: notification of movements "exceeding a total of 25,000 troops," within 250 kilometers of "its frontier facing or sharing with any other European participating state," will be required "twenty-one days or more in advance of the start of the maneuver, or in the case of a manuever arranged at shorter notice at the earliest possible opportunity prior to its starting date."[16] Especially this latter provision dilutes the idea unacceptably for critics, and, added to Western acquiescence on the Soviet and WTO demand that the whole section "rest upon a voluntary basis," this qualification to the twenty-one-day-notice principle hardly provides even verbal assurance against surprise military action. However, it can be argued that no state could depend on such an agreement to increase its security from surprise in any case, and that reliable notification had always depended on "national-technical" means of information.

Thus, the language of the CSCE declaration might be thought in this case, too, to have provided a precedent for future cooperation and to have achieved greater sensitivity to the destabilizing effect of "military activities which could give rise to apprehension, particularly in a situation where the participating states lack clear and timely information." The process, once again, contributed marginally, perhaps, to transformation. The document cannot be thought to have done so.

The CSCE, then, drew many elements of conservation and transformation through the vortex of negotiations. Its efforts on military questions, largely CBM's, were cast in the bipolar framework and its effects were largely related to process, not substance. If NATO's objectives in CBM's are seen as transformationist, these went largely unmet except as the negotiations established the mutually agreed need to reduce uncertainty and ambiguity with respect to troop movement. The hedges written into the document clearly constituted a successful "stonewalling" effort by WTO, a dramatic example of conservationist policy. But expecting dramatic alteration of the security regime from

CSCE always faced two kinds of difficulty: the unrealistic notion that diplomatic agreements can produce reliable security guarantees where interests conflict fundamentally and where shared interests are both difficult to define and obscured by long traditions of hostility, and the mutual expectation that MFR would be the primary focus of any real alteration in the security environment. In the case of the former difficulty, process was the maximum that might be achieved. In the latter, the returns are not yet in. Some successes were scored in freer movement for the transformation perspective, but on the whole each side successfully resisted change where it defined its interests to require conservation. In CSCE neither side surrendered anything important, but neither achieved very great changes.

The process of the talks had its own merit—for the assertion of Romanian foreign policy independence, for the development of NATO cooperation on CBM and "freer movement," for the multilateralization of recognition of the European status quo from the Soviet and Eastern European viewpoints. These achievements ultimately depend for their success on their contribution to the broader process of detente.

MFR

CSCE and MFR have been linked since 1968. In 1973, when the prepatory talks for CSCE got under way before those for MFR, some observers warned that the linkage had been, or was in danger of being, broken. The Nixon administration, over skepticism of some of its foreign allies, asserted that was not the case. In 1975, and after the Helsinki Summit, the Ford administration, and even the president himself in his Helsinki address, was careful to assure that the linkage still exists.[17] Even Brezhnev was sufficiently attuned to the political significance of linkage to pick up the same theme in his speech at Helsinki.[18] The notion that MFR and CSCE were linked had importance precisely because the former was thought by substantial numbers of influential observers to constitute the forum in which the real transformation of Europe's military environment would be addressed.

MFR reveals two general strategies that must be evaluated if we are to understand the prospect for altering the European security environment. First, the strategy to lower forces on both sides equally, or nearly equally, rests on the assumption that something like a satisfactory overall balance of power exists in Europe. If a reasonable balance is thought to exist at present, the tolerances for change probably are substantial; and the security environment might be improved through reductions and other measures, or, at the minimum, the present environment might be maintained at a lower cost in terms of resources. Although this strategy has constituted the basis of Soviet and WTO policy, it also has formed the basis of proposals from some members of the arms control community in the West. Second, the strategy to create a balance assumes that WTO forces are meaningfully superior to NATO ones and that the objective is to obtain disproportionate reductions that might redress this imbalance.[19]

The question of whether change will result from the MFR process, then, depends on the reconciliation of these two separate perspectives—those of "lowering the forces" (MFR) and of "creating a balance" (MBFR). These separate perspectives derive from different assumptions about the current balance of forces in Europe. They also form the basis of different negotiating strategies and perceptions of the bargaining process.

The initial proposals of Vienna reflected the conflicting "lowering the forces" and "creating a balance" perspectives. The WTO countries went to great lengths to argue that even NATO recognized that a rough balance exists in Europe.[20] There is considerable logic to their position, for the contrary assumption would ask that one side surrender its perceived interests while the other side achieves by negotiations a situation it could not attain previously by any other method.

It seems unlikely that NATO will achieve its substantive ends. MFR is not an appropriate forum to create a balance; the goal of promoting that kind of transformation is unrealistic. NATO strategy has been ill-conceived from the beginning. It has not sufficiently engaged real Soviet and WTO security interests to induce the concessions it has sought.

Symbolic First Stage

The Soviet Union has shown considerable interest in a symbolic first step reduction. Leonid Brezhnev first floated this idea in his impromptu news conference with French newsmen near Minsk as early as January 1973.[21] The call for an initial reduction of 20,000 in the November 1973 proposal and in the modification a year later demonstrates considerable persistence for this idea.[22] The proposals are clearly conservationist. They do not seek radical transformation of the military status quo. There are, however, two Soviet motives for some agreement on MFR. First, Brezhnev and the Soviets have an interest in maintaining the momentum of detente as long as the costs are acceptable. Frequent reference to extending detente from the political and economic spheres to the military attest to this motive. Second, a symbolic and equal reduction would help "to clear the air," to record acceptance of the Soviets' preferred "lowering the forces" framework. There is also some logic to the Soviet contention that larger reductions could come slowly and in an ascending scale (5 percent in 1976 and 10 percent in 1977) after good intent is established by means of a symbolic reduction.

However one views the wisdom of proceeding in this manner, one cannot argue that symbolic reductions on the order of one division will alter the security environment of Europe. Nor, for that matter, do the kinds of reductions envisioned in the overall reduction of 17 percent proposed by the WTO constitute such an alteration, even if one ignores the suspicion on each side that the other has increased its forces by something on that order of magnitude since the talks began to be taken seriously in 1972.

National Subceilings

The Soviet effort to design specific ceilings for individual national components of NATO has been directed at the West German armed forces. Such an idea has great promise from the Soviet point of view. It would, of course, prohibit compensating adjustments within NATO for reductions in American or British troops, and would make the composition of NATO forces a matter of multilateral discussion between East and West. On the whole this objective probably reflects the general Soviet motive in the detente process of getting some leverage in the dynamic political development of Western Europe. It both promotes stability in NATO military capabilities and encourages multipolarity within NATO.

These advantages might cut the other way in the long run. It would make Polish, Czech, and East German forces a matter of discussion with NATO, but those questions are decidedly less important to European security than the role and size of the West German forces. In any case, the desire to avoid subceilings is a bogus one. Any reductions will have to specify numbers for component national forces, and substantial future increases in West German forces would be inconsistent with the whole process. What NATO must avoid is negotiations over future composition of its forces, if it wants to pursue a conservationist political strategy.

Composition of Forces

The West has rather glibly assumed that exclusion of air and naval forces and of nuclear capabilities was in its interests. There have been rumors for some time that NATO might sweeten the pot in Vienna by throwing in some "other forces," such as tactical nuclear weapons or some elements of air power. But there is no evidence that these have yet been introduced, however much sense they might make, to induce greater WTO attention to the concerns of NATO about numerical disproportion.

The exclusion of air forces and tactical nuclear weapons always rested on the assumption that the focus of MFR should be to redress NATO inferirority in combat divisions and armor. As such, the limitation sought to transform the military balance. The very notion of pot-sweeteners suggests that the original exclusion probably was never taken seriously as a basis of agreement. And the slowness with which they have been introduced no doubt reflects in part the low priority the Nixon and Ford administrations hve given to Vienna, but also reflects Western European reluctance to see American air forces thinned out in Europe.

To get force reductions, NATO will have to include forces that WTO has an interest in reducing. To obtain transformation of the security environment in any way favorable to it, NATO must promise transformation in ways desirable to the Soviet Union and WTO.

Common Ceilings

This NATO idea has a certain plausibility, but probably is nonnegotiable. It would transform the military environment of Europe more radically than any other thus far advanced. The Soviet arguments against disproportionate reductions apply, naturally, to the goal of achieving a common ceiling of 700,000 men in the region. They point to "historic" reasons for current imbalances—their perceived need to cut the path of invasion—and argue that the present arrangement of forces must conform to national determination of security interests.[23] They also claim that their forces offset other geographical disadvantages such as the American bases circling the Soviet Union and the numerical disadvantage for WTO forces in Southern Europe. But the notion of common ceilings as a goal has a certain logic, and probably is a good issue for holding the feet of WTO negotiators to the fire. It may induce compromise.

The fact is, of course, that the numerical superiority of WTO forces in East Central Europe has been constructed in accord with Soviet military strategy. An overpowering conventional capability poised at the heart of NATO for many years held Paris and Bonn hostage, as a deterrent to American strategic superiority. Should that superiority erode, the conventional threat would take on more the function of tactical choice—to concentrate forces rather than spread them. For the West, however, the spread has been, as WTO spokesmen allege, a matter of NATO's choice. And to expect to redress a posture of choice by inducing the adversary to forfeit advantage derived from his posture of choice may be to expect too much.

THE TWO HALVES OF EUROPE

The fundamental divergence in the two sets of proposals still reflects the conflicting perspectives— NATO's hope "to create a balance" and WTO's desire to "lower the forces." To attempt evaluation of the prospects for transforming or conserving the security environment in Europe by reference to NATO and WTO proposals leads full-circle to the assumptions with which the evaluator started about the nature of the current balance of forces. Whether MFR has the potential to alter the security environment depends, finally, on one's judgment about the relationship of forces-in-being and their purposes.

The notion that the Soviets have real advantages in the present distribution of military forces in Europe supports the assessment of Soviet purpose that suggests that advantages were deliberately created. It is not difficult to make Soviet behavior in MFR look as if it has been designed to conserve advantage, if one is thought to exist. To look at the force balance in that manner will lead once again to assumptions about purpose. It may be that this circle of reasoning is correct: the Soviets and WTO members, having created military advantages, have advanced proposals in MFR that will preserve them or, it is hoped, even improve them. Such zero-sum reasoning, however, should be questioned on two bases: it is tinged with self-serving judgments for NATO and thus requires skepticism by the party thus served, and it reduces the issues to near nonnegotiability, thereby not serving the interests of NATO if reductions are desired, or especially if they are inevitable on the NATO side.

NATO's concern over asymmetries has received publicity, but WTO has concerns about asymmetries as well. The issue is not only, as often seems to be assumed, one of numerical inequality, but rather of reciprocal problems and of force structures that are not identical. NATO, for example, focuses attention on WTO's numerical superiority in Northern and East Central Europe; on the coherence, and therefore the interchangeability, of WTO's logistic and weapons systems; on interior lines of communication and the relative ease and speed of land transportation. and on unitary command structures. But from Moscow's point of view most of these features of European defense carry reciprocal problems. For example, land-based reinforcements and interior lines may be easier to interdict than sea-based ones spread across far greater area. The WTO's numerical superiority in East Central Europe is offset somewhat by inferiority in Southern Europe, and a unitary weapons system may represent disadvantages in research and development even if it offers battlefield advantages.

But Moscow has deeper concerns about asymmetry. It faces the psychological as well as military disadvantage of encirclement, dervied from American strategy of forward deployment.[24] In every sense the targets it must cover are spread across greater area. It also faces the more familiar problem of qualitative imbalances. For example, although its aircraft and tanks are more numerous than those of NATO, those of the latter are more modern and have wider combat radii and greater firepower. In most categories of combat support, NATO technology is more advanced, although it may be that WTO forces have achieved wider deployment of available technology. Even the noncoherence of the NATO front—spread from Norway to Turkey, and including the Baltic, English Channel, and Mediterranean interruptions—might provide advantages in some kinds of scenarios and probably increases tactical options, as Winston Churchill was fond of demonstrating during World War II.

The general question of asymmetries, then, is not as one-sided as it sometimes may appear.

Thus, MFR has posed a classic confrontation between NATO's transformation strategy and WTO's strategy of conservation. NATO proposals to achieve a "common ceiling" and limit forces under negotiation to ground troops and armor have as their purpose the creation of a new balance or the transformation of the European security environment. WTO resistance to those ideas reveals conservationist objectives, ones that the notion of a symbolic first stage reduction is designed to underline.

But this evaluation must be modified by two countervailing pieces of evidence. First, NATO has dominated the definition of what forces would be under negotiation, and a different definition of the composition of those forces might elicit Soviet and WTO interest in transforming the present military environment. Second, WTO has used its proposals for national subceilings to bind NATO against compensating for American reductions in forces by increasing German forces. This notion is clearly designed to cause difficulty in NATO—promote multipolarity—and thereby to transform Europe's present political-military arrangements.

Seen in these terms, NATO's CSCE and MFR strategies seem designed primarily to transform the political and military arrangements that define Europe's security environment. Soviet and WTO strategy in the two conferences, on the other hand, seem designed more to conserve the status quo. These distinctions are not without important exceptions. Each side has attempted to encourage change, to promote diversity or multipolarity in the other, and to limit discord in its own alliance in a manner consistent with interbloc practices for two decades. Old habits die slowly, and the fundamental change in the interbloc diplomacy of CSCE and MFR would appear to be wider tacit acceptance of the limits to which transformationist and multipolar strategies might be taken. This mutual restraint may represent the real accomplishment of detente and measure how well we have learned the lesson that policies of confrontation have failed.

NOTES

1. *Conference on Security and Cooperation in Europe: Final Act*, section "Declaration on Principles Guiding Relations between Participating States," pp. 4, 6. All citations in this chapter are to an unclassified English text used by the American government. Lengthy excerpts are also found in the New York *Times*, July 30, 1975, p. 8.

2. See, for example, David Binder, New York *Times*, April 20, 1974; and Craig Whitney, ibid., September 16, 1974, p. 4.

3. The best descriptions of the mechanical working of the preparatory sessions of CSCE known to this author are in U.S. Congress, Committee on Foreign Affairs,

After the War: European Security and the Middle East (Washington, D.C.: U.S. Government Printing Office, 1973), pp. 21-28; Gotz von Groll, "The Foreign Ministers in Helsinki," *Aussen Politik* 24 (Fall 1973): 255-74; and M. Lvov, *New Times* no. 32 (August 9, 1974): 4-6.

4. For a discussion of the early linkages between these two conferences, see Lawrence T. Caldwell, "Conspiracy, Bargaining, Transformation: Three Views of Soviet Intentions in Europe," *Worldview* (November 1974): 44-48.

5. The most dramatic expression of this view came in an article Solzhenitsyn published in *Le Monde*, May 31, 1975; and in a speech before the AFL-CIO in Washington, "We Beg You to Interfere," Washington *Post*, July 6, 1975, "Outlook" section.

6. The key documents in this campaign were a speech by M. A. Suslov, reported in *Pravda*, June 21, 1972, p. 1, and Zagladin and Shaposhnikov, op. cit. There have been persistent signs that some elements in the Soviet leadership have greater reservations about this aspect of CSCE than others. See, for example, S. K. Tsvigun, *Taynyy front* (Secret Front) (Moscow: Politizdat, 1973); and I. Davydovskaya, "Anticommunism Without a Mask," *Selskaya zhizn*, February 6, 1975, p. 3. These themes have also been echoed in the Eastern European press. See, for example, Jaroslav Brabec, *Smena* (Bratislava) January 21, 1975, p. 2 (Foreign Broadcast Information Service—cited henceforth as—*FBIS*—East Europe, January 27, 1975, p. A1); and Marian Dobrosielski, *Trybuna ludu*, (Warsaw), December 5, 1974, p. 7 (*FBIS*, December 9, 1974, pp. A1-A3.)

7. This theme was developed with exceptional candor by Nikolai Lebedev during the spring of 1975 in "On the Class Nature of Peaceful Coexistence," *Kommunist* no.. 4 (March 1975): 52-62; and "Inspiring Results," *Pravda*, April 8, 1975, p. 4.

8. Suslov, op. cit.; the Brezhnev reiteration of this theme came in a speech during a reception for Fidel Castro, *Pravda*, June 28, 1972, p. 1.

9. *Final Act*, section "Cooperation in Humanitarian and Other Fields," pp.. 61-71; New York *Times*, July 30, 1975, p. 8.

10. *Pravda*, December 22, 1972. The writer is grateful to Stephen Miller of the Fletcher School of Law and Diplomacy, who developed this interpretation while a student at Occidental College.

11. *Final Act*, section "Declaration of Principles Guiding Relations Between Participating States," respectively Principles I, II, IV, and VI, pp. 4, 5, 6, and 8 of typewritten English text.

12. See, for example, D. Tinu, *Scinteia*, January 22, 1975 (summarized in *FBIS*, East Europe, January 23, 1975, pp. A1-A-3), and an Agerpres release on February 19, 1975 (ibid., February 20, 1975, p. A1). Flora Lewis' dispatch from Geneva in New York *Times*, June 30, 1975, p. 6, is revealing on the issue of a follow-on mechanism.

13. *Final Act*, section "Cooperation in the Field of Economics of Science and Technology and of the Environment," subsection "Commercial Exchanges," p. 25 of typewritten English text.

14. See Bernard P. Nossiter, Washington *Post*, February 20, 1975, p. 1; and Reuters dispatch of May 29, ibid., May 30, 1975, p. 19.

15. See Leslie Gelb's report from Bonn, New York *Times*, May 20, 1975, pp. 1,5; Michael Parks, "Kremlin Assured by U.S.," Baltimore *Sun*, May 26, 1975, p. 1; Secretary of State Kissinger's news conference of May 24, 1975, *Department of State Bulletin* 72, no. 1877 (June 16, 1975): 805.

16. *Final Act*, section "Document on Confidence Building Measures and Certain Aspects of Security and Disarmament," subsection I, pp. 18-19 of typewritten English text.

17. Washington *Post*, August 2, 1975, p. A9.

18. New York *Times*, August 1, 1975, p. 2.

19. See John Yochelson, "MBFR: The Search for an American Approach," *Orbis* 17, no. 1 (Spring 1973): 155-75, for a thoughtful analysis of how force reductions

might be accomplished. For conceptual discussion, Christoph Bertram, *Mutual Force Reduction in Europe: The Political Aspect,* Adelphi Paper no. 84 (London: International Institute of Strategic Studies, 1972), remains the best. For authoratative arguments from a Western perspective that the balance does not favor WTO as heavily as usually assumed, the best sources are Alain C. Enthoven and K. Wayne Smith, *How Much is Enough?* (New York: Harper and Row, 1971), pp. 117-42; Timothy W. Stanley in John Newhouse, ed., *U.S. Troops in Europe* (Washington, D.C.: Brookings Institution, 1971); Alain C. Enthoven, "U.S. Forces in Europe: How Many? Doing What?," *Foreign Affairs* 53, no. 3 (April 1975): 513-32.

20. The best summary of the proposals is found in Leslie Gelb, New York *Times,* February 8, 1974, p. 3. Also see the disappointingly unspecific report of the Ad Hoc Subcommittee: U.S. Congress, Committee on Armed Services, *U.S. Military Commitments to Europe* (Washington, D.C.: U.S. Government Printing Office, 1974), esp. pp. 20-21. By far the most explicit commentary from a Soviet source was Yuriy Kostko, "Military Confrontation and the European Security Problem," *Mirovaya ekonomika i mezhdunarodnye otnosheniya* (hereafter MEMO) no. 9 (September, 1972): Once the proposals were tabled in October 1973, the Soviet and WTO press contained many articles attacking the NATO proposal on precisely these grounds. See I. Melnikov, "Vienna–A New Initiative," *Pravda,* November 15, 1974, p. 4.

21. New York *Times,* January 12, 1973, p. 3.

22. For the content of the Soviet proposal put forward on October 31, 1974, see the interview with Oleg N. Khlestov, chief of the Soviet delegation in Vienna, *Izvestia,* December 14, 1974, p. 3; and Bernard Marguerite's analysis in *Le Figaro,* November 11, 1974, p. 1. Also see an article by the East German delegate to MFR, Inage Oeser, "On the State of the Vienna Talks . . .," "*Horizon* no. 47 (1974): 20-21 (in *FBIS,* East Europe, November 19, 1974, pp. A1-A6).

23. See V. M. Komlev, "Making a Common Cause of Military Detente in Europe," *Times* (London), December 19, 1974, p. 14, and his "Realism Is the Key to the Success of the Vienna Talks," *S. SH. A., ekonomika, politika, ideologia* no. 3 (March 1975): 58-61. These arguments were widely used by Soviet experts during this author's visit to Moscow in December 1972, and during a visit by V. M. Kulish and Yu. Kostko to southern California on April 25, 1973.

24. That the United States should reexamine its forward strategy was argued authoritatively in his defense posture statement by former Secretary of Defense James Schlesinger, *Annual Defense Department Report, FY 1976 and FY 1977* (Washington, D.C.: U.S. Government Printing Office, 1975).

10

**EAST-WEST TRADE AND
THE LIMITS OF
WESTERN INFLUENCE**
Roger E. Kanet

INTRODUCTION

In the 1960s it became fashionable in Western analyses of political and economic developments within Soviet-dominated Eastern Europe to focus on those aspects that pointed to expanded opportunities for the Eastern Europeans to exercise decision-making autonomy. The most abhorrent aspects of the Stalinist model of military and political coercion had been abolished in the mid-1950s, and a measure of "liberalization" had already occurred in most of Eastern Europe. It was noted, for example, that some of the early demands that eventually triggered the Hungarian Revolution of 1956 were implemented by Janos Kadar's government within five or six years after the Soviet suppression of the revolution. In addition, Albania had broken completely with the Soviet Union, and Romania was already showing a substantial degree of independence from the Soviet Union in both its domestic and, especially, its foreign policy. "Polycentrism" and "socialist commonwealth of nations" were terms that had replaced the earlier "monolith" and "satellite" in most Western analysis. From the perspective of many Western students of Eastern European affairs, the discussions concerning economic reform (see Chapter 4)—and some of the partial applications of reform—as well as the expanded contacts with the West that seemed to be in the offing were additional indications of both increased Eastern European "liberalization" and "independence" from the Soviet Union.

In the United States analysts such as Zbigniew Brzezinski advocated a new American foreign policy based, at least in part, on "weaning away" the countries

The author wishes to express his appreciation to Ms. Donna Bahry and Mr. William Robinson for their assistance in tracking down data for this chapter.

of Eastern Europe from their continued dependence on the Soviets.[1] The
first, pre-1968, version of the new Ostpolitik of the Federal Republic of
Germany was also oriented toward the expansion of West German relations
with individual Eastern European countries, at least in part at the expense of
the Soviet Union.[2]

In sum, the smaller communist countries that lie between the western
borders of the Soviet Union and Western Europe were viewed as likely targets
of a Western policy of "bridge-building." It was assumed that most of these
countries were increasingly interested in lessening their dependence upon the
Soviet Union and in expanding their contacts—especially in the economic
realm—with the countries of the West. In addition, developments during the
prior decade had resulted in decreasing Soviet control over both the domestic
and the foreign policies of the countries of the area—at a minimum, the
parameters for independent action by the Eastern Europeans seemed to have
widened.

Events since the mid-1960s—especially since the Soviet suppression of
the "liberalization" movement in Czechoslovakia in 1968—have tended to
refute many of the assumptions that buttressed this rather optimistic Western
interpretation of the evolution of Eastern Europe. One of the most important
of these assumptions held that increased Western trade and cultural contacts
would lead to more independence for the Eastern Europeans.

In this chapter I wish to deal with several important and interrelated
developments that are relevant for an understanding both of the position of
Eastern Europe in East-West relations since the early 1950s and the likely
future development of the area. A crucial element of the discussion will focus
on the continuing, even expanding, dependence of the smaller communist
states on the Soviet Union particularly for supplies of raw materials that are
necessary for the economic growth of the area. This economic dependence and
the recent developments in East-West economic contacts that have emphasized
expanded Western contacts primarily with the Soviet Union do not augur well
for the evolution of capabilities in Eastern Europe that would support the type
of movement away from the Soviet Union that was discussed in much of the
Western literature of the mid-1960s. A second important aspect of this study
will be a treatment of both the positive and the negative results of expanded
trade with the West for the Eastern European economies.

EAST-WEST TRADE AND THE ORIGINS
OF DETENTE

In the years immediately following the Cuban missile crisis of October
1962, a new spirit of detente characterized relations between the United States
and the Soviet Union. Both sides appeared to recognize that direct confrontation

of the sort that had occurred in Cuba was far too dangerous to be risked again. Complementing this marginal improvement in American-Soviet relations, however, were the stirrings in relations among some of the European countries. The Soviet Union initiated a campaign aimed, at least in part, against its image as a major military threat to the security of Western Europe. This new approach to Western Europe—at least to some of the countries of the area—found ready response in France, where President Charles de Gaulle had already embarked on the path of reestablishing French grandeur and independence from the United States. Soviet interests in weakening the role of the United States in Europe— and ultimately in the dismantling of the Western alliance system—coincided in part with de Gaulle's policy of independence. De Gaulle envisioned the creation of a united Europe of "fatherlands" from the Atlantic to the Urals. Such a vision was based on two major assumptions: that the ideological and economic differences dividing Europe were soluble, and that the role of the United States in European affairs could—and should—be substantially reduced. By 1964 de Gaulle had begun to initiate the policy by expanding both political and economic contacts between France and the communist countries of the East, including both the Soviet Union and its smaller allies-dependents.[3] From 1960 to 1970 French exports to Eastern Europe almost tripled and imports increased by approximately 230 percent, although trade with Eastern Europe still represented a very small percentage of total French trade.

TABLE 10.1

French Trade with European Members of CEMA, plus Yugoslavia, 1960-73 (million francs)

	Imports	Percent of Total	Exports	Percent of Total
1960	673	2.2	911	2.7
1965	1,402	2.7	1,596	3.2
1970	1,558	1.5	2,503	2.5
1973	3,261	2.0	4,244	2.7

Source: United Nations, *Yearbook of International Trade Statistics* (New York: United Nations, 1961); United Nations *Yearbook of International Trade Statistics* (New York: United Nations, 1966); *United Nations Statistical Yearbook* (New York: United Nations, 1971); *United Nations Statistical Yearbook* (New York: United Nations, 1974).

By 1966, with the creation of the grand coalition of Social Democrats (SPD) and Christian Democrats in West Germany, new developments occurred in the Federal Republic's Ostpolitik. (See Chapter 8.) Willy Brandt and the SPD advocated a normalization of relations with the countries of the East—with the major focus to be placed on Romania, Hungary, and Czechoslovakia. The reaction in Eastern Europe was mixed. Although Romania welcomed this new opportunity to expand its political and economic contacts with the West, and established full diplomatic relations with the Federal Republic of Germany in January 1967, East Germany and Poland, supported by the Soviet Union, condemned the "revanchist" nature of the new "Drang nach Osten" and effectively prevented the success of West Germany's policy in Hungary and Czechoslovakia.

Throughout the mid-1960s and until the Soviet intervention in Czechoslovakia in 1968, relations between Eastern and Western Europe—especially on the economic plane—expanded significantly. Several factors influenced this new flurry of activity. First, and probably most important, was the new political environment that characterized relations between the two superpowers. Despite the expansion of American involvement in Vietnam after 1965 and the ensuing increase in Soviet condemnations, Soviet-American relations did not deteriorate to the level characteristic of the 1950s or early 1960s. Also, the Soviets had initiated something of a peace offensive toward Western Europe, with the exception of the Federal Republic of Germany. Since Soviet control over the policies of the Eastern European countries had been loosened significantly during the prior decade, individual Eastern European countries began to take advantage of their new "freedom of action" to expand contacts with Western countries.

In addition to the general improvement in East-West relations, the economic crisis in which a number of socialist countries found themselves contributed to the growth of trade. By the early 1960s most of the members of CEMA were suffering from declining rates of economic growth. The remedies recommended by the economists included both some form of economic decentralization and expansion of trade with the industrialized West in order to update the technological base of industrial production. The early and mid-1960s witnessed a significant expansion of trade with the West for most of the socialist countries—a trade based increasingly on credits extended by the Western trading partners.

However, by the mid-1960s voices in Eastern Europe were warning of the potential economic damage for the East that might result from the successful economic integration of the economies of Western Europe. For by then the common tarriff barriers of the EEC were already largely constructed—barriers that impeded the growth of the Eastern European exports that were so necessary to cover the costs of increasing imports. The EEC already represented both an attraction and a challenge to the members of CEMA. On the one hand, the success of EEC integration and the impact that expanded trade had had on the rapid growth of the economies in the years immediately following the Treaty of Rome (1957) were obvious. Related to this was the increasing gap in the technological levels of the economies of Western and Eastern Europe taken as

TABLE 10.2

Growth of Eastern European Trade with EEC Members, 1960-68 (million U.S. dollars)

	1960		1965		1968	
	Exports	Imports	Exports	Imports	Exports	Imports
Bulgaria	44	69	113	161	155	216
Czechoslovakia	179	198	271	272	353	398
GDR	136	138	372	385	513	452
Hungary	117	165	212	246	249	278
Poland	254	253	379	320	480	564
Romania	93	112	194	272	312	526
Total	823	935	1,541	1,656	2,062	2,434

Note: Members are Belgium, Denmark, France, West Germany, Ireland, Italy, Luxembourg, Netherlands, and United Kingdon.

Source: United Nations, Yearbook of International Trade Statistics (New York: United Nations, 1961, 1966, 1969).

groups. However, the exclusive nature of the EEC threatened to restrict Eastern European exports at the very time that the socialist countries saw an increasing need for Western industrial goods to bolster their own economies.

By the end of 1967, therefore, East-West contacts had already undergone a substantial degree of change from the situation that had characterized the 1950s and early 1960s. Political, and especially economic, contacts across the postwar political barriers had expanded significantly. In both Eastern and Western Europe there were those who advocated a policy of normalization of relations. However, the events of 1968 that led to the Czechoslovak invasion halted the developments, at least in the short run. By the late summer of 1968, West Germany's new Ostpolitik lay in shambles. The student riots in the spring of 1968 in Paris and the Soviet invasion of Czechoslovakia in August resulted in a serious reconsideration in France both of relations with the East and the future French role in NATO.

EAST-WEST RELATIONS IN THE 1970S

During the period of rapid liberalization in Czechoslovakia in 1968, there were many in the West who expressed the hope that developments there presaged a new era in Eastern Europe that would be characterized by both a liberalization in internal politics and a reduction of hostility and tension in relations between East and West—not to speak of the possibility of increased Eastern European independence.

TABLE 10.3

Growth of West German Trade with Eastern Europe, 1969-74
(million U.S. dollars)

	1969		1970		1971		1972		1973		1974	
	Exports	Imports	Exports	Imports	Exports	Imports	Exports	Imports	Exports	Imports	Exports	Imports
Soviet Union	406	345	422	342	459	367	720	435	1,184	762	1,856	1,272
Bulgaria	63	53	66	65	74	65	98	76	158	106	297	91
Czechoslovakia	211	177	289	189	370	246	385	272	568	378	691	402
East Germany	465	366	515	450	514	510	678	570	850	666	1,101	860
Hungary	91	104	143	134	203	150	265	207	398	318	686	352
Poland	157	137	180	203	221	223	455	310	1,106	464	1,402	555
Romania	187	119	197	159	194	215	300	252	445	327	714	375

Note: The devaluations of the American dollar exaggerate the increase of West German trade with Eastern Europe after 1971. However, even allowing for this bias of the statistics, the increase in total trade, especially of West German exports, is significant.

Sources: All figures except those for trade with East Germany are based on trade statistics of West Germany, and are from International Monetary Fund, *Direction of Trade* (November 1974): 120. Figures for trade with East Germany are from United Nations, *Yearbook of International Trade Statistics,* for 1969-72, and from *Statistisches Taschenbuch der Deutschen Demokratischen Republik, 1975,* for 1973, 1974.

Although the Czechoslovak invasion did result in a flurry of Western activity—particularly discussions about the need to refurbish NATO—it did not have a major lasting effect on Soviet and Eastern European relations with either the United States or Western Europe. In March 1969, at the Budapest meeting of WTO members, the call for an all-European conference on security and peaceful cooperation was repeated. In January of that year France had signed a new trade agreement with the Soviets that called for the doubling of Soviet-French trade within five years, and several months later American-Soviet discussions on various topics were resumed. It was only in their relations with foreign communist parties that the Soviets found the negative results of Czechoslovakia more lasting.

Within a year after Czechoslovakia, therefore, the movement toward expanded East-West contacts was resumed—this time with far more elan and with more tangible results. As already noted, even before 1968 several of the communist states were interested in expanding East-West contacts, especially on the economic level. Romania and Hungary (in addition to pre-invasion Czechoslovakia) had evidenced significant interest in the normalization of relations with West Germany. However, East Germany and Poland had both viewed this increased contact with serious concern, for they saw in it West German efforts to undermine their position in Eastern Europe. For both of them the question of West German refusal to guarantee the territorial status quo of postwar Europe was paramount, and both Wladyslaw Gomulka and Walter Ulbricht had played a major part in condemning the role of West German "revanchism" in the developments in Czechoslovakia in 1968. However, in an unexpected move in May 1969, Gomulka mentioned the possibilities for bilateral talks with West Germany, aimed at the latter's formal recognition of the Oder-Neisse boundary of Poland.[4] Representatives of East Germany viewed the new, more flexible Polish policy toward West Germany with concern, for it presented the possibility of Poland's dealing directly with the West Germans, without necessarily demanding the latter's formal recognition of the de jure existence of East Germany.[5]

In the ensuing two years, after the election of Willy Brandt and formation of the SPD-FDP coalition in West Germany in 1969, a rapid expansion occurred in political contacts between West Germany and its three major Eastern European adversaries—the Soviet Union, East Germany, and Poland. These contacts resulted in a series of treaties that in effect recognized the postwar status quo in Eastern Europe, including both the boundary changes and the existence of a separate German state in East Germany. The agreements eliminated the major obstacle to further expansion of West German economic and political contacts with all of the socialist states. In addition, they removed a major barrier to overall improvements in East-West relations, for they also gave formal Western approval to the political-economic-military position of the Soviet Union in Eastern Europe. In effect, the way in which the negotiations between the West

TABLE 10.4

Average Annual Rates of Growth of National Income, 1960-74
(at constant prices; percent)

	1960-65	1965-70	1960-70	1971	1972	1973	1974
Bulgaria	7.0	8.6	8.2	7.0	7.0	9.7	7.5
Czechoslovakia	1.2	6.9	4.2	5.1	5.9	5.2	5.5
East Germany	3.5	5.2	4.5	4.5	5.8	5.5	6.3
Hungary	4.5	6.8	5.4	6.5	5.1	6.5	7.0
Poland	6.0	6.0	6.2	8.1	10.1	10.0	10.0
Romania	8.9	7.8	8.8	13.0	10.0	10.8	12.5

Sources: Thad P. Alton, "Economic Growth and Resource Allocation in Eastern Europe," in U.S. Congress, Joint Economic Committee, *Reorientation and Commercial Relations of the Economies of Eastern Europe* (Washington, D.C.: U.S. Government Printing Office, 1974), p. 275, table 15, for 1960-72; Alexander Predescu, "New Developments in East-West Economic Relations," *Intereconomics* no. 8 (1975): 251, for 1973-74.

Germans and the three Eastern European states were conducted—by way of Moscow first—gave tacit approval to Soviet claims, as expressed in the "Brezhnev Doctrine," that the Soviet Union has ultimate authority to determine major political developments in the area. Only after having resolved some of the basic differences with the Soviets, primarily on Soviet terms, did West Germany turn to the solution of problems with Poland and East Germany—again largely on terms established by the Eastern European countries.

EEC. CEMA, AND THE GROWTH OF
EAST-WEST TRADE

Among the major concerns of most of the countries of Eastern Europe since the mid-1960s have been the continuing problems that have plagued their economies. Even though the levels of economic growth remained good during this period, by 1970 they leveled off at about 4.5 percent of GNP per capita.[6] Given the fact that EEC growth has been about 4 percent per year and that a significant differential in total economic production in the two regions persists, most of the eastern European regimes are concerned about the necessity of stimulating more rapid economic expansion. More serious, however, is the continuing and persistent technological gap that divides most of the communist economies from those of Western Europe.

Past economic growth in most of Eastern Europe occurred in large part on the basis of the traditional Soviet model of extensive investment policies. Economic recovery and expansion in the first two decades after the war was in most countries, therefore, largely the result of increases in the size of the industrial work force, a high percentage of reinvestment in expanding the economic plant, and a ready supply of raw materials, primarily from the Soviet Union, at prices, after the mid-1950s, that were beneficial to Eastern Europe.* However, since the mid-1960s several developments have occurred that make the growth strategy of the past far less feasible in most of Eastern Europe.

First, as already noted, Eastern European economists have noted the long-term debilitating effects of an economic growth model based primarily on extensive development. Most important has been the failure of the Eastern European economies to become competitive technologically with the economies

---

*According to Western and socialist calculations, concluded before the CEMA price changes of early 1975, raw materials prices in CEMA trade tended to run slightly higher than world market prices, and prices of industrial goods averaged more than one-third higher than world market prices. Since trade between the Soviet Union and Eastern Europe has consisted largely of Soviet raw materials exports in return for Eastern European industrial

of the West. This has become a major factor stimulating Eastern European interest in expanded East-West trade.

A second change that obviously will affect the future growth potential of Eastern Europe (in fact, it has already had an important impact on some of the countries) is the dearth of a surplus population that can be attracted into the industrial sector of the economy. In East Germany, Bohemia and Moravia, and parts of Bulgaria, Poland, and Hungary, most of the surplus rural population has already been absorbed into industry. In addition, since a very large percentage of the female population is employed, there is little likelihood that substantial numbers of additional workers can be brought into the economy from among them. Finally, lower population growth rates over the past decades do not portend well for the future increase of the labor force in Eastern Europe.[7] Both of these recent developments—the decreasing positive results of extensive investments and the general lack of surplus population that can be brought into the industrial sector—have pushed the Eastern European leaders toward an expanded trade with the West composed primarily of Eastern European imports of the products of sophisticated Western technology, as well as of the technology itself.

The third major foundation of economic growth in Eastern Europe since the mid-1950s has been the availability of raw materials from the Soviet Union at costs relatively advantageous to the Eastern European trading partners. However, the situation has shifted drastically during the past few years. By the mid-1960s Soviet economists were pointing to the disproportionately large cost of expanding the production of raw materials as compared with expanding industrial production. A result was the requirement that Eastern European countries invest larger sums in the development of Soviet raw materials production if they were to receive increased deliveries of those raw materials. As Table 10.6 shows, imports of certain crucial raw materials make up an important part of the needs of most Eastern European countries. In addition, imports are increasing far more rapidly than domestic production in several countries (and imports of iron ore and petroleum in virtually all countries). Given the fact that Eastern Europe as a whole is not blessed with large supplies of natural resources (with several exceptions, including Polish coal and Romanian petroleum), expanding industrial growth requires increased imports of raw materials. The combination of worldwide inflation since the early 1970s and the expansion of Soviet exports

---

goods, the latter nations tended to benefit from what, in effect, was a subsidy on raw materials. See Paul Marer, *Postwar Price and Price Patterns in Socialist Foreign Trade* (Bloomington: Indiana University, International Development Center, 1972); J. M. P. van Brabant, *Essays on Planning, Trade, and Integration in Eastern Europe* (Rotterdam: University of Rotterdam Press, 1974), pp. 141 ff.; and Sandor Ausch, *Theory and Practice of CMEA Cooperation* (Budapest: Akademiai Kiado, 1972), pp. 84 ff.

TABLE 10.5

Sectoral Breakdown of the Labor Force in Eastern Europe, 1961 and 1971
(percent of total labor force)

	Agricultural	Nonagricultural	Industrial
1961			
Bulgaria	54.1	45.9	21.8
Czechoslovakia	24.6	75.4	37.6
East Germany	18.1	83.9	40.7
Hungary	35.1	64.9	30.0
Poland	46.2	53.8	23.0
Romania	64.1	35.9	16.7
1971			
Bulgaria	34.8	65.2	30.0
Czechoslovakia	18.8	81.2	38.2
East Germany	12.3	87.7	42.0
Hungary	23.9	76.1	38.3
Poland	36.7	63.3	28.3
Romania	49.7	51.3	24.2

Source: Paul Marer, "Population and Labor Force in Eastern Europe, 1950-1996," in U.S. Congress, Joint Economic Committee, *Reorientation and Commercial Relations of the Economies of Eastern Europe* (Washington, D.C.: U.S. Government Printing Office, 1974), pp. 436-37.

of raw materials to the industrial West has placed the Eastern Europeans in a weaker bargaining position vis-a-vis the Soviets than they had been.* Not only do they find that the prices of the raw materials (and industrial goods) they purchase on the world market have increased significantly, but they are also faced with the substantial increases in the prices that they must pay for raw materials imported from other CEMA countries, primarily the Soviet Union.

As already noted, one of the major assumptions of past Western literature has been that increased East-West contacts are likely to result in increased opportunities for Eastern European countries to become less dependent on the

---

*Planned increases in Soviet trade with the West are to be based largely on the extension of credits to the Soviets that will be repaid primarily by the export of Soviet petroleum and other raw materials. Approximately $9 billion in credits were extended to the Soviet Union by five major Western industrial countries (France, United Kingdon, West Germany, Japan, and Italy) in late 1974 and early 1975. See Dev Mararka, "U.S.-Soviet Detente Starving?," *Christian Science Monitor*, February 25, 1975, p. 1.

TABLE 10.6

Ratio of Imports to Domestic Production
for Selected Raw Materials, 1969-73
(imports/domestic production, based on physical volume)

	1969	1970	1971	1972	1973
Hard coal					
Bulgaria[a]	.085	n.a.	n.a.	n.a.	n.a.
Czechoslovakia	.325	.326	.382	.422	.425
Hungary	—	.478	.485	.452	n.a.
Poland	—	.008	.009	.008	.007
Romania	.030	n.a.	n.a.	n.a.	n.a.
Coke					
Bulgaria	—	.556	.325	.332	n.a.
Czechoslovakia	n.a.	n.a.	n.a.	n.a.	n.a.
East Germany	—	.498	.536	.557	n.a.
Hungary[b]	—	.305	.407	.408	n.a.
Poland	—	virtually all produced domestically			
Romania	2.232	n.a.	2.41	2.547	n.a.
Crude oil					
Bulgaria	14.791	17.054	24.74	33.383	n.a.
Czechoslovakia		virtually all imported			
East Germany		virtually all imported			
Hungary		2.245	2.502	3.068	n.a.
Poland		16.53	19.98	27.96	28.41
Romania		virtually all domestic		n.a.	n.a.
Iron ore					
Bulgaria	.379	.470	.397	.455	n.a.
Czechoslovakia	6.83		n.a.	n.a.	n.a.
East Germany	—	3.530	4.908	n.a.	n.a.
Hungary	—	4.959	4.607	5.073	n.a.
Poland	—	4.637	5.982	7.577	9.673
Romania	1.800	n.a.	n.a.	n.a.	n.a.

Note: n.a. = not available.
[a]Excluding anthracite.
[b]Coal briquettes.

Sources: Bulgaria, *Statisticheski godishnik, 1970*, pp. 120, 342-43; *1973*, pp. 121, 352-53; Czechoslovakia, *Statisticka rocenka CSSR 1970*, pp. 248-51; 419-20; *1974*, pp. 267, 418, 435; Hungary, *Statistical Yearbook 1972*, pp. 119-20, 285; East Germany, *Statistisches Jahrbuch 1972*, pp. 128-29, 325; *1974*, pp, 125-26, 303-04; Poland, *Rucznik statystystyczny 1973*, pp. 174, 322-23, 414; *Statistical Yearbook of Poland 1974*, pp. 96, 195; Romania, *Statistical Pocket Book of the Socialist Republic of Romania 1970*, pp. 104-05, 359-60; *Anuarul statistic al Republicu Socialiste Romania 1974*, pp. 87, 332.

TABLE 10.7

Crude Oil Imports by Eastern European Countries and Percent of
Oil Imports From Soviet Union, 1972-75
(million tons and percent of oil imported from Soviet Union)

	Soviet Union	Others	Percent
1972			
Bulgaria	6.37	1.91	77
Czechoslovakia	11.91	.66	95
Hungary	5.50	–	–
Poland	9.70		–
Romania	nil	2.87	–
1973			
Bulgaria	7.44	–	–
Czechoslovakia	13.05	1,13	92
Hungary	5.76	.78	88
Poland	11.10		–
Romania	nil	4.14	–
1974 (estimated)			
Bulgaria	9.50	1.00	90
Czechoslovakia	14.00	1.50	90
Hungary	5.70	.78	88
Poland	12.5 - 13		–
Romania	–	–	–
1975 (estimated)			
Bulgaria	–	–	–
Czechoslovakia	15.50	2.50	86
Hungary	6.00	.80	88
Poland	13.5 - 14		–
Romania	–	–	–

Notes: Polish figures include all imports of crude oil.

Source: J. L. Kerr, "East European Imports of Crude Oil," Radio Free Europe
Research *RAD Background Report* 12 (Eastern Europe) (January 31, 1975).

Soviet Union. A related argument has focused on the presumed economic
benefits that Eastern Europe is to gain from the expansion of East-West
economic ties. However, this latter argument has tended to downplay the negative implications for Eastern Europe of the substantial increase in world market
prices, the growing balance-of-payments problems of most of the socialist
countries, and the economic problems resulting from these developments. If
anything, these new problems force the Eastern Europeans to turn more to

TABLE 10.8

CEMA Members' Balances of Payments with the Industrial West, 1960-71
(million U.S. dollars; figures are cumulative)

Country	1960	1965	1970	1971
Bulgaria	−100.3	−274.9	−696.5	−787.3
Czechoslovakia	−41.7	−335.8	−798.8	−1021.2
East Germany	−186.0	−512.3	−1014.0	−1237.3
Hungary	−120.8	−401.6	−622.4	−927.9
Poland	−472.4	−966.1	−1160.5	−1157.7
Romania	−	−338.3	−1475.5	−1809.1
Total	−1020.5	−2829.0	−4857.7	−6940.5

Note: These figures include all OECD countries except Greece, Portugal, Spain, and Turkey, plus Australia and New Zealand. However, the greatest part of CEMA trade is with the countries of Western Europe. In addition, most of the balance-of-payments deficit stems from imbalances in the exchange of goods and services.

Source: Edwin M. Snell, "Eastern Europe's Trade and Payments with the Industrial West," U.S. Congress, Joint Economic Committee, *Reorientation and Commercial Relations of the Economies of Eastern Europe* (Washington, D.C.: U.S. Government Printing Office, 1974), pp. 682-724.

TABLE 10.9

CEMA's Balance-of-Trade Deficit with the Industrial West
(billion U.S. dollars)

	1970	1971	1972	1973
CEMA imports	7.6	8.3	10.8	16.4
CEMA exports	6.7	7.4	8.7	12.9
Trade deficit	−1.1	−.9	−2.1	−3.5
Cumulative deficit in trade with West (from 1960)	−5.4	−6.3	−8.5	−11.0*

Note: Figures include all CEMA members' trade with all Western industrial countries.

*Listed as −13.6 in the weekly report of the Deutsches Institut fur Wirtschaftsforschung.

Source: Deutsches Institut fur Wirtschaftsforschung, *DIW—Weekly Report* 40, no. 46 (1973): 418; 42, no. 4 (1975): 27.

TABLE 10.10

Trade Between the EEC and CEMA, 1969-72
(million U.S. dollars)

	1969	1970	1971	1972	1973	1974
Total EEC exports to	111,973	128,287	146,797	174,647	212,664	296,078
Soviet Union	1,565	1,647	1,607	1,985	2,679	3,978
Bulgaria	179	239	247	264	338	585
Czechoslovakia	479	601	704	785	926	1,201
East Germany	673	772	822	1,081	1,216	1,611
Hungary	322	452	569	672	774	1,274
Poland	713	756	900	1,317	2,037	2,928
Romania	542	554	611	799	926	1,314
Total to Eastern Europe	4,473	5,021	5,460	6,903	8,896	12,891
Percent to Eastern Europe	3.7	3.9	3.7	4.0	4.2	4.4
Total EEC Imports from	118,076	134,735	149,661	176,578	215,832	277,275
Soviet Union	1,936	2,095	2,187	2,458	2,846	4,254
Bulgaria	243	258	255	290	268	270
Czechoslovakia	478	531	605	729	833	941
East Germany	646	729	822	959	1,046	1,398
Hungary	348	395	434	607	789	886
Poland	707	855	962	1,205	1,383	1,757
Romania	413	491	542	683	809	986
Total from Eastern Europe	4,771	5,354	5,807	6,931	7,974	10,492
Percent from Eastern Europe	4.0	4.0	3.9	3.9	3.7	3.8

Notes: Devaluations of the U.S. dollar since 1971 exaggerate the increases in the growth of trade. Figures for 1969-72 exclude Ireland for all categories and countries; those for 1973-74 include Ireland.

Sources: International Monetary Fund, *Direction of Trade Annual*, 1969-73. Statistics for East Germany-West Germany trade are from United Nations, *Yearbook of International Trade Statistics*, for 1969-72; *Statistisches Taschenbuch der DDR*, for 1973-74.

TABLE 10.11

Percent of Trade with the EEC for CEMA Members, 1965-73
(percent; trade with EEC/total trade)

	1965		1970		1973	
	Exports	Imports	Exports	Imports	Exports	Imports
Bulgaria	9.6	13.7	9.6	10.6	8.9	10.8
Czechoslovakia	10.1	10.2	13.1	14.6	14.0	13.6
East Germany	12.1	13.7	15.6	16.8	15.4*	19.5*
Hungary	14.0	16.2	18.1	18.0	15.9*	18.6*
Poland	17.0	13.7	17.7	16.8	18.8*	21.5*
Romania	17.6	25.3	23.2	27.2	24.6*	27.8*
Soviet Union	10.2	7.4	10.5	12.1	13.4	12.8

*Figures are for 1972.

Source: United Nations, *Yearbook of International Trade Statistics*, 1965, 1970, 1973.

the Soviet Union, and they provide the foundation for increased economic dependence on the Soviet Union rather than the predicted autonomy.

The Eastern Europeans have discovered that their heavy reliance on imports and the phenomenal growth in trade with the West (imports increased almost threefold in 1969-74 and exports more than doubled) have made them prey to world market inflationary pressures. For example, according to a Polish source, inflationary pressures on imports resulted in losses for the Polish economy of approximately $875 million in 1973 and $1 billion in 1974.[8] However, even before the recent increases in prices of raw materials, the countries of Eastern Europe were faced with substantial and growing deficits in their balance of payments with the West. By 1971 the cumulative balance of payments deficit of the six Eastern European members of CEMA in their transactions with the industrialized West totaled almost $7 billion. (See Table 10.8.) Since the early 1970s the trade deficit has continued to grow, and the total reached $11 billion by the end of 1973 (see Table 10.9) for all CEMA countries including the Soviet Union.[9]

This significant increase in balance-of-trade and balance-of-payments problems is the result not only of inflation in Western markets, but also of the growth of Eastern European imports that is not matched by a comparable increase in exports. An important part of the problem rests with the inability of CEMA members to "break into" Western markets. This results from the inferior quality of many Eastern European products, poor marketing techniques, problems with spare parts and servicing, and the continued existence of some Western barriers against imports from Eastern Europe. The major focus of

CEMA countries during CSCE was on the expansion of East-West trade, and in particular, the elimination of all barriers against the increase of Eastern European exports to the West.

In summary, although the significant expansion in East-West trade has definitely provided the Eastern European countries with needed capital goods and up-to-date technology, it clearly has brought with it serious problems, including vulnerability to worldwide inflationary pressures and increased indebtedness to the West. In addition, the expansion of East-West economic contacts has had an indirect impact on the economic rleationships that exist among the socialist countries themselves, particularly on the prices of raw materials in intra-CEMA trade.

SOVIET-EASTERN EUROPEAN TRADE AND RECENT PRICE CHANGES

Economic growth in Eastern Europe since the mid-1950s has occurred in large part on the basis of large-scale imports of raw materials from the Soviet Union. Ever since the mid-1960s the Soviets have complained that prices paid for raw materials in intra-CEMA trade discriminated against the countries that exported primarily raw materials—for instance, the Soviet Union. This resulted in a virtual Soviet subsidy for Eastern European economic growth, it was argued.[10] In addition, Soviet writers noted that it was increasingly unprofitable for the Soviet Union to provide fuels and mineral resources to meet expanding Eastern European demands. This situation was exacerbated by growing costs to the Soviet Union of developing its reserves, which are primarily in Siberia, and by the relatively low quality of the finished goods that the Soviet Union . received from its CEMA partners in return for raw materials.*

In order to reduce their costs, the Soviets called for direct Eastern European investments in the capital-intensive extraction of fuels and minerals and for a more efficient use of raw materials. Although direct investment in the Soviet economy is not a new phenomenon, its growth since the early 1970s is significant and represents a major burden on the Eastern European economies.[11] More recently, changes in the world market prices of raw materials have provided the impetus to renegotiate intra-CEMA prices, with major increases going to raw materials and fuels. For example, in January 1975 the Soviets raised the

---

*Domestic costs of exploiting Soviet raw material reserves reflect not only a high capital-output ratio, but also relatively high costs for the development of an infrastructure in remote areas of the east and for transporting products to the western border. See I. Dudinsky, "Toplivno-syr'evaia problema stran SEV i puti el resheniia," *Voprosy ekonomiki* no. 4 (1966): 84-93.

price of oil exported to Eastern Europe from 16 to 37 rubles per ton. Overall raw materials prices, including those for oil, seem to have increased approximately 50 percent in intra-CEMA trade, with prices for industrial products increasing substantially less—in the range of 15-30 percent for various categories.[12] The overall impact of the changes in prices is that countries that have been net importers of raw materials and net exporters of industrial goods—as has been the case for all Eastern European countries in their trade with the Soviet Union—will have a deterioration in their terms of trade. Countries like Hungary, for which the most detailed information is available, will have to export substantially more merely to maintain present levels of imports from the Soviet Union.

Although joint investments and price adjustments provide solutions on the Soviet side, they present clear problems for the Eastern Europeans. Because world market prices of some raw materials are comparable with, or even higher than, those within CEMA (especially for petroleum), and because the Eastern Europeans lack the hard currency to purchase on the world market, they have little alternative to paying the increased Soviet prices and investing in Soviet extractive industries. They must deal with a diversion of investment capital that could well be used at home and with inflationary pressures generated by increased resource costs.

These developments in cooperation and trade serve to enhance Soviet economic primacy within CEMA and, with it, Soviet opportunities for exerting economic and political influence. This influence is already visible in the general outlines of future CEMA cooperation envisioned in the 1971 Complex Program. The proposals incorporate the Soviet emphasis on product specialization through bi- and multilateral agreements, and play down or exclude altogether alternative proposals made by Hungarian and Polish economists for the development of convertible currencies and for integration based on the gradual creation of market relations among the members of CEMA.

More recent developments afford additional leverage to the Soviet Union. The development of the EEC into a single market and the requirement that all trade agreements between EEC members and nonmembers be handled at the EEC level have resulted in decisions within CEMA to provide the organization with the authority to negotiate for all of the member countries. The Eastern Europeans, in order to conduct their trade with Western Europe more effectively, have agreed to expand the authority of the central organs of CEMA. This probably will strengthen the position of the Soviet Union within the organization.[13] In addition, the Soviet Union has agreed to cushion the effects of price changes on Eastern Europe by extending credits to cover increased costs, particularly to Hungary.[14] One might wonder, for example, about the increased possibilities for Soviet influence that such credit extensions—and the ensuing economic dependence of the Eastern Europeans—provide. However, Soviet credits also demonstrate the extent of interdependence with CEMA. There can be little Soviet gain, either economic or political, in the long run from an economic slowdown in Eastern Europe; and this fact suggests limits on Soviet efforts to increase export prices and demands for investment funds from Eastern Europe.

EAST-WEST RELATIONS AND PROSPECTS FOR EASTERN EUROPE

One of the arguments of this chapter has been that expanded East-West contacts are not likely to result in significant changes in the relationship between the smaller countries of Eastern Europe and the Soviet Union. In fact, there is good cause to argue (supported by Paul Marer in Chapter 4) that Eastern Europe is in the process of becoming even more economically dependent on the Soviet Union than it has been in the recent past. In addition, the conservative trend that has characterized the recent internal politics of most of the countries does not support the argument that detente and expanded East-West contacts are likely to result in expanded liberalization in Eastern Europe.[15] It should be noted that distinctions should be made among the Eastern European countries. East Germany, because of its relatively high level of technological development and its direct access to the Western European market through its special relationship with West Germany (the absence of customs barriers in "inner-German" trade) would appear to have far better prospects for continued economic growth. In the near future, at least, East Germany should be more capable of expanding its exports to Western markets to cover the costs of needed imports. The weak raw materials base of its economy, however, will potentially limit economic growth of the sort that characterized the 1960s and will continue to tie its economy to that of the Soviet Union. The general improvement in East German-West German relations since the early 1970s and the formal West German recognition of East Germany have eliminated one of the major reasons for the tight East German-Soviet alliance, but the Honecker regime has not indicated any interest in internal liberalization or in deviating from the past policy of unity with the Soviet Union.

In Poland, prospects for the future probably are not as good in the economic sphere as they are in East Germany. The relative backwardness of much of Polish industrial production creates significant problems in matching imports with exports. Although Poland has substantial reserves of hard coal and is expanding both production and exports, it is unlikely that either coal exports or the increase in industrial exports will be able to make up the increasing deficits in Polish trade with the West in the near future. In addition, the Poles are heavily dependent on the Soviets for many of their raw materials, especially petroleum and iron ore. In the political sphere, Edward Gierek and his associates have given no indication that they are likely to indulge in significant experimentation in either the domestic or the foreign policy spheres.

The removal of Rezso Nyers and others closely associated with the New Economic Mechanism from positions of influence in Hungary and the recent purge of social scientists accused of revisionism are both indications of the more conservative trend in Hungarian internal politics. In addition, Hungary's economic position is among the most precarious in Eastern Europe, for it is probably more dependent on raw materials imports than any other Eastern European country. The Hungarians also have discovered that they are unable to cover the costs of their industrial imports from the West because of the general lack of markets for their exports, a problem that faces virtually all the Eastern European countries. This probably will result in a reduction of Western imports and a curtailing of economic development plans.

The economic situation in Bulgaria seems slightly better than it does in some of the other Eastern European countries. Bulgaria's rapid economic growth during the past decade has occurred, to a large extent, without a significant increase in trade with the West. Relative to most of the other countries, therefore, its indebtedness is less. However, like most of the other Eastern European countries, Bulgaria is heavily dependent for raw materials on the Soviet Union and will have to continue to rely on this source. There is no evidence that Bulgaria is likely to shift its domestic or foreign policies away from close association with the Soviet Union.

Since 1969 Czechoslovakia has been among the politically most conservative of the Eastern European regimes. There is no indication that it is about to modify either its internal or its foreign policy. In the economic sphere the Czechoslovaks face among the most serious problems in Eastern Europe. Although more highly developed than the economies of Poland and Hungary, the Czechoslovak economy still suffers significantly from low productivity and antiquated technology compared with the West.

Romania perhaps represents the one country in Eastern Europe that, at least in the long run, has moderately good chances for some type of economic independence from the Soviet Union. This assessment is based on the fact that of all the Eastern European countries, Romania has the greatest domestic supply of raw materials. However, like all of the other countries, it depends on substantial imports of raw materials. and, as the Romanians have discovered, they have been no more capable of covering hard-currency imports with exports than have the other socialist countries. This has required them to reorient their trade away from originally planned increases with the West to expanded trade with other CEMA countries, including the Soviet Union.

In summary, East-West trade, at least in the short run, does not seem likely to significantly affect the relative economic or political dependence on Eastern Europe on the Soviet Union. In fact, expanded East-West economic contacts seem to have had a partially negative impact on Eastern Europe by making its economies more vulnerable to inflationary pressures. In addition, the projected expansion in Soviet-Western trade is likely to cut into the availability of raw materials for other CEMA members, unless Soviet raw material production increases substantially faster than is called for in present production plans. The assumption that expanded East-West contacts are likely to result in a greater degree of economic and political autonomy for Eastern Europe does not appear to be warranted.

NOTES

1. See Zbigniew Brzezinski, *Alternative to Partition: For a Broader Conception of America's Role in Europe* (New York: McGraw-Hill, 1965).

2. See Robert W. Dean, *West German Trade with the East: The Political Dimension* (New York: Praeger, 1974), pp. 30-34.

3. For a discussion of de Gaulle's Eastern policy, see Jean Ethier-Blais, "France's Foreign Policy," in Adam Bromke and Philip E. Uren, eds., *The Communist States and the West* (New York: Praeger, 1967), pp. 117-27.

4. Wladyslaw Gomulka, *Trybuna ludu,* May 18, 1969.

5. See the speech of East German Foreign Minister Otto Winzer, *Neues Deutschland,* November 4, 1969. For an excellent discussion of East German concerns about bilateral negotiations between West Germany and other Eastern European states, see Robin A. Remington, "East Germany: The Politics of Persuasion," in her *The Warsaw Pact: Case Studies in Communist Conflict Resolution* (Cambridge, Mass.: MIT Press, 1971), pp. 134-64.

6. See Thad P. Alton, "Economic Growth and Resource Allocation in Eastern Europe," in U.S. Congress, Joint Economic Committee, *Reorientation and Commercial Relations of the Economies of Eastern Europe* (Washington, D.C.: U.S. Government Printing Office, 1974), p. 273, table 13.

7. See Paul Marer, "Population and Labor Force in Eastern Europe, 1950-1996," in U.S. Congress, Joint Economic Committee, op. cit., pp. 425-28. Also see Karol Szwarc, "Keeping up the Pace," *Polish Perspectives* 12, no. 9 (1975): 41.

8. See Wladyslaw Machejek, "Will the Seventh Congress Forgive?," *Lycie literackie,* January 5, 1975; translated in Radio Free Europe Research [hereafter RFER], *Polish Press Survey* no. 2470. Machejek notes that in 1973 the prices of Polish imports increased by 20 percent (including 56 percent for fuels), and in 1974 fuel prices rose an additional 80 percent. In 1974 Polish imports surpassed exports by 1.6 billion exchange zloty ($400 million). Also see Harry Trend, "Effects of World Price Changes on East European Economies," RFER, *Eastern Europe* no. 5 (June 28, 1974).

9. For two discussions of problems encountered in attempting to derive balance-of-payments or trade figures for CEMA countries, see Lawrence J. Brainard, "Criteria for Financing East-West Trade," in John P. Hardt, ed., *Tariff, Legal and Credit Constraints on East-West Commercial Relations* (Ottawa: Carleton University, Institute of Soviet and East European Studies, 1975), pp. 4-26; Paul Marer, "Foreign Trade," in Carmelo Mesa-Lago and Carl Beck, eds., *Comparative Socialist Systems: Essays on Politics and Economics* (Pittsburgh: University of Pittsburgh, Center for International Studies, 1975), pp. 367-98. In his revised figures, Brainard calculates a total hard-currency indebtedness for the six Eastern European countries at $7.9 billion through 1973, compared with Snell's $6.9 billion through 1971 (Table 10.8). See Brainard, op. cit., p. 13 and Edwin M. Snell, "Eastern Europe's Trade and Payments with the Industrial West," in U.S. Congress, Joint Economic Committee, op. cit., p. 685.

10. See O. Bogomolov, "Aktual'nye problemy ekonomicheskogo sotrudnichestva sotsialisticheskikh stran," *Mirovaia ekonomika i mezhdunarodnaia otnosheniia* no. 5 (1966): 15-27; and I. Dudinsky, "Toplivno-syr'evaia problema stran SEV i puti ei resheniia," *Voprosy ekonomiki* no. 4 (1966): 84-93; and *Resursy i mezhdunarodnoe sotrudnichestvo* (Moscow: Mezhdunarodnye Otnosheniia, 1968). Also see Paul Marer, *Postwar Pricing and Price Patterns in Socialist Foreign Trade* (Bloomington: Indiana University, International Development Center, 1972); J. M. P. van Brabant, *Essays on Planning, Trade, and Integration in Eastern Europe* (Rotterdam: University of Rotterdam Press, 1974), pp. 141 ff.; and Sandor Ausch, *Theory and Practice of CMEA Cooperation* (Budapest: Akademiai Kiado, 1972), pp. 84 ff.; Edward Hewett, *Foreign Trade Prices in the Council for Mutual Economic Assistance* (Cambridge: Cambridge University Press, 1974), esp. Ch. 3; and N. N. Bautina, "The Economic Integration of the Comecon Countries," *Ekonomika i organizatsiia promysh'lennosti* (Siberia) no. 1 (1972): 19-30, summarized in RRG., "Moscow's Efforts to Rig Comecon Prices," RFER, *Communist Area, USSR* no. 1389 (April 20, 1972).

11. See Harry Trend, "New Comecon Joint Investments—But Some Old Problems Remain," RFER, *RAD Background Report* (East Europe) 46 (March 12, 1975). For example, in four cooperation agreements between Hungary and the Soviet Union in 1973 and 1974, Hungary committed investments to the Soviet Union worth 62.4 million rubles for a cellulose project, 1.8 million rubles for an asbestos plant, 17.2 million rubles for an ammonium phosphate facility, and 29.6 million rubles in a fourth agreement. See ibid.; and Harry Trend, RFER, *Hungarian Situation Report* 36 (September 17, 1974): item 4.

12. For the details of the new pricing agreements—based primarily on Hungarian sources—see Harry Trend, "Pieces of Intra-Comecon Price Puzzle Falling into Place," RFER, *RAD Background Report* (Eastern Europe) 34 (February 28, 1975); and RFER, *Hungarian Situation Report* 25 (June 4, 1975): item 1.

13. Alexej Kohout in *Hospodarske noviny*, January 17, 1975; summarized in "The New Comecon Statutes," RFER, *Czechoslovakia Situation Report* no. 4 (January 29, 1975): 12-15. Also see "Comecon Applies for Observer Status at United Nations," *Soviet News* (London), October 8, 1974, p. 371; and Eric Bourne, "East, West Europe Agree to Talk," *Christian Science Monitor*, January 29, 1975, p. 3.

14. See Trend, "Pieces of Intra-Comecon Price Puzzle." The Hungarians also have been seeking credits elsewhere, and in 1974 have received two loans from Kuwait totalling $100 million. RFER, *Hungarian Situation Report* no. 37 (September 2, 1975): 6.

15. See Charles Gati, who takes a similar position in his "East-Central Europe: Touchstone for Detente," *Journal of International Affairs* 28 (1974): 158-74, esp. 172-74.

11

THE EUROPEAN ALLIANCE SYSTEMS: EXPLOITATION OR MUTUAL AID?
Walter C. Clemens, Jr.

INTRODUCTION

The twenty-fifth anniversary of NATO was commemorated in April 1974, and the twentieth anniversary of WTO in May 1975. To what extent are NATO and WTO mirror images of each other? Differently stated, are their similarities more superficial than actual? These questions take on renewed significance as both superpowers and their allies consider troop reductions in Europe and contemplate related problems.

In a world characterized by increasing complexity and—if not interdependence—by heightened vulnerabilities of all to all, other questions, still deeper and more significant, must also be raised about the two alliance systems. To what extent is either an organ for mutual assistance, optimizing the interests of all its members, both large and small? To what extent does either serve the interests of humanity, and not just those of certain elites? To what degree is either a forward-looking, progressive community and not just the embodiment of certain idees fixes from the past?

The unique essence of WTO, according to Soviet commentators, derives from its organic ties with the "community of socialist states" (also called the "socialist commonwealth"), a new kind of international system based on mutual aid and eschewing all forms of exploitation, whether of its own members or of other political actors. This glowing vision was portrayed, for example, in a

Part of the research on this article was carried out under a Rockefeller Foundation humanities fellowship in 1975. An earlier version of the article appeared in *Parameters* 4, no. 2 (1974): 13-22.

speech by Leonid I. Brezhnev, general secretary of the Soviet Communist party, in Warsaw on December 9, 1975. The socialist community, he affirmed,

> ... is a voluntary alliance of equal, sovereign and independent states, which, being socialist ones, draw for strength and well-being only on the free work of their peoples, knowing no exploitation at home and not exploiting the labor or riches of other countries and peoples.

Brezhnev also declared that

> ... [the] socialist community is an alliance of an absolutely new type. It is based not just on the community of state interests of a group of countries but represents a fraternal family of peoples which are led by Marxist-Leninist parties and which are forged into a single whole by a common world outlook, common lofty ideals and relations of comradely solidarity and mutual support. This is an alliance that rests on the permanent identity of positions and actions, which gives additional strength to every one of its participants for tackling national tasks and multiplies manyfold their combined weight and influence on world affairs.

Rejecting critical allegations from putative bourgeois falsifiers and from socialist traitors alike, Brezhnev asserted that

> ... [the] socialist community is the most reliable support of the forces of freedom and progress in the whole world. That is precisely why imperialist reaction is so frenziedly trying to smear it. Using ideological infiltration and economic levers, the bourgeois world stubbornly but unsuccessfully is trying to weaken our unity, trying to undermine the mainstays of socialism, now in one fraternal country, now in another. Traitors to the cause of socialism are slinging mud at our community, are straining to distort both the nature of our relations and our common policy.

These ostensible attributes of the socialist alliance and its fundamental differences from NATO have been elaborated in various Soviet statements:

1. The communique issued by the Warsaw Pact Political Consultative Committee in April 1974.[1]

2. A volume of essays published by the Institute for World Economics and Internal Relations (IMEMO in Russian).[2]

3. Works by Marshal Ivan I. Yakubovsky, commander in chief of the Joint Armed Forces of WTO.[3]

4. Dr. C. V. Kochubei, in a brochure for the Knowledge Society of the Russian Republic.[4]

Each of these documents emphasizes the differences between NATO and WTO, but much of the material they present suggests a more complex picture than the stark black-and-white image conveyed in their initial arguments.

BASIC DISTINCTIONS

The basic distinctions between the two alliances are sharply delineated by IMEMO:

> The Atlantic bloc is not only an organization for the preparation of war and subversive action against socialist countries, but also the leading center for interference in the internal affairs of states in the sphere of activity of that bloc and outside of it, an instrument for the preservation and restoration of reactionary regimes and governments.

While NATO is a kind of twentieth-century Holy Alliance—"the offspring of contemporary Romanovs, Metternichs, and Talleyrands"—WTO "was and remains the firm defender of all revolutionary achievements, the bulwark of socialism and peace in Europe and in the whole world." The two alliances are different with regard to social structure—capitalist vs. socialist; goals—imperialist vs. defensive; and activities—reactionary vs. progressive. The origins of the two alliances also are contrasted: NATO came into being for aggressive purposes; WTO, for self-defense, sparked particularly by the entry of West Germany into NATO in 1955.

YAKUBOVSKY'S FIVE PROPOSITIONS

Marshal Yakubovsky goes so far as to argue that WTO "essentially differs from all past coalitions and from military-political blocs presently linking the imperialist countries." He bases this claim to uniqueness on five main propositions, which do not hold up well, however, if examined against other parts of his essay or other data from the historical record.

Proposition 1. The WTO is "a voluntary alliance." Even if this were true, it is hardly unique among alliances, such as those formed prior to World War I, although there is always an element of "necessity" resulting from the material environment in which states consider whether to ally with other states.

Neither WTO nor NATO provides for withdrawal from the alliance until a fixed term has elapsed—1974-75 for WTO, 1969-70 for NATO. France, however, withdrew in stages from the military activities and organization of NATO through the 1960s—a point documented by IMEMO—without encountering major opposition from her alliance partners, even though de Gaulle's policies caused them serious economic, logistic, and strategic difficulties. Disputes over use of bases and other problems aggravated NATO's internal problems during the 1973 Middle East war, setting the stage for many members to go it alone in trying to cope with the oil shortages and price hikes in the winter of 1973-74. Although France has now resumed some integrated military activities within the NATO framework, Athens—in the 1974 Cyprus confrontation—declared that Greece would no longer take part in the military organization of NATO (thereby heightening doubts about the legality or desirability of leaving nuclear weapons in Greece or Turkey under joint controls with the United States).

The preferences of the hegemonical alliance power also have been defied by Romania. Although she has not formally withdrawn from the military structure of WTO, Romania has balked at permitting WTO maneuvers in her territory and has severely limited her participation in such maneuvers elsewhere. Bucharest also has called for changes in WTO structure and operations, advocated an end to alliances more vociferously than her WTO partners, and threatened armed resistance to any WTO invasion.

As a result of her deviant behavior, Romania has been subjected to more intense threats and pressures from her putative allies than the criticisms that other NATO members directed against France and Greece for their autonomous stands. Considering Moscow's proven willingness to use force to enforce its will in Eastern Europe, it is hardly surprising that Romania in the mid-1970s was much more submissive to the Kremlin than France or other NATO members were to the United States.

The April 1974 WTO communique affirmed that friendship among members offers a model of "a new type of interstate relations, of a truly democratic society, an example of the socialist way of life." What we know from history, including Soviet-sponsored subversive activities in Yugoslavia,* however, suggests a less rosy image. At least three WTO members seem to have considered complete withdrawal from the Soviet system. Hungary was invaded in 1956 by Soviet forces when Premier Imre Nagy proclaimed the country's neutrality. One reason for the WTO intervention against Czechoslovakia in 1968 was that military planners in Prague considered scenarios for nonalignment. Only Albania—separated from other WTO nations by Yugoslavia—has gone her way untouched, proclaiming in 1968 that she had withdrawn from WTO. Her legal right to do so, however, has not been recognized in Moscow. Yakubovsky says only that in 1962 Albania ceased "participation in the work" of WTO. The IMEMO study puts the date still earlier, saying that Albania "stopped taking part in the activities of the Warsaw Treaty Organization in 1960-61 and virtually withdrew from it."

---

*Not a WTO member, but a socialist state by its own definition.

Judging by the early demise of the Czechoslovak experiment in "socialism" with a human face" in 1968, the Soviets would have intervened earlier and with greater force had they been confronted with a situation in their camp analogous to that of Portugal in 1975.

Though Western political processes fall short of any democratic (or functional) ideal, the NATO governments appear in 1974-75 to have given little (if any) more assistance to noncommunist factions struggling for power in Portugal than Moscow did to the leftist factions, even though the future political complexion of an important strategic link in NATO was at stake.

The extent to which freedom of action characterizes the internal as well as the external politics of NATO was also illustrated in American-Turkish relations in 1974-75. Turkey defied Washington in using American arms to invade Cyprus; the American executive branch could not prevent Congress from embargoing future arms shipments to Turkey, with the result that American bases were curtailed in that country; resolute defiance of the United States became an issue in Turkish domestic politics, just as pro-Greek sentiments activated much action in the American Congress. A vital segment of the Western alliance was allowed to unravel for over a year before the executive branches and legislatures of both governments concurred in a compromise solution restoring a modicum of functional coordination.

Even if the WTO member had chosen to denounce the pact in 1974-75, when its terms specifically permit withdrawal, every WTO ally is also bound to the Soviet Union and to other WTO members by a series of bilateral agreements that could easily be exploited by Moscow to achieve a considerable degree of control over the lesser partner. For example, the terms of the Czechoslovak-Soviet treaty, revised and renewed in 1970, give legal status to the principle of the "Brezhnev Doctrine," which asserts that the interests of the "socialist commonwealth" take precedence over those of "national sovereignty." In the language of the 1970 treaty: "The support, strengthening and defense of the conquests of socialism, achieved at the expense of heroic efforts and selfless labor of each people, is the common international duty of the socialist countries." This provision, according to S. V. Kochubei, "reflects as in a mirror the main principle lying at the basis of the military and other forms of collaboration of the countries of socialism—proletarian internationalism."[5]

Similar language found its way into the new treaty of friendship between Moscow and East Germany, signed on October 7, 1975. This treaty gave further substance to Soviet-East German unity, for it committed both sides to long-range coordination of their national economic plans and to military assistance without the territorial limitation to Europe still contained in WTO and the earlier friendship treaties. This meant, as *Sueddeutsche Zeitung* commented on October 8, that "if the Chinese come, the Germans have to go to the front," with mounting pressures on the other WTO allies to do the same.

While Soviet spokesmen intermittently deny that there is any such notion as a "Brezhnev Doctrine," and often champion "non-interference in domestic affairs," they continue to uphold the basic concept through the euphemism "socialist internationalism," a slogan repeated, for example, in Brezhnev's December 9, 1975, speech in Warsaw.

WTO, in sum, is no more voluntary than other alliances; probably it is less so, given the hegemonic position of the Soviet Union within the alliance.

Proposition 2. WTO is based on "the principle of total equality of participants." Some animals, as George Orwell observed, are "more equal than others." Yakubovsky and IMEMO affirm the leading role of the Soviet Union within WTO in providing armaments and combat materiel, strategic doctrine, and organizational forms. They could (but do not) also confirm the leading role played by Soviet personnel in commanding the various organs of WTO. They explicitly cite the historical precedents for multinational cooperation in the contingents from various Eastern European countries fighting with the Red Army in 1918-21 and again during World War II. According to Yakubovsky, by 1945 the total number of foreign units formed in the Soviet Union "amounted to 557,000 men." He continues:

> The Soviet Army provides its comrades-in-arms with the broad opportunity to adopt everything valuable that it has amassed in theory and practice. The friendly armies naturally regard Soviet military science as the deep Marxist-Leninist theoretical generalization of the experience of creating and improving socialist armies under conditions of the complete victory of socialism and the all-out building of communism.

The motto of the fraternal armies, their commander in chief writes, is "to learn from the Soviet Army means to learn to win."

The IMEMO study dwells on the "personal union" between the hegemonic power in NATO and the armed forces of its allies, a union personified by the commanding position of American generals and admirals, seconded most often by British officers, at the top of the NATO hierarchy.

Yakubovsky stresses the "latitude for broad initiative and creativity of all [WTO] participants...." But he also notes that the plans for closer economic integration, adopted by CEMA, will contribute greatly to the military as well as to the economic power of the alliance. While Yakubovsky probably is correct in assuming that closer economic integration among WTO allies would strengthen their military and economic power, it seems certain that such a tendency would reduce the latitude enjoyed by some members. Romania has resisted such integration since the early 1960s. In the wake of the Czechoslovak events of 1968-69, however, the Kremlin has mounted strong efforts to integrate economic and scientific work, directed by various institutes in Moscow.

It is difficult or impossible to recall a historical case where the other members of a multilateral alliance have been so overshadowed by one hegemonical power. The relative power of the United States in NATO, for example, is less than that of the Soviet Union in WTO. Two other NATO powers have their own nuclear arsenals, contrasted with Moscow's monopoly in WTO. Whereas most NATO members have indirect access to American nuclear warheads, there is no evidence that WTO allies have any warheads at their disposal but only delivery systems, such as short-range surface-to-surface missiles.

For better or worse, the IMEMO study probably is correct in asserting:

> The decisive material force in the Warsaw Treaty Organization is the USSR. To her falls the main share of military expenditures. The armed forces of the USSR and their technical equipment occupy the predominant position, both in quantity and in quality.

It goes on to affirm that the nuclear-rocket potential of the Soviet Union "protects not only the state interests of the USSR but also the state interests of other countries of the Warsaw Pact, all socialist countries, guarantees them from aggression, and ensures their development on the communist route chosen by them." Soviet predominance is manifested by the fact that command of the air defense system covering the entire WTO area is now centralized in Moscow and directed by the commander in chief of the Soviet Air Defense Forces, Marshal P. F. Batinsky. Thus, the Eastern Europeans remain totally dependent upon Moscow not only for strategic deterrence but also for air defense.

Though the Soviet Union opted in the early and mid-1970s to strengthen the armed forces of her Eastern European allies, qualitatively and quantitatively, the fact remains that they have been denied access to the most modern Soviet fighter-bombers, interceptor aircraft, surface-to-air missiles and tanks—even though some of these weapons have long been available to Third World clients such as Syria, a condition that can only irritate Eastern Europeans. Though interceptors such as the MIG-25 and SU-15 were shown in the Soviet Union as early as 1967, by 1975 they had still not entered service in the Eastern European air forces. (In 1974, however, the SU-20 bomber, capable of Mach 1.6 speeds, was put into service in Poland as well as in the Soviet air force. But it is outclassed in almost every respect by the F-104 and F-4 made available to American allies beginning in 1958 and 1962, respectively.)

Proposition 3. The "alliance of the socialist countries is a genuinely defensive organization," whereas the "military blocs of the imperialists serve aggressive aims and are directed against the socialist countries and against all freedom-loving peoples. . . ." Yakubovsky immediately qualifies the word "defensive," however, by saying that WTO "pursues no aims other than the defense of its revolutionary attainments and the cause of peace." He also confirms WTO's willingness to give "fraternal assistance" to its members and to other fraternal countries:

> Such was the case in 1956-58 when the resolve of the socialist countries to defend the peace halted the aggression against Egypt, Syria and Iraq. In 1956, the Soviet Union rendered fraternal assistance to the Hungarian people in putting down the counterrevolutionary uprising that was launched by internal reactionary forces with the direct participation of the West. In 1961, an imperialist provocation against the GDR was averted and in the following year support was rendered to revolutionary Cuba. In 1967, the fraternal socialist countries resolutely supported the Arab nations that were subjected to Israeli aggression. The assistance rendered in 1968 by five socialist countries to the fraternal people of Czechoslovakia in defending the attainments of socialism which were menaced by internal counterrevolutionary and international reactionary forces was a clear demonstration of the power of proletarian internationalism.

Without debating Marshal Yakubovsky on the particular events that he cites, it seems clear that many observers—and many participants in these events—would question whether those WTO actions were "defensive." Indeed, the cases that Yakubovsky mentions could be used to contradict his further assertion that the WTO participants "threaten no one, claim no foreign territory, and do not intervene in the internal affairs of other countries." One might recall also the Soviet argument that the medium-range ballistic missiles installed in Cuba in 1962 were "defensive weapons." To be sure, the policies of certain NATO powers in the Third World since the mid-1950s can be called "defensive" only by stretching the meaning of the term quite broadly. They cannot, however, be attributed to some decision by "NATO," since the *casus foederis* clauses of the NATO Charter apply only to an attack in Europe, in America, and in the Atlantic Ocean north of the Tropic of Cancer.

According to Yakubovsky, the aggressive forces of the United States and her allies are engaged in heavy defense expenditures, and they plan to increase tensions and preparations for war with the socialist countries. Yakubovsky enumerates American nuclear forces—land and sea-based missiles, bombers, warheads deployed in Europe—and asserts that they have been "designated to deliver a surprise nuclear strike against the socialist countries." On the other hand, Yakubovsky says of WTO strategy:

> Collective defense in Europe, based on the joint action of the Unified Armed Forces that are prepared not only to ward off any attack by the aggressor but also to crush him outright, is the military-strategic basis of the military alliance of the fraternal peoples and their armies.

While we should not rely on Yakubovsky for an authoritative assessment of American or NATO strategy, his statement on WTO plans might well indicate genuine Soviet aspirations, if not current planning. His formulation resembles that of former Defense Minister R. A. Malinovsky and other Soviet marshals who have dealt in circumlocutions, such as a "timely blow," to convey what Western strategists speak of as a preemptive strike.

Preemption, of course, could be thought of as a defensive or as an offensive strategy. Soviet deployment of "heavy" missiles or American deployment of MIRV might be interpreted as part of such a strategy, the aim of which could be to neutralize the enemy's second-strike response capability. Given the variety and quantity of strategic forces possessed by each superpower, it seems quite doubtful that either could be deprived of an assured-destruction, second-strike capability. To use the language of preemption, nonetheless, is to inflame the tensions that Yakubovsky accuses NATO alone of kindling.

Other WTO commentaries roundly denounced the doctrines enunciated by American Defense Secretary James Schlesinger in 1974-75 for intimating that the United States might be the first to initiate battlefield use of nuclear weapons in Europe or even a "selective" strike against the Soviet Union. Unlike the situation in the 1950s and 1960s, however, when the Soviet Union flatly asserted that any use of nuclear weapons would trigger an all-out holocaust, Soviet doctrine and military maneuvers in the early 1970s hinted at the possibility that nuclear exchanges could be "limited," even in Europe.

Proposition 4. "Unlike NATO, the Warsaw Pact is not a narrow, closed military organization. The Treaty is open to other nations irrespective of their social and government system. . . . The only prerequisite of membership is the willingness to promote the unification of the efforts of peace-loving peoples in the interest of peace and the security of peoples."

This proposition is contradicted by Yakubovsky's further assertion that WTO rests upon "firm political, economic, ideological, and military-strategic foundations," including a "common social and government structure."

He continues:

> Common political ground is the basis for socialist international relations between friendly nations in all areas, including the military area, since all socialist countries now have a common enemy—imperialism, and the threat of imperialist aggression is a threat to all socialist countries.

Indeed, throughout the essay Yakubovsky states that WTO consists of "socialist countries." As Czechoslovakia experienced in 1968, however, deviation from the Soviet definition of "socialism" can trigger WTO intervention. And Moscow has sustained a diplomatic effort over several years to persuade its WTO allies to declare their readiness to take part in "defensive actions" against another putatively socialist state—China.

An even stronger pressure for conformity among the members of WTO is that the character of each country's policies—economic, military, political—is determined by its Communist party. As Yakubovsky puts it: "The fact that Communist and Workers' Parties manage all the defenses of socialist countries is of paramount importance to the development and strengthening of the military alliance of these countries." These parties and their governments act as a "united front," and their governments act as a "united front in the international arena." The heads of the parties and of the government take part in the work of the Political Consultative Committee (PCC), which heads the WTO and to which foreign ministers and other officials are summoned to participate.

Given its underlying characteristics, WTO seems to be much more "closed" than NATO. Member states of the Atlantic alliance are more diverse, ranging along a wide economic spectrum from public to private ownership and control, and from highly democratic to highly authoritarian political and social systems. NATO has expanded its ranks twice, in 1952 and 1955, whereas WTO has not enlarged its original membership. Indeed, Albania has declared her withdrawal from WTO and no other socialist states have joined, although some, notably Outer Mongolia and China, have bilateral alliances with Moscow.

Finally, Yakubovsky uses the term "narrow" to contrast strictly military alliances with WTO, the latter being engaged in the promotion of economic and other forms of cooperation. In fact, however, both alliances have expressed their interest in promoting nonmilitary cooperation inter se and with each other. They have, for example, addressed themselves to pan-European security and, since the late 1960s, to ecological planning and controls.

Proposition 5. "Unlike NATO," Yakubovsky writes, "troops of the Warsaw Pact continue to be directly subordinate to the national commands, another fact attesting to the mutual respect for the sovereignty of allied nations." At the same time, he continues: ". . . the creation of the United [or Combined] Armed Forces has immeasurably increased the defensive might of socialist countries since the best trained troops with a high degree of combat readiness were assigned for these purposes."

These remarks of Yakubovsky and similar statements in the IMEMO study are of interest, not only for comparisons with NATO but also because they terminate speculations by some Western observers about the meaning of "the new statutes of the Unified Armed Forces and the Joint Command," approved by the Budapest meeting of the PCC in March 1969. Some observers concluded that tighter integration of WTO forces had been accomplished, units from each army being earmarked for subjugation to direct orders from a Soviet officer in time of an emergency. From these two authoritative Soviet works, however, it appears that the various national armies remain physically distinct from Soviet forces and directly subordinate to their own national authorities. In the words of the IMEMO report: the Unified Forces are controlled by the commander in chief "through his deputies, who are representatives of the national commands."

The degree of WTO coordination also has been stressed by Yakubovsky on the basis of large-scale maneuvers, such as the "Comrades-in-Arms" exercise held in East Germany and in the Baltic Sea in 1970. "In terms of its military-political significance, scope, and results it was the most significant of all the years of existence of the Warsaw Treaty Organization." The exercise included the troops of "all seven armies and the forces of three fleets." (The first WTO exercise involving more than one fleet seems to have occurred in 1969, when Bulgarian and Soviet fleets participated. According to Bulgarian sources, however, Romania did not participate, although it would have been logical for her to do so.)

Yakubovsky also notes that the Committee of Defense Ministers organized at the March 1969 PCC meeting "has been established and is now functioning." Since 1969, "The functions of headquarters and other organs of control of the Unified Armed Forces have been expanded."

On these points of the Yakubovsky and IMEMO studies, little qualification seems necessary. The main question to be posed is whether the degree of integration achieved is that which Moscow wanted. It is more likely that the Soviet Union sought greater centralization of WTO forces at the March 1969 meeting of the PCC, but that this was successfully blocked by Romania and perhaps by Czechoslovakia, still represented in Budapest at that time by Alexander Dubcek. Indeed, for months after the PCC session in Budapest, rumors circulated throughout Europe that the conference almost broke down over Soviet efforts to induce WTO members to cooperate actively with the Soviet Union in her struggle with China.

Though the details of the 1969 reorganization and its implementations are by no means clear, Lawrence T. Caldwell has pieced together the command structure shown in Figure 11.1. According to Caldwell:

> The PCC provides broad foreign policy coordination among the Pact states and apparently receives reports from the Committee of Defense Ministers as well as directly from the Commander-in-Chief on military questions. Marshal Yakubovsky's presence at PCC meetings when the Defense Ministers have not been in attendance suggests (1) that the Committee of Defense Ministers essentially affords a channel of communication with national defense planners; (2) that the Committee of Defense Ministers has little advisory responsibility outside of the roles of its members in national governments; and (3) that the PCC is advised on military considerations fundamentally by the Commander-in-Chief.

He infers, however, that the Military Council

> ... probably does report to the defense ministers either in the Committee of Defense Ministers or individually within national decision-making structures; thus, it carries out a communications

FIGURE 11.1

WTO Command Structure

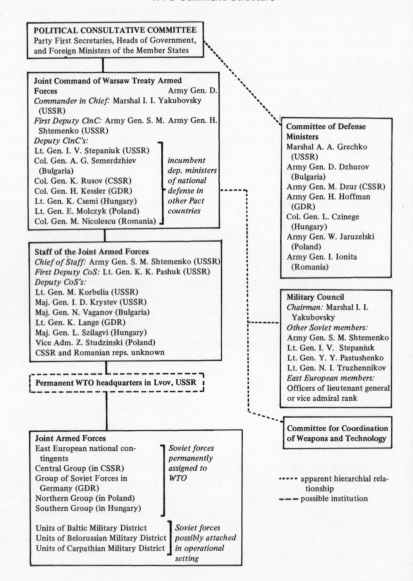

POLITICAL CONSULTATIVE COMMITTEE
Party First Secretaries, Heads of Government,
and Foreign Ministers of the Member States

**Joint Command of Warsaw Treaty Armed
Forces**   Army Gen. D.
Commander in Chief: Marshal I. I. Yakubovsky
 (USSR)
First Deputy CinC: Army Gen. S. M. Army Gen. H.
 Shtemenko (USSR)
Deputy CinC's:
Lt. Gen. I. V. Stepaniuk (USSR)
Col. Gen. A. G. Semerdzhiev   *incumbent*
 (Bulgaria)   *dep. ministers*
Col. Gen. K. Rusov (CSSR)   *of national*
Col. Gen. H. Kessler (GDR)   *defense in*
Lt. Gen. K. Csemi (Hungary)   *other Pact*
Lt. Gen. E. Molczyk (Poland)   *countries*
Col. Gen. M. Nicolescu (Romania)

Staff of the Joint Armed Forces
Chief of Staff: Army Gen. S. M. Shtemenko (USSR)
First Deputy CoS: Lt. Gen. K. K. Pashuk (USSR)
Deputy CoS's:
Lt. Gen. M. Korbelia (USSR)
Maj. Gen. I. D. Krystev (USSR)
Maj. Gen. N. Vaganov (Bulgaria)
Lt. Gen. K. Lange (GDR)
Maj. Gen. L. Szilagvi (Hungary)
Vice Adm. Z. Studzinski (Poland)
CSSR and Romanian reps. unknown

Permanent WTO headquarters in Lvov, USSR

Joint Armed Forces
East European national con-   *Soviet forces*
 tingents   *permanently*
Central Group (in CSSR)   *assigned to*
Group of Soviet Forces in   *WTO*
 Germany (GDR)
Northern Group (in Poland)
Southern Group (in Hungary)

Units of Baltic Military District   *Soviet forces*
Units of Belorussian Military District   *possibly attached*
Units of Carpathian Military District   *in operational*
                                     setting

**Committee of Defense
Ministers**
Marshal A. A. Grechko
 (USSR)
Army Gen. D. Dzhurov
 (Bulgaria)
Army Gen. M. Dzur (CSSR)
Army Gen. H. Hoffman
 (GDR)
Col. Gen. L. Czinege
 (Hungary)
Army Gen. W. Jaruzelski
 (Poland)
Army Gen. I. Ionita
 (Romania)

Military Council
Chairman: Marshal I. I.
 Yakubovsky
Other Soviet members:
Army Gen. S. M. Shtemenko
Lt. Gen. I. V. Stepaniuk
Lt. Gen. Y. Y. Pastushenko
Lt. Gen. N. I. Truzhennikov
East European members:
Officers of lieutenant general
or vice admiral rank

**Committee for Coordination
of Weapons and Technology**

· · · · · apparent hierarchial rela-
       tionship
— — possible institution

Source: Lawrence T. Caldwell, "The Warsaw Pact: Directions of Change," *Problems
of Communism* 24, no. 5 (September-october 1975): 1-19, at 8. Caldwell cites the following
sources: Malcolm Mackintosh, "The Warsaw Pact Today," *Survival* (May-June 1974): 123;
R. W. Herrick, "Warsaw Pact Restructuring Strengthens Principle of National Control,"
Radio Liberty Dispatch (March 6, 1970): 6-8; A. Ross Johnson's chapter (Chapter 3) in this
book; CIA, *Reference Aid: Directory of USSR Ministry of Defense and Armed Forces
Officials* (Washington, D.C.: 1974).

function. The Joint Command oversees military operations and issues broad policy guidance for the Staff of the Joint Armed Forces. . . . The Staff, then, directs actual training and implements the policies of the Joint Command.[6]

Though the Eastern European armies remain subordinate to their own national authorities, according to the 1969 agreements, the International Institute for Strategic Studies posits that in time of war, all WTO forces would be operationally subordinate to the Soviet High Command.[7]

In NATO, by contrast, some national forces are subject to the supreme commander of NATO, while some remain under national command, except for West German forces, all of which are NATO-committed. At the same time, there are other possibilities in NATO for bilateral or multilateral coordination among subsets of the entire membership—for instance, on nuclear operations and strategy—to which there is no known analogue in the WTO. (Only certain members of both alliances, however, have been full participants in the MFR negotiations taking place in Vienna since 1969.) Thus, while the WTO forces are less integrated in some respects than NATO's, they are more dependent upon the hegemonical power of the alliance.

The more open-ended character of NATO may permit it to adjust to changing circumstances with greater flexibility than WTO. This character creates dangers as well as opportunities. In the future we might still see the formation of a European nuclear force within NATO, joining the nuclear forces of Britain and France. If supranational cooperation progresses still further in Europe, it is at least conceivable—but not at all likely—that West Germany might participate in a European nuclear force in ways skirting the original intent of the West European Union and the Non-Proliferation Treaty. Such developments would doubtless create tensions within NATO as well as between the two alliances.

SYMMETRIES AND ASYMMETRIES

Analysis of the key propositions in the Soviet argument suggests that WTO is not so unique as Moscow claims. In some ways it resembles NATO and in some respects it differs. Let us now examine more analytically the symmetries and asymmetries between the two alliances.

Origins

Both alliances claim to be a response to aggressive action from the other side. NATO claimed to be a response to Sovietization in Eastern Europe and to fears of Soviet pressures against Western Europe. WTO, however, was created in

May 1955, when international tensions were easing, because of changes in Soviet policy toward Austria, Finland, Yugoslavia, and arms control. The main Western event to which WTO responded was West Germany's entry into NATO under the terms of the London-Paris accords for the West European Union, which were signed in late 1954 and ratified in the spring of 1955. The fact that little military coordination took place among WTO allies until the early 1960s suggests that WTO was formed more for political and diplomatic purposes than for defensive (or offensive) military ones. Moscow had a network of bilateral alliances in Eastern Europe before and after the creation of WTO, making a multilateral alliance superfluous unless it promoted coordination or interpretation more than the bilateral treaties did.

Structure

The military capabilities of both alliance systems overlap in many ways, but there also are many asymmetries—a fact of life that makes it more difficult to reach any negotiated accord on a formula for "mutual and balanced force reductions."

Even the number of men under arms in both alliances cannot be assessed by a simple head count. NATO divisions contain many more men per unit than WTO divisions, which leads Western pessimists to count division strengths, while their WTO counterparts prefer to emphasize numbers of troops. According to the International Institute for Strategic Studies, combat and direct support troops available in 1975 were as shown in Table 11.1. These figures do not include dual-based brigades of American forces stationed in the United States, but they do include Soviet troops stationed in the western Soviet Union. Although Western pessimists can point out the short distances that Soviet troops have to move to reach Central Europe, WTO pessimists can count the American

TABLE 11.1

NATO and WTO Support Troops, 1975

	Northern and Central Europe	Southern Europe
NATO	675,000*	575,000
WTO	895,000	345,000
of which Sovet Union	595,000	115,000

*Includes 50,000 French troops stationed in Germany.

Source: International Institute for Strategic Studies, *The Military Balance, 1975-1976* (London: the Institute, 1975), pp. 96-102.

TABLE 11.2

Balance of Tactical Aircraft in Northern and Central Europe

	NATO	WTO	Soviet Union/WTO
Light bombers	150	225	200
Fighter/ground-attack	1,250	1,325	900
Interceptors	350	2,000	950
Reconnaissance	300	475	350

forces deployed in North America and the commercial and military aircraft that could lift them to Europe in a crisis.

Generally, while NATO pessimists emphasize gross, quantitative discrepancies, their Eastern counterparts worry more about the quality of Western forces and technology.

More glaringly, the above figures say nothing about the combat reliability of WTO compared with NATO troops. Under what conditions would Czechoslovak or Romanian formations, for example, fight loyally with the Soviet Union? To what extent would Soviet troops be committed to ensuring that their allies did not fight against them instead of with them?

In Northern and Central Europe, NATO was thought in 1975 to possess about 7,000 main battle tanks (not counting 810 French tanks), compared with about 19,000 WTO tanks, of which 11,500 were in Soviet forces.

While WTO outnumbers NATO in numbers of tanks by more than two-to-one, Western tanks—those in service and those in development—are judged to be qualitatively superior. The Western alliance is also strong, and becoming stronger, in highly accurate antitank weapons, raising questions about the rationale behind continued Soviet production of tanks that are becoming increasingly vulnerable.

The United States and her allies had more than 7,000 tactical nuclear warheads stationed in Europe in 1975, over twice the number available to WTO, most of which are thought to be stockpiled not in Eastern Europe but in the Soviet Union. Some of the NATO weapons were obsolete and others were deemed redundant; hence NATO's decision on December 12, 1975, to propose withdrawing 1,000 American tactical nuclear weapons and 29,000 American troops from Central Europe in exchange for the retirement from Central Europe of a Soviet army of about 1,700 tanks and 68,000 men. Though Moscow might not judge this to be an advantageous trade, some American State Department officials thought the Kremlin might respond with some other quid pro quo to keep the MFR talks alive.

In Northern and Central Europe the balance of tactical aircraft in operational service was assessed by the International Institute for Strategic Studies as shown in Table 11.2. Similar disparities were found in Southern Europe.

But the main asymmetries lay in the missions presumably assigned to each set of air forces, in the much larger number of aircraft available for reinforcement in the West, and in the qualitative superiority not only of the NATO aircraft but of the training of their crews.

Thus, NATO forces are strong in aircraft capable of deep penetration and bombing missions into Soviet territory, as well as of tactical support of ground combat units. Soviet aircraft are more numerous, but are geared more to an interceptor role than are NATO's fighter-bombers.

Except for France, however, no NATO member possesses intermediate range ballistic missiles (IRBMs), while the Soviet Union continues to deploy about 600 IRBM and medium range ballistic missile (MRBM) forces against European targets. Britain and France have a powerful strategic capability, however, thus creating (with China and the United States) at least four independent nuclear threats to the Soviet Union, which monopolizes the strategic forces available to WTO.

Indeed, none of the comparisons in "theater forces" take full account of American forward-based systems—land- and sea-based aircraft (plus submarines) stationed in or near Europe, capable of attacking the Soviet heartland or supporting battlefield operations in Europe proper. With the advent of highly accurate, radar-evading cruise missiles, these aircraft and submarines must take on still greater significance for Soviet planners.

Given the vocal support for a strong NATO from leaders in Peking in the early and mid-1970s, the Kremlin would have to consider whether China would stand aside or take advantage of any WTO-NATO engagement in Europe. Even without Chinese-American collusion, Peking might choose to create a two-front war for the Soviet Union in the event of a European conflict. At a minimum, China compels the Soviet Union to keep large numbers of troops and other forces deployed eastward.

The European balance also depends on the overall strategic equations between the Soviet Union and the United States, which also are complicated by great asymmetries. But, although the Soviet Union leads in some areas of strategic weaponry, the United States still enjoys a commanding advantage not only in numbers of warheads but also in most qualitative aspects of the strategic arms race, such as accuracy.

Functioning

Both alliances profess to have a basically defensive character, but WTO has been used primarily to enforce Soviet policy preferences regarding the internal affairs of member states, such as Hungary and Czechoslovakia. France and Greece, in contrast, have formally left the military organization of NATO, and could have denounced the treaty as well, without suffering major pressures from other NATO members.

NATO is cemented by a common Western heritage shared by most of its members. A common Western political culture also buttresses an informal consensus that runs deeper than enforced ideological conformity. Indeed, the sacerdotal character of communist ideology probably aggravates disputes among WTO members on matters affecting their particular interests.

Although the United States is more physically remote from her alliance partners in Europe, she shares more culturally with them than the Soviet Union does with many members of WTO. Czechoslovakia, for example, is strongly linked with Western culture, while the Soviet Union has experienced strong Byzantine and Asian influences.

In terms of power relationships, the Organization of American States is more similar to WTO than is NATO. And Washington's willingness to enforce its will has been much greater in Latin America—Guatemala, Cuba, the Dominican Republic, Chile—than in Europe. In short, the domain covered by the Monroe Doctrine is much more analogous to that regulated by the "Brezhnev Doctrine" than is NATO.

Soviet security has been directly affected by the buffer area of Eastern Europe, while Realpolitik dictates that American security is less directly affected by the fortunes of Western Europe. This means that the internal affairs of the other WTO members are of a greater importance to Moscow than are those of other NATO partners to the United States. By the same token, however, America's remoteness from Europe creates greater doubt in European chancelleries about the extent to which there would be an automatic American response to aggression against Washington's NATO allies. A reduction in American forces stationed in Europe would aggravate doubts about the American commitment, moreso than a reduction, or even a complete withdrawal, of Soviet forces would affect European perceptions of Moscow's interests in Europe.

Taken together, the members of NATO are more advanced economically than most countries of WTO. The economic and demographic resources of Western Europe approach those of either superpower. Eastern Europe's resources, by contrast, do not match even those of the Soviet Union. Most of the European members of NATO also have a much longer and more positive experience in transnational and supranational cooperation than the Eastern European members of WTO have.

Although nationalism gains freer expression in the West than in the East, reflected even in military deployments of Greece against Turkey and of Iceland against Britain, it remains a potent divisive force in Eastern Europe as well—not just in boundary and minority problems that continue to simmer, but in deep fears and resentments against economic integration that has produced, and could again result in, exploitative arrangements.

Western European union has been supported by the United States—at least until economic developments of recent years compelled all parties to commence a reappraisal—while Moscow has sought to force integration of the Eastern European economies with that of the Soviet Union. The Eastern European governments tend to remain heavily dependent upon the Soviet Union, not only militarily but also economically and politically.

PROSPECTS

The MFR negotiations and multilateral talks on European security add great strains to the cohesion of both alliance systems.[8] Within each bloc, governments are weighing the pros and cons of three basic approaches:

1. Preserving bloc-to-bloc relationships, whether for confrontation or for negotiation, or both.

2. Pursuing bilateral relations with nations of the opposite bloc, regardless of interalliance developments, in such areas as trade, arms control, and war prevention.

3. Seeking to transcend the long-familiar bloc structures to develop new forms of cooperation—international, transnational, supranational.

Thus, the April 1974 communique from Warsaw reaffirmed the "invariable" readiness of all WTO members "to disband the Warsaw Treaty Organization simultaneously with the disbanding of the North Atlantic Treaty Organization or, as an initial step, liquidation of their military organizations." Although the document pledged WTO efforts in behalf of "equal cooperation" with all European states, WTO countries nevertheless promised to strengthen their defenses and to develop close participation so long as the blocs remain and disarmament measures have not been implemented.

The tighter reins that Moscow imposes on its alliance partners, compared with Washington's, should help sustain the solidarity of WTO, at least in the short run. In the longer term, however, resentments of these controls will continue to fester in Eastern Europe, as they have in the past. This produces a situation that tends to appear more stable than NATO, where disagreements are often more open. But externally imposed discipline is less viable over time than restraints that are self-chosen.[9] In a crisis situation, WTO forces and populations probably would be less reliable than those of NATO. Were communist parties to gain greater weight in the governments of Portugal, Italy, or other NATO countries, however, the reliability and coherence of the Western alliance would become much more dubious than it has been historically. Although less monolithic for political bargaining purposes, the Western alliance may have more staying power and flexibility to accommodate changing times and new problems. Such are the liabilities and advantages of a freer association.

AID OR EXPLOITATION?

The historical record suggests that WTO is unique—not for being a voluntary alliance of equals dedicated to enhancing their common aims, but for providing the legal and military framework that for decades helps a hegemonical power to impose its will upon weaker neighbors who, given a free choice, might well opt for nonalignment or even participation in the security operations of the opposing camp. The historical record indicates that this institution, like other exploitative arrangements among nations, tends toward instability, despite surface harmonies.

To be sure, the ruling regimes in Moscow, East Berlin, and some other WTO capitals do share some interests that have been advanced by the mechanisms of WTO. As Lawrence Caldwell notes, some Eastern European elites, like those of the Soviet Union, derive both legitimacy and prestige from the workings of their alliance, while "the diplomacy of intra-Pact affairs and East-West negotiations under Pact sponsorship also provides international political training for East European cadres. . . ."[10] For those Eastern European regimes that seek to show their independence from Soviet dictation, however, the enforced integration in WTO affairs is a liability.

On balance, WTO has been manipulated by Moscow for its own purposes, with only secondary or tertiary attention to its allies' interests. Indeed, the East German government has often feared that its vital interests would be sacrificed upon the altar of peaceful coexistence, and other Eastern Europeans feared that their incipient autonomy might be destroyed in the new wave of Cold War. The Soviet Union has paid, and continues to pay, a price for this exploitation, a cost expressed in cynicism and distrust at high levels, and popular resentment—even to the point of intermittent rebellions—against the Soviet system in most, if not all, of Eastern Europe. Even the most Slavophile and left-leaning of the Eastern Europeans in 1945, the Czechs and Slovaks, have been alienated by Soviet policies. (Analogous costs have been run up for the United States as a result of numerous heavy-handed American interventions in Latin America and other parts of the world, though not, I would argue, in Europe, where the American presence has generally been welcomed by the majority of the population as well as by the NATO governments.)

Few, if any, Western governments depend to any significant degree upon NATO for their legitimacy (though this may well have been the case in Konrad Adenauer's Germany). As in Eastern Europe, some NATO governments gain points with their own peoples by defying the alliance leader and taking their own course, at least part-way. The NATO autonomists never seem to go more than part-way, however, because they continue to appreciate the value of the Western alliance in restraining the military and political potential of Moscow, a force that could again be activated, as in 1968. By contrast, there probably is rather little fear among WTO governments that any NATO power, even West Germany, would ever seek to dictate political concessions from military strength.

To the extent that exploitation exists in NATO, it probably tends to be manipulation of the hegemonical power by the lesser members rather than vice versa, as in the East. This paradox is explained by the theory of "collective goods." As Mancur Olson and other economists have pointed out, a "collective good" such as security usually is not funded to optimal levels unless all beneficiaries are compelled to contribute. Failing such coercion, there is a tendency for the strongest, most interested party to provide the collective goods to the degree it believes necessary for its own reasons, while others often take a "free ride" or at least pay a discount fare.[11]

This helps explain why American defense expenditures per capita in 1974 averaged twice those of most NATO members. The net gains and contributions of the various NATO members are quite difficult to compute, however, and are rendered still more complex by the ability of the American aircraft industry to win contracts with other alliance members. A promising development in "mutual aid" during 1975 were the signs that many of the new contracts awarded to American firms would be shared with European producers.

MUTUAL ANACHRONISM?

The most important common feature shared by the two alliance systems is their anachronistic existence beyond the early years of the Cold War. Both alliance systems, concentrating the largest and most powerful forces ever amassed in peacetime, are directed against security problems of the past rather than those of the future. The greatest threats facing members of both alliances are probably ecological, as environmental and economic pressures rise. If this assessment is correct, both sides should curtail their Cold War disputation and commence joint action to reduce deployments and enhance mutual trust.

To be sure, both NATO and WTO provide mutual assistance against external attack by the other. Whether the costs and dangers entailed in these systems of collective security are warranted is another matter. Why should rational actors in the richest nations in history maintain the most deadly (and costly) armies in history? The answer is that each alliance perpetuates a perceived need—or at least a justification—for the other. To that extent, both NATO and WTO do a disservice to their constituent peoples, compelling them to maintain higher levels of arms and military manpower than necessary.

Even if we grant that each superpower continues to harbor hostile plans against the other, are any of the scenarios for limited war in Europe really credible?[12] Would not any conflict in Europe—especially if one or both sides resorted to tactical nuclear weapons (often more powerful than the Hiroshima bomb)—escalate to global dimensions? Can either side be credited with real statesmanship when neither acts to circumvent this spiraling balance of terror?

Both alliances would benefit their peoples far more if they took a sober look at the real, rather than the imagined, dangers to their security and other vital interests in the years ahead. These dangers arise basically from the economic and environmental problems that, in different ways, plague the industrially developed as well as the developing countries. These difficulties, joined with the aspirations for a better life among the have-nots of the Third World, and linked with the spread of nuclear and other advanced weaponry, pose the most urgent threats to the security of the northern nations, whatever their ideology.

Both alliances would profit their members far more if a wider vision of mutual interest could be implemented as the basis for policy, one that comprehended the transcendent problems of global politics rather than the cliches of the Cold War. Security, in the long run, may lie more in the formation of pan-European electric grids and fuel networks than in deterrence and early warning systems, and in coordinated development projects aimed at the economic well-being and social justice in the Third World rather than quarrels over the short-run allegiance of rival factions in Angola or Laos.

NOTES

1. Text reprinted in *Survival* 16, no. 4 (July/August 1974): 198-200.

2. *Sovremennye problemy razoruzheniia* (Moscow: Mysl', 1970), published for the Institute of World Economics and International Relations. Chapter XI, by I.A. Koloshov, is entitled "The North Atlantic Alliance, the Warsaw Treaty Organization and the Problem of Their Dissolution [*rospusk*]," pp. 262-90. Another relevant chapter is VIII, by M. P. Shelepin, "Nuclear-Free Zones," pp. 166-97.

3. Marshal Ivan Yakubovsky, "Bastion of Peace and National Security," *Voenno-istoricheskii zhurnal* no. 3 (March 1971): 20-31. In 1975 Yakubovsky was credited with editing a book entitled "Combat Alliance of the Fraternal Peoples and Armies." For a more legalistic treatment, see A. S. Bakhov, *Organizatsiia Varshavskogo dogovora (pravovye aspekty)* (Moscow: Nauka, 1971).

4. S. V. Kochubei, *NATO i voprosy evropeiskoi bezopasnosti* (Leningrad: Obshchestvo "Znanie" RSFSR, Leningradskaia Organizatsiia, 1974). A more general and objective treatment of European security problems may be found in a book edited by V. V. Zagladin, *Problemy sovremennoi Evropy* (Moscow: Mysl', 1974), which includes chapters on NATO and on "military detente," but omits the polemical comparisons between NATO and WTO provided in the works discussed in the present chapter.

5. Kochubei, op. cit., pp. 25-26.

6. Lawrence T. Caldwell, "The Warsaw Pact: Directions of Change," *Problems of Communism* 24, no. 5 (September/October 1975): 1-19, at 6-7.

7. International Institute for Strategic Studies, *The Military Balance, 1974-1975* (London: the Institute, 1974), p. 11.

8. Text of the Helsinki agreement, "Conference on Security and Co-Operation in Europe, Final Act," U.S. Department of State Publication 8826, August 1975 (mimeo.).

9. A major work on WTO points to greater flexibility and consultation among its members in the crises of 1968-70 than in those, say, of 1956-60; see Robin Allison Rem-

ington, *The Warsaw Pact: Case Studies in Communist Conflict Resolution* (Cambridge, Mass.: M.I.T. Press, 1971).

10. Caldwell, op. cit., pp. 18-19.

11. For analysis, see Bruce M. Russett, *What Price Vigilance?* (New Haven: Yale University Press, 1970), Ch. IV, "Alliances and the Price of Primacy." Russett finds that WTO spending did not conform to the theory until the mid-1960s, which he attributes to Soviet coercion in the earlier years (p. 115). The most serious types of Soviet exploitation of WTO, however, have been more political and ideological than economic. There simply is no Western analogy to Soviet use of WTO and Soviet armies stationed in Eastern Europe to maintain ideological standards of alliance members (though one motive for maintaining American, British and French troops in West Germany was to ensure that the country did not become remilitarized in ways that could threaten any of its neighbors).

12. Various scenarios are discussed in R. J. Vincent, "Military Power and Political Influence: The Soviet Union and Western Europe," *Adelphi Papers* no. 119 (London: International Institute for Strategic Studies, 1975).

12

THE DOMESTIC ROOTS
OF FOREIGN POLICY
IN EASTERN EUROPE
Bogdan Denitch

INTRODUCTION

The publication of a serious book on the international politics of Eastern Europe, with a number of scholars contributing papers on various aspects of foreign policy development there, marks a shift in the way that the Eastern European states are viewed by the academic world in the United States. The consensual wisdom of the scholars in the field of comparative communist studies has, for most of the post-World War II period, held that with the exception of Yugoslavia, and later Albania and Romania, there was, for all practical purposes, no such thing as a foreign policy for the Eastern European states, and that their posture had to be understood primarily in terms of the long-range policy interests of the Soviet Union. That consensus of course reflected the reality of the 1950s and early 1960s and the growing attempts to integrate Eastern Europe as a Soviet-led counterbloc to NATO and the European Common Market (EEC).

Today the Eastern European states are increasingly perceived as stable polities by both the outside world and their own ruling elites and, consequently, as moving from a relationship of subservience to one of a partnership with the Soviet Union. Consequences of this development are that the traditional interests of the individual Eastern European states are increasingly asserting themselves, and that within the framework of the alliance they increasingly pursue policies based on the interests of their own ruling elites that often, but not always, coincide with the general interests of the bloc and the Soviet Union.[1]

Major accelerating factors in this development have undoubtedly been the development of Ostpolitik under Willy Brandt and of the American-Soviet detente in the Nixon-Kissinger era. Both developments provided a framework for an increasing differentiation within the bloc vis-a-vis Western Europe, the United States, and each other.

GROWTH OF INTRABLOC DIVERSITY

Before turning to the specific domestic roots of foreign policy of the Eastern European states, it is useful to classify those polities in terms of the degree to which the present regimes successfully maximize the traditional (pre-communist) aims of those states and the consequent legitimation of those regimes among their own people. If we use this criterion as a yardstick, Albania, Yugoslavia, and Romania clearly are governed by elites that have successfully and aggressively asserted an independent role that is often disproportionate to the economic, political, and demographic strength of the country. They are clearly, therefore, regimes that can harness the themes of nationalism, national pride, and independence from bloc politics, and thus can mobilize support of elements of the population that do not necessarily accept the sociopolitical programs of the ruling parties.

To a lesser extent, the same can be said for Poland, which has emerged as a major Eastern European power with increasing economic weight in an energy-dependent Europe. Bulgaria and Hungary can be viewed essentially as "stand pat" nations whose traditional territorial claims have not been successfully asserted and whose nationalist feeling is exacerbated by the presence of real or imagined irredenta—in the case of Hungary, the large Hungarian minorities in Transylvania, Czechoslovakia, and Yugoslavia, and in the case of Bulgaria, the traditional claims to Yugoslav and Greek Macedonia. In both cases, no likely prospect exists for the fulfillment of those claims and no aid of a practical nature from WTO can be expected. However, both countries have had moderate economic successes of sharply different types, and in both cases the prospect of continued stable rule makes the regimes increasingly act as the repositories of national sentiments and aims.

East Germany represents a special case, since it explicitly cannot fulfill the traditional national aims of unification and is, in terms of foreign policy, simultaneously preoccupied with its relationship with West Germany and the continual need to contrast its internal social order and foreign policy with that of the Federal Republic, while also acting as the most developed, most modernized, and most efficient ally of the Soviet Union in the area. For East Germany, the alliance probably is indispensable for the very existence of the state and regime.

Czechoslovakia, after the traumatic "Prague Spring," is a more complicated case, since the national unification and integration have not been adversely affected by membership within the bloc; the regime itself has developed a shaky legitimacy primarily because of its generally unsuccessful path of economic development in the 1960s and the abrupt crackdown on the experimentation of the Dubcek era that might have created a Czech variant of the road to socialism capable of mobilizing support and compliance.

In terms of the traditional approach to the legitimation of regimes, which stresses that support and compliance are critical in determining whether a regime has achieved legitimacy, it is clear that all of the regimes discussed are high on compliance but support varies, particularly in terms of foreign policies.[2]

Support is probably highest in Albania, Yugoslavia, Romania, and Poland. The aggressive assertion of Albanian national claims, its obvious independence from its neighbors, and the hostile stance it takes toward the Eastern European bloc probably have wide support and acceptance throughout the population. In Yugoslavia we are on much firmer ground, for voluminous data exist in the form of public opinion polls and studies by opinion-makers and journalists, all of which indicate that the greatest area of consensus has, since the mid-1960s, been in the field of foreign policy, which is seen as logical, consistent with national interest, and successful in maintaining national independence while obtaining a fair amount of foreign credits and aid.[3]

In Romania, this support can be inferred if only because of the repeated appeals of the regime to national pride, to the specific Romanian path to socialism, to a dynamic and independent foreign policy, to increasing economic contacts with Western Europe, and to the successful management of the traditional territorial dispute with Hungary, which was settled after World War II in favor of Romania.* Poland is somewhat more complex, for large territorial losses in the east were more than made up by major territorial acquisitions from Germany and the chronic minority problem that plagued the pre-World War II Polish state has been replaced by the creation of what is one of the more homogeneous national states in Europe. The remnant of the German ethnic minority has been traded to West Germany in the recent settlements for closer economic relations and the increasing recognition of the legitimacy of the new western frontiers of Poland. The acquisitions were economically greater than the losses, and a foreign policy calculated to obtain treaties acknowledging and legitimizing the Oder-Neisse border obviously had broad support. Since the acquisition also meant that Poland was able to move into the ranks of major coal-producing and coal-exporting countries, a long-range policy of economic

---

*The territorial settlement is successful from the point of view of Romanian national tradition, in that the dispute in Transylvania was settled in Romania's favor, although the national question in Transylvania, with the large Hungarian and Saxon minorities, remains a problem that clearly will have to be resolved, within the present frontiers, between Romania and Hungary.

development in Poland reinforced the regime's claims to be successful guardian of Polish national interests.

DOMESTIC ROOTS: NATIONAL IDENTITY AND SECURITY

The domestic roots of foreign policy can first be treated generally for the region as a whole by examining the local bases of policies common to the countries of the region. With the exception of East Germany, the assertion and maintenance of national independence and the fulfillment of the traditional desire to establish homogeneous nation-states unifying the fragmented populations of Eastern Europe obviously played a major role in legitimating the regimes as the repositories of national traditions for ever-increasing numbers of people. It is useful to remember that the fragile Versailles settlement lasted only twenty years, while the Yalta and Teheran settlements are completing their third decade with no visible realistic challenges to the territorial settlement (and thus to the existence of the individual Eastern European nations as nation-states). One could therefore argue that whatever else were the consequences of the dependence on the Soviet Union and the political systems that were consequently imposed, that dependence has not jeopardized—on the contrary, it has guaranteed—the continued existence of independent Eastern European states. It also has made unrealistic any possibility of German revanchism, which evidently could have been a problem at least for Poland, with its major territorial acquisitions, and for Czechoslovakia, which forcibly expelled over 3 million Sudeten Germans as a part of the postwar settlement. The borders are generally acknowledged to be stable, and claims against the Eastern European states are unlikely to be asserted.

The imposition of the settlement on the Eastern European nations also has frozen other potentially dangerous frontiers that naturally lent themselves to claims and counterclaims. Whatever the other limitations of the Helsinki talks, they represented a major step in obtaining international recognition for the postwar settlement, shifting the basis of that settlement from one endorsed exclusively by the protective power to one recognized by the West as well, and have therefore opened up further possibilities for increasing multilateral East-West European contacts. The agreements can be seen as representing a formal end of a claim to legitimacy by the various emigre groups.

Thus the frontiers in Transylvania, the Yugoslav-Albanian frontier, the status of Macedonia, and the Hungarian-Czechoslovak border have assumed a stability and legitimacy they did not have before World War II. Therefore, neither German claims for the lost territories nor potential territorial intrabloc conflicts were permitted to surface. One consequence of the stability of the boundaries, insofar as there are ethnic minorities involved, is that the fate of those minorities has to be determined within the present frontiers. No redrawing of frontiers in Eastern Europe is likely in the foreseeable future, if for no other reason than that the Soviet Union has no intentions of permitting that Pandora's box to be opened. This differs dramatically from the chronically unstable situation in the region between the two world wars.[4]

A possible exception to this generalization exists in Yugoslavia, where it is not external guarantees, but the repeatedly stated readiness of the Yugoslavs to defend their sovereignty and national independence, that reassures the local populace that no partitioning or redrafting of the frontiers is likely. The 1975 agreements with Italy over the Trieste frontier area removed the last outstanding border dispute with a neighboring power, and formalized stable and friendly relations on what would otherwise be a frontier lending itself to irridentist claims.

CONSEQUENCES OF MODERNIZATION AND ECONOMIC DEVELOPMENT

Once the basic national existence has been given a stable, long-range framework, several other forces shape foreign policy. First, a unifying characteristic of all of the regimes has been their commitment to rapid industrialization and overall economic development since World War II.[5] The performance of the Eastern European polities, with the notable exception of Czechoslovakia, can be increasingly perceived as relatively successful compared both with the prewar regimes and with a Western Europe and capitalist world that are subject to unemployment, inflation, and economic crises. The Eastern European regimes, on the contrary, can be described—whatever else may be their problems—as stable, conservative polities in which socioeconomic development probably will continue along predictable lines.[6]

The evolution of these societies is, of course, reinforced by the changing economic relationship between the Soviet Union and its Eastern European allies. In the period immediately following World War II, the relationship was seen both locally and by foreign observers as one of economic subordination to the interests of the Soviet Union; and it could have been defined as an exploitative one in which the economic agreements provided aid for the Soviet Union's reconstruction and the export of technologies somewhat more advanced than those of the Soviet Union. That relationship is no longer the dominant mode in the area. On the contrary, the Soviet Union is the supplier of essential raw materials and energy sources, including oil and natural gas, and cannot be said to have a less developed technological infrastructure than its Eastern European allies. Although East Germany is more developed, particularly in the chemical industry, the Soviet situation as a major source of energy for itself and the bloc leads to an increasing division of labor in intrabloc relations, and probably will lead more and more to a specialization of the Eastern European economies in those fields where they have a historical or actual advantage: consumer goods, electronics, and light manufacturing.

However, the Soviets are in a superior position to obtain high-level Western technology, given their situation in the world market; and it is my opinion that the technological gap between Eastern Europe and the Soviet Union will increasingly shift so that some of the Western technology will be made available to the Eastern European states by the Soviet Union. Consequently the domestic perception of relations with the Soviet Union no longer is a major problem for the Eastern European regimes, whose subservience to the Soviet Union was previously seen by much of the public as a betrayal of national interests. The stability of the Eastern European economies rests on an increasing division of labor within CEMA and is underpinned by access to the raw material resources of the Soviet Union. This situation probably will increase independent arrangements by individual Eastern European states directly with the West, since the old intrabloc autarchy is now economically more of a liability than an asset to the Soviet Union's own economic development and needs.

The rapid industrialization and urbanization of the Eastern European states has created broad new groups of persons whose relatively high social mobility is directly linked to the existence of the present regimes. There are now new technological and white-collar workers who are simultaneously the product of these regimes and the politically most articulate and vociferous citizens. Their own needs and desires, after three decades of development, are for a life style appropriate to their present rank, which is interpreted in terms of life styles of the prewar and pre-communist middle and professional classes. Simply stated, increasingly large groups now exist that demand some of the amenities traditionally associated with middle-class European life, and the regimes are pressed to fulfill these needs in a number of ways.[7]

The first and most obvious is the desire for more and better consumer goods of a type not produced domestically. Therefore, the pressure for increasing trade and contact with the West will continue. Second, for the technological and scientific communities, intellectual contact with their colleagues and peers, and access to universities and research findings, are essential; and consequently increasing pressure can be expected for broader cultural and scientific exchanges. So long as these groups were primarily the residues of the prewar middle classes and were viewed as hostile to the ruling parties, the pressure was resisted with varying degrees of rigidity. The new technocrats, scientists, and administrators, however, are products of the new societies; and more often than not they are integrated politically into the ruling party. Therefore, these same demands today assume a different dimension and increasingly are met with a positive response, since they came from groups fundamentally loyal to the regime and represent demands that can be granted without shifts in the priorities of the regime. More simply put, the new middle classes are raising demands for individual advancement and a socially stable environment within the framework of the regime goals rather than representing a demand for the restoration of class privileges to groups whose interests were linked with the pre-communist regimes.[8]

The demand for consumer goods and the ability to travel and consume the cultural goods of the West is, of course, not limited to the technocrats and the new middle class; it can also be found among increasingly large segments of the working class. For a number of reasons this is becoming a more acute problem. To begin with, the working classes are large and resemble the classic industrial proletariat of advanced industrial societies. Unlike the earlier newly industrialized peasants, the present working classes of Eastern Europe are potentially much more powerful and, as the 1970-71 events in Poland show, are capable of successfully asserting classic trade union and class demands without external leadership. It is my opinion that this trend will continue, particularly given the special nature of political socialization in the Eastern European countries. These are, after all, workers who have been repeatedly told that they are the rulers of their countries, the carriers of historical progress, and the backbone of industrial development. They are therefore unlikely to accept growing social differentiation in life style and access to consumer goods, which would be the consequence of further improvements in the standard of living of the technocrats and the middle class. They also are far better educated and more aware of the range of possibilities outside their own countries. Radio and television are perhaps more corrosive of social stability in Eastern Europe when they advertise consumer goods and show vignettes of daily life in the West than when they engage in anti-communist propaganda.[9]

Whatever the causal linkages, I am postulating increasing workers' demands for a change in living standards and life styles in the immediate and not-too-distant future. A complicating factor is the regime's propaganda stressing its economic successes. If one is continually told that the country is developing rapidly and that Five-Year Plan after Five-Year Plan has been a brilliant success, it would be an odd person indeed who did not begin to ask when there will be better personal living standards. Therefore the pressures for increasing contact with the Western European economies and the demand for trade and credits are likely to assume a greater urgency, since trade can be viewed as stabilizing the domestic situation, in addition to any other economic consequences it might have.

The new and growing weight of the working class as a part of the political public is likely to have several additional foreign policy impacts. First, given the current attempts toward a merger of the communist and noncommunist world trade union federations in a context where the working classes, and eventually the trade unions, are likely to assume increasingly independent roles in Eastern Europe, one can postulate that the regimes in that area will be pressed to seek contacts and alliances with trade unions and communist and working-class parties in the West, and that actions like East Germany's recognition of Franco's Spain will become increasingly difficult. In a context in which the Western

European communists or socialists have more and more prospects of political power, the relative weight of those parties vis-a-vis the Eastern European regimes is augmented, since they will no longer be merely opposition parties whose ideological differences irritate; with access to power, they will represent alternate Western European establishments that may well have common interests with the Eastern European states in emphasizing European regional concerns independent of both American and Soviet ones.[10] It is hard to imagine that the present line of the Italian communists on European security and independence go unnoticed in sections of the Eastern European political establishment. On the other hand, it is politically far more difficult to maintain a stance of hostility and isolation from socialist states in Western Europe than from a Western Europe seen primarily as a junior ally of the United States. A part of this process can be seen in the increasingly close relations between Poland and Sweden.

Second, an increasingly assertive working class, while providing a barrier against the embourgeoisement of those societies, also may well exert pressures toward the greater production of consumer goods within the area as a whole, and consequently toward a lowering of the domestic arms budgets and a revival of the idea of a neutral and independent Europe.

Two more general tendencies can be seen in Eastern Europe. One is the relative advantages given by the type of underdevelopment characteristic of Eastern Europe in the current economic era. For example, Poland's lack of success in modernizing its energy sources by switching from coal to the "more modern" fuel, oil, is clearly a blessing. Although the present oil requirements of Eastern Europe are in good part covered by the Soviet oil surpluses, the ability of Eastern European economies to utilize alternative energy sources, primarily coal, makes them less subject to energy crunches, and thus to external pressure, than the more advanced economies are. Further, the centralized planned economies find themselves more capable of restraining energy consumption by the population than the Western European societies do. Thus, in individual consumption, the relative absence of a huge private investment in transportation—that is, the small number of passenger cars—is a phenomenon that may be envied by some of the prosperous European nations. Less investment in energy consumption for heating and lighting the cities, and less stress on energy-consuming gadgetry permit those economies to adapt more flexibly to the realities of an energy-scarce world.

Second, the Eastern European countries are relatively rich in raw materials, particularly in agricultural goods, although these resources have been inadequately developed. The potential that exists there, however, will favorably affect the economies and societies in an era of increasing shifts in the pricing policies between the manufactured goods and raw materials.

The general point, however, is that a number of the amenities characteristic of Western European and American life were dependent on a peculiar arrangement of the world economy that provided for cheap energy and raw materials and expensive manufactured goods. The fact that the Eastern European nations have less of an investment in that type of modern sector and a heavier investment in public goods and public consumption will probably be seen in the future not as the result of bad planning and mismanagement but as the result of the wisdom of the economic planners and political leaders. All this means that the Eastern European countries will have less reason to expect disadvantageous deals in their contacts with Western Europe. The consequent growing self-confidence of the ruling elites probably will accelerate tendencies toward greater all-European economic integration.

The self-confidence of the elites in Eastern Europe has not been seriously challenged by what many observers have seen as the major single weakness of the communist nation-states, the lack of integration of the peasantry in the new nations, and their alleged hostility to the regimes. In my view, this problem has been much exaggerated by Western observers, often influenced by exiled leaders of former peasant and smallholder parties. The problem of the Eastern European regimes has been not so much with peasants as a social group, but with the relative inefficiency of agriculture.[11] In point of fact, no serious challenge to any regime has been posed by the peasantry since the end of World War II; and when one thinks of the challenges of the workers' revolts in East Germany, of the riots in Poznan in Poland, of the Polish October of 1956, of the abortive Hungarian revolution, and of the "Prague Spring" of 1968, what comes through quite clearly is that the peasantry in these cases was passive, and that insofar as the regimes did face internal challenges, they came from workers and sections of the intelligentsia, modern urban rather than traditional rural groups.

The peasantry in Eastern Europe does not represent a problem, in my opinion, for a number of factors, of which repression is only one, and probably the least important one. To begin with, all of the Eastern European regimes provided for a great deal of social mobility from the countryside during the rapid urbanization and industrialization that followed World War II. The young, the bright, and the ambitious—the natural potential leaders of rural discontent— have all had the option of leaving the countryside, and have done so en masse. In many of the Eastern European countries, the rural population is overwhelmingly old and female, and therefore quite passive. The bias against agriculture, coming as it did from both ideological sources and the reality of rural over-population, probably will be reversed, given the shifts in the world prices of agricultural products and the increasing emphasis on economic criteria in decision-making within Eastern Europe.

The country-city cleavage manifested in anti-peasant politics in the past and a relative neglect of agriculture are therefore almost sure to be reversed in the foreseeable future. On the one hand, this will mean a greater emphasis on food production; on the other, a conciliatory policy toward the rural population will result in increased stability of the regime and willingness to increase foreign contacts.

The last of the general forces in domestic life with an impact on foreign policy to be discussed briefly is the Roman Catholic Church, which is the major nonestablishment force in Poland and Hungary and an important force in Czechoslovakia and Yugoslavia. As the regimes have moved toward a greater stability and legitimacy, the direct confrontation between the church and the party, and the consequent strains in relationships to the rural populations, have increasingly receded. It is obvious that both the Vatican and the communist elites desire to coexist on a long-range basis. Misunderstandings and differences of interest of course will continue to exist. No lay government is ever likely to fully satisfy the church's claims in the field of education, birth control, and the establishment of independent organizations for the socialization of the young. On the other hand, the degree of toleration toward the church and its activities in Eastern Europe increasingly resembles that of societies that practice separation of church and state and in which the Catholics are a minority. The normalization of these relations has several consequences for foreign policy. First, it means an end of the perception that the world outside, especially the church, is engaged in a permanent crusade against the governments of Eastern Europe. Second, it means that the Christian Democratic parties of Western Europe can move from their rigid anti-communist stance, and therefore will accelerate the possibilities of contact and trade. Third, the absence of major church-state confrontations creates less pressure for emigration and a greater likelihood of a more open border policy on the part of the Eastern European regimes.[12]

RETURN TO TRADITION

As a part of the normalization of the Eastern European states, we can observe the reassertion of certain traditional relationships in foreign policy and in international contacts. For example, it is useful to remember that most of the Eastern European countries have traditionally had relatively little contact with the United States, and considerably more contact with their Eastern and Western European neighbors. Almost unnoted by American scholars and observers, a reassertion of certain traditional cultural ties has been slowly growing. There has been a steady increase of contacts since the mid-1960s between Poland and France, a link that is historical and that certainly was aided by the common antipathy of the two countries toward any talk of German reunification. The Hungarians have increasing contacts with Austria, a cultural tie that surely warms many a middle-aged heart; the East Germans are tacitly, as a part of Ostpolitik, treated as belonging to a nonexistent unified Germany in dealings with the Common Market; on the other hand, the Yugoslavs and the Bulgarians have reverted to their traditional hostile relations, and little love seems lost between Romania and Hungary. In many ways, the foreign policy predilections of the ruling elites and the educated publics of Eastern Europe would strike a historian as familiar, with a notable change in the role of the Soviet Union in the area.[13]

The linkages that are created and maintained in this manner are welcomed not only by the regime but also by the publics of the Eastern European states, since they represent a return to a familiar normalcy and dampen the shock that rapid modernization and social change have created among the middle classes of Eastern Europe. There is something reassuringly familiar in Warsaw today when one finds that graduate students plan to study in Paris; in Budapest, where a portly technocrat plans a weekend in Vienna; and when a communist Bulgarian professor asserts boundary claims against Yugoslavia in a language not one whit different from that of the right-wing Bulgarian intellectuals between the two world wars.

The wild cards in the deck are, of course, Yugoslavia and Albania. While many of the general considerations affecting the other Eastern European countries apply to them, including the reassertion of certain traditional relations (Albania's major economic trading partner is Italy), the fact that they are not a part of WTO or CEMA makes them different in interesting ways. The central policy considerations of the Albanian elite are evident. A tiny country with a substantial irridenta in Yugoslavia, it is caught in a dilemma: on one hand, Albania would normally assert territorial claims against a neighbor that has close to a million Albanians living within its borders; but on the other hand, it has to face the reality that the existence of an independent Yugoslavia, outside WTO, is a major guarantor of an independent Albania. This preoccupation with the preservation of national independence explains why this most Stalinist of states bitterly denounced the Soviet intervention in Czechoslovakia and asserted that it would be ready to aid Yugoslavia in maintaining its sovereignty and independence. As a result, Albanian-Yugoslav relations have been steadily improving, and Albanian trade depends on good relations with the Yugoslavs. Other than that, about the only relations that Albania has in Europe are with Italy and France.

The Yugoslav case is far too complex to be discussed at length. However, there are certain major outlines of Yugoslav policy that can be viewed from the domestic angle. First, Yugoslavia's position outside the two blocs has required that it energetically seek contacts, and ties, and potential allies outside Europe. Therefore, the Yugoslavs probably pay more attention to the United Nations and to the Third World than any other European country. They see their special position in the U.N. and their ties with Third World countries as partly a guarantor of their continued independence and existence, but they also see the Third World countries (at least potentially) as future trading partners whose markets will not depend on the state of the Cold War or the state of Yugoslav-Soviet relations.[14]

Second, the Yugoslavs are further affected by several immediate considerations. They have a large number of immigrant workers in Western Europe whose fate and whose return are a continual problem of domestic policy. This requires a series of bilateral arrangements protecting the Yugoslav workers in West Germany, Belgium, and Sweden; increasingly close contact between the Yugo-- slav trade unions and the Western European trade unions; and the maintenance of cultural and educational institutions for those workers in the countries where they are temporarily working.[15] All of those considerations dictate a very active foreign policy emphasizing governmental, economic, trade union, and academic contacts.

Third, since the Yugoslavs have an open-frontier policy and have abolished visas by bilateral agreements with many countries, a special problem has emerged in maintaining their equidistance from the two major power blocs. The problem is that although possibilities of contact and travel are theoretically equally open to Western and Eastern Europe, both economic and cultural ties tend to tilt toward Western Europe and the United States. Yugoslavs go to work in West Germany and not East Germany; Yugoslav enterprises seek to trade on the Western markets; and Yugoslav intellectuals, artists, and scholars maintain their contacts almost exclusively with Western European and American centers. This situation creates an asymmetry that goes a long way to explain the relatively hostile tone taken by the Yugoslav press and some of the authorities toward excessive contacts with the West; and it is sometimes seen as threatening the delicate balance required by a policy of nonalignment. The real difficulty is in increasing the contacts with Eastern Europe and the Soviet Union.

The pressures toward imports of consumer goods and for access to Western cultural commodities are likewise not a particular problem in Yugoslavia, which both imports and manufactures those goods and has Western films and books readily available. However, a specific problem for Yugoslavia is that it, more than any other Eastern European country, simultaneously hails and is threatened by a Soviet-American detente. While coexistence between the two power blocs and a lowering of the tension in Europe, especially in the Mediterranean basin, are in the long-range Yugoslav interest, too close an agreement between the Russians and Americans may—and this is probably a nightmare for Yugoslav foreign policy-makers—involve trade-offs jeopardizing Yugoslavia's present situation outside both blocs. In plain language, increased Soviet influence in Yugoslavia may be a part of a deal. The experience of Cyprus and the continuing crisis in the Middle East contribute to this sense of unease.

The detente between the United States and the Soviet Union, emphasizing the dominance of the major powers, has been paralleled by an increasing disarray of the Third World nonaligned bloc, as individual powers that had formed that bloc have moved to a closer relation with one of the major powers. This trend in the Middle East, in India, and in some of the African states is a serious setback for a policy the Yugoslavs have spent so much time, resources, and energy in developing. As of this writing, of the figures who were central to that bloc, only President Tito remains alive and in power; Nehru, Sukarno, Nasser, and Nkrumah are dead. It is therefore likely that Yugoslavia will seek to neutralize and avoid hostile confrontations with either of the major blocs, and that it will adopt a considerably lower profile in foreign policy. The Yugoslav policy will, in my opinion, remain firmly committed to independence and, internally as well as externally, will crack down on any moves challenging this independence and seeking closer integration with either bloc. The recent appearance and subsequent arrest of Cominform sympathizers—presumably Soviet-inspired—is an indicator of this continuing and consistent policy. On the other hand, the state of the Yugoslav economy requires credits and markets; and therefore far greater emphasis on economic arrangements of a bilateral and multilateral character can be expected.

In conclusion, the Eastern European states are increasingly differentiating in their foreign policy approaches, although they are still subject to a number of constraints—especially those countries that are in WTO and CEMA. The basic pressures domestically are generated by the creation of a new middle class of technocrats, scientists, and administrators who desire commodities and cultural goods that would require increasing contacts between Eastern and Western Europe, and by a growing and powerful industrial working class whose needs for consumer goods have to be satisfied if the regimes are not to face internal challenges to their norms and claims to legitimacy. Detente has accelerated the need of the Eastern European countries to individually seek their own economic and political links, since in the Soviet-American detente the interests of minor allies, both Western and Eastern European, often appear to be overlooked or ignored. The tendency therefore will be toward greater intra-European integration and an opening up of economic and cultural contacts between Eastern and Western Europe. This trend will be reinforced by the needs of Western Europe to maintain greater independence and cohesion in a situation where American and European interests often do not coincide, particularly given the need for the Western European trade and energy interests to be separated from the vagaries of American policy. The natural trading partners and the traditional cultural ties of Eastern European countries are in Western Europe, and it will therefore be a delicate balancing act between the need to maintain intra-bloc solidarity and economic ties, on the one hand, and an opening to greater contact with Western Europe, on the other hand, that will dominate the policies of Eastern European elites in the 1980s. As the regimes increasingly appear to be stable and legitimate, the reluctance to engage in broad contacts outside their system of alliances will diminish.

NOTES

1. Ghita Ionesco, *The Politics of the European Communist States* (New York: Praeger Publishers, 1967); H. Gordon Skilling, "Interest Groups and Communist Politics," *World Politics* 18, no. 3 (April 1966): 417-42.

2. Bogdan Denitch, *The Legitimation of a Revolution: The Yugoslav Case* (New Haven: Yale University Press, 1976), pp. 197-99.

3. *Opinion-Making Elites in Yugoslavia*, Allen H. Barton, Bogdan Denitch, and Charles Kadushin, eds. (New York: Praeger Publishers, 1973), presents a summary of joint Yugoslav-American work in this field. Other major sources are the annual reports of the Center for Public Opinion Research of the Institute of Social Sciences in Belgrade since 1956; reports of the Center for Public Opinion Research of the Institute of Social Research in Zagreb; and, in English, *Some Yugoslav Papers Presented to the VIIIth ISA Congress in Toronto* (Ljubljana: University of Ljubljana, 1976).

4. Peter Sugar and Ivo Lederer, *Nationalism in Eastern Europe* (Seattle: University of Washington Press, 1971), pp. 360-62, 434-36.

5. Neil Smelser, "Mechanics of Change and Adjustment to Change," in B. Hoselitz and W. Moore, eds., *Industrialization and Society* (Paris: UNESCO, 1973), pp. 87-96.

6. William Shawcross, *Crime and Compromise: Politics of Kadar's Hungary* (New York: Dutton, 1974), pp. 280-84.

7. Ota Klein and Jindrich Zelerny, "Dynamics of Change: Leadership, the Economy, Organizational Structure and Society," in R. Barry Farrell, ed., *Political Leadership in Eastern Europe and the Soviet Union* (Chicago: Aldine, 1970), pp. 199-224.

8. Chalmers Johnson, ed., *Change in Communist Systems* (Palo Alto, Calif.: Stanford University Press, 1970), esp. R. V. Burks, "Technology and Political Change in Eastern Europe," pp. 265-312, and Dankwart A. Rustow, "Communism and Change," pp. 343-58.

9. Frank Parkin, *Class Inequality and Political Order* (New York: Praeger Publishers, 1971), pp. 167-80.

10. Neil McInnes, *Communist Parties of Western Europe* (New York: Oxford University Press, 1975), pp. 183-204.

11. A. L. Stinchcombe, "Agricultural Enterprise and Rural Class Relations," in R. Bendix and S. M. Lipset, eds., *Class, Status and Power* (London: Routledge & Kegan Paul, 1966), pp. 248-72.

12. Bogdan Bociurkiw and John Strong, *Religion and Atheism in the USSR and Eastern Europe* (New York: Macmillan, 1975), pp. 124-38.

13. Paul Lendvai, *The Eagles in the Cobwebs* (New York: Anchor, 1970), pp. 44-52.

14. Lars Nord, *Non-Alignment and Socialism* (Stockholm: Raben & Sjogren, 1974), pp. 124-49; and Leon Mates, *Non-Alignment: Theory and Current Practice* (Belgrade: Institute for International Politics and Economy, 1972), pp. 18-24.

15. Stephen Castles and Godela Kosak, *Immigrant Workers and Class Structure in Western Europe* (New York: Oxford University Press, 1973), pp. 40-52.

13

EXTERNAL INFLUENCES
ON EASTERN EUROPE
Andrzej Korbonski

INTRODUCTION

Anyone trying to evaluate external influences on Eastern European politics is faced with a difficult task. According to a dictionary definition, "to evaluate" means "to determine or set the value or amount of" or "to appraise." The same dictionary defines influence as "the capacity or power of persons or things to produce effects on others by intangible or indirect means."[1] In other words, assuming that we accept the above definition, our task is to measure the power of "persons or things" external to Eastern Europe to cause certain events to occur there. However, if we broaden the above definition somewhat, we may simply rephrase the question, which would then call for the appraisal of the impact of foreign influences on Eastern European politics.

While any attempt at estimating the power of an institution or an organization, of a country or a group of states, is tricky enough, any effort to evaluate the effect of that power is even more difficult.[2] It is obvious that in order to be able to do so, we would require at least concrete evidence or data indicating the existence of external influences affecting the region, and a method of measuring their impact on the given polity or polities.

Throughout history, Eastern Europe, if only because of its geographical location, has been on the receiving end of foreign influences. The region has been an object rather than a subject in international politics, and although some of the countries in the area may periodically have influenced their immediate neighbors, Eastern Europe has, by and large, been strongly influenced by either the West or the East. In a sense it can be argued that the establishment of communist regimes in Eastern Europe after World War II did not represent a major deviation from past patterns but was simply a logical continuation of a lengthy historical process.

Although even at the height of the Stalinist empire, Eastern Europe did not constitute a hermetically "closed" system, the idiosyncratic nature of communist regimes makes it difficult, if not impossible, to gather data that would enable us to determine the impact of external influences on the foreign and domestic politics of the region and of its component parts. For various reasons, the major gap in our knowledge of communist politics concerns the "input" side of political processes, which is where the weight of foreign influences would be most felt. Although some progress has been made in this respect, we still have to rely on the "outputs" as the best source of data illustrating the performance of the system. The only other thing we can do is to make some more or less informed guesses regarding both foreign and domestic inputs into the decision-making process.

Since it is still impossible to trace, much less evaluate, foreign influences on Eastern European politics, one option open to us is to utilize the available data to show the level and extent of interaction between Eastern Europe and various environments with the aid of different models and/or approaches, on the assumption that interaction implies interdependence and, hence, influence.

Thus, for example, we may want to insert Eastern Europe into the communication or transaction model and to calculate all kinds of flows between that area and other environments.[3] The economic and other data appearing in the national statistical yearbooks are generally recognized as reflecting reality, and they provide sufficient raw material for empirical investigations.

Another alternative would be to look at Eastern Europe from the point of view of transnational relations.[4] Although in this case the data base leaves much to be desired, there is little doubt that some interesting work can be done in this respect, especially if, instead of focusing on transnational relations, we concentrate on transgovernmental relations.[5]

Still another possibility is to apply the linkage concept to the study of the relationship between Eastern Europe and other areas.[6] As in the transnational approach, the lack of data limits the utility of this method, although the prospects are not entirely unpromising.

Partly because of the scarcity of data, Eastern Europe has not figured prominently in the literature experimenting with these three approaches. Thus far, the transaction model has proved to be most popular; and several writers have utilized it, mostly in their research on Eastern European regional integration.[7] As for the transnational approach, to the best of my knowledge, the *tabula* continues to be *rasa*.[8] The linkage concept has been introduced into the study of Eastern European politics somewhat self-consciously, partly by adherents of the transaction model and partly by those eager to dismantle the barriers separating communist politics from the rest of comparative politics and international relations, and to bring the former into the mainstream of "modern" social science research.[9] By and large, however, both the quantity and the quality of output have not been very impressive, especially when compared with the work done with respect to other parts of the world.

The purpose of this essay is quite limited and modest. Above all, it is not an attempt to postulate new hypotheses regarding Eastern Europe's interaction with, or dependence on, the outside world, nor is it an effort to test some existing hypotheses utilizing one or more of the approaches mentioned above. It is intended, instead, to be partly a checklist and partly an attempt to draw up an agenda for future research. Thus, first, I shall list and discuss the various environments that, in my opinion, have tended to exert some influence on Eastern Europe since the 1950s and still do so today. I also shall examine the conditions of influence transmission and the agents, channels, and targets of influence penetration. Finally, I shall briefly evaluate the impact of foreign influences in five cases of Eastern European politics that, in my view, provide good examples of the presence or absence of external influences.

My examination will be confined to the seven countries of Eastern Europe (Albania, Bulgaria, Czechoslovakia, East Germany, Hungary, Poland, Romania) and will exclude the Soviet Union. In contrast with other external influences, the impact of Soviet pressures on Eastern Europe has been thoroughly examined in the literature (including Chapters 2-4 of this book), resulting in a high degree of consensus that Moscow's influence in that region has been, is, and will continue to be significant.[10] For the purpose of this chapter, then, I shall take it as given and shall focus on analyzing influences emanating from external environments other than the Soviet Union.

In view of this decision, I will examine whatever evidence there is of non-Soviet external influences in Eastern Europe, with special emphasis on the sources of these influences, the way in which they were transmitted to the region, and the targets they were most likely to hit. Needless to say, the discussion will be descriptive and historical, as well as intuitive and impressionistic. The political systems will be defined broadly enough to include both the economic and the social components. Simply put, this chapter is intended to draw attention to a relatively unexplored aspect of international politics in a regional context.

EASTERN EUROPE AND FOREIGN ENVIRONMENTS

Like all other regions, Eastern Europe as a whole and its individual components can be viewed as belonging to a number of environments, however defined.* Thus, when looking at the area it may be useful to think of it in terms of multiple and/or "overlapping" memberships or "identity references,[11] whether in such formal organizations as CEMA and WTO today or the Cominform in the past, or as part of less well-defined entities, such as the "socialist commonwealth of nations" or the international communist camp—or, to make it still broader, as belonging to the family of European or even industrialized nations. It is a truism that membership in these formal or informal groups subjects both the region and the individual countries to external influences while providing an opportunity for the area to exert its influence on other regions or countries.

One of the most interesting and significant changes in the international environment has been the expansion in the number of multiple memberships experienced by Eastern Europe.[12] Without going into the reasons for this phenomenon, there is considerable evidence indicating growing awareness in some Eastern European countries of being part of Europe or of having much in common with industrial or modern societies. At the same time, some individual states have been gravitating in the direction of more narrowly defined environments, such as the Balkans (Bulgaria and Romania) or the Baltic area (East Germany and Poland). Finally, some countries tend to identify themselves as members of universes with which otherwise they have relatively little in common (Romania and the Third World).

All this has meant that ever since the collapse of the Stalinist colonial empire in the mid-1950s, Eastern Europe has been subjected to a growing volume of influences from the outside, not only because of the gradual, partial lifting of the "iron curtain," but also because of the proliferation of memberships in the various environments. Although the former process probably was more important, since it permitted a greater flow of foreign influences into the area, the latter phenomenon was perhaps more interesting, in that it exposed the region and its individual members to new and unexpected pressures. It also should be mentioned that one of the most significant additional consequences of de-Stalinization in Eastern Europe was the lowering of barriers between individual countries in the region, which until then had tended to be rather isolated from each other, perhaps even more so than from the West.

As will be shown below, the character of the influences generated by the different environments varied greatly. Some of the pressures, such as those caused by industrialization, technological progress, or the scarcity of natural

---

*For the purpose of this discussion I shall define the concept of environment in Deutschian terms of "marked discontinuities in the frequency of transactions and marked discontinuities in the frequency of responses." Karl W. Deutsch, "External Influences on the Internal Behavior of States," in R. Barry Farrell, ed., *Approaches to Comparative and International Politics* (Evanston, Ill.: Northwestern University Press, 1966), p. 5.

resources, were global, secular and long-term. Others tended to be confined to certain geographical regions and to be of shorter duration, as exemplified by the Cold War environment or, possibly, the current East-West detente. Still others were restricted to only a few countries and lasted a relatively short period of time: the influence of Titoism between 1948 and 1956, the impact of events in Hungary and Poland in 1956, and the reverberations of the "Prague Spring" in 1968, are cases in point. All these pressures, alone or in combination, had an effect on Eastern European societies.

CONDITIONS OF INFLUENCE PENETRATION

In attempting to appraise the impact of external influences on any political system, one quickly becomes aware of the complexity of the process of political penetration. In some cases the process can be deceptively simple, as shown by the experience of Eastern Europe after World War II, at least until the mid-1950s. With the Soviet Union as the hegemonical power in the area that insisted on absolute conformity to the Stalinist model, the latter was rather quickly imposed on the satellite countries in the name of "one road to socialism."[13] In that particular period, the Soviet Union clearly was interested not only in spreading its influence, but also in revolutionizing the political, economic, and social systems in the region. It apparently was prepared to take drastic action to accomplish that goal. The Soviet Union succeeded in reaching its objective partly because, for various reasons, local ruling elites were receptive to influences emanating from the East, and partly because it was able to isolate the area from all other influences.

From the perspective of more than twenty years, the Stalinist empire may appear more as an aberration than as a model to be emulated in the future. However, some lessons can be drawn from it. Thus, it appears that the necessary and sufficient condition for the smooth penetration of political influence from the center to the periphery is that the hegemonical power must be ready and willing to exert its influence and its junior allies must be equally ready and willing to receive it.

Does this condition obtain in the mid-1970s? The answer is both "yes" and "no." In order to be more precise, it may be useful to analyze the situation from the macro and micro levels. With the former one can look at the changes in both the international environment and the national elites in the individual Eastern European countries. The latter allows one to deal with the specific conditions in the area as a whole, and in particular countries, that tended to facilitate or hinder the process of penetration.

Starting with the macro level, in the second half of the 1950s the superficially tightly knit Soviet colonial empire was replaced by a much more loosely structured alliance. Although the Soviet Union remained the hegemonical power in the region, the emergence of polycentrism within the international communist environment and the seeming breakup of the bipolar system in favor of a multi-polar international system dramatically changed the conditions of penetration by exposing Eastern Europe to influences other than those of Moscow, which then had to compete with other power centers for influence in the region. Some of these changes in the international communist camp clearly occurred with the tacit approval of the Kremlin, while others obviously were beyond its control. For our purposes the important fact is that the hegemonical power no longer insisted on absolute conformity but was willing (if not forced) to open the area to outside influences.

The other condition—the existence of a homogeneous elite receptive to Soviet pressures—also has undergone some changes. On the one hand, the centrifugal tendencies generated by the abandonment of the doctrine of "one road to socialism" destroyed the fabric of uniformity in the region; and the national decision-makers in some Eastern European countries, who in the past were only too eager to absorb and internalize Soviet influences, began to take advantage of new opportunities offered by the expanding range of multiple memberships and to adopt some political and economic innovations from sources other than the Soviet Union. On the other hand, the process of decompression throughout the area unleashed powerful political, economic, and social forces that contributed to the appearance of serious systemic crises in some countries, which also tended to increase the receptivity to non-Soviet ideas.

Hence the emergence of polycentrism in international communism meant that in the mid-1950s, Eastern European polities became exposed to influences stemming not only from the Soviet Union but also from China and Yugoslavia. The influence of the latter was quite direct and can be documented rather satisfactorily; but the impact of China, although mostly indirect, has been perhaps even more profound.[14] It is a matter of record that China played a major role in the Hungarian and Polish upheavals of October-November 1956 and that it contributed signally to the process of "desatellization" culminating in the defection of Albania from Moscow to Peking. Although China's influence in Eastern Europe declined after the formal appearance of the Sino-Soviet rift, it has by no means disappeared completely. The continuing challenge to Moscow's hegemony in world communism provided the individual Eastern European states with a certain freedom by offering an alternative to the Kremlin's leadership. Only two countries, Albania and Romania, made good use of this opportunity, mainly because of the internal developments in China, especially the "Cultural Revolution," which destroyed most of the credit and goodwill accumulated by Peking in Eastern Europe in the second half of the 1950s. In this respect Romania's attitude was unique and reflected the peculiarity of the leadership's clear determination to keep open as many options as possible.[15] There is little doubt that China's harsh rhetoric throughout the 1960s had the opposite effect from the one originally intended; it brought the majority of Eastern European countries closer to the Soviet Union.

Yugoslavia's influence, very powerful in the 1950s, declined markedly in the following decade. Without going into the causes of the decline, here also internal developments made it much less attractive as a model to be emulated. The Tito-Khrushchev reconciliation of 1955 legitimized Titoism to some extent, thereby making it a tempting proposition; but this was no longer true in the era of "many roads to socialism." Rampant inflation, virulent local nationalism, persistent unemployment, and continued and growing regional socioeconomic differences tended to deter even the most sympathetic Eastern European leaders from imitating the Yugoslav experience.

The disintegration of the Soviet monolith also resulted in some lowering of barriers between individual Eastern European countries, which meant that contacts and communication among them increased greatly. Hence, in addition to influence from the Soviet Union, China, and Yugoslavia, the countries in the region became exposed to influences generated by each other. Obviously, the impact of these influences varied considerably from country to country and was the result of several factors: the relative status and/or prestige of a given country within the area, the character and duration of the influence, and the depth of the potential changes induced by that influence.

Using this crude checklist we can speculate about the degree of influence exerted by individual bloc members upon the rest of the region since the mid-1950s. Poland probably exerted strongest influence in the area from 1956 until at least the end of 1957.[16] The reverberations caused by the Hungarian revolt, while powerful, were much shorter-lived. In contrast, the impact of the 1968 political liberalization in Czechoslovakia was taken much more seriously by almost the entire region. Finally, although Romania has been following a semi-independent line since 1963, it appears that its influence in the last dozen years or so has been virtually nil. There is no doubt that the differences in impact reflected the status of a given country as perceived by others. After the Soviet Union, Poland was seen as the strongest member of the European communist alliance, and the changes occurring there during 1956 appeared almost revolutionary. Czechoslovakia enjoyed considerable prestige in the region even prior to the communist take-over, and this clearly helped to make its influence so pervasive in 1968. On the other hand, most likely for historical reasons, Romania has never had great influence in the region; therefore its post-1963 policy has lacked the kind of credibility necessary to ensure its acceptance by others.

Insofar as the character and duration of a given influence are concerned, there have also been some interesting differences. Influences that impinged directly on the political system took a long time to be absorbed, if they were absorbed at all, whereas those that touched upon politics indirectly—for example, through the economic and/or social systems—were relatively more easily handled. The most striking example here was the spreading of economic reforms throughout the region, beginning with Czechoslovakia in 1964-65, moving into Hungary in 1968, and reaching other countries in the early 1970s. Similarly, influences impinging on the conduct of foreign policy seemed to be more easily received and absorbed than pressures aimed at influencing the domestic political system, which tended to be strongly resisted.

So far we have discussed the influences resulting from changes in the international and regional communist environments. But what about the impact of changes in other types of environments that also affected Eastern Europe? It seems clear that the impact of these influences was not less profound than that of the pressures from within the communist camp.

For example, the first, however feeble, attempts at East-West detente, manifested in the "spirit of Geneva" in 1955 had major repercussions in Eastern Europe by removing the specter of an immediate armed confrontation, thereby ipso facto lessening the dependence of the smaller countries on the Soviet Union for protection against intervention from the West, and strengthening the individual national regimes. Subsequent steps in the rapprochement between the superpowers, marked by the various arms control agreements, increase in personal contacts, and growth in economic and cultural relations, had far-reaching repercussions in Eastern Europe.

One of the most interesting changes in the international environment in the 1960s was the return of Western Europe to the forefront of international politics. At the same time both parts of Europe rediscovered that they formed a single continent and had shared many historical and cultural values and traditions for centuries. The initiative for the intra-European rapprochement came from the West, and was spearheaded by Charles de Gaulle and Willy Brandt. Its timing proved to be most auspicious, for most of the Eastern European countries welcomed the new approach as providing them with additional elbow room and offering tangible advantages in the form of increased trade, credits, and technology transfers.

By now it should be apparent that the macro effect of the influences stemming from the growth in the multiple and/or overlapping memberships in various types of environments has given Eastern Europe as a whole, as well as the individual countries, greater autonomy vis-a-vis the Soviet Union and other members of the alliance.

However, although the significant changes in the international and regional environments greatly affected the conditions and process of influence penetration at the macro level, this did not mean that Eastern Europe became an "open" region where foreign influences of all sorts could freely compete for supremacy. This clearly was not so, and there was (and is) a limit to that competition and to the "free flow of people and ideas" that proved to be the most hotly contested and controversial "basket" at the 1975 Conference on Security and Cooperation in Europe (see Chapter 9). Although in recent years the Soviet Union has been surprisingly flexible, relaxed, and even permissive with regard to the appearance of various external influences in Eastern Europe, which until relatively recently has been rather isolated from the outside, there is no doubt that the Soviet Union remains the hegemonical power in the region and that it alone determines the threshold that foreign influences cannot cross.[17]

In his pioneering article on the diffusion of political innovation, Zvi Gitelman, on the basis of the historical experiences since 1960, suggested some "rules of the game" governing the process of transmitting innovations within the Soviet bloc.[18] The list is quite exhaustive and attempts to pinpoint aspects of communist political systems that the Soviet Union, as the hegemonical power in the region and the guardian and interpreter of Marxist-Leninist orthodoxy, considers permanent and inviolate, subject to change only by its own force or influence.

Some of the rules appear clear-cut and unambiguous, such as those related to the leading role of the party, censorship of the mass media, and open criticism of the Soviet Union. Others, however, tend to be somewhat ambivalent. Thus, according to Gitelman, "perhaps the cardinal rule in innovation diffusion among socialist countries is that the innovator should never claim to be elaborating an alternative, competitive 'model' of socialism."[19] While the statement may be formally correct, in practice it may be argued that in Eastern Europe there are almost as many "models" as there are countries; and even though national decision-makers take care not to advertise their innovations and pay obligatory homage to the Soviet model, the growing systemic differentiation has been taking place for some time and has been perceived by both the national elites and the national publics.

The same can be said about another condition suggesting that any pressure or influence aimed at inducing a country to leave either WTO or CEMA would be automatically barred by the Soviet Union.[20] Again, this condition may be valid in theory but, for some time now, Romania has been a member of both organizations mostly on paper without incurring Soviet sanctions.

The ambiguity surrounding the "rules of the game," which, by the way, apply not only to the diffusion of innovation within the communist block but also to the transmission of influences into the region, arises from the fact that the Soviet Union is both a player and an umpire, and thus can change the rules as often as is necessary.

Now that the various types of external influences impinging on Eastern Europe at a macro level, as well as the conditions of their penetration, have been discussed, it is necessary to examine how external influences are transmitted at the micro level. This means, above all, looking at the agents, channels, and targets of penetration.

AGENTS, CHANNELS, AND TARGETS OF PENETRATION

Agents of penetration or transmission have been of several kinds. The global and regional environments have been discussed. There have been (and still are) other agents or "linkage groups" that, intentionally or not, directly or indirectly, serve as "transmission belts" for influences, views, and ideas into Eastern Europe.

One of them has been the network of international organizations headed by the United Nations and its various specialized agencies. Czechoslovakia, Poland, and Yugoslavia were among the original signatories of the United Nations Charter in 1945, most of the remaining countries were admitted in 1955, and East Germany became a member in 1974. Several countries belong also to the General Agreement on Tariffs and Trade (GATT) and the International Monetary Fund; and there is little doubt that these agencies act as both agents and channels of influence transmission and penetration.

The same is true of other international bodies with more restricted membership. Several Eastern European states are represented on the Eighteen Nations Disarmament Committee, Hungary and Poland served on the international commissions supervising armistice in Indochina.

It may be assumed that most, if not all, of these organizations did not see themselves as active agents of influence diffusion that would have a serious effect on the political systems of the member countries. Indeed, most of them would strenuously deny harboring such intentions, and it was largely for that reason that many of the Eastern European countries were able to join.

At least two organizations that did not include East European countries probably had a greater impact on Eastern Europe than most of the organizations that included them: NATO and EEC. In both cases the impact was indirect and took several years to develop, yet the "demonstration effect" was unmistakable. Although six years elapsed between the creation of NATO in 1949 and the establishment of WTO in 1955, there is no doubt that the latter was strongly influenced by the former. This can be seen not only in the WTO Charter but also in the discussions justifying WTO's formation.[21] There are also some striking parallelisms in more recent developments within both alliances.

The establishment of CEMA in 1949 is said to have been decided by the Soviet Union in direct response to the Marshall Plan and the formation of the European Economic Community (EEC). Although CEMA remained largely moribund for the first decade of its existence, its revival in the late 1950s and early 1960s probably was at least partly due to the success of the EEC.[22]

Next to international organizations, probably the most significant agents of influence diffusion were individual countries. In some cases their influence was direct, purposeful, and intentional; at other times it was indirect, ad hoc, and almost accidental. As suggested earlier, the most potent agents were other communist states, such as China and Yugoslavia and, to some extent, Czechoslovakia, Hungary, and Poland. Among the noncommunist countries the United States, France, and West Germany played the major role in influence transmission.

The impact of American policy on Eastern Europe varied rather sharply after World War II. Until 1952 the region seemed to represent a major target of

American policy, culminating in the "liberation doctrine" of John Foster Dulles. Soon thereafter, however, the doctrine lost its credibility and was replaced by the slogans "peaceful engagement" and "bridge building," both of which became a cover for a policy of "benign neglect" vis-a-vis Eastern Europe.[23] It can be argued that since the mid-1950s, direct American influence in the region has been minimal, although indirect influence of the two policies mentioned above, which were part of the early stages of East-West detente, was not inconsiderable.

France, under Charles de Gaulle, and West Germany, led by Willy Brandt, penetrated Eastern Europe more deeply than the United States did. In contrast with the latter, both countries clearly were interested in the region, although for different reasons. There is evidence suggesting that de Gaulle viewed Eastern Europe as part of "Europe from the Atlantic to the Urals," and that he had consistently called for the reduction of Soviet control over the area.[24] Moreover, his attempt at an independent foreign policy, reflected in the open challenge to American hegemony and in France's withdrawal from NATO, was bound to find a sympathetic echo among the Eastern European states.

Although West Germany's Ostpolitik took several years to become credible, its impact probably was even more striking, especially in Czechoslovakia, East Germany, and Poland. Although in a sense Bonn's policy paralleled that of Paris by emphasizing the unity of Europe, its greatest importance lay in removing or minimizing the points of tension that had threatened the European status quo. The recognition of the Oder-Neisse line, the disavowal of the Munich Treaty, the agreement on the status of West Berlin, and the recognition of East Germany as a separate state were the milestones in the West German rapprochement with Eastern Europe and in the growth of West German influence in the region.

Thus far we have treated the international organizations and individual countries as "rational actors" engaged in generating influence that eventually reached and affected Eastern Europe. We will now examine the role of the international and national actors actually involved in influence transmission.

The international organizations that had communist countries as members performed several functions: they were used as listening posts; they acted as instruments of education and socialization; and they served as channels of communication. For example, the Eastern European employees of the United Nations Secretariat and of the specialized agencies, most of whom served for several years at a time, tended to acquire firsthand exposure to foreign influences; and it may be assumed that upon their return home, they were likely to disseminate some of the information and experiences gained abroad.

Probably the most important role in this respect was played by such international economic organizations as GATT, the United Nations Food and Agri-Culture Organization, the United Nations Conference on Trade and Development, and the United Nations Economic Commission for Europe (ECE). In addition to the functions mentioned above, they have served as instruments of technological progress and have imposed certain conditions upon their members. In the case of the Eastern European countries, this usually meant liberalization of their economic systems, especially in the area of foreign trade.

Moreover, membership in other groupings, formal or informal, influenced Eastern European politics indirectly by providing an additional legitimacy to the national communist regimes and expanding their room to maneuver. This was particularly valid for countries like Romania that have been challenging the hegemony of the Soviet Union. It is obvious that Romania's membership in, and/or identification with, non-European communist states and Third World countries, as well as its efforts to cultivate bilateral relations with several Western countries, strengthened its drive toward partial autonomy, making it difficult for Moscow to coerce it into total submission.[25]

Within individual countries there have been two major categories of transmission belts: governments and "transnational organizations"— nongovernmental institutions and groups.[26] In the former, it often has been the top foreign policy-makers, who either personally acted as architects of a new approach toward Eastern Europe (Presidents de Gaulle and John Kennedy, Chancellor Brandt, and American Secretary of State Henry Kissinger), or who at least were willing to legitimize and follow a policy initiated by their predecessors (Presidents Lyndon Johnson, Richard Nixon, and Georges Pompidou, and Chancellor Helmut Schmidt). The parliamentary bodies and the bureaucracies were either negative or indifferent; and the initiative usually tended to originate in small advisory councils composed, frequently, of individuals with academic backgrounds (Zbigniew Brzezinski in the United States; Egon Bahr and Horst Ehmke in West Germany). The new policy was soon reflected in the output of governmental and semipublic broadcasting services that tended to soften past criticism of the Eastern European regimes and to present more "balanced" reporting.

Although the benevolent attitude of the top decision-makers was not a necessary and sufficient condition of new approaches undertaken by nongovernmental bodies, it was helpful. Thus, although labor unions in some Western countries (such as the United States) remained very critical of the regimes of Eastern Europe, certain Western European unions (such as those in West Germany) actively supported the reestablishment of closer relations between both parts of Europe. In the United States and West Germany, business and industrial associations favoring expansion of economic contacts between East and West either put pressure on their respective governments or established direct connection with the Eastern European regimes. Such political parties in Western Europe as the West German Social Democratic party and the British Labour party openly favored rapprochement with Eastern Europe, while others remained either hostile or ambivalent.* Private American foundations, among

---

*Paradoxically, one of the most influential Western political parties in Eastern Europe was the Italian Communist party, whose official pronouncements were studied with great care by the local political elites.

which the Ford Foundation was by far the most prominent, financed a series of academic and cultural exchanges with several Eastern European countries; and a similar task was accomplished by public agencies in France, West Germany, and Great Britain. Various other institutions—universities, tourist and youth organizations, and ethnic associations—stimulated contacts and exerted influence on the people-to-people level.

A separate, important chapter in the history of influence transmission was written by the Roman Catholic church, especially in countries with a predominantly Catholic population, such as Poland. Following the establishment of a modus vivendi between the church and the party in 1956, the contacts between the Polish clergy and the Vatican began to multiply at various levels. The Holy See itself, starting in the late 1960s, inaugurated an active foreign policy of its own, aimed at improving relations with Czechoslovakia, Hungary, and East Germany. While the effect of that policy cannot be easily ascertained, it most likely was not inconsiderable.*

The final question concerns the Eastern European targets of political penetration—individuals, groups, and institutions that were exposed to foreign influences, intentionally or not.

In the communist regimes the obvious target was the ruling political elite, particularly the members of the top party hierarchy—the politburo and the secretariat. While it is impossible to appraise the degree of receptivity to foreign influences among the top decision-makers, we can determine the range of opportunities open to them, and examine their personal backgrounds, which may offer some additional clues to their sensitivity to outside pressures. In the case of the top leaders, one opportunity was provided by personal contacts between the Eastern Europeans and their counterparts in other parts of the world. In this respect Presidents Tito and Nicolae Ceausescu clearly led the way, closely followed by Edward Gierek. These three leaders have paid numerous visits to the West; and Gierek, who lived for several years in France and Belgium, apparently speaks fluent French. In contrast, many of the past and present East European leaders (Wladyslaw Gomulka, Erich Honecker, Gustav Husak, Janos Kadar, Antonin Novotny) have had little or no direct exposure to Western influences.

Available personal background data provided no significant insights as to which of the top leaders might prove particularly sensitive to outside influences. The best that can be done is to suggest that regardless of their family, educational, or professional backgrounds, some Eastern European leaders appeared to

---

*The Vatican's policy toward Eastern Europe, inaugurated during the pontificate of Pope John XXIII and continued under his successor Paul VI, represents a fascinating exercise in high politics which thus far has not been satifactority analyzed (or understood) in the West.

be psychologically more "open-minded" to outside influences and stimuli than others, as reflected in different behavior patterns of Gomulka and Gierek, Walter Ulbricht and Honecker, or Novotny and Alexander Dubcek.

Insofar as the rest of the hierarchy was concerned, the pattern was modeled largely by the top elite. Thus Polish, Romanian, and Yugoslav party and government bureaucrats have had more personal contacts with the non-communist world than their counterparts in Bulgaria, Czechoslovakia, East Germany, and Hungary, although the East German officials have had a long record of negotiations with their opposite numbers in the Federal Republic.

One of the key target groups was the experts and techniciams. Some of them were employed by international organizations. Others participated in scholarly exchanges and/or joint research projects. Still others worked abroad, mostly in Third World countries, as part of foreign aid or international development programs. With the expansion of economic relations with the non-communist world, growing numbers of Eastern European specialists have participated in bilateral negotiations concerning trade and industrial cooperation.

A separate target audience was the intellectuals, who traditionally enjoyed considerable status and prestige in Eastern European societies and probably had suffered more than other groups from being isolated. The writers, artists, and academic personnel, especially in humanities and social sciences, benefited from greater freedom of travel to, and the flow of ideas from, the West. They took advantage of international cultural exchanges and meetings sponsored by governmental and private organizations in the West, and they were largely responsible for the intellectual ferment in several Eastern European countries.

Another target of external influences was the Eastern European youth. The importance of this particular target needs no elaboration, although it was hardly a homogeneous group and some of its subgroups were more sensitive to outside influences than others. The most visible subgroup was the university students, who also had the greatest opportunity for contacts abroad through academic exchanges, youth festivals, and tourism.[27] The most numerous components, the young industrial workers, had much less exposure but, according to available evidence, were not entirely isolated; young peasants, however, tended to be nearly totally deprived of foreign contacts. The Eastern European working class has the potential to become a very important linkage group if the Yugoslav experience has any bearing on the region.[28]

The public at large, politically the least relevant social group, has been increasingly subjected to the economic "demonstration effect," mostly through exposure to foreign consumer goods, publications, films, plays, and television.*

---

*". . . the demonstration effect on the international plane is determined by two factors. One is the size of the disparities in real income and consumption levels. The other is

Visits from relatives and friends living abroad and personal contacts with foreign tourists completed the picture.

EVALUATING EXTERNAL INFLUENCES ON EASTERN EUROPEAN POLITICS

One possible way of analyzing the effect of foreign influences on Eastern Europe and on the individual countries is to examine the process of political, economic, and social change in Eastern Europe and then try to discover how much of it was due, directly or indirectly, to the influence of external factors.

The process of change in Eastern Europe has not been neglected in the literature.[29] Although there is still a lack of consensus among scholars as to the suitability of a particular analytical model for the study of Eastern Europe, and although there is still disagreement regarding the definition of the concept of "change" as opposed to "development" and "modernization," there clearly is a high degree of agreement that the Eastern Europe of the mid-1970s is different from that of twenty years earlier. We may not be ready to measure exactly the degree and rate of change, but the transformation of the region has been unmistakable if uneven.

In the absence of a full-fledged analysis of change in the area, it may make sense to examine briefly some of the milestones in the process in chronological order, indicating their dependence on external factors.

The Polish and Hungarian Crises of 1956

There is little doubt that the impact of foreign influences on the origin of the upheavals in Hungary and Poland was quite powerful, yet it can also be easily exaggerated. Although the Soviet Union, China, and Yugoslavia all had exerted influence on Eastern Europe in the mid-1950s, the fact that dramatic reaction occurred in only two of the countries indicated the presence in them of key internal conditions that proved to be especially sensitive and receptive to outside pressures.[30] The latter were generated almost exclusively by the international communist environment, with the West remaining essentially passive, although its implicit acceptance of the principle of "peaceful coexistence," emphasized by the Geneva summit meeting of 1955, helped to ensure an important background condition for the events of 1956. The pressures stemming from

the extent of people's awareness of them." Ragnar Nurkse, *Problems of Capital Formation in Underdeveloped Countries* (Oxford: Oxford University Press, 1957), pp. 61-67. Large parts of Czechoslovakia, East Germany, and Hungary can receive television programs from Austria and West Germany, including West Berlin.

the international communist camp clearly were intended to induce change in Eastern Europe, although their ultimate consequences obviously were unanticipated.

The Albanian-Romanian Syndrome of the 1960s

The defection of Albania in 1961, and the loosening of Romania's ties with the rest of the Soviet-dominated alliance beginning in 1963, were influenced by outside factors, although their immediate impact was less significant than in Poland and Hungary. Both states took advantage of the continuing escalation of the Sino-Soviet conflict, yet domestic considerations also played an important role in the decisions.

Enver Hoxha's perception of past and future patterns of communist international relations and his total control over the Albanian political system made it relatively easy for him to make the switch. The Romanian situation was more complex. Although the Sino-Soviet rift played a role in convincing the Romanian leadership that the time was right to initiate the process of desatellization, and while both Gheorghe Gheorghiu-Dej and Nicolae Ceausescu appeared to be firmly in control, one can speculate that external influences were present that were absent in Albania. On the one hand, de Gaulle's initiative, followed by the first version of Brandt's Ostpolitik, created a favorable climate for such a move. On the other hand, growing contacts with the West may have opened the eyes of the Romanian decision-makers to the growing technological gap between East and West, and persuaded them to limit their participation in CEMA, which they perceived as a brake on their country's economic development, and to favor expanded economic cooperation with the West.

Since the mid-1960s, the course of Romanian domestic and foreign policy has continued to reflect a mixture of foreign influences and purely domestic values and traditions. On the domestic political scene, Ceausescu seems to have been impressed by the experience of China and, more recently, by that of North Korea. His foreign policy appears to represent an attempt to take advantage of all opportunities offered Romania by its formal or informal identification with various international environments. In the final analysis it is difficult to say whether internal or external influences have had a stronger impact on Romania's politics, although my own view is that the former have had the upper hand.[31]

The Eastern European Economic Reforms of the 1960s

There is no doubt that the economic reforms conducted in several Eastern European countries throughout the second half of the 1960s represented a major watershed in that region's political, economic, and social development.[32] Perhaps one of the most fascinating features of the reforms was the fact that, by and large, the decision to get them under way was the outcome of internal rather than external pressures. To be sure, the overall climate of incipient detente provided the necessary background condition that made it possible for the "iron curtain" to be lifted somewhat, permitting a flow of information from the West, including some personal contacts. Nevertheless, the impetus for the reforms was born within the region alone.

The reasons for the reforms have been widely discussed.[33] The first serious reform in Czechoslovakia, starting in 1964-65, was mostly an indigenous phenomenon with some relatively minor inputs from other communist states. Although East Germany was the first to proclaim a major reform of its economy, in the summer of 1963, its most important effect was in showing the Czechoslovak reformers how not to conduct their own reform.[34] On the other hand, many of the ideas that were eventually incorporated into the final reform blueprint came from Polish economists, who, after being in the forefront of revolutionizing communist economic theory in the late 1950s, were, in the 1960s, forced to abandon the practical implementation of their ideas by the increasingly conservative Gomulka regime. Their works, however, were either translated or read in the original; and they played a seminal role in laying the theoretical foundations for the Czechoslovak reforms.

It was then the turn of the Hungarian reformers to learn the lessons from their Czechoslovak counterparts. Preparations for the Hungarian New Economic Mechanism started after the main outlines of the Czechoslovak reforms were agreed upon. The latter went into partial effect in January 1967, and the former was formally inaugurated a year later. In the course of the preparatory work, there were frequent contacts between both sets of planners; and in the final analysis it was Hungary that enjoyed "the advantage of being second."[35]

The much less extensive reforms undertaken by the remaining countries in the region undoubtedly were influenced by the demonstration effect, especially of the Hungarian reform, which almost from the start proved to be an unmitigated success. In this case, however, the additional stimulus came also from the rapid expansion of East-West economic relations, which made it easier to overcome the resistance of the anti-reform opposition.

The Czechoslovak Crisis of 1968

A good case can be made showing that the liberalization process in Czechoslovakia in 1968 was pursued despite, if not against, influences emanating from both East and West, and that as such it was perhaps the best example of a far-reaching political change in Eastern Europe achieved without any major input from outside.

It is beyond the scope of this chapter to go into the origins of the "Prague Spring" except to emphasize that they had their source in domestic problems and issues.[36] Reference has already been made to the Czechoslovak economic reform, which was essentially an internal phenomenon. The Czechoslovak ruling elite at both the top and middle levels probably was more isolated from the West than any other elite in Eastern Europe, with the possible exception of that in Bulgaria. The same probably was true for the professional and cultural elites, who had not had the advantage of educational and cultural exchanges and contacts with the West that were enjoyed by their Polish, Hungarian, and Yugoslav opposite numbers. The working class and the youth were also insulated from foreign influences. Indeed, with the possible exception of Bulgaria and East Germany, Czechoslovakia maintained the traditional coercive political system longer than any other member of the communist bloc.

Once the process of liberalization was initiated in the spring of 1968, the country found itself under considerable foreign pressure: explicit from the other alliance partners and implicit from the leader of the Western camp, the United States. The former is well documented, but the latter continues to be an object of controversy even today. Every effort was made by Washington not to give the slightest encouragement to the Dubcek regime, for fear of antagonizing the Soviet Union; and this lack of support or even interest was well understood in both Moscow and Prague. Indeed, the only visible support for the Czechoslovak cause came from the two maverick East European countries, Romania and Yugoslavia, and from some equally maverick Western communist parties, mainly those of Italy and Spain.

The impact of the Czechoslovak events on the rest of Eastern Europe and on the Soviet Union is well known, and its magnitude and depth were the chief forces behind the Soviet decision to terminate the liberal experiment in August 1968. The strong areawide receptivity to Czechoslovak ideas and the almost total indifference to Romania's drive toward greater autonomy are perplexing, however; and this contrast illustrates the complexity of international relations and domestic politics within the region.

The Polish Crisis of 1970

Like the Czechoslovak crisis of 1968, the Polish crisis of 1970 was by and large rooted in internal problems. Throughout the 1960s, Poland presented a paradox. On the one hand, after a brief period of rising expectations in the late 1950s, the country entered a period of political and economic stagnation interrupted only by the brief but violent interlude of March 1968. On the other hand, no country in the area, except Yugoslavia, had had closer relations with the West and, hence, the opportunity to absorb and assimilate Western influences. Poland not only received American loans, including Public Law 480 foodstuff shipments, but also was the beneficiary of the highly valued most-favored-nation treatment by the United States. Its relations with France and most of the other Western European countries were improving, West Germany being the conspicuous exception, at least until 1969. More scholars, students, and intellectuals from Poland visited and studied in the West than from any other country in the region.

Yet when the crisis came in December 1970, ignited by the Baltic coast riots that toppled Gomulka and replaced him with Gierek, it was very much a domestic affair, sparked by the opposition of the workers to drastic price reforms that resulted from a decade of economic mismanagement and political indifference. Neither East nor West exerted any visible pressure on the country, either before or after the explosion.*

Although the Polish crisis was not the direct consequence of foreign influences, it caused some reverberations throughout Eastern Europe, apparently even the Soviet Union. The open revolt of the workers, the favored class in all communist societies, was seen as a danger sign that might be replicated elsewhere. Shortly thereafter, several countries were forced to take measures aimed at improving the standard of living of the population, either by expanding the output of consumer goods or by eliminating or postponing planned price increases.[37]

CONCLUSIONS

On the basis of the foregoing discussion several tentative conclusions suggest themselves:

1. Since the mid-1950s, Eastern Europe has been increasingly exposed to foreign influences emanating from a variety of environments.

2. Although the influence of the Soviet Union has remained crucial, its impact has been, by and large, stabilized if not somewhat reduced.

3. The effect of Western political influences has been steadily declining since its high point in the mid-1950s.

4. Most dramatic changes in Eastern European politics have been caused by domestic rather than by foreign influences.

---

*Interestingly, there is some suggestion that Gomulka was hoping that the impact of a major international event would offset the impact of a major domestic event. Thus, although the negative popular reaction to drastic price reform in December 1970 apparently was fully or partly anticipated by the Polish leadership, it also was assumed that the positive effect of the signing of the Polish-West German treaty, just prior to the reform, would largely offset the negative impact of the price increases.

What about the future? Judging from past and present experience, a good case can be made that the current trends will continue for some time. It may be assumed that the Soviet influence in Eastern Europe will not change in the foreseeable future. At the same time, there are no visible signs that Western interest in, and influence on, the region will be drastically modified: although its decline may stop, it will at best be stabilized rather than reversed. The much-heralded Conference on European Security and Cooperation, for example, is not likely to bring about any striking changes; and if Eastern European politics is going to be transformed in the future, it will be the result of internal rather than of non-Soviet external pressures.

There is, however, one possibly important exception that ought to be mentioned: the growing global pressure on certain raw materials, especially fuels, and the resulting worldwide inflation. As long as Eastern Europe was isolated from the rest of the world, it was relatively immune to international economic disturbances. However, as soon as the region became more open, it was exposed to a host of economic problems that it was neither prepared for, nor able to handle. If the global crisis continues and if the individual Eastern European countries cannot find means of coping with it, one possible solution is to raise the barriers and become insulated once again. From this it is only a short step to reimposition of highly centralized economic controls and, eventually, the return to a coercive political regime.

While the above scenario may never be played, its actual implementation is hardly unrealistic, considering the importance and complexity of external influences in Eastern Europe.

NOTES

1. *The Random House Dictionary of the English Language*, unabridged ed. (New York: Random House, 1967), pp. 493, 730.

2. For an interesting discussion of the concept of power as the capacity to influence, see J. David Singer, "Inter-Nation Influence: A Formal Model," *American Political Science Review* 57, no. 2 (June 1963): 420-30.

3. Karl W. Deutsch, "External Influences on the Internal Behavior of States," in R. Barry Farrell, ed., *Approaches to Comparative and International Politics* (Evanston, Ill.: Northwestern University, 1966), pp. 5-26. Also see Steven J. Brams, "Transaction Flows in the International System," *American Political Science Review* 60, no. 4 (December 1966): 880-98.

4. For the original definition of the concept of transnational relations, see Joseph S. Nye, Jr., and Robert O. Keohane, "Transnational Relations and World Politics: An Introduction," *International Organization* 25, no. 3 (Summer 1971): 329-49.

5. Robert O. Keohane and Joseph S. Nye, Jr., "Transnational Relations and International Organizations," *World Politics* 27, no. 1 (October 1974): 43.

6. The best-known definition can be found in James N. Rosenau, "Toward the Study of National-International Linkages," in James N. Rosenau, ed., *Linkage Politics* (New York

and London: Free Press, 1969), pp. 44-63. For a more recent statement, see James N. Rosenau, "Theorizing Across Systems: Linkage Politics Revisited," in Jonathan Wilkenfeld, ed., *Conflict Behavior and Linkage Behavior* (New York: McKay, 1973), pp. 25-56.

7. For one of the earliest attempts, see Michael P. Gehlen, "The Integrative Process in East Europe: A Theoretical Framework," *Journal of Politics* 30, no. 1 (February 1968): 90-113. Also see David D. Finley, "Some International Pressures and Political Change in Eastern Europe," paper presented at the Western Slavic Conference, San Francisco, October 1973.

8. Neither Peter D. Bell ("The Ford Foundation as a Transnational Actor") nor Ivan Vallier ("The Roman Catholic Church: A Transnational Actor"), both in *International Organization* 25, no. 3 (Summer 1971): 465-502, had anything to say about Eastern Europe, although both organizations have been quite active in the region.

9. The single essay in Rosenau, *Linkage Politics*, op. cit., dealing with the Communist world (R. V. Burks, "The Communist Politics of Eastern Europe," pp. 275-303), is essentially cast in the traditional mold, in which the use of the linkage concept is more or less incidental. For an excellent recent attempt, see William Zimmerman, "National-International Linkages in Yugoslavia: The Political Consequences of Openness," paper presented at the an annual meeting of the Americal Political Science Association, New Orleans, September 1973).

10. For a recent analysis, see Vernon V. Aspaturian, "The Soviet Impact on Development and Modernization in Eastern Europe," in Charles Gati, ed., *The Politics of Modernization in Eastern Europe* (New York: Praeger, 1974), pp. 205-53.

11. I borrowed the term "identity reference" from Kenneth Jowitt, who discussed it in the East European context in Sylvia Sinanian, Istvan Deak, and Peter C. Ludz, eds., *Eastern Europe in the 1970s* (New York: Praeger, 1972), pp. 180-84.

12. For an interesting discussion of this process, see William Zimmerman, "Hierarchical Regional Systems and the Politics of System Boundaries," *International Organization* 26, no. 1 (Winter 1972): 25-36.

13. For the classical treatment of this period, see Zbigniew Brzezinski, *The Soviet Bloc*, rev. and enl. ed. (Cambridge, Mass.: Harvard University Press, 1967), Chs. 5-7.

14. Ibid., Chs. 9, 12.

15. Robert R. King, "Rumania and the Sino-Soviet Conflict," *Studies in Comparative Communism* 5, no. 4 (Winter 1972): pp. 373-412.

16. For a discussion of one aspect of that influence, see Andrzej Brzeski, "Poland as a Catalyst of Change in the Communist Economic System," *Polish Review* 16, no. 2 (Spring 1971): pp. 3-24.

17. J. F. Brown, "The 'Socialist Commonwealth,'" *Problems of Communism* 23, no. 1 (January-February 1974): 76-79.

18. Zvi Gitelman, "The Diffusion of Political Innovation: From Eastern Europe to the Soviet Union," *Sage Professional Papers in Comparative Politics* 3, no. 27 (1972): 29-33. Also see his "The Impact on the Soviet Union of the East European Experience in Modernization," in Gati, op. cit., pp. 256-74.

19. Gitelman, "The Diffusion of Political Innovation," pp. 30-31.

20. Ibid., p. 31.

21. Andrzej Korbonski, "The Warsaw Pact," *International Conciliation* no. 573 (May 1969): 8-9, 12. For a useful comparison of both NATO and WTO, see *The Warsaw Pact—Its Role in Soviet Bloc*, a study submitted by the Senate Subcommittee on National Security and International Operations, 89th Congress, 2d Session (Washington, D.C.: U.S. Government Printing Office, 1966).

22. Marshall D. Shulman, "The Communist States and Western Integration," *Problems of Communism* 12, no. 5 (September-October 1963): 47-54.

23. The initial call for a new American involvement in Eastern Europe appeared in Zbigniew Brzezinski and William E. Griffith, "Peaceful Engagement in Eastern Europe," *Foreign Affairs* 39, no. 4 (July 1961): 642-54. For an up-to-date account of that involvement, see Charles Gati, "The Forgotten Region," *Foreign Policy* no. 19 (Summer 1975): 135-45.

24. For an interesting account, see Earl Fry, "Executive Policy-Making in Gaullist France: The Case of Franco-Soviet Relations, 1958-1964" (unpublished Ph.D. diss., UCLA, 1975), passim.

25. For a perceptive account, see Kenneth Jowitt, "Political Innovation in Rumania," *Survey* 20, no. 4 (Autumn 1974): esp. 133-134, 141-144. The early stages of Soviet-Romanian relations are discussed in Fritz Ermarth, "Internationalism, Security and Legitimacy: The Challenge to Soviet Interests in Eastern Europe," *Rand Memorandum* RM-5909-PR (1969): passim.

26. For a definition of transnational organizations, see Samuel P. Huntington, "Transnational Organizations in World Politics," *World Politics* 25, no. 3 (April 1973): 333.

27. The impact on the Polish youth of the Fifth World Youth Festival, held in Warsaw in the summer of 1955, is well analyzed in Flora Lewis, *A Case History of Hope* (Garden City, N.Y.: Doubleday, 1958), pp. 55-69.

28. The Yugoslav experience is discussed in William Zimmerman, "National-International Linkages in Yugoslavia: The Political Consequences of Openness."

29. Among the recent studies are Charles Gati, ed., *The Politics of Modernization in Eastern Europe* (New York: Praeger, 1974); Paul Shoup, "Eastern Europe and the Soviet Union: Convergence and Divergence in Historical Perspective," in Henry W. Morton and Rudolf L. Tokes, eds., *Soviet Politics and Society in the 1970s* (New York and London: Free Press, 1974), pp. 340-68; and Andrzej Korbonski, "Prospects for Change in Eastern Europe," *Slavic Review* 33, no. 2 (June 1974): 219-39.

30. Brzezinski, op. cit., pp. 200, 205-06.

31. See Jowitt, "Political Innovation in Rumania," passim.; and Trond Gilberg, "Ceausescu's Romania," *Problems of Communism* 23, no. 4 (July-August 1974): 29-43.

32. Andrzej Korbonski, "Political Aspects of Economic Reforms in Eastern Europe," in Z. A. Fallenbuchl, ed., *Economic Development in the Soviet Union and Eastern Europe*. Volume 1 and 2 (New York: Praeger, 1975).

33. For two comprehensive accounts, see Gregory Grossman, "Economic Reforms: A Balance Sheet," *Problems of Communism* 15, no. 6 (November-December 1966): 43-55; and Morris Bornstein, ed., *Plan and Market* (New Haven and London: Yale University Press, 1973).

34. Personal interviews, Prague, October 1966.

35. Personal interviews, Budapest, January 1970.

36. An extensive bibliography dealing with the Czechoslovak events is in Michael Parrish, *The 1968 Crisis: A Bibliography 1968-1970* (Santa Barbara, Calif.: ABC-CLIO, 1971).

37. Personal interviews in Budapest and Bucharest, July and October 1971.

14

A FRAMEWORK FOR VIEWING DOMESTIC AND FOREIGN POLICY PATTERNS
James A. Kuhlman

INTRODUCTION

Scholars and decision-makers alike have taken too long to conceptually acknowledge an established pattern of events (underlined for Americans in recent years by the crises in Vietnam and the Middle East) in the global political environment: the interrelationship of political processes occurring at different levels—local, national, and international. Increasingly, national actors tend to view domestic and foreign policy decision-making in the same overall framework.

Thus it is logical that American writers on political affairs should attempt to use theories and models constructed at one level of analysis, such as the state public policy literature, and apply that experience to regional and international politics.[1] The American federal system affords an interstate, multilevel laboratory with abundant data from which international-relations theorists may easily benefit. The increased attention to parallels of domestic and foreign affairs began with a series of theoretical essays and empirical attempts at applying simple models in the mid-1960s, stressing similarities and differences in structures and processes at various political system levels.[2] Before long, attention to parallels led to focus on linkages between national and international phenomena.[3]

Linkage theory carried a very important message to area specialists working on behavior of the Soviet-Eastern European community. The emphasis on domestic influence in foreign policy behavior brought traditional assumptions about the "satellite" status of Eastern European nations into more critical perspective. The enlargement of frameworks to encompass domestic and foreign policy patterns not only added insight into individual "balancing acts" of

internal and external behavior by Eastern European elites, but also put their relations with the Soviet leadership into a more substantive and sophisticated
national context. This, plus knowledge of the theoretical aspects of socialist
international relations, allowed a more complete picture to be drawn in that area
of the world.

While one may speculate that this sudden scholarly awareness of the
complementarity of analysis at national and international levels rises simply
from the fact that findings are more available and advanced on the national level,
rapid change in the character of the international level necessitated radical
reformulations of existing approaches.[4] International economic events gave
natural emphasis to the concept of integration, a conceptual counterpart to the
obsession with development (or modernization) in comparative politics. Whatever the reason for the new notions, a framework within which scholars not only
can pursue correlations between domestic and foreign policy patterns but also
can "pretheorize" about possible causal relationships of the two policy areas is a
contributon to common sense and comparative inquiry. The decision-maker, if
successful, accomplishes some degree of coordination between his domestic
policy and the foreign policy of the nation. Modeling that policy process, therefore, begs an appropriately parallel framework that can be used by the scholar in
his attempt to answer the questions posed in the international system.[5]

Perhaps nowhere in the international system is the linkage between domestic factors and foreign policy more evident than in Eastern Europe. The regional
subsystem is bound tightly together by ideology and events; and at least intuitively, one expects a high degree of uniformity in the external relations of the
Soviet-Eastern European bloc members.[6] The concepts of development and integration are obviously interrelated in Soviet strategy with respect to CEMA. The
command-oriented economic systems in the various people's republics are
paralleled by a regional attempt to integrate plans, on the one hand, while such
regional integration is reinforced by the progress of the market-integrated subsystem of Western Europe, on the other hand.[7]

Both national and international factors are crucial in the maintenance of
an alliance system.[8] Maintenance of the regional subsystem in Eastern Europe is
achieved by adherence to a domestic model of socialism, a political process
directly contributing to bloc behavior in foreign policy. From this notion one
would expect to find domestic policy uniformities paralleled by foreign policy
patterning among the party-states with similar domstic structures and processes.
Conversely, where one finds dissimilar domestic policy behavior in a cross-
national examination of Eastern European systems, foreign policy behavior
should differ correspondingly. Domestic policy occurs in an environment con-
sisting of national, regional, and international factors, and, of course, subsets at
any given level. Likewise, foreign policy is conditioned by factors from all such
levels.

Balancing the domestic and foreign policy orientations in relation to over-all objectives and goals of a national leadership becomes a delicate and difficult task. Although one may make a cursory review of the domestic and foreign policies of Bulgaria and Czechoslovakia, and conclude that both internal and external orthodoxy are maintained, there are alternative models from which one may gain insight into differences within the regional subsystem.

For instance, it is generally assumed that Hungary has taken a somewhat liberal and experimental domestic path with respect to market innovations in the economic sector. The Hungarian literature about and experience with the New Economic Mechanism points to an internal flexibility not yet shared in Bulgaria, Czechoslovakia, and other Eastern European states, with the notable exception of Yugoslavia. Yet in foreign policy the Hungarian line is most orthodox and inflexible, deviating very little from the Soviet posture. In contrast with the Hungarian model, the Romanian balancing act features external flexibility with internal rigidity. The variety of decision-making strategies pursued by Eastern European elites is evidence enough that, despite regional subsystem mainte-nance, variations do occur within the bloc. Why and in what ways such variance in domestic and foreign policy patterns manifests itself is a subject of signifi-cance, one that necessitates an approach capable of illuminating the parameters of the problem, even if it does not produce the answers.

MODELING THE POLICY PROCESS

The analytic framework found in Figure 14.1 posits an overall strategy for viewing cross-nationally the patterns in the public policy process, both domestic and foreign, in the Soviet-Eastern European subsystem. Though this framework does have some of the formal attributes of a model, with the use of analogies, metaphors, theories, and empirical referents, one should be cautious in assuming any causal connections between components in the model.[9] Rather, this model implies an approach that underlines important features of domestic systems and their relationships, more specifically their correlations, with characteristics of foreign policies of those systems. Before reviewing details of the interrelation-ships among components of the model, certain aspects of the model, as derived from general theories and assumptions about policy-making in communist sys-tems, should be stressed.

The funnel-of-causality metaphor utilized in Figure 14.1 is not intended to treat domestic factors of the communist states as necessarily deterministic in relation to foreign policy outputs. What the funnel construction does allow is an emphasis on the process of policy determination and an explicit ranking of the least-to-most influential factors in a given setting (or on a given issue). All factors of relevance to this geographical area in general, or to an issue area in particular,

FIGURE 14.1

A Framework for Public Policy Processes
in the Soviet-Eastern European Bloc

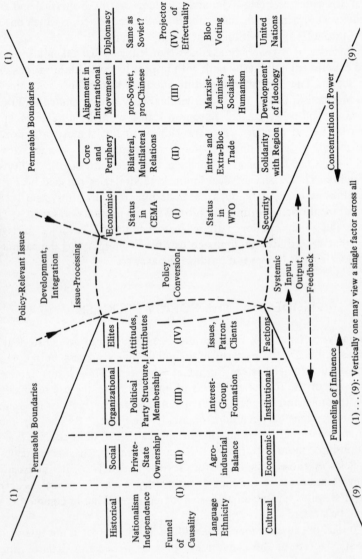

Source: Data compiled by the author.

are seen as funneled or processed from the open end to the point of policy conversion. It is only at the point of conversion that specific relationships between
independent and dependent variables in the policy process may be investigated
(see Figures 14.2 and 14.3 below). Similarly, the projector employed in the foreign policy sector of the model does not imply a direct image reflecting domestic
determinants onto the international system. Rather, the analogy is one wherein
certain foreign policy behavior is considered more indicative of an integrated,
bloc-oriented (or highly focused) pattern, while other behavior patterns may be
viewed as less reflective of bloc behavior (more diffused).

Though such crude devices as the funnel and projector do not lend themselves to exact parallels between theoretical and substantive processes in Eastern
European policy behavior, they do provide a scheme for visualizing the relative
salience of broad categories of data. Historical-cultural, socioeconomic, organizational-institutional, and elite-faction variables are positioned in the funnel in
ascending order of importance. Literature on policy-making in general, and on
communist systems in particular, indicates that party elites and hierarchical
organization are very crucial to system functioning, with socioeconomic and
historical-cultural less important conditioning factors in the policy process.

More acutely important for the modeling of the policy process itself, however, is the pinpointing of specific factors in each of the four broad categories
that might make a difference in domestic policy orientation. Examples of
historically recurrent and culturally significant factors in Eastern Europe are
identified in the funnel as the degrees of ethnicity and nationalism within the
country and, relatedly, the linguistic consistency in the nation. Quite obviously
the numerous nationalities in Yugoslavia and the Soviet Union, conflict between
Czechs and Slovaks, and disputes between Bulgaria and Yugoslavia over
Macedonia influence policy within and between the socialist states.[10] The relative ethnic homogeneity of East Germany and Poland also conditions policy
outputs and outcomes in those states. Within the socioeconomic sector of the
model, two principal characteristics are stressed in terms of importance for the
policy process and its outcomes. Economic development literature emphasizes
the general impact of the agriculturally based versus industrially based economy,
and Eastern Europe in particular brings this point to the surface because such
distinct types and levels of development are present. Contrasting industrial-
technological systems such as East Germany and Czechoslovakia with relatively
underdeveloped, agriculturally oriented systems such as Bulgaria and Romania,
one would expect to see policy variations patterned after such differences. Even
more insight could be gained in the context of socialist domestic structures by
ascertaining the degree of public to private ownership in both the industrial and
the agricultural sectors.[11]

Of increasing importance, as indicated in the funnel dynamics of the
model, are the organizational and elite factors involved in the policy process.
Though numerous organizational and institutional characteristics influence

policy to some degree, two particular aspects are explicitly cited in Figure 14.1 as having impact generally in all communist systems in Eastern Europe. Despite the traditional notions that the party-states are uniformly one-party systems with little or no pressures and interests from the outside being brought to bear upon the political system, there are differential roles played by party structures, legislatures, constitutions, and interest groups across the bloc.[12] The roles of the Polish legislative body (Sejm) and the three political parties (Polish United Workers party, Democratic party, and United Peasant party) provide an example of a setting somewhat more complex than that generally accepted to be the case in a communist party-state, although the tendency to take such pluralistic structure at face value in the political process should be avoided.[13] Yet federal constitutional structures in Czechoslovakia and Yugoslavia, the roles of the trade unions across several Eastern European countries, and other organizational-institutional factors in each of the Eastern European systems have some modifying effect on the policy process.[14]

Of course elites occupy the sector closest to the point of policy conversion, if for no other reason than that they are necessary, and in hierarchical systems sometimes even sufficient, for the policy-making process itself. All conventional wisdom and traditional literature on communist states would agree to the positioning of party elites as the single most influential factor in the political process, yet attitudinal and background characteristic variations within and across countries cannot be overlooked.[15] Moreover, factions within party and non-party elite groups can be significant influencers of outcomes, either as factions that form around specific identities (perhaps as in patron-client relationships) or as issue-oriented factions.

ISSUES AND OUTCOMES IN THE POLICY PROCESS

Issue variability involves not only the elite sector but also the permutations of all variables in the model.[16] Though Figure 14.1 isolates important differences within each broad category of factors in the policy process, the specific items are included here as representative of generally held assumptions about the nature of critical aspects of socialist polities. Not only would the order of importance of these factors change with changes in issues under consideration, or thought to be "policy relevant," but specific issues may argue for the selection of particulars not included in the itemization in Figure 14.1. Dimensionality and direction of flow through the funnel and the projector sectors are critical to the modeling and understanding of policy in socialist systems. Before discussing the foreign policy projector metaphor in the model, the multivariate and cross-national dimensions of the process should be outlined.

The student of Eastern European politics must constantly be sensitive to, but in control of, immense complexity represented in Eastern Europe. By disciplining oneself to view the dynamics of the model in their horizontal and vertical patterns, comprehension of the interplay of actors and events may be achieved. It should be obvious that the requirements of model-building that lead to categorization of four major sets of factors influencing policy in Eastern European systems do not in real political processes produce equally neat, discrete, and compartmentalized clusters of politically relevant factors. Moving from the first (historical-cultural) to the fourth (elite) sector of the funnel is an incremental process in reality. Socioeconomic conditions in a given country are conditioned by historical-cultural factors. The organizational structure of the political system flows directly from historical and economic characteristics of the country. Elites, though salient in policy-making, rarely operate in a historical-cultural, socioeconomic, or organizational vacuum, regardless of the degree of centralization of authority in the system.

Depending upon the policy-relevant issue, this horizontal flow may occur in different modes. One could conceive of the general incremental buildup of influence through the four sectors of the funnel to the point of actual conversion; but in addition a single determinant in one category could be brought to bear upon the salient factor in another—for instance, ethnicity being directly reflected in factions within the elite sector. This direct influence also may reverse itself in the natural flow of the funnel, as in the case of a leader pursuing a particular economic policy regardless of the domestic makeup of the economy. Elite-designated campaigns for industrialization in essentially pastoral systems could be examples of such reverse flow.

Vertically viewed, one may consider the cross-national variations on a single variable influence in the policy process. The nine countries (Albania, Bulgaria, Czechoslovakia, East Germany, Hungary, Poland, Romania, the Soviet Union, and Yugoslavia) of Eastern Europe may be compared in terms of attributes and capabilities in each of the four sectors. As stated at the outset of this chapter, if domestic political and economic development and international political and economic integration are the predominant policy-relevant issues, the determination and correlation of these four categories in the funnel in connection with foreign policy patterns on the projector side should become evident. The model in Figure 14.1 may only serve to generate hypotheses of a highly speculative nature about the specific determination and correlation between domestic and foreign policy patterns (permutations among variables in the funnel and projector). The public policy process and identification of independent-dependent variable relationships in that process must depend on detailed data presented in measurable format or indexes. Figure 14.2 presents a design for such research, treating the broad categories of the model in Figure 14.1 in a more specific manner.

Foreign policy patterns in Figure 14.1 are viewed systemically as outputs, to some degree determined by the domestic variables funneled into the public policy process. This overall approach, it should be emphasized, allows for a

FIGURE 14.2

Research Design for Domestic Policy Behavior

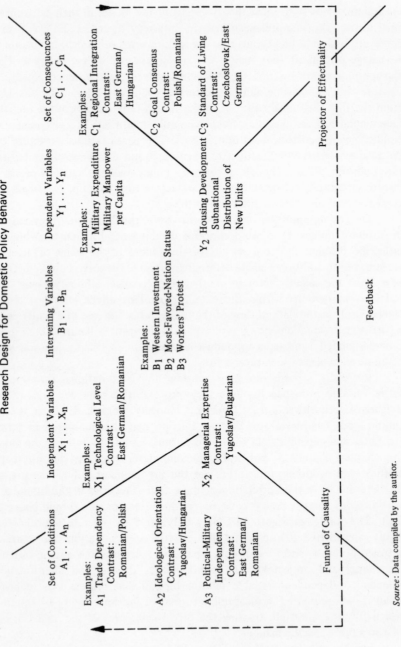

Set of Conditions
$A_1 \cdots A_n$

Independent Variables
$X_1 \cdots X_n$

Intervening Variables
$B_1 \cdots B_n$

Dependent Variables
$Y_1 \cdots Y_n$

Set of Consequcnces
$C_1 \cdots C_n$

Examples:
A_1 Trade Dependency
Contrast:
Romanian/Polish

A_2 Ideological Orientation
Contrast:
Yugoslav/Hungarian

A_3 Political-Military
Independence
Contrast:
East German/
Romanian

Examples:
X_1 Technological Level
Contrast:
East German/Romanian

X_2 Managerial Expertise
Contrast:
Yugoslav/Bulgarian

Examples:
B_1 Western Investment
B_2 Most-Favored-Nation Status
B_3 Workers' Protest

Examples:
Y_1 Military Expenditure
Military Manpower
per Capita

Y_2 Housing Development
Subnational
Distribution of
New Units

Examples:
C_1 Regional Integration
Contrast:
East German/
Hungarian

C_2 Goal Consensus
Contrast:
Polish/Romanian

C_3 Standard of Living
Contrast:
Czechoslovak/East
German

Funnel of Causality

Feedback

Projector of Effectuality

Source: Data compiled by the author.

282

feedback process by which subsequent developments at the domestic level are conditioned by foreign policy events (conditions A_1 ... A_n in Figure 14.2). As with domestic factors in the funnel, four major categories of foreign policy behavior are listed in the projector. Beginning with political-military and economic organizations, WTO and CEMA, the focus of bloc behavior becomes more diffused as one moves toward the open end. Secondary to actual organizational participation, but still significant in the foreign policy process, is a sector describing the nature of relations between Eastern European countries of the periphery with the dominant or core country in the region.* Proceeding outward in the projector, foreign policy orientations vis-a-vis international communism are indicated, finally leading to a category indicating actions with respect to the international system in general. As postures toward development become progressively channeled into elite decisions, indications of integrative behavior become more intense. Moving outward in the projector, foreign policy factors become less relevant to the integrative process and at the same time provide more flexibility with respect to bloc behavior.

Specific indicators within each broad category of foreign policy behavior are given, again with the caveat that the particular selection offered in Figure 14.1 represents only often-used and conventionally supported indexes of behavior. Depending upon bloc or regionally identified policy-relevant issues at hand, different variables, and different weights attached to these same variables, could be envisioned. In general, however, the specific features of the projector can account for a great deal of variance in Eastern European behavior. Economically and politically it is important to assess the actual participation of Eastern European states in CEMA and WTO.[17] Relatedly, the nature of relationships among smaller Eastern European countries with the Soviet Union is particularly important. Increasingly, one suspects that the integrated and coordinated behavior of states under CEMA auspices does not simply mean Soviet economic and political hegemony but, rather, the existence of negative feedback for the Soviet Union: the flexibility associated with coalitions of lesser partners in multilateral frameworks. Thus any change from bilateral to multilateral structures within CEMA trade agreements or the WTO Treaty of Friendship and Mutual Assistance would be important to note. Similarly, shifts in the intrabloc versus extrabloc trade ratios for Eastern European states are important indicators of foreign policy behavior.[18]

---

*Though the terms "core" and "periphery" are defined differently in the context of the Soviet Union (a separate subordinate system) and other Eastern European countries (with a core and periphery) by the authors originating the concepts, in this chapter the Soviet Union is considered core but part of the Eastern European subsystem. See Louis J. Cantori and Steven L. Spiegel, *The International Politics of Regions: A Comparative Approach* (Englewood Cliffs, N.J.: Prentice-Hall, 1970).

FIGURE 14.3

Research Design for Foreign Policy Behavior

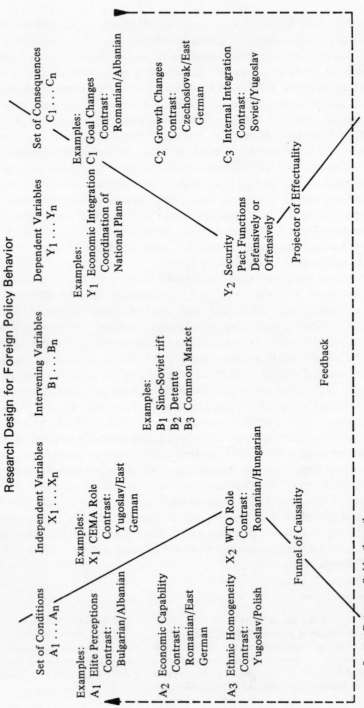

Set of Conditions $A_1 \ldots A_n$	Independent Variables $X_1 \ldots X_n$	Intervening Variables $B_1 \ldots B_n$	Dependent Variables $Y_1 \ldots Y_n$	Set of Consequences $C_1 \ldots C_n$

Examples:

A_1 Elite Perceptions
Contrast:
Bulgarian/Albanian

A_2 Economic Capability
Contrast:
Romanian/East German

A_3 Ethnic Homogeneity
Contrast:
Yugoslav/Polish

Examples:

X_1 CEMA Role
Contrast:
Yugoslav/East German

X_2 WTO Role
Contrast:
Romanian/Hungarian

Examples:

B_1 Sino-Soviet rift
B_2 Detente
B_3 Common Market

Examples:

Y_1 Economic Integration
Coordination of
National Plans

Y_2 Security
Pact Functions
Defensively or
Offensively

C_1 Goal Changes
Contrast:
Romanian/Albanian

C_2 Growth Changes
Contrast:
Czechoslovak/East German

C_3 Internal Integration
Contrast:
Soviet/Yugoslav

Funnel of Causality

Projector of Effectuality

Feedback

Source: Data compiled by the author.

284

Specific indicators related to international communism that were selected for purposes of illustration in the model are the alignment in the Sino-Soviet conflict and positioning in the ideological transition away from orthodox Marxism-Leninism toward socialist humanism. Both factors are critical in the development of bloc policy behavior and represent outcomes on issues that remain crucial to the international relations of Eastern Europe. The positions of Albania and Yugoslavia, one having chosen the Chinese wing of the movement and the other with substantial spokesmen in the socialist humanist school, are evidence of the weight of these factors.[19] Finally, the projector includes a sector on broad international patterns. One method of ascertaining behavior in this area would be to look for differences between diplomatic relations of Eastern European countries distinct from those of the Soviet Union. Bloc versus nonbloc voting in the United Nations would be another indicator, with easily accessible data, in the last sector.

Figure 14.2 posits a research strategy for identifying independent-dependent relationships in the domestic policy process; Figure 14.3 designates a strategy for similar findings in the foreign policy or projector sector of the model. Again, factors from the funnel and projector are seen in Figure 14.3 simply as conditions and consequences of the actual policy conversion sector. Figures 14.2 and 14.3 appropriately fall within that conversion sector, treating the inputs (funnel) and outputs (projector) simply as influences upon the policy process.

VARIATIONS AMONG EASTERN EUROPEAN PUBLIC POLICIES

It remains for researchers to establish concrete similarities and dissimilarities within and between the domestic and foreign policy patterns in Eastern Europe. The empirical and methodological deficiencies in comparative communist studies noted for some years now have yet to be corrected.[20] Despite increasing amounts of data, comparability is at a premium, not only across Eastern and Western boundaries but also within the socialist community itself. Yet some preliminary notions and tentative hypotheses may be drawn from an examination of data that are available, such as indicators of national development and regional integration.

One of the primary conclusions about the domestic structures within Eastern Europe is that production has shifted markedly from an agricultural orientation during the early 1950s in almost all systems, save East Germany and Czechoslovakia, to a situation in which industry prevails over agriculture almost everywhere (see Table 14.1). This general phenomenon leads to expectations of increased rates of growth in gross national product per capita; but because of the technology lag and administrative instability and experimentation, such expected growth rates have not been forthcoming.[21] Excluding Bulgaria and

TABLE 14.1

Comparison of Eastern European GNP
by Industrial Origin, 1950 and 1972
(percent)

	Industry and Handicrafts	Agriculture and Forestry	All Others*	Total
Bulgaria				
1950	15.9	41.3	42.8	100.0
1972	39.0	21.1	39.9	100.0
Czechoslovakia				
1950	34.8	23.9	41.3	100.0
1972	47.7	11.7	40.6	100.0
East Germany				
1950	36.0	15.3	48.7	100.0
1972	47.4	9.2	43.4	100.0
Hungary				
1950	25.3	29.7	45.0	100.0
1972	37.3	17.1	45.6	100.0
Poland				
1950	22.0	36.9	41.1	100.0
1972	29.3	19.6	51.1	100.0
Romania				
1950	21.3	42.2	36.5	100.0
1972	41.8	24.5	33.7	100.0

*Includes construction, transport and communications, trade, housing, and government and other services.

Sources: For Bulgaria, Tsentralno Statistichesko Upravlenie, *Statisticheski godishnik na Narodna Republika Bulgariia* (annual); for Czechoslovakia, Federalni Statisticky Urad, *Statisticka rocenka Ceskoslovenske Socialisticke Republicy* (annual); for East Germany, Staatliche Zentralverwaltung fur Statistik, *Statistisches Jahrbuch der DDR* (annual); for Hungary, Kozponti Statisztikai Hivatal, *Statisztikai evkonyv* (annual); for Poland, Glowny Urzad Statystyczny, *Rocznik statystyczny* (annual); and for Romania, Directia Centrala de Statistica, *Annuarul statistic al Republicii Socialiste Romania* (annual).

TABLE 14.2

Indicators of Comparative East-West Economic Strength, 1972

Item	Unit	Western Europe	United States	Canada	Australia	Japan	Total	Soviet Union	Other Eastern Europe[a]	People's Republic of China	Other-Asian Communist Areas[b]	Cuba	Total	Rest of World
Population[c]	Millions	396	209	22	13	106	746	248	107	878	36	8.8	1,278	1,836
GNP (at market prices)	Billion dollars	1,144	1,155	103	53	341	2,796	549	206	141	8	4.8	909	634[e]
Per capita GNP (at market prices)[d]	Dollars	2,891	5,532	4,714	4,069	3,218	3,751	2,217	1,931	160	216	545	711	345[e]
Foreign Trade														
Imports (c.i.f.)	Billion dollars	199.1	55.6[f]	18.9[f]	4.7[f]	23.5	301.8	16.0[f]	24.3[g]	2.7	1.4	1.3	45.7	76.3
Exports (f.o.b.)	Billion dollars	188.7	49.7	20.2	6.7	28.6	293.9	15.4	24.9	3.0	0.5 1971	0.8	44.6	65.9
Trade balance	Billion dollars	-10.4	-5.9	+1.3	+2.0	+5.1	-7.9	-0.6	+0.6	+0.3	-0.9	-0.5	-1.1	-10.4
Production														
Coal[h]	Million MT	344	539	17	64	27	991	544	366	340	32	none	1,282	143
Crude steel	Million MT	165	121	12	7	97	402	126	45	23	3	0.2	197	26
Electric power	Billion KWH	1,306	1,853	238	63	414	3,874	858	284	95	20	5.4	1,262	438
Crude petroleum	Million MT	22	467	77	16	1	583	394	19	30	insig.	0.1	443	1,474
Primary aluminum	Thousand MT	2,521	3,729	998	206	1,015	8,479	1,800	390	280	insig.	none	2,470	415
Motor vehicles	Thousands	12,551	11,271[i]	1,474	446[j]	6,297	32,039	1,379	610	100	12	none	2,101	1,018
Passenger cars	Thousands	11,241	8,824[i]	1,154	367[j]	4,022	25,608	730	420	insig.	insig.	none	1,150	772
Commercial vehicles	Thousands	1,310	2,447[i]	320	79[j]	2,275	6,431	649	190	100	12	none	951	246

Notes: Data shown are the latest available at time of publication, but are subject to revisions.

All figures are rounded, but computations for per capita figures are based on unrounded data.

Some data represent new estimates, and therefore are not comparable with data published in the 1972 edition of the "Indicators."

All data for *People's Republic of China, Other Asian Communist Areas,* and *Cuba* are rough estimates.

[a]Includes Albania, Bulgaria, Czechoslovakia, East Germany, Hungary, Poland, and Romania.

[b]Includes Mongolia, North Korea, and North Vietnam.

[c]Mid-1972.

[d]For the Western countries, currencies are converted into dollars at April 1973 exchange rates, as published by the International Monetary Fund. The GNP values for the Communist countries are calculated with the aid of the Gilbert–Kravis method; see e below.

[e]For details on methodology, see "The Planetary Product in 1972; Systems in Disarray," RESS 46, September 20, 1973.

[f]Imports f.o.b.

[g]All imports are f.o.b. except Hungary's, which are c.i.f.

[h]Hard coal and lignite in terms of hard coal equivalents.

[i]Factory sales.

[j]Including assembly.

Source: Bureau of Public Affairs, Office of Media Services, U.S. Department of State, "Special Report: 1972 Indicators of Comparative East-West Economic Strength" (Washington, D.C.: the Bureau, October 25, 1973) (mimeo).

Romania, rates fall below the average for the European Economic Community.[22] Data in Table 14.1 (within bloc) and Table 14.2 (across regions) provide ample evidence of the saliency of factors in the socioeconomic sector of the funnel or domestic side of the model. Economic development will continue to influence public policy directions. The growth in the industrial sectors puts a dual pressure upon Eastern European countries to extend trade dependencies on the West for technology, on the one hand, while increasing intra-CEMA activity for guarantees of raw materials, reduction of production duplication, and lowering the cost of research and development.[23]

Implicit in the domestic and foreign policy data from the Eastern European systems may be the notion that development and integration concepts represent linkage issue areas. Individual development strategies by each country have obvious implications for integration of the planned economies. Such strategies may not only differ in terms of independence vis-a-vis Moscow, or Bulgaria in contrast with Romania, for instance, but may also evidence interesting variations in the domestic models employed, as can be seen in Hungary and Poland. While political advantage may accrue to the Soviet Union in this situation of domestic development dependency and regional integrative process, it may well be argued that economic disadvantages for the superpower are inherent in the Soviet-Eastern European relationship. (See Chapter 4.) The potential for this economic burden on the Soviet system to become political influence from Eastern Europe to the Soviet Union is a consideration certain to occupy scholars and decision-makers in the decades to come.*

It is conceivable that the Soviet Union could default on the economic responsibility for Eastern European development, perhaps as a result of Soviet domestic deficiencies, though Soviet political objectives and military capability undoubtedly mitigate against such a public policy outcome. Pressure for changes in domestic and foreign policy patterns in the socialist community will have to originate with the Eastern Europeans. Reform of economic structures in the quest for development by the less-advanced countries in the region may well be the source for altering past patterns of public policy in the Soviet framework.

---

*Though the Yugoslav reforms are given the widest treatment in the literature, the Hungarian example is more germane to the point here, in that Hungary remains in the mainstream of the CEMA structure. See in particular William F. Robinson, *The Patterns of Reform in Hungary: A Political, Economic and Cultural Analysis* (New York: Praeger Publishers, 1973); Istvan Friss, ed., *Reform of the Economic Mechanism in Hungary* (Budapest: Akademiai Kiado, 1971); and Otto Gado, ed., *Reform of the Economic Mechanism in Hungary: Development 1968-71* (Budapest: Akademiai Kiado, 1972).

NOTES

1. For examples of the most advanced theoretical and empirical material from state public policy analysis, which can be used heuristically within international studies in general and will be evident in this approach to Eastern European foreign policy-making, see especially Thomas R. Dye, *Politics, Economics and the Public: Policy Outcomes in the American States* (Chicago: Rand McNally, 1966); and *Understanding Public Policy* (Englewood Cliffs, N.J.: Prentice-Hall, 1972); Richard I. Hofferbert, *The Study of Public Policy* (Indianapolis: Bobbs-Merrill, 1974); Yehezkel Dror, *Public Policymaking Reexamined* (San Francisco: Chandler Publishing Co., 1968); Ira Sharkansky, *Regionalism in American Politics* (Indianapolis: Bobbs-Merrill, 1970); and James E. Anderson, *Public Policy-Making* (New York: Praeger Publishers, 1975).

2. These early essays all in some degree follow the morphology-then-process logic of James N. Rosenau in "Pre-Theories and Theories of Foreign Policy," in R. Barry Farrell, ed., *Approaches to Comparative and International Politics* (Evanston, Ill.: Northwestern University Press, 1966), pp. 27-93. Also from the Farrell volume see in particular Chadwick F. Alger, "Comparison of Intranational and International Politics," pp. 301-29; Raoul Naroll, "Scientific Comparative Politics and International Relations," pp. 329-38; and Oliver Benson, "Challenges for Research in International Relations and Comparative Politics," pp. 338-59.

3. Linkage theory and its development in recent years may be best represented by the series of volumes under the editorship of James N. Rosenau. See in particular his *Domestic Sources of Foreign Policy* (New York: Free Press, 1967) and *Linkage Politics: Essays on the Convergence of National and International Systems* (New York: Free Press, 1969), esp. R. V. Burks, "The Communist Polities of Eastern Europe," pp. 275-304. For the first comprehensive attempt at application of linkage theory to communist systems, see Jan F. Triska, ed., *Communist Party-States: Comparative and International Studies* (Indianapolis: Bobbs-Merrill, 1969).

4. A point noted by James A. Caporaso, *The Structure and Function of European Integration* (Pacific Palisades, Calif.: Goodyear Publishing Co., 1974), pp. 1-2.

5. For elaboration of this argument for increased complementarity in models of actors and analysts in international relations theory, see James A. Kuhlman, "Changing Patterns in East-West Relations," in James A. Kuhlman and Louis J. Mensonides, eds., *Changes in European Relations* (Leiden, Netherlands: A. W. Sijthoff Publishers, 1976).

6. For an empirical attempt at describing this external uniformity in behavior, see P. Terry Hopmann, "International Conflict and Cohesion in the Communist System," *International Studies Quarterly* 11, no. 3 (September 1967): 212-36.

7. For analysis of the impact of one European subsystem upon the other, see Werner J. Feld, "The Utility of the EEC Experience for Eastern Europe," *Journal of Common Market Studies* 8, no. 3 (March 1970): 236-61; and E. S. Kirschen, "Reflections on Economic Integration in Western and Eastern Europe," *Annals of Planned and Central Economy* 43, no. 1 (January-March 1972): 15-25. The issue of national development and international integration in Eastern Europe in its political and economic dimensions is discussed in James A. Kuhlman, "Eastern Europe," esp. the section "Economics of Interdependence/Politics of Regions," in James N. Rosenau, Kenneth W. Thompson, and Gavin Boyd, eds., *World Politics* (New York: Free Press, 1976), pp. 444-65. For Eastern European discussions of the interrelationship of development and integration objectives, see in particular Tibor Kiss, *International Division of Labour in Open Economies, with Special Regard to the CMEA* (Budapest: Akademiai Kiado, 1971); and Sandor Ausch, *Theory and Practice of CMEA Cooperation* (Budapest: Akademiai Kiado, 1972).

8. For a full discussion of this point, see Ole R. Holsti, P. Terrence Hopmann, and John D. Sullivan, *Unity and Disintegration in International Alliances: Comparative Studies* (New York: John Wiley & Sons, 1973), pp. 48-59.

9. The use of the term "model" here is close to that of Abraham Kaplan, *Conduct of Inquiry: Methodology for Behavioral Science* (San Francisco: Chandler Publishing Co., 1964), p. 265: "A more defensible usage views as models only those theories which explicitly direct attention to certain resemblances between the theoretical entities and the real subject matter. With this usage in mind, models have been defined as 'scientific metaphors.'" For the specific construction of the funnel of causality employed in Figure 14.1, see Angus Campbell, Philip E. Converse, Warren E. Miller, and Donald E. Stokes, *The American Voter* (New York: John Wiley & Sons, 1960).

10. For an excellent survey of the nationalities problem, see Peter F. Sugar and Ivo J. Lederer, eds., *Nationalism in Eastern Europe* (Seattle: University of Washington Press, 1969).

11. Very helpful with description, data and hypotheses concerning socioeconomic factors are works by Frederic L. Pryor: *Public Expenditures in Communist and Capitalist Nations* (Homewood, Ill.: Richard D. Irwin, 1968) and *Property and Industrial Organization in Communist and Capitalist Nations* (Bloomington: Indiana University Press, 1973).

12. On this point see the seminal article by H. Gordon Skilling, "Interest Groups and Communist Politics," *World Politics* 18, no. 3 (April 1966): 435-52.

13. If one cannot call the Polish party structure monolithic, it is at the very least "hegemonic," as noted by Jerzy J. Wiatr, "The Hegemonic Party System in Poland," in Erik Allardt and Stein Rokkan, eds., *Mass Politics: Studies in Political Sociology* (New York: Free Press, 1970), pp. 312-22.

14. For general background on parties, governments, and constitutions, respectively, in the party-states, see Ghita Ionescu, *The Politics of the European Communist States* (New York: Praeger Publishers, 1967); H. Gordon Skilling, *The Governments of Communist East Europe* (New York: Thomas Y. Crowell, 1966); and Istvan Kovacs, *New Elements in the Evolution of Socialist Constitution* (Budapest: Akademiai Kiado, 1968).

15. For excellent collections of comparative communist elite analysis, see R. Barry Farrell, ed., *Political Leadership in Eastern Europe and the Soviet Union* (Chicago: Aldine Publishing Co., 1970); and Carl Beck et al., *Comparative Communist Political Leadership* (New York: David McKay Co., 1973).

16. For the issue-processing approach as included in this model, see Herbert J. Spiro, "Comparative Politics: A Comprehensive Approach," *American Political Science Review* 56, no. 3 (September 1962): 577-95. For an overall evaluation of the systems-oriented approach to communist political behavior, see William A. Welsh, "The Usefulness of the Apter, Easton, and Spiro Models in the Study of Communist Systems in Eastern Europe," *Newsletter on Comparative Studies of Communism* 5, no. 4 (August 1972): 3-21.

17. Though with a different research design in mind, participation in CEMA and WTO, as well as the trade indicators mentioned in the second sector of the projector of Figure 14.1, are used as variables in the assessment of bloc conformity by William R. Kintner and Wolfgang Klaiber in their *Eastern Europe and European Security* (New York: Dunellen Publishers, 1972). The best, though dated, work available on CEMA is in Michael Kaser, *Comecon: Integration Problems of the Planned Economies* (New York: Oxford University Press, 1967). For WTO participation, see Robin Alison Remington, *The Warsaw Pact: Case Studies in Communist Conflict Resolution* (Cambridge, Mass.: M.I.T. Press, 1971). A classic study of the comprehensive organizational framework in the bloc is in Kazimierz Grzybowski, *The Socialist Commonwealth of Nations: Organizations and Institutions* (New Haven: Yale University Press, 1964).

18. For theory and data, respectively, concerning the foreign trade of Eastern European states, see Imre Vajda and Mihaly Simai, eds., *Foreign Trade in a Planned Economy*

(Cambridge: Cambridge University Press, 1971); and Paul Marer, *Soviet and East European Foreign Trade 1946-1969: Statistical Compendium and Guide* (Bloomington: Indiana University Press, 1972).

19. For the most representative works of the socialist humanist school, see Adam Schaff, *Marxism and the Human Individual* (New York: McGraw-Hill, 1970); Leszek Kolakowski, *Toward a Marxist Humanism: Essays on the Left Today* (New York: Grove Press, 1968); and Svetozar Stojanovic, *Between Ideals and Reality: A Critique of Socialism and Its Future* (New York: Oxford University Press, 1973).

20. For example, see Frederic J. Fleron, Jr., "Soviet Area Studies and the Social Sciences: Some Methodological Problems in Communist Studies," *Soviet Studies* 19, no. 3 (January 1968): 313-39. Also see the symposium "Comparative Politics and Communist Systems," *Slavic Review* 26, no. 1 (March 1967): 1-29.

21. See Thad P. Alton, "Economic Growth and Resource Allocation in Eastern Europe," in U.S. Congress, Joint Economic Committee, *Reorientation and Commercial Relations of the Economies of Eastern Europe* (Washington, D.C.: U.S. Government Printing Office, 1974), p. 256.

22. Ibid., p. 293.

23. A conclusion reinforced in J. T. Crawford and John Haberstroh, "Survey of Economic Policy Issues in Eastern Europe: Technology, Trade, and the Consumer," ibid., pp. 32-50.

SELECTED BIBLIOGRAPHY

Alperovitz, Gar. *Cold War Essays*. New York: Anchor Books, 1970.

Aspaturian, Vernon V. *Power and Process in Soviet Foreign Policy*. Boston: Little, Brown, 1971.

Aspaturian, Vernon V. *The Soviet Union in the International Communist System*. Stanford: Hoover Institution Studies, 1966.

Bromke, Adam, ed. *The Communist States at the Crossroads*. New York: Praeger, 1965.

Bromke, Adam, and Teresa Rakowska-Harmstone, eds. *The Communist States in Disarray, 1965-1971*. Minneapolis: University of Minnesota Press, 1972.

Bromke, Adam, and Philip E. Uren, eds. *The Communist States and the West*. New York: Praeger, 1967.

Brzezinski, Zbigniew K. *Alternative to Partition*. New York: McGraw-Hill, 1965.

Brzezinski, Zbigniew K. *The Soviet Bloc: Unity and Conflict*. Cambridge: Harvard University Press, 1967.

Burks, R. V., ed. *The Future of Communism in Europe*. Detroit: Wayne State University Press, 1968.

Burnham, James. *Containment or Liberation*. New York: John Day, 1953.

Byrnes, Robert F. *The United States and Eastern Europe*. Englewood Cliffs, N.J.: Prentice-Hall, 1967.

Campbell, John C. *American Policy Toward Eastern Europe: The Choices Ahead*. Minneapolis: University of Minnesota Press, 1965.

Campbell, John C. *Tito's Separate Road: America and Yugoslavia in World Politics*. New York: Harper & Row, 1967.

Clemens, Diane S. *Yalta*. New York: Oxford University Press, 1970.

Collier, D. S. *Western Policy and Eastern Europe*. Chicago: Regnery, 1966.

Collier, David S., and Kurt Glaser, eds. *Western Integration and the Future of Eastern Europe*. Chicago: Regnery, 1964.

Dallin, Alexander, and Jonathan Harris, eds. *Diversity in International Communism*. New York: Columbia University Press, 1963.

Davis, Lynn E. *The Cold War Begins: Soviet-American Conflict Over Eastern Europe*. Princeton, N.J.: Princeton University Press, 1974.

Djilas, Milovan. *Conversations with Stalin*. New York: Harcourt, Brace, and World, 1968.

Ermarth, Fritz. *Internationalism, Security, and Legitimacy: The Challenge to Soviet Interests in East Europe, 1964-1968*. Santa Monica: The Rand Corporation, 1969.

Farrell, R. Barry. *Yugoslavia and the Soviet Union, 1948-1956*. Hamden, Conn.: Shoe String Press, 1956.

Fisher-Galati, Stephen, ed. *Eastern Europe in the Sixties*. New York: Praeger, 1963.

Floyd, David. *Rumania: Russia's Dissident Ally*. New York: Praeger, 1965.

Gaddis, John L. *The United States and the Origins of the Cold War, 1941-1947*. New York: Columbia University Press, 1972.

Gamarnikow, Michael. *Economic Reforms in Eastern Europe*. Detroit: Wayne State University Press, 1968.

Gati, Charles, ed. *The Politics of Modernization in Eastern Europe: Testing the Soviet Model*. New York: Praeger, 1974.

Griffith, William E., ed. *Communism in Europe*. Cambridge: The M.I.T. Press, 1964 and 1966.

Griffith, William E. *Albania and the Sino-Soviet Rift*. Cambridge: The M.I.T. Press, 1963.

Grub, Phillip and Karel Holcik, eds. *American-East European Trade: Controversy, Progress, Prospects*. Washington, D.C.: National Press, 1969.

Grzybowski, Kasmierz. *The Socialist Commonwealth of Nations*. New Haven: Yale University Press, 1964.

Gyorgy, Andrew, ed. *Issues of World Communism*. Princeton, N.J.: D. Van Nostrand, 1966.

Hamm, Harry. *Albania: China's Beachhead in Europe*. New York: Praeger, 1963.

Hammond, Thomas T., ed. *The Anatomy of Communist Takeovers*. New Haven: Yale University Press, 1975.

Ionescu, Ghita. *The Break-up of the Soviet Empire in Eastern Europe*. London: Penguin, 1965.

Jowitt, Kenneth T.A. *Revolutionary Breakthroughs and National Development: The Case of Romania, 1944-1965*. Berkeley: University of California Press, 1971.

Kaser, Michael. *Comecon: Integration Problems of the Planned Economies*. New York: Oxford University Press, 1967.

Keesing's Research Report. *Germany and Eastern Europe Since 1945: From the Potsdam Agreement to Chancellor Brandt's "Ostpolitik."* New York: Charles Scribner's Sons, 1973.

Kertesz, Stephen D., ed. *East Central Europe and the World*. Notre Dame, Ind.: University of Notre Dame Press, 1962.

Kertesz, Stephen D., ed. *The Fate of East Central Europe: Hopes and Failures of American Foreign Policy*. Notre Dame, Ind.: University of Notre Dame Press, 1956.

King, Robert R., and Robert W. Dean, eds. *East European Perspectives on European Security and Cooperation*. New York: Praeger, 1974.

Kintner, William R., and Wolfgang Klaiber. *Eastern Europe and European Security*. New York: Dunellen, 1971.

Kolko, Joyce and Gabriel. *The Limits of Power: The World and United States Foreign Policy, 1945-1954*. New York: Harper & Row, 1972.

Korbel, Josef. *Detente in Europe: Real or Imaginary?* Princeton, N.J.: Princeton University Press, 1972.

Kovrig, Bennett. *The Myth of Liberation: East-Central Europe in U.S. Diplomacy and Politics Since 1941*. Baltimore: Johns Hopkins University Press, 1973.

Lendvai, Paul. *Eagles in Cobwebs: Nationalism and Communism in the Balkans*. New York: Doubleday, 1969.

London, Kurt, ed. *Eastern Europe in Transition*. Baltimore: Johns Hopkins Press, 1966.

Lowenthal, Richard. *World Communism: The Disintegration of a Secular Faith*. New York: Oxford University Press, 1964.

Ludz, Peter C. *Two Germanys in One World*. (Atlantic Papers 3/1973.) Westmead (England): Saxon House, 1973.

Lundestad, Geir. *The American Non-Policy Toward Eastern Europe, 1943-1947*. New York: Humanities Press, 1975.

McNeal, Robert H., ed. *International Relations Among Communists*. Englewood Cliffs, N.J.: Prentice-Hall, 1967.

McVicker, Charles. *Titoism: Pattern for International Communism.* New York: St. Martin's Press, 1957.

Maddox, Robert J. *The New Left and the Origins of the Cold War.* Princeton, N.J.: Princeton University Press, 1973.

Merkl, Peter. *German Foreign Policies, West and East.* Santa Barbara, Calif.: ABC-Clio, 1974.

Morris, Bernard S. *International Communism and American Policy.* New York: Atherton Press, 1966.

Myers, Kenneth A. *Ostpolitik and American Security Interests in Europe.* Washington, D.C.: Georgetown University Press, 1972.

Nagorski, Zygmunt, Jr. *The Psychology of East-West Trade: Illusions and Opportunities.* New York: Mason & Lipscomb, 1974.

Planck, Charles R. *The Changing Status of German Reunification in Western Diplomacy, 1955-1966.* Baltimore: Johns Hopkins Press, 1967.

Prpic, George J. *Eastern Europe and World Communism.* University Heights: John Carroll University, 1966.

Pryor, F. L. *The Communist Foreign Trade System.* Cambridge: Harvard University Press, 1963.

Radvanyi, Janos. *Hungary and the Superpowers.* Stanford, Calif.: Hoover Institution Press, 1972.

Remington, Robin A. *The Warsaw Pact: Case Studies in Communist Conflict Resolution.* Cambridge: M.I.T. Press, 1971.

Reorientation and Commercial Relations of the Economies of Eastern Europe. Washington, D.C.: GPO, 1974.

Rubinstein, Alvin Z. *Yugoslavia and the Nonaligned World.* Princeton, N.J.: Princeton University Press, 1970.

Schwartz, Harry. *Eastern Europe in the Soviet Shadow.* New York: John Day, 1973.

Shub, Anatole. *An Empire Loses Hope: The Return of Stalin's Ghost.* New York: Norton, 1970.

Shulman, Marshall D. *Beyond the Cold War.* New Haven: Yale University Press, 1966.

Skilling, H. Gordon. *Communism, National and International: Eastern Europe After Stalin.* Toronto: University of Toronto Press, 1964.

Stokke, Baard R. *Soviet and East European Trade and Aid in Africa.* New York: Praeger, 1968.

Toma, Peter A., ed. *The Changing Face of Communism in Eastern Europe.* Tucson: University of Arizona Press, 1970.

Triska, Jan, ed. *Communist Party-States: International and Comparative Studies*. New York: Bobbs-Merrill, 1969.

Triska, Jan F. and David Finley. *Soviet Foreign Policy*. New York: Macmillan, 1968.

Ulam, Adam B. *Expansion and Coexistence*. New York: Praeger, 1968.

Ulam, Adam B. *Titoism and the Cominform*. Cambridge: Harvard University Press, 1962.

Whetten, Lawrence L. *Germany's Ostpolitik: Relations Between the Federal Republic and the Warsaw Pact Countries*. New York: Oxford University Press, 1971.

Wiles, P.J.D. *Communist International Economics*. New York: Praeger, 1968.

Windsor, Philip, and Adam Roberts. *Czechoslovakia 1968*. New York: Columbia University Press, 1969.

Wolfe, Thomas W. *Soviet Power and Europe, 1945-1970*. Baltimore: Johns Hopkins University Press, 1970.

Zartman, I. William, ed. *Czechoslovakia: Intervention and Impact*. New York: New York University Press, 1970.

Zinner, P. E., ed. *National Communism and Popular Revolt in Eastern Europe*. New York: Columbia University Press, 1957.

CHARLES GATI is Professor and Chairman in the Department of Political Science at Union College and Visiting Professor of Political Science at Columbia University. He is the editor and coauthor of *Caging the Bear: Containment and the Cold War*, and editor of *The Politics of Modernization in Eastern Europe: Testing the Soviet Model*, 2d printing (New York: Praeger Publishers, 1976), and has written on Soviet foreign policy, American foreign policy, and Eastern European politics for scholarly periodicals and books.

VERNON V. ASPATURIAN is Evan Pugh Professor of Political Science and Director of the Slavic and Soviet Area Studies Center at Pennsylvania State University. He is the author of *Process and Power in Soviet Foreign Policy, The Soviet Union in the World Communist System, The Union Republics in Soviet Diplomacy,* and coauthor of *Foreign Policy in World Politics* and *Modern Political Systems: Europe.* He also has published in scholarly periodicals and books.

LAWRENCE T. CALDWELL is Associate Professor of Political Science at Occidental College. He has written on Soviet foreign and military policies and issues of European security for scholarly periodicals.

WALTER C. CLEMENS, JR., is Professor of Political Science at Boston University and an Associate of the Russian Research Center at Harvard University. He is the author or coauthor of seven books, including *The Superpowers and Arms Control*, and has written on the Soviet Union, Sino-Soviet relations, and arms control for scholarly books and periodicals.

BOGDAN DENITCH is Associate Professor of Sociology at Queens College/CUNY, and Visiting Associate Professor of Political Science and Senior at the Research Institute on International Change, Columbia University. He is the author of *The Legitimation of a Revolution: The Yugoslav Case*, and co-editor of *Opinion-Making Elites in Yugoslavia* (New York: Praeger, 1973), and has written on comparative sociology and political science for scholarly books and periodicals.

TROND GILBERG is Associate Professor of Political Science at Pennsylvania State University. He is the author of *Modernization in Romania Since*

World War II (New York: Praeger, 1974) and *The Soviet Communist Party and Scandinavian Communism: The Norwegian Case*, and has written on Eastern European politics in scholarly periodicals and books.

ANDREW GYORGY is Professor of International Affairs and Political Science at the Institute for Sino-Soviet Studies of George Washington University. He has written and edited several books, most recently *Nationalism in Eastern Europe* and (with Peter Toma and Robert Jordan) *Basic Issues in International Relations*, and has contributed to scholarly books and periodicals.

A. ROSS JOHNSON is a Senior Staff Member at The RAND Corporation. He is the author of *Yugoslavia: In the Twilight of Tito*, and has written on Eastern European political and military affairs for scholarly books and periodicals.

ROGER E. KANET is Associate Professor of Political Science at the University of Illinois. He has recently edited *The Soviet Union and the Developing Nations, Soviet and East European Foreign Policy: A Bibliography* and (with Donna Bakry) *Soviet Economic and Political Relations with the Developing Countries*. He also has contributed to scholarly books and periodicals.

ANDRZEJ KORBONSKI is Professor of Political Science at the University of California at Los Angeles. He is the author of *The Politics of Socialist Agriculture in Poland, 1945-1960*, and has written on various aspects of Eastern European politics and economics, problems of Eastern European integration, and East-West trade for scholarly books and periodicals.

BENNETT KOVRIG is Professor in the Department of Political Economy and in Erindale College at the University of Toronto. He is the author of *The Myth of Liberation, The Hungarian People's Republic*, and several chapters and articles in scholarly books and periodicals.

JAMES A. KUHLMAN is Associate Professor of Government and International Studies at the University of South Carolina. A specialist on Eastern European politics and international relations, he is coeditor of *The Future of Inter-Bloc Relations in Europe* (New York: Praeger, 1974) and *Changes in European Relations*, editor of *The Foreign Policies of Eastern Europe: Domestic and International Determinants*, and contributor to scholarly books and periodicals.

PAUL MARER is Associate Professor of International Business and Director of the East Europe Program of the International Development Research Center at Indiana University. A specialist on Soviet, Eastern European, and East-West trade, his publications include *Soviet and East European Foreign Trade*,

1946-1969: Statistical Compendium and Guide, Postwar Pricing and Price Patterns in Socialist Foreign Trade, and *US Financing of East-West Trade*. He also has written numerous articles and chapters on related topics for scholarly books and periodicals.

ROBIN REMINGTON is Associate Professor of Political Science at the University of Missouri and a research affiliate of the Massachusetts Institute of Technology Center for International Studies. Her publications include *Winter in Prague: Documents on Czechoslovak Communism in Crisis* and *The Warsaw Pact: Case Studies in Communist Conflict Resolution*. She has written on Eastern European politics for scholarly books and periodicals.

THE FUTURE OF INTER-BLOC RELATIONS IN EUROPE
edited by Louis J. Mensonides
and James A. Kuhlman

POLITICAL DEVELOPMENT IN EASTERN EUROPE
edited by Jan F. Triska and
Paul M. Cocks

THE INFLUENCE OF EAST EUROPE AND THE SOVIET WEST
ON THE USSR
edited by Roman Szporluk

POLITICAL SOCIALIZATION IN EASTERN EUROPE:
A Comparative Framework
edited by Ivan Volgyes

THE SOCIAL STRUCTURE OF EASTERN EUROPE: Transition
and Process in Czechoslovakia, Hungary, Poland, Romania, and
Yugoslavia
edited by Bernard Lewis Faber

CHANGE AND ADAPTATION IN SOVIET AND EAST EUROPEAN
POLITICS
edited by Jane P. Shapiro and
Peter J. Potichnyj

FROM THE COLD WAR TO DETENTE
edited by Peter J. Potichnyj and
Jane P. Shapiro